Nectar & Ambrosia

An Encyclopedia of Food in World Mythology

Nectar & Ambrosia

AN ENCYCLOPEDIA OF FOOD IN WORLD MYTHOLOGY

TAMRA ANDREWS

ABC-CLIO

Santa Barbara, California
Denver, Colorado
Oxford, England

Library of Congress Cataloging-in-Publication Data

Andrews, Tamra, 1959–
    Nectar and ambrosia: an encyclopedia of food in world mythology /
    Tamra Andrews
    p. cm.
    Includes bibliographical references and index.
    ISBN 1-57607-036-0 (hard : alk. paper)
    1. Food—Folklore. 2. Food habits—Folklore. 3. Food—Symbolic aspects. I. Title.

GR498 .A53 2000
398.27—dc21   00-010485

04 03 02 01 00   10 9 8 7 6 5 4 3 2 1

ABC-CLIO, Inc.
130 Cremona Drive
P.O. Box 1911
Santa Barbara, California 93116-1911

This book is printed on acid-free paper ∞.

*To my husband, Carlton,
and my children, Cristen and Carolyn.*

CONTENTS

Preface, ix
Acknowledgments, xi
Introduction, xiii

Nectar and Ambrosia, 1

Appendix I, Food Myths by Culture, 253
Appendix II, Food Functions, 259
Bibliography, 265
Index, 275

PREFACE

An immutable bond exists between the people of the world and the foods we consume. Food is our subsistence, our life thread, the sole reason we continue to live and thrive. In the ancient world, people created myths to reinforce their bond with the world around them and with the gods and goddesses they believed were responsible for human life and sustenance. Deities of the earth and soil made the fields sprout with grain. Spirits of the animals gave their bodies freely in sacrifice. From the plains of ancient Sumer to the fields of the New World, fertility goddesses guaranteed continued life, spouted milk from their breasts, and nurtured the world. In ancient times, food was magical: It was earth goddess and animal spirit, life and rebirth, nectar and ambrosia.

Nectar and *ambrosia* are words coined by ancient mythmakers to describe the foods of the immortals—what these people believed the gods consumed to sustain their life in the heavens. The mere sound of these words conjures up images of Zeus and the Olympians reclining on clouds and sipping from golden chalices; but more importantly, it evokes the mystery and magic that people long ago assigned to the consumables of their world. The foods people knew and loved grew by the grace of their most beloved deities, sprouted from fields covered with sacred soil, and hung from mythical trees of life that grew in the

minds of mythmakers, and in magic gardens somewhere in the otherworld. Food was most definitely a divine gift. The gods possessed it, so the people sanctified it, and they believed that it was only by divine grace that the gods shared the miracle of food with human beings.

Nectar and Ambrosia provides an alphabetically organized survey of foods that have played important roles in myth—both those consumed by mortals and those consumed by immortals. It includes foods in all major food groups as well as some intoxicating drinks and consumable herbs and spices. Particular foods were selected for attention on the basis of their popularity in myth, their distribution in geographical areas, and their familiarity in the world today. Because so many books already exist that trace the history of various foodstuffs and discuss the medicinal value of plants and herbs, I made every attempt to restrict the scope of this book to food mythology. But because history and medical science do interact with food myths and beliefs, I embellished the narrative with enough historical background and medical lore to explain the reasons for the development of particular beliefs and rituals. The references cited at the end of each entry provide additional historical and mythological background that some readers might wish to pursue.

The myths and legends of the world's foodstuffs have been and continue to be intimately connected with ritual practices. People recognized the importance of food in every part of the life cycle: They used food in rites and ceremonies connected with planting and harvesting; with hunting; and with birth, death, and marriage. In most of these rituals, food was both consumed by the masses and offered to the deities. But the people had to exercise great care in choosing appropriate foods, and they had to interpret the gods' wishes and determine which foods they prized and which they despised. For reasons largely grounded in myth, people considered certain foods sacred and other foods strictly taboo. *Nectar and Ambrosia* includes foods of both categories—those considered taboo and thus strictly avoided, and those considered highly desirable and thus fitting fare for the highest and most venerated gods.

People from all areas of the world created food myths linking the foods they consumed with the deities they worshiped as creators and providers. In *Nectar and Ambrosia,* I have focused on the foods with the richest bodies of myth surrounding them; yet I have made every attempt to give equal treatment to food myths in all major world areas. Foods, beverages, herbs, spices, and confections appear in a single, continuous alphabetical listing, with extensive cross-references for accessibility. References at the end of each entry refer readers to sources of additional information that are listed in full in the bibliography at the back of the book. Because of the wide range of concepts pertinent to a discussion of food myths, cohesiveness, as well as accessibility, was a major concern. For this reason, in addition to a detailed subject index, the book includes two appendixes that tie together major concepts: an appendix of world cultures refers readers to foods and food myths of specific cultures; and an appendix of food functions provides explanations of major categories of foods (such as forbidden fruits, elixirs of life, and foods for the dead) and refers readers to the encyclopedia entries pertaining to each category.

Because the subject of food mythology encompasses so many concepts, I found it necessary to reach into the literature of numerous academic disciplines for information. Anyone who intends to delve further into the myths and legends of the world's foodstuffs will find it necessary to do the same. In addition to reviewing primary sources of myths as well as the ancient works of Pliny, Aristotle, Herodotus, Theophrastus, and Dioscorides, I drew upon a number of secondary sources pertaining to food history: books on festivals and holidays, on ethnobotany, on the rites and rituals of agriculturists and hunter-gatherers, and on mythology and legend. Among the references I consulted most frequently are *Funk and Wagnall's Standard Dictionary of Folklore, Mythology and Legend* and Sir James G. Frazer's *The Golden Bough.* Some of the most fascinating books about food mythology are those by renowned cultural geographer Frederick J. Simoons. *Food in China, Eat Not This Flesh,* and *Plants of Life, Plants of Death* all contain a wealth of fascinating information as well as exhaustive bibliographies. For accessing individual food myths from various cultures, the *Stith-Thompson Motif Index of Folk Literature* is an indispensable guide.

Most of the foods discussed in *Nectar and Ambrosia* are foods people today eat as a matter of course. We down bread with no thought to the miracle of the harvest, and we devour meat with no concern for the sacrifice of the animals. We indulge in alcoholic beverages simply to have a good time, not to elevate our minds to a higher, more spiritual plane. Most people today take food for granted, while most people of the past considered it a sacred and precious gift. Some of us do address our god when receiving our foodstuffs, however. Christians ask God to "give us this day our daily bread," and thank him "for these thy gifts, which we are about to receive." But more often than not, such prayers are recited by rote. In the past, all was different. Magic and sanctity existed everywhere; and food, because it guaranteed life, was the most magical and most sacred force of all.

ACKNOWLEDGMENTS

Writing *Nectar and Ambrosia* was a monumental task; not only was I venturing into unfamiliar territory but I was attempting to cull and make sense out of an immense quantity and variety of information from areas such as anthropology, ethnobotany, cultural geography, food history, symbolism and superstition, and of course, mythology and religion. There are many wonderful books in these areas, and so many authors who have done pioneering and fascinating research, authors whom I will never know personally but to whom I will always be grateful.

I'd like in particular to thank Dr. Frederick J. Simoons, renowned cultural geographer and the author of several highly respected works in the area of food mythology. His books *A Ceremonial Ox of India, Eat Not This Flesh, Food in China,* and most recently, *Plants of Life, Plants of Death* proved indispensable, as did his numerous journal articles and our personal correspondence. Our conversations were always intellectually stimulating and invaluable, and I grew to rely on him to clarify concepts and to answer many of my questions. I want to express my gratitude to him for his knowledge, his encouragement, and the unselfish gift of his time.

I would like also to thank Jonathan Sauer, the renowned plant geographer, for providing references and input on plant history; and William (Buddy) McNiece, a former Baptist minister, for his input on the meaning of foods in the Bible.

I also would like to express my gratitude to the University of Texas for their outstanding libraries and the wealth of information they provided me, and to the Austin Public Library. Both of these institutions served as second homes during my research. I would like to thank the editors and personnel I worked with at ABC-CLIO as well: particularly Jack Zipes, the renowned expert on fairy tales and consultant for ABC-CLIO, for his input on the meaning of food in fairy tales; and my editors Todd Hallman and Martha Whitt, for their help and attention to my manuscript.

Permissions editor Liz Kincaid also did an excellent job in choosing the illustrations. As was the case during the production of my first book, *Legends of the Earth, Sea and Sky,* everyone at ABC-CLIO who has been involved in the production of this book was helpful and accommodating always.

Last but not least, I'd like to thank my husband, Carlton, and my two daughters, Cristen and Carolyn—Carlton, for his continued support and encouragement, and for putting up with my computer angst time and time again; and Cristen and Carolyn, for once again patiently putting up with their eternally busy, and often distracted, mother.

INTRODUCTION

Food myths and food symbolism permeate ancient literary traditions. To people of times past, food was not mundane; it was magical. It was not only a means of sustenance but an affirmation of resurrection and renewal in the world.

The eternal quest for food greatly influenced the themes underlying the most ancient religious doctrines. According to the Upanishads, the sacred scriptures of Hinduism, human beings consist of "the essence of food." According to the Hindu Sanskrit poem the Bhagavad Gita, "From food do all creatures come into being." Early people were preoccupied with food; they considered it a gift from the gods, and as such, the most auspicious offering. The gods gave wild plants and animals to the people, and then taught them the arts of domestication and cultivation. So people returned the gift. The ancient Sanskrit scriptures say that food is God, because like God, it sustains all life, all human beings. For this reason, the scriptures say, human beings must worship food as they worship God. They must treat the two with equal reverence. The prophets and mythmakers of the ancient world made it perfectly clear why people sanctified their foodstuffs and why they made them the objects of sacred rituals—because without food, no life could exist at all.

Volumes of ancient wisdom survive in the sacred texts of the Hindus and in other religious doctrines that originated in prehistory. The creators of these doctrines believed in the unity of life; they embraced the concept that humans share a common soul or spirit with the lowliest plants and animals. This understanding of soul led to the sanctification of food, the respect for sacrifice, and the quest for ritual purity. Endowing all living things with soul or spirit made people conscious of what they should and should not consume. It made them conscious of what kinds of consumables please the gods and what offends them. It's interesting that so many groups of people describe a mystical relationship they maintain with plants and animals. It appears that people have a hard time denying the feeling that some strange, immutable bond unites the lives of plants and animals with their own.

Today, the domestication of plants and animals and the consumption and preparation of food constitute significant rituals of daily life; but in the past, they defined religious life. Perhaps nothing better illustrates the contrast between ancient and modern belief systems than the perception of food. The primary value of food was always to provide sustenance; but in ancient cultures, it fed the soul as well as the body, and it acted as a means of worship and a social binder. Food rituals continue to tie societies together. By eating roast goose at Christmas, eggs at Easter, and even celebratory cakes at birthdays, people continue the food traditions set by their ancestors. Most food festivals people celebrate today have their basis in some ancient thank offering, or sacrifice, or prayer.

Food means different things to different people. To some it means nothing more than physical satisfaction. People tend to forget that in the past, food provided an affirmation of God's presence. In myths, food symbolizes wealth and prosperity, fertility and renewal. It purifies, poisons, incites passion, and grants fertility. It elevates the mind, facilitating communication with the gods. Sometimes, it bestows immortality. People of the past created food myths rich in symbolism, myths perhaps intended to keep accumulated knowledge alive from generation to generation. The mythmakers put their faith in the goddess of the earth; they saw the earth goddess provide, and they rejoiced.

People rejoiced, feasted, created food myths, and performed food rituals because they recognized how vital a role food played in the cycle of life. Food was the very symbol of life, created by divine intervention; it came forth from nature, so people connected food with the earth and the waters and with the fertility gods who controlled them. In mythological belief, this connection to the deities made food a magical substance. In myths, each food had a magical origin. It arose from the womb of the earth goddess or from the body of a murdered god. The theme of gods and other mythological heroes dying to allow food to sprout from their bodies revealed the ancient knowledge of life from death. The earth died each winter yet sprouted new life each spring. That was part of the magic. Myths attesting to the magic of food involve trees full of immortal fruits, magic pans of buffalo meat, and cauldrons full of mead that miraculously yield inexhaustible supplies. The Norse thunder god Thor performed a most amazing feat when he resurrected his goats. He waved his hammer like a magic wand over their dead bones, and with his energizing storm power, restored them to life. The myth of Thor illustrated the power the gods had over fertility and food supply. The theme of resurrection crops up time and time again in food myths. In Greek myth, the earth goddess Persephone retreated to the underworld each winter but returned each spring, bringing the grain with her. In Japanese myth, bears gave their bodies in sacrifice, but their spirits did not die; instead, they retreated to their mountain homes, and then returned in the bodies of other bears, which again gave their bodies in sacrifice. Death and resurrection defined the cycle of life, and food formed its basis.

Food represents hope; it symbolizes life. Because long ago people endowed the earth and the animals with magic powers, survival meant propitiating the nature spirits—those deities who controlled the fertility of the soil and the availability of game. Almost every existing plant and animal became the subject of a legend explaining its origin. Hunters felt the need to explain how the animals migrated to their hunting grounds, and agriculturists felt the need to explain how the plants arose from the soil. The ancients regarded both hunting and agriculture not as scientific endeavors but as religious arts. Because they deeply believed that gods and spirits controlled the fertility of the earth, they viewed foodstuffs too as sacred and full of spirit. The ancients spun myths around these spirits to tap into their powers, and they left them offerings of food to ensure that these spirits would act benevolently toward humans and continue to provide. The gods and goddesses who controlled food, and indeed personified food, symbolized life as well. What powers these deities and their sacred foodstuffs possessed! The myths tell of salmon that granted wisdom, fruit that granted immortality, and hidden strengths in all sorts of consumables, real or imagined. The ancients searched for magic in food just as they did in every other element of their world.

The sanctification of food and the acceptance of food as magic leads to a rethinking of the meaning of sustenance. Myths and legends surround almost every food plant and every game animal, and when people take time to dissect those myths, common, everyday plants come to life and assume new meaning, and the animals people butcher without thought seem to give up their spirit to feed others. When people read the myths and gain a true understanding of the thought processes behind them, they begin to think of plants and animals not simply as foods but as powerful spirits, spirits who can intoxicate, cure, grant fertility, bring good fortune, or banish demons. In this way of thinking food certainly does become God, full of spirit and full of magic. In a world long ago where food formed the basis of myth, life, and ritual, consuming a plant or an animal meant to absorb its magic powers.

A myths, Zeus and Jupiter manifested themselves in oak trees, as booming sounds of thunder rustled through the branches of these trees like the voices of powerful deities. Teutonic myth-makers named Thor, their thunder god, as god of the oak, and the Russians did the same with their thunder god, Perun. In Celtic myth, the oak was sacred to Dadga, their omnipotent god of both earth and sky. The Druids believed that eating the acorns of their sacred oaks aided their powers to divine the future.

Due to the importance of the acorn, early foragers felt the need to explain why the oak, and the food it produced, existed. Ancient people so venerated the oak tree that some believed it was the first tree created. Some early mythmakers even said that human beings sprang from the plant. Such myths were told by many nonagricultural peoples of North America, many of whom gathered acorns from the forests long before they learned other means of finding food.

In a legend from the Luiseños of California, the oak arose from the body of Wyot, the son of Night and Earth. Wyot served as guardian of all living things. He foretold his own death, instructing his people to make a basket for his ashes. From those ashes the first oak tree grew. In some versions of the myth, Wyot's spirit became the bright star Vega, and his people sent various birds to the star to ask Wyot how they might use this oak tree. A hummingbird finally succeeded in reaching the star and returned with the news: Wyot had told the hummingbird that he gave the oak to the people, the animals, and the birds as a gift of sustenance.

To Native Americans in California, acorns were, in past times, the staff of life. In fact, many of these people relied on them for sustenance into the early 1900s. Acorns are still an important food for some Native Americans, who grind them into meal and make them into porridge, breads, and cakes. They also incorporate acorns into their rituals and

ACORNS

Most people today don't think of acorns as food, but in fact, acorns were one of the earliest foods. The classical myths list them as one of the foods people subsisted on during the Golden Age, when food was abundant and there was no need for farming. Long before the advent of agriculture, foragers relied on acorns for survival, particularly in Europe, where people considered the seeds of the oak tree a symbol of fecundity and immortality. In Roman myth, early humans lived on leaves and grasses until the goddess Ceres replaced these foods with acorns. The people of ancient Rome made them into bread during wars and famines. Though these early acorn breads eventually gave way to flat breads made out of barley, the Romans obviously recognized acorns as a valuable and nutritious food source. The Romans dedicated the acorn to Jupiter, their sky god, because in myth, the oak tree provided Jupiter with shelter at the time of his birth.

Acorns were abundant in lands covered with vast forests of oak trees, and, not surprisingly, the sanctity of acorns goes hand in hand with the practice of oak worship. Early people first worshipped oak trees for the food they produced, and people in Greece, Rome, Germany, and the Slavic lands associated the oak with the gods who controlled rain, thunder, and the fertility of the earth. In the classical

1

ceremonies. In the past, some California tribes held an annual celebration of acorns, at which time people gathered under certain oak trees and pleaded with them to produce abundant supplies. This type of first-fruit ceremony involved a tribal priest who impersonated the vegetation god and a group of women who gathered the acorns and then pressed them into mush. After cooking the mush over a fire, the people held a feast.

The California Indians told numerous legends about gathering and cooking acorns. In a Yurok myth, Coyote learned the hard way the correct method of preparing them. When Coyote first tasted these foods, he enjoyed them immensely. The people who had fed them to him explained that to prepare acorns himself, he should soak them in water, press them, and then wait several days before eating them. Coyote didn't believe these people. He much preferred to try drowning the acorns in the river, then gathering them from the riverbank afterward, which the people suggested when he refused to accept the correct method. Coyote tried this with his grandmother's acorns, and she got quite angry when he lost them all—after dumping them in the river, he couldn't find a single one. Coyote's grandmother refused to give him more acorns after that. But with no acorns to eat, Coyote nearly died of starvation. His grandmother finally relented, and acorn mush saved Coyote.

Oak trees take a long time to produce, but when they do, they produce an abundant food supply. For this reason many people who consumed them believed they symbolized the perfection that can be achieved after long, concentrated effort. (*Funk and Wagnall's* 1972; Wilkins et al. 1995)

See also Almonds; Chestnuts; Hazelnuts; Mesquite; Peanuts; Pines and Pine Nuts; Walnuts

AGAVE
See Pulque

ALCOHOLIC BEVERAGES
The consumption of alcohol played an integral role in the belief systems of nearly all early cultures. The peoples of Oceania and most of North America considered alcohol contradictory to their beliefs; but people in much of the Old World and in Mesoamerica used intoxicating beverages to enhance their ritual and spiritual lives. Alcohol consumption in the ancient world was a matter of public endeavor, originally undertaken to achieve a spiritual communion with the deities. Drinking was a religious act, often considered so sacred that it was reserved for priests and shamans—those with the real power to commune with the divine.

Alcoholic beverages often figured in ancient myths. Just as people felt the need to explain the origin of the world and of natural phenomena in the earth, sea, and sky, they felt the need to explain the origin of their sacred beverages; for, like the wind and the rain and the majestic mountains, these beverages too had mysterious properties. In Hindu myth, the drink soma arose from the primordial ocean. Mead, a drink of the Germanic peoples, spouted from the udders of Odin, the great god's goat. The wine of the ancient Greeks was a divine gift from the god Dionysus. Since the gods consumed these beverages in myths, followers of these gods drank them in their honor. Dionysus, for instance, was invoked and honored in the imbibing of the sacred Greek beverage (grape wine), and those who partook of it shared in his divinity.

Many ancient peoples viewed intoxication as an element of worship. Because the gods gave humans the gift of ecstasy, people participated in drinking much as they did in prayer. They elevated their mental state to reach that of the deities. This practice in part reflected a belief that substances capable of altering mental states had a supernatural influence, and that beverages such as wine and beer had a spirit, or perhaps were spirits in themselves. Soma, the magical elixir of ancient India, was both a drink and a god; worshipers of the great

Liturgical banquet relief, 2700–2344 B.C. *Alcohol consumption in the ancient world was a matter of public endeavor, originally undertaken to achieve a spiritual communion with the deities. (Erich Lessing/Art Resource, NY)*

god Indra drank it to please him. The Aztecs drank the alcoholic beverage pulque at every major religious occasion, and they believed that they had to get drunk to please the gods. The worship of Dionysus also involved drinking to intoxication. When followers reached a state of religious ecstasy, they believed they had entered Dionysus's realm.

This deification of alcohol contrasts with the view taken by Muslims, Jains, and higher-caste Hindus today, particularly Brahmins and Vaishnavas (devotees of Vishnu). Many Hindus, following the sacred text of the Vedas, eschew alcohol as a polluting substance that violates ritual purity. Modern Hindus label alcohol a "hot" food, meaning that it is thought to interfere with physical strength, to stimulate sexual behavior, and to promote other forms of behavior deemed undesirable. The hot-cold classification of foods is based on their perceived impact on a person's physical condition: The consumption of healthful, or "cold" (typically, vegetarian), foods paves the way for spiritual purity (though it alone does not create spiritual purity); the consumption of "hot" foods (like meat, for instance) works against purity. Hindus place alcohol in the same category as meat for two reasons: In addition to its "hot" nature and its negative spiritual effects, the consumption of meat violates ahimsa (the principle of noninjury to living things). Higher-caste Hindus reject alcohol also because the brewing process involves killing insects. For those devoted to ahimsa, the act of killing any living creature further contributes to the consumer's spiritual impurity.

Pious Hindus, Buddhists, and people in other Eastern religions make ritual purity a primary goal. They believe that because alcohol interferes with mental clarity, it interferes with the mind-set they need to achieve—ultimately, it keeps them out of heaven and away from the gods. Many others hold the view that altered states bring one closer to the gods, and intoxication is embraced not only by cult worshipers but often by those believed to have true power. In much of the world, shamans who consume alcoholic beverages do so to make contact with supernatural forces. They believe the alcohol elevates their minds to a state beyond the ordinary, where the forces of the otherworld reside. (Marshall 1979; Simoons 1998; Toussaint-Samat 1992)

See also Ayahuasca; Balche; Beer; Chicha; Kava; Mead; Pulque; Sake; Soma; Wine

ALLIGATOR AND CROCODILE

People dining in the southeastern United States today may not be surprised to find alligator on the menu. After years of myths that labeled the alligator a frightful water monster, alligator meat came into acceptance as a medicinal substance, then as a southern specialty in trendy Cajun cuisine. But just as crocodiles served as food for people of the Old World, alligators served as food for people living in the bayous and swamplands of the southeastern United States, even in prehistory. The Native Americans used the skin to make drums and the flesh for food and medicine. They believed that alligator meat had healing properties and that it gave strength to whomever consumed it.

When the Europeans arrived in southeastern America, they quickly "discovered" the alligator and recognized the similarities to serpentlike monsters they knew from Old World legends. They transferred these legends to the creatures they saw swimming in the lagoons and bayous, creatures that looked foreboding and evil, like the Nile crocodile and the Leviathan of the Mediterranean. In the Old World, people in ancient Egypt ate crocodiles from the Nile, and so did people in other parts of Africa; however, they also feared crocodiles as creatures of evil. Later Europeans feared the alligators of North America as well. In legend, the Nile crocodile swallowed one stone for each person he devoured—that's how he counted his victims. Then European explorers in America found stones in the alligators' stomachs, which gave credence to the myths.

The alligators' stomach stones were simply fragments of stone, glass, and wood made smooth from the action of gastric juices. After the initial fear of crocodiles dissipated, the early Americans utilized the stones. They ground them into powder and assigned them medicinal and aphrodisiacal powers.

Though for a long time early settlers in America avoided consuming alligators because they feared eating anything that might eat them, they eventually changed their view. The consumption of alligators became popular primarily among black slaves, who knew the legends and lore of Africa and the crocodiles that resided there. In later years, however, more people began to consume the flesh of alligators, as well as the fat and the eggs, just as the Native Americans did. They learned to rely on the animal for both food and medicine. The healing properties assigned to alligators seemed linked to the fact that many people worshipped the animal; some even considered it their totem, an animal who guarded and protected them. While alligator worship prevented some people from killing these creatures, it encouraged others to utilize their products. People of many tribes thought alligator teeth counteracted poisonous snakebites, relieved pain of other sorts, and even guarded against witchcraft. They also believed that alligator fat relieved fever and cured arthritis and that alligator blood cured eye irritations.

As common as alligators were to the Native Americans, the ancient Chinese, it appears, incorporated these animals into their mythology even more. The Chinese also ate alligators, ones that inhabited the lower Yangtze River. It appears likely that Chinese dragon myths stemmed from early perceptions about alligators. Both dragons and alligators symbolize the underworld, earth energies, and the power of the waters. In legend, dragons control the waters. They reside there, as do alligators, and they hibernate in the winter before emerging in the spring and bringing rejuvenating rains that renew the earth. When the dragons emerge, they rise to the sky and battle

with each other, their enormous feet pressing on the clouds and pushing out the water. In reality, alligators do emerge in the spring just as the rains begin to fall. They too hibernate in the winter, when Chinese hunters find it easiest to hunt and kill them for food. (Glasgow 1991; Robbins 1999)

ALMONDS

The almond tree originated in the Middle East and western Asia, and since prehistory people considered it a symbol of sweetness and fragility. In the spring, the tree was one of the first to bloom, and late frosts could easily destroy its delicate buds. If the almond tree survived the frosts, it soon became a bestower of a wealth of gifts. In addition to providing nuts, oil, and shells for fuel, the almond tree was aesthetically pleasing, with lovely flowers and beautiful leaves. So the almond tree inspired divine worship.

Ancient mythmakers commonly said that gods turned people into trees; that was how they explained the origins of various plants. In the Greek myth of Phyllis, a Thracian princess, Athena fashioned this conversion to honor Phyllis for her faithfulness. The princess fell in love with Demophon, a young man who had fought in the Trojan War and whom she met and married when he stopped in Thrace on his way home. Phyllis killed herself a short time later, after Demophon went to Athens and did not return. In death, she was transformed into an almond tree. When Demophon finally returned to Thrace, he embraced the tree, and it instantly blossomed.

Several Moroccan folktales tell of princesses who became almond trees. Allah changed the princess Jasmina into an almond tree after her lover died in battle, and the tree blossomed each year on the anniversary of her lover's death. The generous princess Hatim gave away much of her father's riches to the poor, which enraged him so much that he demanded that she choose between exile or death. The princess chose to be killed. Allah changed her into an almond tree because the almond tree, like Hatim, gave its gifts freely to the poor. Poor people could rely on the almond tree to provide.

In these and other instances, the almond tree was female. The mythic figure of the tree as woman, or as mother, is common to many cultures, and the almond is but one example. Perhaps the ancients identified the tree as feminine also because the almond nut has a shape similar to that of the womb. But the mythmakers of Phrygia, a region that today is in central Turkey, identified the almond as male rather than female, and in fact, referred to the nut as "the father of all things." A myth from this area told of the virgin goddess Nana, who conceived a child after carrying a ripe almond in her bosom. (In other versions it was a pomegranate.) She conceived Attis, a vegetation god—the Babylonian equivalent to the Greek Adonis. In another variation of the Attis myth, the daughter of the Phrygian River god Sangarius conceived the child after she fell in love with the almond tree and ate its fruit. In the Greek version, the mother of Adonis transformed herself into the almond tree and then gave birth to him.

The identification of the almond as father or as mother reflected the fact that almond blossoms herald the spring and thus the birth of vegetation. Because the almond tree blossoms suddenly, the Hebrews considered it a symbol of haste, and because the almond tree that survives the frosts bestows gifts of nuts and oil, they considered it a symbol of vigilance. Trees in other lands held particular prominence in the myths and the almond was no exception. People revered the almond tree as a provider—of life, of love, and of happiness. (Folkard 1892; Goor and Nurock 1968; Reed 1992)

See also Acorns; Chestnuts; Hazelnuts; Peanuts; Walnuts

AMARANTH

Amaranth refers to various types of weedy plants of the genus *Amaranthus,* some of which are high-protein grain crops. These plants are native to tropical and subtropical regions of the world, and people have eaten the leaves and the seeds since antiquity. The grain amaranths were essential food plants of the Aztecs, plants they had consumed for thousands of years before Cortez and the Spaniards banned their use. Amaranth seed could be ground into flour, cooked into porridge, popped and eaten like cold cereal, or mixed with honey and made into a sweet bread or unleavened cake. As an essential part of ancient ritual, the Aztecs ground these seeds into flour and formed sacred images of their deities from the dough.

Scholars today recognize that amaranth contains more protein than other grains, but the Aztecs, and the Maya before them, appeared to believe that amaranth contained magic. In addition to eating the unleavened cakes as communion bread, the Aztecs drank the grain in a concoction mixed with the blood of their sacrifice victims. Because they incorporated amaranth into their religious rituals, Cortez forbade its cultivation. Cortez wanted to convert the Aztecs to Christianity, and amaranth played an important role in their worship of pagan gods.

Cortez made every attempt to eradicate amaranth. He sent soldiers out to burn the fields and destroy the *chinampas,* or "floating gardens," of Tenochtitlán, the Aztec capital, which had produced primary food crops including amaranth for hundreds of years. The Aztecs had built an empire and developed a highly advanced agricultural society, and Cortez destroyed it. But amaranth was such a vital part of the Mesoamerican culture that people continued to grow the grain in secrecy. This crop meant survival to the Aztecs. It was not only an essential food but also an important symbol, one that, because of its ceremonial significance, cemented their culture together.

The Aztecs worshipped Huitzilopochtli, their war god, with the use of amaranth. They ground the seeds into a paste they called *zoale* or *tzoalli,* formed dough images of

Huitzilopochtli from it, then ate the images as communion bread, believing it to be the flesh and bones of their god. The feast of Huitzilopochtli included human sacrifice and utilization of the sacrificial blood to consecrate one gigantic dough image of the god. Everyone in the city attended this ceremony, and each person was forbidden to eat anything that day except the amaranth dough, sweetened with honey. After much dancing and many games and sacrifices, all performed for the deities, the priests broke the tzoalli into small bits and everyone ate them. All those who received this communion partook in the divinity of Huitzilopochtli. Then they offered amaranth seeds to him, the seeds that the Aztecs believed formed the basis of their idol's flesh and bones.

The Aztecs used tzoalli in numerous rituals and made images not only of Huitzilopochtli but of other important deities as well. They used amaranth to make images of Chicomecoatl, the goddess of crops; of Xiuhtecutli, the god of fire; of Omacatl, the god of feasts; of Macuilxochitli, the flower god; and of the Tlaloques, the gods of rain. They fed amaranth to people before they sacrificed them. They fashioned all kinds of animals from the dough. The Aztecs made birdlike images of Xocotl out of amaranth dough; Xocotl appeared to be some kind of bird deity. They carried the dough idols to the tops of trees, then threw them down to the ground where they broke into pieces and people consumed the fragments. They also used amaranth dough to make little hills—images they placed in shrines and worshipped as part of a festival honoring their hills and mountains. People formed images of the principal mountains out of the dough, then put idols alongside them.

Amaranth had, in large part, defined a culture, both as a religious symbol and as a staple food. It had grown in Mesoamerica in abundance, so it enabled the people to survive when other crops failed. Amaranth served not only as a source of carbohydrates but also as an essential source of protein for people who did not have the ability to domesticate animals. Because scholars recognize the nutritive value of this grain, amaranth has made a comeback recently in America. In present-day Mexico, people continue to use amaranth to make cakes, candies, and sweet tamales called *chuales,* which bear a remarkable resemblance to the food of the ancient Aztecs. Mexicans today make a sweet bread called *alegria* from a dough of amaranth seeds and molasses, and they make chuales out of bean paste covered with amaranth flour. They prepare these products on All Soul's Day, or the Day of the Dead, as well as on other Christian feast days, which suggests a relationship to the ancient tzoalli and connects the use of amaranth with religious ritual.

People of the Old World and the Americas appeared to connect amaranth with their ideas of God, heaven, and the afterlife. Swiss peasants wore wreaths of amaranth on Ascension Day, the feast day of the Lord's ascent to heaven, and the Greeks used amaranth flowers to decorate their churches and to adorn images of their gods. In ancient Greece, amaranth symbolized immortality, so the people used it as a funeral flower, placing it on graves as a dedication to the dead. Homer said that the Thessalonians used crowns of amaranth at the burial of Achilles. People considered amaranth an emblem of immortality because it never faded. People of western China call amaranth seed "millet from heaven," in keeping with an ancient belief that amaranth covered the fields of paradise. (Cole 1979; Duran 1971; Foster and Cordell 1992)

See also Bread; Cake; Corn; Grain; Millet; Oats; Quinoa; Rice; Rye; Wheat

AMBROSIA
See Nectar and Ambrosia

APPLES
The apple has an extensive mythological history. It appears in the lore and legends of countries around the world as a mystical, enchanted

fruit. The apple was a magic object in the myths of Scandinavia, Ireland, Iceland, Germany, Brittany, England, and Arabia. There were apples that sang, apples that nourished people for long periods of time, and apples whose aroma alone provided sustenance. In Arabian myth, Prince Ahmed of the Arabian Nights had apples that cured every known human disorder. In many cultures the apple guaranteed fruitfulness. The apple served as a healing object, a love charm, a fertility amulet, and a means of divination. In many traditional myths, eating apples led to immortality.

The Latin name for the apple is *Pomma,* which is also the generic Latin word for fruit; Pomona was the Roman goddess of gardens and fruit trees. Apples were popular fruits in the classical world, and the ancient Greeks served them at every meal. But the Greeks tended to call any strange fruit an apple, distinguishing them only by their country of origin. They called citrus fruits "Persian apples," for instance, and apricots, "Armenian apples." Perhaps for this reason, scholars dispute whether the golden apples in Greek myth were actually apples or some other kind of fruit, possibly oranges.

The golden apples of Greek myth surfaced when the sky god, Zeus, gave them to his goddess, Hera, as a wedding present. Hera gave the apples to the dragon, Ladon, to guard in the Garden of the Hesperides. The ancient Greeks said that in this garden, a tree grew that bore the magnificent fruit. Heracles wanted the fruit because it bestowed immortality, and he obtained it by tricking Atlas, the owner of the garden, and slaying the dragon. However, the apples retained their magic only in the Garden of the Hesperides, and when Heracles discovered this, he had to return them.

Magic apples appear in several other myths as well. In the popular myth known as the Judgement of Paris, the goddess of discord threw a golden apple marked "for the fairest" into the midst of a wedding feast for Thetis and Peleus attended by all the Greek gods and goddesses. (This apple was commonly called the Apple of Discord.) Three goddesses—Hera, Athena, and Aphrodite—claimed the apple, so Zeus asked Paris, a shepherd, to decide who was worthy. Each of the goddesses offered Paris great gifts, but the shepherd awarded the apple to Aphrodite, who offered him Helen, the most beautiful woman in the world. For the Greeks, the apple was a feminine symbol, the inside of which resembles the female genitalia, and it was commonly identified with Aphrodite, the goddess of love, fertility, and fruitfulness.

The symbolic association of the apple with fertility appears in Norse myths as well, perhaps because the people in these frigid lands welcomed the appearance of apple blossoms as a sign that the earth had survived the winter. The apple served as a fertility symbol when the Norse sun god Frey sent golden apples to the frost giantess Gerda as a marriage offer. An apple served a similar purpose when Odin sent the wife of Rerir an apple. She ate the apple and soon afterward gave birth to a son whom she named Volsung. In later myths, Volsung had an apple tree in the center of his hall, symbolizing the continuation of the family line.

Perhaps the most noted apples of Norse myth belonged to the goddess Idun. These apples bestowed immortality, and Idun guarded them and doled them out to aging gods to restore their youth. The great value of these apples made them targets for theft; and Loki, the trickster, did indeed steal them—along with Idun—for the giant Thiazi. But when the gods began to wither away, Loki was forced to give them back. Loki disguised himself as a falcon, turned Idun into a hazelnut, and flew away with her in his claws. He returned Idun to Asgard, the home of the gods, where she once again used her apples to restore the gods' health and youth.

Irish mythmakers told similar stories of apples and nuts, giving them the ability to bestow both youth and immortality. In one Irish legend, a woman from the otherworld gave apples to the hero Candle, and they nourished him for an entire month, then made him

Heracles in the Garden of the Hesperides. (Alinari/Art Resource, NY)

immortal. In another Irish legend, the smith god Lugh punished the three sons of Tuleran for killing his father, and that punishment involved retrieving three apples of immortality—a seemingly impossible task.

People familiar with the biblical story of Adam and Eve know the significance of the apple. It was the forbidden fruit, a magic fruit, and a symbol of temptation, guarded by a serpent who served a function similar to the dragon Ladon's role in the Garden of the Hesperides. Dragons and serpents often guarded apples in the myths. In a Polish legend, a hawk, rather than a dragon or a serpent, guarded the apples. In this story the apples grew on a tree at the entrance to a golden castle on a mountain of ice that seemed impossible to reach. The hero of this story, much like Heracles, killed the hawk, gathered the apples, and rescued a princess.

In myths, legends, and folklore around the world, apples hold appeal for everyone—gods, royalty, and commoners alike—as a magnificent and often magical fruit. The Celtic paradise, called Avalon or the Islands of the Blessed, was generally believed to be full of apple trees. Here too the apple was clearly the fruit of immortality, and some said it symbolized springtime and bliss, the kind of bliss only attainable in heaven. Some scholars have suggested that Avalon was a real place, possibly at Glastonbury in Britain, a fertile area of abundant fruit that was surrounded by marshes and could easily have been considered an island. The Celts revered apples and attributed to them the power to enchant, mystify, and grant wishes. (Davidson 1988; Folkard 1892; Graves 1988; Toussaint-Samat 1992)

See also Apricots; Bananas and Plantains; Lemons and Citrons; Oranges; Pomegranates; Quinces; Tomatoes

APRICOTS

Apricots grow in parts of Central Asia, Korea, Siberia, and northern China. Symbols of these delectable fruits appear on oracle bones of the Shang dynasty, from the eighth to the twelfth centuries B.C. Most likely, apricots were domesticated in China, then spread westward via Armenia. Certainly apricots grew abundantly in Asia and the Middle East, and they grew there long before apples. Before the seventeenth century, many kinds of fruit were called apples, usually distinguished by their place of origin or by some other identifying characteristic. The ancients called apricots Armenian apples, or golden apples. Certainly they were golden in color, and they smelled delicious. It's quite likely that apricots were the forbidden fruit that tempted Eve in the Garden of Eden.

Ancient myths commonly place apricots in paradise. These "golden apples" grew abundantly in the Holy Land, and scholars therefore have argued that apricots, not apples, hung from the biblical Tree of Knowledge. Furthermore, the apples that grew in this area had far less flavor than apricots, whose appearance and aroma conjured up images of godly delights of nectar and ambrosia. In Babylonian myth, after the creation of the world, when a worm begged the sun god Shamash for food, Shamash offered him apricots. Apricots seemed a fitting food for a sun god to possess; they were golden like the sun, and their sweet aroma typified the smells associated with celestial deities. Some ancient people believed the apricot to be a prophetic or oracular tree, and decidedly magical. In China, Confucius compiled some of the most important religious books of China in an apricot grove. After he completed his work, Confucius erected an altar in the grove to thank God for allowing him to finish his work. This endowed the apricot with even greater legendary significance among the Chinese.

In Chinese mythology, the apricot was one of the five renowned fruits of antiquity, along with the plum, the peach, the jujube, and the chestnut. In Chinese symbolism, apricots represent timidity. Like many fruits, they're also seductive; they have a soft, fleshy texture and a sweet, mildly pungent aroma. Fruits with these characteristics have often been used as aphrodisiacs and love charms. Apricots, when cut, resemble the yoni, or the female genitalia, as do other fruits such as almonds, figs, apples, and pears. All these fruits evoke the symbolism of love and sex. The Chinese say that the kernels of the apricot resemble the slanting eyes of Chinese women, and for this reason they consider the fruit a female symbol. In folktales, apricots often represent lust; and people in England once believed that to dream of apricots brought good fortune, especially in love. (Moldenke and Moldenke 1952; Reed 1992; Toussaint-Samat 1992)

See also Apples; Lemons and Citrons; Quinces

ARECA NUTS
See Betel Nuts

ARTICHOKES

Thousands of years ago, wild artichokes grew on the hills of Greece, Egypt, and parts of Asia. Some scholars have identified these as globe artichokes, the vegetable familiar to people today; others, as cardoons, the artichokes' predecessor. Cardoons are wild thistles with sharp prickles on the ends of the leaves. Ancient people familiar with these plants consumed the large flower buds in salads, stews, and soups.

Artichokes are one of the world's oldest cultivated vegetables, grown extensively in Greece and Rome. They were highly esteemed in Tudor England, and the British exported them to other parts of Europe. Yet, however edible these wild "thistles" may have been, the ancients certainly recognized the symbolic implications of the sharp leaves. When the Bible's Job contrasted prosperity and usefulness with cruel suffering, he did so by metaphorically contrasting thorns and weeds with wheat and barley—in other words, thistles, which caused pain and suffering, with grain, which brought happiness and prosperity. Job's thistles may have been cardoons rather than globe artichokes, but artichokes were also denigrated for their sharp prickles. In one myth, a beautiful young girl named Cinara angered a god, who turned her into an artichoke. (The scientific name for artichoke is *Cynara scolymus.*) Although the gods often changed humans into plants to honor them and reward them with immortality, the transformation of Cinara was clearly a punishment. (Soyer 1977; White 1934)

ASPARAGUS

In ancient times, asparagus grew wild in eastern Europe and the Mediterranean region. Cattle used to graze on asparagus growing on the steppes in Russia and Poland, but people did not consume it except in medicines. The first asparagus varieties were bitter to the taste, but cultivation eventually yielded sweeter varieties. The Greeks likely cultivated asparagus by 200 B.C. and held the vegetable in high esteem.

The Greeks weren't the only people of the ancient world to venerate asparagus: Archaeologists have found representations of the asparagus plant in ancient tombs, indicating that the Egyptians used it in funerary rites. The Romans valued asparagus as food. People in the British Isles used it to make wine, since asparagus thrived in this area and grapes did not. The people of Britain considered grape wine a drink of the rich, but they used plants such as asparagus and turnips to make wine that the poorer people could afford.

People all over Europe found uses for asparagus. They used the plant not only for eating and drinking but also for making garlands. The Greeks used asparagus for making bridal garlands and for weaving baskets used in the Greek harvest festival, the Thesmophoria. This may have had some connection to the phallic shape of the emergent asparagus shoots and their subsequent role in myth and symbol. The Greeks dedicated asparagus to Aphrodite, the goddess of love, and to Perigune, a goddess of the cornfield, who hid behind a bush of asparagus to escape her wicked father.

The Greek myth of Perigune begins with Perigune's father, Sinus, who lived on the isthmus of Corinth and personified the north wind. Sinus was a bandit, strong like the north wind, and he acquired the name Pitokamptes, or Pine Bender, for his ability to bend the tops of pine trees down to the ground with his bare hands. Sinus typically asked travelers he encountered on the isthmus to help him bend down the pine trees, and when they did, he quickly releasd his hold and sent the unwitting victims catapulting to their deaths. But the Greek hero Theseus put an end to that. When Theseus encountered Sinus, he released his hold first, and the infamous Pine Bender never terrorized anyone again. After Theseus killed Sinus, he noticed Sinus's daughter Perigune hiding behind an asparagus bush, terribly frightened. She was talking to the asparagus, and promising the plant that if it hid her safely, she would never harm it. Because Perigune had connections not only to the asparagus plant but also to the cornfield and the fertility of the land, the use of asparagus in her myth likely reflected its phallic symbolism. Perigune emerged from behind the asparagus and immediately fell in love with Theseus. Soon she bore him a son, Melanippus, who became the ancestor of the Ioxids, who venerated asparagus. (Baumann 1993; Graves 1988)

AVOCADOS

The Mayan, the Aztec, and the pre-Incan peoples of Peru all cultivated avocados. These fruits likely originated in Mexico in pre-Aztec times, though scholars have discovered depictions of the fruit on pottery from all three of these ancient civilizations. They've also found avocado seeds in archaeological sites in Mexico dating from 8000 to 7000 B.C. The pre-Columbian Americans subsisted on a low-fat diet consisting primarily of beans, corn, squash, tomatoes, and chili peppers. The Aztecs also consumed a grain called amaranth, and the Peruvians consumed a grain called quinoa and

hundreds of varieties of potatoes. Avocados provided these people with the essential oils their other staple foods lacked, and supplied vitamins and nearly twice the amount of protein they received from other fruits.

The seeds of avocados germinate easily, and the people of pre-Columbian America consumed a large quantity of avocados. They also extracted oil from the avocado seeds to light their lamps and to use in cooking. Few products in history have achieved such consistent regard as oil, and all sorts of vegetable oils achieved ritual significance for their use in anointing. The pre-Columbian Americans held the avocado in high esteem. This fruit, often called the alligator pear, was shaped like a pear, and the Maya and the Aztec peoples saw it as a symbol of the human heart. The Aztecs also likened avocados to testicles.

A myth from South America explains the growth of avocado trees throughout the forests of Guiana. A man named Seriokai loved avocados, and he spent a lot of time traipsing through the forests with his wife, climbing avocado trees and gathering stores of the ripe fruits. One day, Seriokai's wife attracted the attention of a tapir, and the tapir and the woman fell in love. The woman desired the tapir so desperately that she planned to leave her husband and steal away with the animal into the forest. An opportunity presented itself one day while Seriokai was up in an avocado tree gathering fruit. When he descended the trunk, his conniving wife struck him with the ax she had been carrying to chop firewood. Seriokai fell to the ground, horribly wounded, and his wife ran off with the tapir and left her husband for dead.

Fortunately for Seriokai, a friendly neighbor came along, and seeing the injured man, picked him up and nursed him back to health. But his wife had struck him in the leg, and it took a long time before Seriokai could walk again. During this time, the woman and the tapir had traveled far, and avocado trees had sprung up along their path where the woman had dropped seeds. Bent on revenge, Seriokai used the avocado trees to find her. He found large trees, then smaller ones, then mere sprouts, and finally avocado seeds—and his wife's footsteps. He spotted the tapir and shot him with an arrow. According to legend, Seriokai, his wife, and the tapir live on in the sky—Seriokai as the hunter Orion, his wife as the Pleiades, and the tapir as the Hyades. (Bayley 1913; Skinner n.d.)

See also Pears

AYAHUASCA

Ayahuasca is a hallucinogenic beverage consumed by people in the Amazonian rain forests and in areas of the Andes. It goes by many other names as well, including *caapi, kahi, pinde,* and *yaje.* The drink is a primary tool of South American shamans, who believe it enables them to foretell the future, diagnose illnesses, and predict disasters, and to travel through time to see their gods and ancestors. Ayahuasca means "vine of the soul," which refers to the

drink's ability to free the spirit. Those who consume ayahuasca believe that their souls transcend the earth, wander around for a while communing with the spirits, and then return to their bodies. Some native South Americans continue to use the drink ceremonially—for instance, in healing rituals. Colombians still use it in adolescent initiation rites.

Hallucinogens play a significant, and according to some observers, an all-encompassing role in the mythology and beliefs of South American tribal societies. Native tribes of this continent, past and present, have accumulated tremendous knowledge of plants and their properties, and they know how to utilize those plants for magico-religious purposes—to heighten the senses, cure diseases, and commune with spirits. Ayahuasca is just one of many hallucinogenic drinks people make from the plants in their world; the South American tribes concoct it from several species of woody liana, which have psychoactive effects due to the beta-carboline alkaloids in them. The preparation of ayahuasca involves scraping the bark

Peruvian shaman mixing a medicinal drink from the ayahuasca plant. (AFP/Corbis)

from the stem, then cutting up the bark and either boiling it or kneading it in cold water, and occasionally adding the leaves of other plants.

The drink is bitter and nauseating, but effective. It can cause an overwhelming sense of euphoria and produce colorful visions. Those who have drunk ayahuasca reportedly experience a sensation of flying or of being lifted into the air. South American shamans say they ascend to the top of the Milky Way. Different plant additives produce different effects: One additive produces visions in red, while another one produces visions of green snakes. Frequently the consumer sees either snakes or jaguars, and shamans sometimes say they become jaguars while thus intoxicated. Partakers of the drink may see the gods, their ancestors, or animals, and report that they gain an understanding of reality and social order.

Because of the telepathic powers attributed to ayahuasca, the beverage and the plants play a significant role in native mythology and beliefs. The plants themselves are considered gifts from the gods, and their power is said to come from supernatural forces within their tissues. In one origin myth of ayahuasca, the sun father impregnated the first woman, who then gave birth to the narcotic plant. The child lived to an old age, all the while guarding his hallucinogenic powers. (Balik and Cox 1996; Ratsch 1992; Schultes and Hofmann 1979; Spruce 1980)

See also Alcoholic Beverages; Balche; Beer; Cactus; Chicha; Coca; Kava; Mead; Nightshades; Ololiuqui; Pulque; Sake; Soma; Tobacco; Wine

BALCHE

Balche is a kind of mead, an intoxicating beverage consumed by the ancient Maya and by some of their descendants today. These people make the drink in a trough or a canoe, which they fill with water and honey, adding chunks of bark and roots from the balche tree. The mixture begins to ferment immediately. It results in an inebriating drink the people consume during rituals and believe to have magical powers.

The peoples of Mesoamerica have long held the balche tree and their mysterious beverage sacred. Because the drink had strong religious significance to the Maya, the Spaniards banned the beverage in an attempt to convert them to Christianity. The ban was observed until a Maya named Chi convinced the Spaniards that balche had important health benefits and that many Maya were dying as a result of the prohibition. The Spaniards then lifted their ban, and balche rituals resumed.★

A typical ritual of the ancient Maya involved the ceremonial use of balche during severe droughts to encourage the rain gods to release the waters. These ceremonies lasted three days. On the third day, the participants sacrificed hens to the Chacs, who sent the rains. Because the croaking of frogs typically heralded the rains, young boys were chosen to represent frogs, and were tied to altars and forced to croak. The Maya poured balche down the throats of the hens before they sacrificed them, and they filled thirteen gourds full of balche and offered them to the Chacs. Then everyone assembled for the ritual drank balche as well, and the shaman sprinkled it on the altar thirteen times.

The ancient Maya considered their sacred drink a purifier as well as an inebriant. To make it particularly powerful, they often used it in enemas and administered it rectally. Mayan healers also used balche for divination. They did this by placing a quartz crystal into the mixture, letting the balche sit overnight, then consuming the drink, sometimes with ololiuqui (hallucinogenic morning glory seeds) and thornapple to aid their visions. After the drink took effect, those who partook said they could see the future.

Some Mexicans today perform rituals similar to those of the ancient Maya. The Lacandon, descendants of the ancient Maya living in Chiapas along the Mexican-Guatemalan border, believe that the gods gave balche rituals to them, and that because the gods themselves first became inebriated by the beverage, the people from then on had a duty to imitate the inebriation of the gods and to experience that same exhilaration. The Lacandon chant incantations while preparing the balche. The brewer summons the spirits of all the poisonous animals and plants and asks them to put their poisons into the balche to make it strong. Sometimes the brewer adds actual toads and frogs to the mixture, then lets the drink ferment for a few days. First, the brewer offers his drink to the gods; then later, the people partake of it, usually just before dawn. The Lacandon call the balche brewer "Lord of the Balche" and they identify him with Bohr or Bol, the god of inebriation. They believe that if Bol gets angry, the drink will fail to work properly.

Those who consume the balche feel a sense of euphoria. Their senses sharpen, their muscles relax, and like ritual consumers of inebriating

_____

★*Chi* was also the Mayan word for inebriating drinks.

15

e world over, they feel closer to the ... hey perform the ritual to elevate their ... ds to a higher level and to maintain harmony between earth and the sky world.

Balche pleases the gods, and it also cleanses the people who consume it. Participants in the rituals consume large quantities of the balche, and then vomit, urinate, and have intense bouts of diarrhea. They drink all of the beverage and then fall asleep. They awake with clear minds and purged bodies.

The ancient Maya had numerous gods of inebriation, and Acan served as the god of balche. The name Acan means "bellowing," and perhaps refers to the uproarious noise the Maya made after becoming intoxicated on their sacred drink. (Coe 1994; Ratsch 1992)

See also Alcoholic Beverages; Ayahuasca; Beer; Cactus; Chicha; Kava; Mead; Ololiuqui; Pulque; Sake; Soma; Wine

BAMBOO (SHOOTS)

Bamboo is a sacred plant of India, and in China and Japan, a symbol of strength, vitality, durability, and longevity. The Japanese also consider it a lucky plant; they believe it has the power to bring good fortune. The bamboo is hardy, long-lived, and stays green through all the seasons. Because the bamboo has strong roots and always grows upright, the Chinese say that the plant shows strength of character. The roots of the bamboo thrive even under ice and snow, and in spring they put out multiple shoots, a further indication of strength and vitality.

The bamboo is a useful tree—so much so that the Vietnamese called it a gift from the gods. All parts of the tree have economic value, including the shoots, which were a significant food source in ancient times, and the seeds, which served as a reliable staple in times of famine. All parts of the bamboo tree are believed to have medicinal properties as well, particularly the leaves.

The fact that the bamboo leaves stay eternally green made the plant not only a symbol of longevity but also of tenderheartedness. In Chinese legend, a boy named Meng Tsung went to a bamboo grove and cried because his dying mother wished for nothing but to eat bamboo shoots in the middle of winter. Miraculously, the roots sprouted to feed his mother. This legend reveals that the Chinese believed their beloved bamboo to be compassionate. Perhaps this is why they often depict Kuan-yin, their goddess of mercy, holding a bamboo branch in her hand.

The Indians as well as the Chinese hailed the properties of bamboo. They too took note of its long life and perpetual foliage, and they labeled it a symbol of friendship because it remains steadfast and true even during hard times. Many peoples of India believed the plants to be caretakers of their agricultural fields and their villages, and some villages worshiped them as gods. Although some people of India believed evil spirits inhabited the bamboo, many others believed that the plant warded off evil. They used it in marriage ceremonies and kept it in the rooms of women giving birth, to keep evil spirits from inhabiting their newborn babies. Bamboo has long been associated with fertility because the plant grows rapidly and in clusters, which symbolize offspring. The mythmakers of India identified bamboo with sacred fire as well. They believed that fires in the jungle ignited when bamboo stems rubbed together. In Indian myth, the bamboo grew from the ashes of a girl who burned herself on a funeral pyre. The girl, Murala, was of the highest social caste, the Brahman. When she discovered that she had unwittingly married a man of lower caste—which would bring great humiliation on her family—she committed suicide; and with this act, she gave the gift of bamboo to the world. (Hu 1991)

BANANAS AND PLANTAINS

Bananas are thought to have originated in Southeast Asia. The first wild banana trees produced hard, seedy fruits unlike the fleshy, tasty fruit of today's cultivated varieties. The ancient hunter-gatherers of this region likely utilized the plant fibers in various ways rather than consuming the fruit as food. From the Asian lands, the banana traveled in prehistoric times across the Indian Ocean to Africa, and thence westward. The banana and the closely related plantain appear in myths around the world. In Europe, Asia, Africa, Oceania, and the Americas, the banana quickly became an invaluable source of food.

The word *banana* is of West African origin, and both the fruit and the tree play an important role in the myths and beliefs of people around the African continent. Many Africans link the tree to fertility. The Antaivandrika of Madagascar even say they descended from the banana tree, which they call the vandrika. As their legend has it, a boy was born from the tree, and that boy became the progenitor of the tribe. The Baganda of Uganda say that women who give birth to twins can fertilize banana trees, or that banana leaves can impregnate women, as if by magic. Because the Baganda regard the banana as a twin of a child, they customarily plant the woman's placenta under the root of a banana tree, then they guard the tree to make sure no one eats its fruit. Presumably, the Baganda believe the tree's roots absorb the spirit of the child, and the tree's leaves gain fertilizing abilities. They also believe that if someone violates the tree, and thus the child's spirit, by eating its fruit, the living child thought to be the twin of the tree will die shortly thereafter.

The Chinese tell a legend about the Banana Maiden, a spirit of the banana tree whose life had a mysterious connection to the life of a young woman. It begins with two banana growers named Wang and Li, best friends who made their living together, tending a large grove of banana trees. Each of the men had a child—Li had a boy, and Wang, a girl—and the children grew up and fell in love. However, the father of the young boy died before his son reached maturity. After Li's death, Wang refused to let his daughter marry Li's son. In-

stead he promised her in marriage to a wealthy old man who was, in fact, the evil spirit of a thousand-year-old banyan tree.

The Banana Maiden—the spirit of the banana tree, which bore a remarkable resemblance to Ts'ui-lien, the young woman—intervened to help the young couple. The Banana Maiden gave the young man Ch'ing-sung a banana leaf and instructed him to place the leaf in his love's wedding chair, which at that very moment was en route to her new husband's home, carrying Ts'ui-lien within it. Ch'ing-sung did as he was told, and miraculously, the banana leaf replaced Ts'ui-lien's body. Saved from the evil spirit, she returned to Ch'ing-sung and became his bride. The evil old man, of course, became enraged at this, and he tracked Ts'ui-lien to her new home and killed her by puncturing her lung with a poisoned needle. But the Banana Maiden let her own blood flow into the wound and restored the young woman to life. At the same time, life drained from the Banana Maiden, and she lost her human form and became a banana tree.

The prominence of plantain in mythology is not surprising, because in the areas conducive to their growth, the trees grew abundantly. They reproduced rapidly, and perhaps for this reason, mythmakers used them as fertility symbols. The Hindus used bananas in marriage ceremonies, presenting the newly married bride with a banana as a symbol of fruitfulness and the ability to bear sons. In Hindu myth, the plantain tree was an agricultural deity called Navapatrika, said to be the incarnation of both Parvati, the wife of Shiva, and of Lakshmi, the wife of Vishnu. In Hindu ceremonies, worshipers commonly offered the precious fruit, as well as the leaves, to Vishnu, Lakshmi, and other high deities. In one ceremony, they offered banana leaves to Ganesha, the elephant-headed god who brought good luck and prosperity, and in another they offered banana fruit to their sun god. Sometimes during these ceremonies the worshipers killed a chicken and sprinkled the blood of the chicken on the banana, which they then offered to

The Hindus offered bananas to these ed deities because they venerated the plant. The Buddhists venerated the banana as well. They considered it a symbol of Kali in her role as goddess of agriculture.

India is a land rich in food myths, and food plays a vital role in the religion of the people. Numerous Hindu rituals are centered on food, particularly on the fruits of trees; Hindus venerated many kinds of trees as incarnations of gods or as their sacred abodes. Shiva meditated under a tree and obtained enlightenment, as did Buddha. Trees, like gods, bestow life; food is similarly life-giving. Food and trees also represented fertility. This symbolism made foods that come from trees particularly effective as ritual tools and offerings.

Both the fertility connection and the considerable economic value of the banana plant led to its ritual use. Every part of the banana benefited people, from the stalks to the leaves and fruit. In one Hindu legend, Bimma created the plantain tree; and because Rama was jealous of Bimma for creating such a useful plant, he put a curse on the tree so that it would die after producing only one crop of fruit. But apparently Rama's curse didn't work. The plantain is a perennial, and it continues to produce fruit season after season, without the need for pollination or fertilization of its flowers. Another Hindu legend explains the tree's unusual characteristic: A father attempted to marry off his five daughters: Mango, Tamarind, Fig, Jasmine, and Plantain. The father succeeded in finding husbands for all except Plantain, who wanted children but no husband. That is why the plantain bears fruit without pollination, and why its fruit has no seeds.

The people of India told these legends of the plantain because they believed the fruit worthy of divine status. Revering the plant, they immortalized it in myth. Some people of India continue to believe that bananas bring good fortune. In the ancient world, and in eastern Asia particularly, people elevated the banana to even higher status; they considered it the source of good and evil, the forbidden Tree of Knowledge in the Garden of Eden. Other fruit trees share the same distinction, and no one knows for certain whether the original mythic forbidden fruit was a banana, an apple, an orange, a grape, a fig, or a pomegranate. But certainly, many ancient people who ate bananas revered them, and offered bananas to their deities. Many people believed banana trees, and indeed all plants, had souls. Some people in the Solomon Islands believe that the souls of the dead inhabit banana trees, and they refuse to eat bananas, for fear of eating a dead friend or relative. (Barooah 1992; Goor and Nurock 1968; Gupta 1991; Hu 1996; Lehner and Lehner 1973; Majupuria 1988)

BAOBAB

The baobab is said to be the largest tree in the world, and it appears in many African myths, particularly of Senegal, where baobabs flourish and may live up to 5,000 years. Baobabs have seeds, leaves, and fruit that Africans over the centuries have prized both for food and for medicinal purposes. Africans also worship the trees, by virtue of their sheer size. Baobab trees in Senegal are reputedly the largest, thickest-trunked trees in the world, some of them up to 100 feet around. They look strange and supernatural, with contorted branches that make the trees appear as if they were planted upside down. In Arab legend, the Devil planted the first baobab upside down, and in Bushman legend, the hyena did it. As the Great Spirit formed the world, he assigned each animal a tree to plant, and the hyena, upset at having gotten the baobab, thrust its branches into the ground to play a trick on nature.

The baobab commands respect, and people in Africa have worshiped these trees since antiquity. Goats often nibble the young saplings, but the ones that survive grow so large that people hesitate to cut them down. Some people believe that these trees miraculously appear in the earth fully matured—they assign them that much power and magic. The people of Africa utilize every part of the baobab trees,

The baobab tree, with its thick trunk and contorted branches, led people of Africa to worship the trees and create legends to explain its supernatural appearance. (Craig Lovell/Corbis)

and they even hollow out the gigantic trunks to make storage buildings, temporary homes, and graves, particularly for poets, clowns, and musicians. Because these "magic" people reputedly got their inspiration from the Devil, people hesitated to bury them in the ground or at sea for fear of killing the fruits or the fish. But the baobab tree served the purpose well. In fact, it served numerous purposes, including the provision of food, medicinals, rope, paper, and various household utensils. These trees, the people believe, are protected by powerful tree spirits, spirits who gather underneath the branches at night. The spirits don't seem to mind if people make use of the tree, it appears, but they get extremely angry if people fell the tree for wood. In part because the African people fear angering these spirits, the baobab tree receives the utmost respect and reverence. In South Africa, people sometimes consider the baobab tree a bad omen, and they believe that the branches swaying in

the wind alerts the people to the presence of evil spirits.

People in Africa have assigned the baobab tree all kinds of supernatural powers, including the power to protect against smallpox and other diseases, to herald epidemics and the arrival of important visitors, and to make barren women fertile. Even in modern times desperate women sometimes sacrifice goats and cocks under a particular baobab tree, believing its powers of fertility strong enough to grant them children. Anything with that much power commands respect, as does anything that provides food for the people. The vitamin-rich leaves can be eaten fresh, or dried and powdered and added to soups. The seeds can be roasted or made into cakes, or ground and used as a substitute for coffee. The baobab fruit, called Ethiopian sour gourd or monkey bread, grows like cucumbers and has the nutritive value of citrus fruits. People use it to make acidic drinks with water or milk or they use the fruit matrix as a substitute for baking powder. Traditional dishes made of baobab fruit gained cultural significance in many African societies; in addition to relying on this food to fill a nutritional gap in areas that lack citrus fruits, people eat the fruit at baptismal ceremonies and religious festivals. The baobab tree has fed Africans in times of scarcity since ancient times. One clan of people in southern Rhodesia made the baobab tree their totem, believing that their ancestors lived almost exclusively on the fruit. (Owen 1970; Simoons 1998)

BARLEY

The cultivation of barley, one of the world's oldest cereal grains, dates back to the Stone Age in Europe. Barley was a staple food and thus a plant of life, like rice. In Greek myth, it is the grain most closely associated with Demeter, the earth goddess and goddess of the cultivated soil. An entire religion developed around Demeter, called the Eleusinian Mysteries, and the barley that rose from the land served as the focus of this agricultural cult. Initiates to the Eleusinian Mysteries were offered the promise of rebirth after death; and they witnessed just such a rebirth when they saw the sacred barley seed sprout from the ground.

In ancient times, many cultures had agricultural myths affirming a belief in resurrection. Barley, one of the oldest grains, became a symbol not only of resurrection but also of the mythological dying and rising god or goddess. In Greek myth, Demeter died and was resurrected, as was her daughter, Persephone, having been abducted by Hades, descended with him to the underworld, then returned back to earth. Demeter followed in pursuit, searched throughout the underworld for her daughter, and finally found her with Hades. Demeter struck a bargain with Hades, who promised to permit Persephone to return to the land of the living for a part of each year. The journey of the mythical mother and daughter to the underworld symbolizes the "death" and burial of the planted barley seed, and the emergence of the new sprouts from the ground is symbolically explained by the goddess's return from the underworld.

In Egypt, the dying and rising god Osiris fulfilled the same mythic role. Barley was the most ancient staple grain of Egypt, and Osiris, as god of agriculture, personified the Nile and its power to make the barley grow. In myth, the evil Seth murdered Osiris, dismembered his body, and strewed the body parts across the land as if sowing barley seed. But the Nile rose each year, flooding its banks and fertilizing the soil. And each year, like Persephone, Osiris returned to life just as the barley emerged from beneath the ground.

Barley is a cultivated plant, not a wild one, and in Greek myth, this quality was symbolized by Demeter's acceptance of Persephone's absence. The barley seed, in other words, was temporarily entrusted to the dark earth but would continue to return to the light, the renewal of life guaranteed. The cults of both Osiris and Demeter celebrated the mystery of resurrection through the rebirth of barley. In the cult of Osiris, worshipers planted wooden funerary beds with sprouted barley to symbolize resurrection and rebirth. They made necklaces out of barley and placed them on mummies—a practice most likely connected with the myth of Osiris. In the Eleusinian Mysteries, worshipers considered the cultivation of barley the ultimate mystery, and they experienced that revelation by consuming a seemingly magical potion and reliving Demeter's myth.

The revelation at Eleusis was key to Demeter's agricultural cult. But to experience this mystic revelation, adherents of the cult had to partake of a magical potion—a drink that most likely contained barley as a primary ingredient, given the belief that the mystery was embodied in the barley itself. When the initiates consumed their magical drink, they experienced visions as well as vertigo, tremors, and cold sweats—all symptomatic of a hallucinogen of some sort. Many scholars have

Osiris, the Egyptian god of agriculture, personified the fecundating power of the Nile and the ability of the river water to make the barley grow. Worshippers of Osiris planted wooden funerary beds filled with sprouted barley to symbolize his death and rebirth. (Werner Forman Archive/Art Resource, NY)

identified this hallucinogen as ergot, a fungus that invades barley and when consumed produces effects similar to those of LSD. Ergot of rye was most prevalent in ancient times; but ergot of barley existed too, and quite likely, the barley on the Rarian plain next to Eleusis had ergot. The ergot could be scraped off the barley and mixed with water and mint. Ergot causes purplish spikes to appear on the grain, and the ancients linked the color purple with the power of the underworld; in other words, with Demeter and Persephone. The use of barley to make intoxicating beverages was not unique to the Greek world; ergot-infected barley was quite possibly the primary ingredient used in the ritual Indian beverage called soma, and fermented barley has been used since antiquity to make wine. The oldest known recipe for barley wine was found on a Babylonian brick tablet dating back to 2800 B.C.

The prevalence of barley in the Old World made it the focus of myth wherever it grew. The ancient Egyptians said that barley grew from man and wheat from woman; and the ancient Chinese considered barley a symbol of male potency. In biblical parables, however, barley served as a symbol of poverty and even worthlessness, because however prolific, it was consumed primarily by the poor. Barley was far from worthless to the peasants of the world, however, and many agricultural peoples celebrated its birth each spring with a feast in honor of the barley god. In the Estonian tradition, barley originated with the god Peko. The peoples of ancient India dedicated barley to high gods such as Varuna and Indra, whom they credited with ripening the grain, making it an essential object in their religious rituals. (Darby et al. 1977; Schultes and Hofmann 1979; Schultes and von Reis 1995; Wasson et al. 1978; Wilkins et al. 1995)

See also Cake; Corn; Grain; Millet; Oats; Rice; Rye; Soma; Sorghum; Wheat

BASIL

The early lore surrounding basil identified it variously as a creation of the Devil or of a god. In the Middle East, basil was associated with mourning and death, and in Greece, with hatred and misfortune. In ancient Rome, it was associated with fertility, love, and sexual stimulation. Other ancient peoples connected the herb with dragons. Some say that sweet basil got its name from a legendary dragonlike creature called the basilisk, the very sight of which brought instant death to onlookers. But nowhere is the mythology of basil so rich and so pervasive as in India, where it is among the most sacred of plants. There it is worshiped as a deity in itself and invoked for protection against evil spirits.

Worship of holy basil continues in India today, and has become particularly pervasive as the worship of Vishnu, or Vaishnavism, spread throughout the country. This holy basil is not the commonly known sweet basil indigenous to the tropics and appearing in myths of the Mediterranean but a plant called *tulsi* or *tulasi,* which was incarnated in myth as the goddess Tulasi, the wife of Vishnu, one of three supreme deities of the Hindu pantheon. Tulasi was more widely known as Lakshmi, the goddess of fortune and fertility, and among the most highly revered Indian goddesses. According to one legend, this goddess fell under a demon's curse and was born into the world as the basil plant. Variations of this legend exist, explaining not only how the basil plant became sacred to Vishnu but also how Tulasi became his wife.

The origins of India's sacred basil are retold in the legend of the demon king Jalandhara.

He had a magnificent kingdom and was married to Tulasi, who at that time was called Vrinda. Brahma had shown Jalandhara favor, granting him power and agreeing not to kill him, provided that Jalandhara's wife Vrinda remain faithful to her husband. But Jalandhara was a demon after all, and in Hindu myth, the demons continually waged war against the gods. Jalandhara stole the ocean jewels from Indra, and among them the magic elixir of life, which made the gods immortal. In revenge, Vishnu assumed the guise of Jalandhara and tricked Vrinda into cheating on her husband. According to one version of this legend, Jalandhara cursed her and turned her into a basil plant. In another version, Jalandhara was killed, and Tulasi burned herself in grief. In her honor, the goddess Parvati planted tulasi at the funeral pyre. Vishnu realized he was wrong to trick Tulasi, and the plant became holy to him. Because the spirit of the goddess was said to enter the plant each evening, anyone who caused injury to a basil plant incurred the wrath of Vishnu.

The people of ancient India treated this plant with the utmost respect, and still do so today. They plant it in their homes, carve rosary beads out of the plant's wood, and take care to include it in their meals. Devotees of Vishnu, in particular, observe this reverence to Tulasi. They believe that their god's powers purify the area around the plant. In ancient times, some of these worshipers made sure to put sprigs of the holy basil in their mouths when they were dying, and considered it a means to salvation.

Because Tulasi, or Lakshmi, was the wife of Vishnu, rituals involving her plant symbolize the marriage of the basil plant to Vishnu, often represented as a stone. Tulasi is decorated and presented to Vishnu during the month of Kartika, the Hindu marriage season; and because the god Krishna is an incarnation of Vishnu, sometimes Tulasi is married to him as well. In one variant of the legend of Jalandhara, Jalandhara cursed Vrinda and turned her into the tulasi plant; but Tulasi, in her rage at

In Hindu mythology, Lakshmi, the goddess of fortune and fertility, manifested herself as Tulasi, the personification of the basil plant. (SEF/Art Resource, NY)

Vishnu's trick, cursed Vishnu and turned him into a stone. When Vishnu's worshipers marry the basil plant to the stone, the god himself is said to live within it. When worshipers marry the basil plant to Krishna, they do so because in legend, Krishna's wife saved their marriage by meeting the gods' demand for Krishna's weight in gold. Gold alone did not equal Krishna's exact weight, so his wife added a tulasi plant to make up the difference. Ever since then, Vaishnavas have celebrated the ritual marriage between the god and goddess, and they often refer to the sacred plant as "Krishna Tulasi."

Tulasi takes precedence in the worship of Vishnu and his incarnations, especially Rama and Krishna, but this sacred plant has its own well-established place in mythology. Some legends trace the origin of tulasi to the primordial milk ocean; others place the plant at the meeting point between heaven and earth, the sacred Ganges River flowing at its roots. Tulasi is a manifestation of Vishnu; but Brahma, the creator god, lives in its branches, and other gods in the Hindu pantheon reside in its leaves. Worshipers of Vishnu in particular use the tulasi leaves as food offerings. They believe that because the plant represents his consort, Tulasi, food is unacceptable to Vishnu without these leaves, and that it is the goddess in her vegetal form who makes the ordinary food offering sacred.

The dietary use of tulasi is insignificant in comparison with its ritual and medicinal uses. To many, tulasi is the holiest of all plants, much too sacred to be used for ordinary nourishment. Rituals involving tulasi center around the notions of sanctity, purity, good health, and the fertility of women. Women, in particular, worship tulasi, and in return the goddess within the plant grants them the children or husbands they desire. Tulasi also has the ability to make poor people wealthy and to drive away demons. Tulasi purifies, kills evil sprits, and even wards off death. Neither Yama, the death god, nor any of his messengers tread where the tulasi plant is found. People through-

out India keep a twig of tulasi in their homes, believing that it brings them good luck and guards them from evil. Tulasi is also said to know the future, and some Indians use the plant also in divination. (Folkard 1892; Gupta 1991; Majupuria 1988; Simoons 1998)

See also Herbs

BEANS

Beans commonly appear in folklore and legends as magical objects. Some traditional societies revered them—particularly, various tribes of North America, who immortalized them as one of a trio of primary food deities, along with corn and squash. Other societies, though they considered beans magic, avoided them, associating them with death and decay. Numerous cults in Greece and Rome, and the Hindus of India, considered the eating of beans evil. The association with evil magic stemmed largely from the notion that beans contained the souls of the dead. The association with good magic stemmed from the bean's ability to germinate quickly, bean stalks shooting to the sky to provide a convenient path to the otherworld.

The popular tale of "Jack and the Bean-stalk" is just one of many stories in which magical beans hit the ground, and soon after, bean stalks shoot up into the sky world. Because of beans' tendency to sprout and grow relatively quickly, the ancient Egyptians thought they symbolized immortal life. The Egyptians buried beans in tombs, and later discovered that when exposed to light and moisture, they sprouted—even after being buried for thousands of years. So it appears that the Egyptians connected beans with death but also with resurrection. They called the place where the souls of the dead awaited reincarnation "the bean field." Perhaps because of the bean's association with the dead, Egyptian priests held the legumes sacred and refused to eat them.

Perhaps nowhere did beans achieve the reverence that they did in North America, however. Early agriculturists relied on beans as a staple crop because all of the plant can be eaten, and the plants typically yield a large harvest. Furthermore, the plants grow and mature quickly, which led the people to give them starring roles in their myths and legends. The Native Americans considered beans a sacred gift from the Great Spirit and from the earth goddess who provides life and sustenance. The sacred beans the goddess delivered to the ancient tribes were what are today known as green beans, a New World domesticate of the fava beans of the Old World. But whereas green beans achieved widespread use and reverence in the New World, fava beans achieved infamy in the Old: The Native Americans connected beans with life, not with death; but people in parts of the Old World associated beans with underworld spirits and decay.

Beans were considered unacceptable foods in several Old World cultures—for example, in the cult of Demeter and in some of the other most prominent cults in Greece and Rome. In Greek myth, the earth goddess Demeter gave food plants to humans as gifts but excluded beans because she considered them unworthy. Greek oracles thought eating beans would cloud their vision; Hippocrates thought that eating them would weaken the eyesight. Both the fava bean of the classical world and the urd bean of India suffered poor reputations in part because of their black seed coats. In ancient thought, the color black symbolized the underworld and the death gods who inhabited it. The fava bean was domesticated around 7000–6500 B.C. Although beans might have been regarded as a healthy source of nourishment initially, in later years, the Greeks and Romans scorned them. The Romans offered bean soup to Carna, who served as the goddess of health and the protector of vital organs but who was also a deity of the underworld. The Romans used beans in numerous magical rites connected with deities of the dead; with Carna; with Tacita or Muta, another death goddess; and with the bean goddess Fabula, whom Romans honored during the annual festival of the dead.

Beans, though nutritious, were black nevertheless, and black foods reputedly pleased dark deities. The Hindus associated black urd beans with Rahu, the eclipse demon; Sani, an evil planetary god; and Ravana, a demon reputedly reborn in the form of urd seed. The people made offerings of urd seed to counter the evil influence of these deities, most commonly to Yama, the god of death, and to the ancestral spirits who shared his realm.

Much of the popular disdain for beans had to do with the belief that the bean plants harbored dead souls. In one respect, this likened bean eating to cannibalism. The priests of Jupiter recognized this connection, and refused fava beans as food. These Roman priests had to avoid contact with the dead and with anything associated with them, so they couldn't even speak of beans, let alone eat them. The followers of Orpheus and Pythagoras likewise avoided beans. Because of the bean's connection with death, Orpheus and Pythagoras considered beans polluting foods.

Though many Indo-Europeans shunned beans, Pythagoras instigated perhaps the most famous ban on them. Pythagoras lived in the sixth century B.C., and he founded a philosophical and religious movement with strict rules, many of them pertaining to diet. In ancient times, Pythagoras was perceived as a god, his religion largely dependent on ancient superstitions and permeated with rules based on magic. The bean ban was quite likely one such rule. Pythagoras believed in the transmigration of souls, the unity of all living beings, and thus the unacceptability of consuming flesh foods. The concept of beans containing souls of the dead likely stemmed from the notion that they bore the character of human flesh. Pythagoras, it appears, classified beans with flesh; he likened them to testicles, comparing their smell to that of semen and their texture and appearance to that of testicles or human embryos.

People who drew the connection between beans and sex organs linked these foods to the generative principle. This led to the belief

In stories such as "Jack and the Beanstalk," magic beans shoot to the sky world to illustrate the ability of bean plants to germinate quickly. (Library of Congress)

that chaste people should avoid eating beans, perhaps because they stimulated sexual desire. People in Vedic India associated urd beans with passion; they used them as love charms because they considered them an aphrodisiac and believed that they had the ability to produce sperm and thus lead to the bearing of offspring—particularly, male offspring. Beans may have contained the souls of the dead, but they also represented the embryo and the embryonic state; so people in some early cultures used them as ritual offerings during marriage ceremonies to represent the ancestral male, soon to be reborn as a new male to carry on the family line. Beginning in the early sixteenth century, people in England, France, Germany, and Belgium began putting a bean in Twelfth Night Cake, and whoever got the bean got to be king—king of the bean, that is. It has been suggested that this practice had possible links to fertility cults, particularly those related to the sowing or harvesting of crops, which in turn stem from ancient beliefs in the bean's generative power.

The belief that beans contained life forces or souls led to all kinds of beliefs and practices. Pythagoras knew that beans caused flatulence, and he seemed to consider this evidence of the life within them. Perhaps, too, he embraced the belief that at the origin of the world, beans and humans emerged from the same primeval slime. This common origin meant that beans and humans were composed of the same matter, which reinforced the comparison of bean eating to cannibalism. Like eating human flesh, or flesh of any kind, bean eating polluted the body with decaying matter. The flatulence caused by eating beans also linked them to polluting matter. Furthermore, beans have hollow stems with no joints, which the ancients perceived as a path to the earth world from the land of death beneath it. Just as Jack climbed up the bean stalk to the sky, dead souls climbed up the bean stalk from the underworld.

The link the ancients recognized between beans and death has been widely documented. But more recently, some scholars have come to believe that the ban Pythagoras instigated on beans had something to do with favism, or rather a fear of favism, a hereditary disease in Greece that was linked to the fava bean. But long before Pythagoras, other peoples also had banned beans, and such food taboos were largely based on magico-religious beliefs. Bean taboos were common in Egypt, particularly among the priests, as well as in many societies in Africa. In any case, Pythagoras prohibited the consumption of beans under any circumstances, possibly even under threat of death. He also forbade the cultivation of the bean vine. In legend, Pythagoras died while fleeing from an enemy during the war between Acragas and Syracuse because he refused to escape by crossing a bean field. No one knows for sure whether the legend is true, but it certainly seems plausible. If indeed Pythagoras did believe that beans harbored souls of the dead, he likely would have refused to cross a bean field, which in his mind might well have led to a death much worse than murder by enemy troops. It was said that Pythagoras not only believed that dead souls resided in beans but that they could emerge from the plants and enter human bodies. Given the fact that Pythagoras based an entire religion largely on magic, it seems likely that he greatly feared possession by spirits of the underworld. (Andrews 1949; Burkert 1972; Detienne 1977; Foster and Cordell 1992; Simoons 1998; Toussaint-Samat 1992)

See also Blood and Flesh; Corn; Eggplant; Lupines; Meat; Peas and Lentils; Soybeans; Squash

BEAR

Ancient bear hunters considered these strong, majestic animals both humanlike and godlike. Bears stand erect, as people do, yet they exhibit such tremendous strength and bravery that they appear to have supernatural powers. This strength elevated the bear to revered status among early hunters, and it led to

Ainu men capture a bear and then threaten it with bows and arrows as part of the Ainu Bear Festival in Japan. (Hulton Deutsch Collection/Corbis)

widespread rituals accompanying the killing and eating of the animal. The Ainu of Japan developed what may well be the most elaborate of all bear rituals. They considered the bear an earthly messenger of high gods, and believed that if they treated the animal respectfully before slaughtering and eating it, the bear's spirit would give the gods a positive report of their pious actions.

The Ainu were, essentially, bear worshipers, and their elaborate rituals achieved widespread fame. But they were not the only bear hunters who had a doctrine and ritual of showing respect to their prey both before and after the kill. Many North American hunters killed and ate bear, and most of them apologized to the animal spirit before taking its life. They also left the dead bear sacrificial liba-

tions. The rituals surrounding the bear hunt offered assurance that the spirit world would not take offense or perceive the killing and eating of the animal as disrespectful. The correct performance of these rituals offered assurance that the spirits would not punish the hunters but would reward them by sending more game to their hunting grounds.

North American bear hunters typically practiced magic in pursuit of their game. Their tribal shamans were believed to possess the ability to communicate with the animals' spirits by going into trances and traveling to the otherworld. Early hunters typically believed that game animals were a gift from the spirits. Shamans could persuade the spirits to send the animals, but it was up to the hunters to perform the rituals and show the animals proper signs of respect. If they did so, the animals gave themselves voluntarily in sacrifice, and the animal spirits were then reborn in the bodies of other animals, reincarnated for the purpose of feeding the people.

Native North Americans attributed great significance to the rituals of hunting and killing bear, perhaps partly because many native peoples recognized a similarity between bears and humans. The Pueblo, for instance, likened the skin of the bear to the scalp of a man, and thus killing a bear was tantamount to killing a man: Those who succeeded could join the warriors' society.

The hunt and kill was equally important to the Ainu, in whose culture the bear meat held special significance. The Ainu believed that they partook of the bear's strength and courage when they consumed its flesh and blood. In ancient times, this was common reasoning among many people who consumed animals as well as among cannibals who consumed the blood and flesh of tribal chiefs and of those chosen to represent their deities. They consumed the bodies of their victims largely out of reverence, believing that they absorbed their strength and life force in eating their flesh and drinking their blood.

The bear festival traditionally practiced by the Ainu would appall today's animal advocates; but the Ainu performed it as a sacred act, in the earnest belief that they were thereby pleasing and appeasing the animal spirits. The ritual began when a bear cub was brought to the Ainu village and suckled by one of the women. The people raised this animal as they would a child until it got too large, and then confined it in a cage for several years, until the time was right to slaughter and eat it. The Ainu honored the bear as they would a god while it was alive; yet in the end, they killed him. But they apologized to the gods before they did so. Everyone from the village attended the feast. The people celebrated the departure of the bear god's spirit, and they sent him away with plenty of cake and wine to take into the next world. After they killed the bear, the men

sometimes drank the bear's blood to become as brave as the bear. Yet they treated the dead animal as an honored guest. They placed bowls of food in front of the bear, symbolically offering the revered animal some of its own meat, as well as millet and fish. After the bear symbolically partook of the boiled flesh, the festival participants would partake from the same bowl. They consumed the entire bear, leaving only the bones, teeth, and claws.

The Ainu bear ritual has changed somewhat since ancient times, but the tradition still survives. These people believe the bear has superhuman powers, regarding it as a powerful god who rules in the mountains. Some of the Ainu say they descended from the bear, yet they consume bear meat as staple food. Respect is the key. The Ainu nurture and love the bear before they kill it. They even hang the bear's skull on a post outside their huts and propitiate the spirit by leaving the skull libations of millet, beer, and sake. Sometimes they offer it rice or potatoes. Making offerings to the bear's skull reflects a common belief among early peoples that the soul of the animal resided in the head.

The Gilyaks of eastern Siberia have festivals and beliefs about bear hunting similar to those of the Ainu. The Gilyaks also worship and respect the animal, yet they capture, kill, and eat it as well. They also offer the dead animal libations of food, including its own flesh. Native Siberian hunters today still adhere to strict rules surrounding the bear hunt, performing rituals that emphasize the appeasement of the animal's soul. Siberian hunters also believe that when shown proper respect, the animals give up their lives freely.

In Finnish myth, Vainamoinen, the magician, hunted the bear, and from the start of the hunt to the consumption of the flesh Vainamoinen sang praise to the animal. He played his harp and recounted the myth of the bear's birth. Those who attended the feast invited the God of the Forests to partake, believing the bear's flesh worthy of the deities and infused with the divine spirit. The Ainu believed that the bear was given to them for sacrifice, and therefore they considered the worship, slaughter, and consumption of the animal their sacred duty and God-given privilege. (Campbell 1988; Frazer 1950; Pavlik 1997)

See also Blood and Flesh; Meat

BEEF

Cattle were domesticated in the Middle East and southeastern Europe in early antiquity, by 6000 B.C. It is possible that cattle were first domesticated for ritual purposes. Both cows and bulls were important religious symbols—bulls as sky gods, and cows as earth or mother goddesses. Worship of these deities involved sacrifices, and people often believed that the flesh from the animal that symbolized them was what these gods desired most.

Beef was offered to gods in many cultures. This generally meant that the priests or the rulers who presided over the sacrificial ceremonies also ate beef, and in some cases, commoners did as well. The ancient Greeks ate beef, and so did the Mesopotamians, the Celts, the Germanic peoples, and the priests of ancient Egypt. Even the high priests of ancient India offered cows for sacrifice and consumed beef in their rituals. Religious Hindus today hold cows sacred and wouldn't dream of killing the animal and consuming its flesh. But in the early Vedic era, the cow had not yet come to be so venerated and was still considered an acceptable food.

From the Vedic period onward, Hindu priests gradually began to eliminate meat from their diets. By the time of the Rig Veda, around 1000 B.C., the priests forbade the slaughter of cows; then after Krishna was deified, they considered cow slaughter the height of sacrilege. Many Hindus today worship Krishna as the Supreme Lord, an incarnation of Vishnu

In the Hindu religion, Krishna grew up among milkmaids, called Gopis, and he grew to value their precious cows as providers of essential nourishment. Because these cows provided Krishna with their strength-giving milk, Krishna's worshippers view all cows as sacred. (Borromeo/Art Resource, NY)

as the preserver of world order. They also call him the Divine Cowherd. Krishna himself venerated the cow, as the animal had always served as his provider. According to legend, Krishna grew up among milkmaids, called Gopis, and he grew to value their precious cows as providers of essential nourishment. Because these cows provided Krishna with their strength-giving milk, Krishna's worshipers viewed all cows as sacred. When Krishna died, his followers deified him, and by extension, cows as well.

The worship of Krishna certainly plays a large role in the rejection of beef by Hindus today, but it is likely that the original ban on cow slaughter arose to promote the advancement of agriculture. Agriculture was hard work, and to succeed, people had to stop killing cattle and concentrate on cultivating the land. Buddhist and Jain influences in India also led to the promotion of vegetarianism in general. The Buddhists and Jains embraced the principle of ahimsa, or noninjury of living things, and prohibited animal sacrifice of any kind. Ahimsa expressed a belief in the fundamental unity of all life, and the Brahmans who embraced this concept rejected the meat sacrifice that defined ancient Vedic rituals. When the Brahmans adopted ahimsa, they argued that the sacrifices in the Vedas were only symbolic, not real, because the gods, they believed, did not eat meat. Milk then became the ritual food of Hinduism, later joined by other dairy products, such as curds and butter.

The concept of the sacred cow had much to do with the animal's popular association with fertility and motherhood. Hindus who venerate cows liken them to mothers, since they provide life-giving nourishment in the form or milk and butter. But even long before Krishna's deification, Hindus worshiped cow goddesses and considered their milk a sacred substance. Early peoples of Mesopotamia and Egypt similarly likened cows to mother goddesses, and possibly the pre-Aryan people of the Indus Valley did as well. In Egypt,

the goddesses Hathor and Nut served as the great mothers of the world, and both were depicted as celestial cows who fed princes and pharaohs, high gods, and departed souls with their streams of heavenly milk.

Cow goddesses and other female deities possessed great power because they nourished the world. They also gave birth to other divinities who nourished the world; so cows epitomized both fertility and motherhood. In Hindu thought, people have the responsibility to feed and nurture cows and the sacred duty to protect them from being slaughtered and eaten. Many Hindus today believe that if they care for cows properly, these sacred animals will bring them good fortune, just as they brought Krishna good fortune, strength, and even immortality. Even in the early Vedic period, when priests did sacrifice cows, they likely only sacrificed barren cows and never fertile ones. The concept of motherhood was always sacred, and the maternal cow was worshiped as Surabhi, the cow goddess. Surabhi, in fact, was said to have created the cosmic waters. She released a sacred stream of fluid from her teats and created the ocean of milk from which the world began.

While the Hindus gradually moved toward avoiding the consumption of beef and holding cows sacred, people in other parts of the world continued to consume the flesh of cows in quantity. Many of them also venerated cattle, particularly bulls; but unlike the Buddhists and later Hindus, they considered this veneration a good reason for sacrificing the animals to their gods. The Vikings sacrificed bulls to their fertility gods and to the thunder god Thor—just as Vedic priests sacrificed bulls to Indra, the god of thunder and storm. Bulls symbolized storms because they bellowed like thunder. It was thought that the thunder gods would relish the flesh of such animals.

Some early people who slew sacrificial bulls used the body parts for divination. The Irish bull feast, or *tairbfeis,* included the eating of a bull's flesh and the drinking of its blood. It was believed that the participants in the ritual

Cow grazing in the temple of Shiva. (Library of Congress)

feast would have dreams foretelling important future events if they slept on the hide of the bull they had eaten. In an Irish legend, a Druid consumed the ritual bull, slept on its hide, and dreamed of Conaire, who arrived the next day to become ruler of Tara, the royal court and historic seat of Irish kings. (Harris 1985; Simoons 1994)

See also Blood and Flesh; Butter; Meat; Milk

BEER

The consumption of beer has played a role in myth and religion since antiquity. The ancients often considered beer the beverage of choice, because of the risk of drinking contaminated water. People have been brewing beer for thousands of years, some say even back to the Pleistocene era. Ancient people discovered that fermented grains produced intoxicating effects, so they considered the brew a gift from the gods. Not only did it elevate their minds to a higher state but if crops failed, people could rely on beer for survival; so the gods indeed gave human beings something of great value.

The discovery that fermented grains produced intoxicating effects greatly affected agricultural societies all over the world. In most parts of the world, people brewed beer of some sort from cultivated grains, from an early stage in their agricultural histories. Egyptians made beer from fermented barley; Tibetans and Africans used millet; Nubians and Assyrians used oats; and the peoples of the Americas used maize. People even made beer from seeds, twigs, leaves, and roots of plants such as sassafras, ginger, or spruce.

The first brewers likely made their beers by accident. In order for fermentation to take place, the grain had to get wet, germinate, and then dry. Quite likely, someone left their barley out in the rain and then tried to salvage it.

The ancient Egyptians credited Osiris, the god of agriculture, with the discovery of beer. He made the beer out of germinated barley and sacred water from the Nile, then left the mixture out in the sun and forgot it. When Osiris came back, the mixture had fermented, and it tasted so good that he gave it to human beings as a gift. This account explains the process now known as malting. When the grain got wet and sprouted, enzymes in the barley converted starches to sugars; and as the grain dried, those sugars met with yeasts in the air, and fermentation began.

Because fermentation produced a substance that could alter minds, the process itself seemed mystical, and early peoples often connected beer brewing with the deities who watched over them and protected them, like Osiris. Others devised gods who personified the brewing process. The Celts had Braciaca as their god of malt and intoxication. The Teutonic people had Gambrinus, a mythical Flemish king who was said to have invented hopped beer. The hop plant is a vine of the mulberry family that has grown wild since ancient times, but it was not cultivated for flavoring beer until several hundred years ago. Long before then, however, people used other additives for flavoring: dates, honey, and herbs and spices of all sorts—even henbane, rosemary, and mandrake, plants believed to have magical properties.

The production of beer changed dramatically during the Industrial Revolution, when giant breweries arose; but in the early days, the production of beer was a crude and simple procedure. Once people learned what had to happen to the grain, they developed a way to control the process. In the early days of brewing, women made beer by chewing the grain, spitting it into a large vat, adding water, and heating the mixture. They used their saliva as a fermenting agent, then they buried the vats underground. In the absence of air, the enzymes in their saliva changed the starch in the mashed grain to sugar, and the production of alcohol began.

Women brewers, called brewsters, controlled the production of beer in ancient times. Tales of these brewsters surface frequently in the myths. In Mesopotamia, Siduri, a woman brewer, gave beer to the Sumerian king Gilgamesh. In the Finnish epic *Kalevala,* women brewers are frequently mentioned. Just as early brewers were most often women, the deities of beer were most often goddesses. In Egyptian myth, Hathor-Sekmet was the beer goddess, worshiped as such because Ra, the sun god, succeeded in transforming her from a wild lioness into a frivolous woman by feeding her a red-dyed beer she mistook for blood. As a result of Ra's trick, the fierce lioness failed to destroy humankind, and drunkenness became a symbol of gaiety.

Some of the best-known myths of beer and drunkenness arose from Germanic folk epics, in which departed heroes drank beer in the otherworld. In these tales, cauldrons and kettles played important roles; and in this case, male deities generally owned the cauldrons and the beer within them. Odin, the sky god, had a beer hall in Valhalla, and Aegir, the sea god, brewed beer in his underwater hall. Like the beer of Goibniu of Celtic myth, the brews of Odin and Aegir featured prominently in the otherworld. Goibniu was the god of beer and the host of the otherworld feast called the Feast of Age: His beer removed the bonds of age, in essence bestowing immortality. Mythical beers as elixirs of life obviously paid tribute to beer's intoxicating effects. Because it altered consciousness, beer seemed magical, and because it elevated the mind, it appeared to bridge the gap between humans and gods.

Intoxication and beer drinking assumed tremendous importance to the pagan peoples of Europe. They associated their high gods with magic meads and drinking rituals, and they held boisterous beer parties in honor of these gods. At these carousals, beer was consumed so that the gods would leave the heavens, come to earth, and join in the revelry. This ancient beer cult was the predecessor of the German Oktoberfest and similar beer festivals, although the modern beer festival has lost its element of religious fervor. Beer was also a logical choice for religious offerings. In Finnish myth, Ukko, the sky god, received sacrifices of sheep as well as beer and other alcoholic beverages. His worshipers placed their offerings in a chest and carried them to Ukko's mountain, where they believed the god appeared during the night and consumed what they left. They also poured part of the beer and liquor onto the ground to make the earth fruitful and to ensure a drought-free summer.

Finns believed that beer pleased the spirits, and that the gods would thank them for their gift with fruitful harvests. The pleasurable effects of alcohol led many to believe that the gods desired beer. In some of the ancient drinking rituals, people consumed large quantities of beer because they believed that drunkenness pleased the gods. Other people, however, shunned drunkenness and alcohol altogether. The Aztecs, for instance, had gods who killed drunks by drowning. In Aztec culture, beer drinking was reserved primarily for priests participating in religious rituals, and it was generally forbidden to commoners.

Inebriation could be frightening, making people capable of "going berserk." In Germanic lands, the word *beer* is related to both *bear* and *berserk,* and berserk described the state achieved by drinking too much. Odin's followers, the Berserkers, consumed large quantities of beer, then ran wild through the countryside dressed in bear skins and ready to fight. Their drunken state made them impervious to pain, and they worked themselves into such a frenzy that they howled and roared like bears as they savagely attacked their enemies. (Bickerdyke 1965; Darby et al. 1977; Elkhort 1991; Lehner and Lehner 1973; Toussaint-Samat 1992)

See also Alcoholic Beverages; Ayahuasca; Balche; Chicha; Kava; Mead; Pulque; Sake; Soma; Wine

BELLADONNA
See Nightshades

BETEL NUTS
Betel nuts come from the areca palm tree, considered by Hindus one of the most sacred of plants. Areca palms are native not only to India but also to Malaysia, Ceylon, the Philippines, and the Melanesian islands, where their nuts frequently were used as offerings to the gods. In Hindu India, betel nuts still accompany each and every Brahmanic religious ceremony. Participants use the nuts and leaves to adorn images of Vedic deities, who like the fruit of the areca palm, embody auspiciousness and purity.

Today betel or areca nuts are one of the world's leading stimulants, particularly in the Far East, where they are considered powerful aphrodisiacs. In traditional cultures, the nuts and the leaves still bear a deep religious significance. Betel leaves are triangular and identified with the vulva, and nuts have always symbolized fertility—thus the betel nut's association with Lakshmi, the Hindu fertility goddess. Both Lakshmi and the elephant-headed god Ganesha are personified in Hinduism by the betel nut. Hindus associate the nut with Ganesha because both are believed to bring good fortune, wealth, and prosperity.

Hindus past and present offered betel nuts to both Lakshmi and to Ganesha as well as to Agni, the god of fire. But today they incorporate betel nuts into popular customs as frequently as they do in religious rituals. In Hindu custom, a gift of these nuts to guests symbolizes hospitality and friendship. The Melanesians use them in marriage ceremonies as symbols of affection and peace. The Newars of Nepal also incorporate betel nuts into marriage rituals. The parents of the girl present betel nuts to the parents of their prospective son-in-law, and after the couple marry, the new bride presents betel nuts to her husband and his family. People in India typically present betel nuts, wrapped in the leaves of the sacred plant, to wedding guests. These marriage customs likely developed because of the betel nut's association with fertility; the nuts, encased in the leaves, symbolize the ripening of fruit within

The Hindus associate betel nuts with the elephant-headed god Ganesha because they consider it fortuitous to possess the nuts. Ganesha, the Hindus believe, brings good fortune, wealth, and prosperity to his worshippers. (SEF, Art Resource, NY)

the womb. The custom of wrapping the betel nuts likely stems from the myth of Deva-damani, who entered the court of King Vikramaditya with betel nuts enveloped in leaves.

The frequent use of betel nuts as offerings underscores their value to Hindus. In one tradition, the betel nut tree originated in the celestial sphere, and the Hindu god Arjuna stole a branch from this celestial tree and planted it on earth. In another tradition, Shiva

became annoyed with the betel plant and asked it to descend to earth, but decreed that the people on earth should worship the plant. For one reason or another, the betel plant no longer grew in heaven but only on earth, and the gods coveted it. For this reason, people made offerings of betel nuts to appease the gods. They also placed betel nuts in the mouths of the dead. Because the Hindus believed no betel nuts grew in heaven, they sent the dead to their afterlife with one last taste of the valued food. (Gupta 1991; Majupuria 1988; Ratsch 1992)

See also Coca; Coffee; Cola Nuts; Tobacco

BILVA FRUIT

The bilva, or bel tree, is one of the most sacred trees of India and one that plays a large role in Hindu myths, particularly those surrounding Shiva. Shiva, sometimes called Bilvadanda, lives in the bel tree and thus the Hindus consider the tree itself a vegetal form of the god. According to legend, the god Vishnu had two wives, Lakshmi and Saraswati, and he loved Saraswati more, so Lakshmi began to worship Shiva. She engaged in meditation to commune with Shiva, and she finally turned into the bilva tree. Among pious Hindus, the worship of Shiva, called Shaivism, stands in opposition to the worship of Vishnu, called Vaishnavism, and while Vaishnavism worship involves tulsi, or holy basil, Shaivism worship involves the bilva tree. Since Lakshmi's meditation, Shiva has lived in the bilva tree, and his worshipers sanctified the tree at that time.

The bilva tree produces orange pulpy fruits that some Hindus identified with the breasts and milk of Lakshmi. In worshiping Shiva, Lakshmi offered the god a thousand lotus buds every day. One day she lacked two buds, so she planned to cut off her breasts and offer them instead, because her husband, Vishnu, had likened her breasts to lotus buds. Lakshmi cut off one breast, and Shiva was satisfied. He decreed that the breast would grow into the bilva tree. Because the tree grew from the breast of Lakshmi, bilva fruit and leaves became sacred offerings. The bilva leaves also achieved sanctity because of their trifoliate arrangement. In Hindu belief, most plants with a trifoliate arrangement of leaves were associated with the trinity of Brahma, Vishnu, and Shiva, and they were offered to all three gods. But the bilva was offered primarily to Shiva. The three leaves signify the three functions of Shiva—creation, preservation, and destruction—as well as his three eyes.

Hindu myths offer numerous explanations for the sanctity of the bilva tree and its leaves and fruit. One myth tells of a hunter who climbed a bilva tree in order to hide and to spot a deer he wanted to shoot. The hunter got bored sitting in the tree, so he began picking off the leaves and throwing them down, and they happened to fall onto an image of Shiva underneath the tree. Miraculously, the god appeared to the hunter and told him that he made himself visible because he considered even the accidental fall of leaves on his image a means of worship. So bilva leaves became a common offering to Shiva. The plant has long been considered valuable as medicine and for its cooling ability. At the beginning of the universe, when the gods and demons churned the ocean of milk to get soma, the elixir of life, poison arose from the ocean before the soma, and Shiva held it in his throat, presumably to keep the poison from contaminating the waters. Hindus offer bilva leaves to Shiva to cool the heat he felt in his body after drinking the poison.

The Hindus attribute all kinds of medicinal properties to bilva fruits. Their uses range from curing dysentery to promoting fertility—not surprising, given the fruit's resemblance to breasts and its association with the breasts of Lakshmi, the goddess of love and fertility. Some people think the fruit signifies the head of Shiva and will not eat it.

In Hindu myth, the bilva tree grew either from the breast of Lakshmi or from her dung (Lakshmi was born a sacred cow). But although most Hindus consider bilva fruit sacred, most tribal people of India do not: In tribal legend, the bilva tree sprang from the testicles of a pig, which many consider an unclean animal. (Barooah 1992; Gupta 1991; Simoons 1998)

See also Lotus

BIRDS' NESTS

For 1,500 years, the Chinese have considered birds' nests a valuable and even magical delicacy. Edible nests are served in Hong Kong, Thailand, Indonesia, Burma, Malaysia, Vietnam, the Philippines, and the people of these areas prize them as miracle medicines, aphrodisiacs, purifiers, and even agents of longevity. Nests as food items don't come from just any birds, however, but from a particular kind of bird thought at first to be a sea swallow and now known to be a swiftlet. The tiny swiftlets build their nests primarily in sea caves, and highly skilled harvesters risk life and limb scaling the rocks to pry their nests off the cave walls. In order to retrieve the nests, many harvesters find it necessary to use tools reputed to have magic powers.

Swiftlets weave nests not of straw or sticks, like other birds, but of their own saliva—gummy, spaghetti-like strands secreted by glands under their tongues. This nest-building process, the birds, and the food they produce have long been considered magical. The birds feed on flying insects, but for centuries the Chinese believed they fed only on the sea foam that blows in the wind. Believing the birds contained the essence of sea foam, the Chinese endowed the nests with all the properties they knew existed in the sea. They considered the nests rich in mineral salts but also much more mysterious elements, such as the phosphorescence that lights up the oceans. They also believed the nests contained the miraculous qualities of the creatures that created them—notably, the strength and perseverance it took to survive the ferocious monsoon winds and to thrive on a diet of sea foam.

A combination of all of these mystical elements convinced superstitious nest harvesters to use what they believed to be magical tools to retrieve their precious swiftlet nests. Believing the birds magical, these harvesters thought that the gods protected the birds, and that if the harvesters failed to use magical tools, the gods would become angry with them and cause them to fall to their deaths on the cave floors. Harvesters today continue to take the time to master this dangerous business, knowing that people in many Asian lands pay exceptionally high prices for their products. Despite the relatively low nutritive value of the nests, people continue to esteem their properties. They are believed to cure skin and lung diseases, improve the immune system, and endow with wisdom, strength, virility, and longevity. Because of these persistent, centuries-old beliefs, some harvesters have been able to build a lucrative (although in many places illegal) business trade in the birds' nests. Nests of top quality—in particular, white nests retrieved from cave walls before the female swiftlet has laid her eggs—may sell for several thousand dollars a pound. (de Groot 1983; Elkhort 1991; Simoons 1991)

BLACKBERRIES

Blackberries grow on woody plants with cane-like stems, commonly known as bramble bushes. They were probably one of the earliest foods, and through the ages have often supplied poor people with food in the summertime. It was commonly said that the Devil hated blackberries, a belief that may have arisen from the blackberry's association with Christ. In Christian legend, the burning bush was identified as a bramble, Christ's crown of thorns was said to be made from the bramble's branches, and Christ's blood was thought to have manifested itself in the dark berries. The blackberry bush symbolized virtue, perhaps because of its connection with Christ, and purity because of its connection with the fire of the burning bush.

The bramble bush grows abundantly in woodlands and scrublands, particularly in the eastern part of North America, along the Pacific coast, and in the British Isles and western Europe. The plant flowers from May through September, and in early October the uneaten berries begin to decay. Mythmakers commonly attributed this decay to the Devil, who is said to have appeared on Old Michaelmas, or St. Michael's Day (10 October), and cursed the plant. St. Michael was an archangel, an archetype of Christ, and it was on this day that St. Michael defeated the forces of evil and banished the Devil from heaven. According to legend, when the Devil fell from heaven, he landed in a bramble bush. In some legends, the Devil returns to the bramble bush each year on this day and stamps on the branches. In other legends he spits or urinates on the berries. In either case, the Devil himself halts the production of fruit. Some say that anyone who dares to eat blackberries after St. Michael's Day will suffer disastrous consequences within a year's time.★

Many of these early beliefs about the Devil and blackberries survive today in western Europe. In Ireland, blackberries are eaten past St. Michael's Day until Halloween, when in Irish legend the Devil's goblin assistant, Phooka, appeared as some kind of animal and withered the berries either by throwing a cloak over the bushes or by crawling around on top of them. In parts of Great Britain, witches were often said to wither the blackberries. A legend from Cornwall also reveals a connection between the blackberry and evil forces. In this legend, a wicked witch changed a kind princess named Olwen into a blackberry bush. Olwen had a cruel twin sister named Gertha, whom the father of these two girls favored most. A prince came along asking for milk one day, and Olwen kindly gave it to him. Knowing that the prince would be back for

★ Michaelmas today is celebrated on 29 September, but in past times, before the shift from the Julian calendar to the Gregorian calendar, it was celebrated on 10 October.

her, Olwen's father sent her away to a witch so that his other daughter, Gertha, could have the prince. But the prince wanted only Olwen, and when the two of them fell in love, the witch in her anger changed Olwen into a thorny blackberry bush by the side of the road. A wizard helped the prince win his lover back, however. He instructed the prince to fly to the bush, in bird form, and bring back a ripe berry. This the prince did, and the wizard reversed the spell.

Most traditional legends about the blackberry described it as a fruit of ill omen. Blackberries were considered fairy food, and it was believed that anyone who ate them might well be doomed to remain in the fairy realm forever. Touching blackberries, fairy fruit or not, could bring bad luck. In Greek myth, when Bellerophon tried to seize the gods' powers by riding the winged horse Pegasus to the top of Mount Olympus, he fell into a blackberry bush instead (just as the Devil had when he fell from heaven). The thorns blinded and maimed him, condemning him to the life of an outcast. (Folkard 1892; *Oxford Dictionary of Plant-Lore* 1995; Reed 1992; Skinner n.d.)

See also Blueberries; Cranberries; Elderberries; Gooseberries; Mulberries; Raspberries; Strawberries

BLOOD AND FLESH

People in traditional cultures consumed blood and flesh based on the mythological notion that blood contained life force and soul. This reflected the early belief that a human body had magical properties. Early people made a connection between death, flesh, blood, and spirit. They observed that a person died when blood flowed from the body, so they surmised that blood contained the person's principal essence, and that essence escaped in the blood that flowed during death.

People have long expressed the belief in blood as the essence of life in sacraments ranging from holy communion to rituals involving cannibalism and human sacrifice. Participants in these rituals consumed blood and flesh, or a representation of blood and flesh, to partake of divine spirit. The transformation of one substance into another, and specifically the transformation of bread and wine into flesh and blood, was called the doctrine of transubstantiation. For centuries people consumed breads in human likeness to represent godly flesh and they drank red wine to represent godly blood. Today these sacraments may be simply symbolic; but in times past, many people believed the bread and the wine actually did take on divine properties. The ability of an earthly material to stand in for a divine substance is exemplified in the Catholic doctrine of transubstantiation, which holds that consecrated bread and wine literally become the flesh and blood of Christ, while also remaining bread and wine. In other cultures and religions the communion is often more symbolic, but the underlying notion of eating divine flesh and blood remains.

In some religions, blood served as a communal drink shared between humans and gods. The idea of blood covenants permeated ancient thought, and human sacrifice pervaded much of the Old World. Human sacrifice and cannibalism are usually associated with the Aztecs of Mexico and with societies in Oceania and South America, but cannibalism commonly occurred in Europe as well. The ancient Europeans performed blood sacrifices in public, as did the ancient peoples of the Americas. Certainly the Aztecs during Montezuma's time engaged in the practice, as did the Incas and the Caribs. All these peoples wove the necessity for blood and flesh into their myths. In the Aztec myth of the Five Suns, Tonatiuh, the fifth and current sun, needed blood in order to rise. So from that mythical time long ago when the Aztec gods gathered in the city of Teotihuacan and sacrificed themselves for the sun, people have continued the practice. Commonly, after the sacrifice, they consumed the flesh. Not only did the Aztecs consider this consumption a blood covenant but they also adhered to a

An Aztec priest sacrificing a human heart to the war god, Huitzilopochtli. The Aztecs believed that the gods both required and desired blood and flesh. (Library of Congress)

hierarchy of food and drink from these sacrifices. They considered the heart and blood of a hero more nutritious than that of a slave or a commoner, for instance.

Ancient people ate human flesh to acquire the outstanding qualities of the person they consumed. By eating brains the consumers gained wisdom, and by drinking blood they nourished their souls. The Greeks and others of the ancient world believed that the soul resided in the head. Headhunters of central Celebes and the East Indies also consumed certain parts of their victims, believing that human blood and brains would make them brave. For the same reasons, early people made love potions from reproductive organs; the Australians ate the testicles of the kangaroo, for instance, and some peoples of North America ate the testicles of the beaver. The Aztecs considered the human heart, as the vital organ of the body, the most valued sacrifice and the most appropriate food for their gods.

In early religions, worshipers considered sacrifices part of a blood covenant with the gods. Myths often revealed that the gods wanted blood and flesh. In the Aztec myth, Tonatiuh, the Sun, required it in order to rise, and in Greek myth, the high god Zeus demanded it. In Hesiod's *Theogony,* Prometheus tried to trick Zeus by disguising an offering of bones—the least desirable portions of an ox—as its flesh and blood. Some scholars assert that this myth not only reveals the belief in the primary importance of blood sacrifice to the gods but also the essential role of flesh in civilized life. Enraged by Prometheus's deception, Zeus denied fire to humankind. From then on, mortals had to show their inferiority to Zeus and the other gods by making animal sacrifices, reflecting the ranking of humans between divinity and bestiality. This myth has appeared in different sources and has been interpreted in different ways, but it appears to emphasize the importance of blood sacrifice and the belief in blood as the most precious offering of all. Some believe that all liquid substances used in offerings represented blood. Blood fueled the soul with energy and life force. (Camporesi 1995; Carrasco 1995; Frazer 1950; Tannahill 1975; Wilkins 1995)

See also Bread; Meat; Ox; Wine

BLUEBERRIES

Blueberries and their European relatives, bilberries (or whortleberries), have enjoyed celebrity as firstfruits for centuries. They ripen from mid- to late summer, when early peoples often held harvest festivals to thank the nature gods for the sun and the rain and their generous provisions of food. In ancient Ireland, people gathered bilberries during Lughnasad, a harvest festival held around 1 August to honor the sun god Lugh. This was the first of four annual Celtic harvest festivals, held at a specific site on the river Boyne. On the nearby hilltops, bilberries grew in abundance and provided people with ripe, juicy fruits to celebrate the season.

Harvest festivals typically involve the offering and consumption of firstfruits, and during Lughnasad, the people picked the first bilberries of the season. The people recognized that Lugh ripened the berries, and that the earth goddess in a sense had given birth to them. Lughnasad ritualized the union between the sun god and the earth goddess by turning the harvest festival into a kind of marriage rite. In marrying men and women who had gathered for the occasion, the pagan Celts rejoiced in the fruitful marriage of the sun and the earth. Ancient legends relate stories of men destined to be Ireland's kings mating with old hags and transforming them into beautiful women. The kings, who assumed the role of sun gods, married the hags, who represented Ireland in the winter. The hags' transformation after their marriages represented the transformation of the barren winter landscape into the fruitful fields of spring. The multitude of bilberries at Lughnasad attested to the land's fruitfulness. The people climbed the nearby hills and picked them, a practice that has continued at modern-day festivals, even though most of the other rituals of ancient Lughnasad have faded.

Bilberries continue to grow abundantly on the hilltops near the river Boyne. They thrive in moist, peaty soils and grow throughout the hill districts of Great Britain. A certain species of bilberry, the whortleberry, also grows in the volcanic soils of Hawaii. These whortleberries are sacred to the volcano goddess Pele, and people traditionally have offered these fruits to Pele before partaking of the harvest themselves.

Whortleberries are a species of myrtle, and the people of Greece referred to the fruits of their myrtle plants as myrtleberries. They grew on the coasts of the Mediterranean Sea, and the ancient Romans told the myth of Myrtillus to explain how they got there. Myrtillus was the charioteer of Oenomaus, the king of Pisa and the father of Hippodamia. Oenomaus had chosen Myrtillus as his charioteer because Myrtillus was the son of Mercury, the swift messenger of the gods. Oenomaus decreed that whoever wished to marry Hippodamia had to best him in a chariot race; because he had Myrtillus to drive his chariot, he thought no one could compete. But Pelops, one of Hippodamia's suitors, paid Myrtillus a large reward to disable Oenomaus's chariot. Oenomaus was fatally injured in the race, and as a dying request, he asked Pelops to throw Myrtillus into the sea. The traitorous Pelops obliged. Mercury, however, intervened, changing his son into the seaside plant that produces myrtleberries, or bilberries. (Folkard 1892; *Funk and Wagnall's* 1972; *Oxford Dictionary of Plant-Lore* 1995)

See also Blackberries; Cranberries; Elderberries; Gooseberries; Mulberries; Raspberries; Strawberries

BREAD

Bread was perhaps the most important food to all cultures that baked, and one of great symbolic importance. It served as the basis for some the most celebrated feasts of the ancient world, and it gained even more significance in early Christian times because the apostles of Christ ate it at the Last Supper. In many cultures people have baked loaves in particular shapes to reinforce mythic symbols. Bread baked in moon shapes symbolized death and rebirth. Breads baked with sun symbols stamped on them symbolized fertility and regeneration. Bread baked in ellipsoid forms suggested the female genitalia; bread baked in phallic forms suggested the male genitalia; and both symbolized fertility or reproduction. Bread making involved utilizing grain, which died and was resurrected with the seasons. Bread, by its very nature, symbolized life, regeneration, and the cyclical nature of existence.

People have baked bread in one form or another for at least five millennia, and although most considered it a luxury until a few centuries ago, bread quickly became the staff of life. Porridge was the staff of life long before bread. The first "breads" were in fact cereals, soaked and pressed into cakes and then dried, either on hot stones or in the sun. Anthropologists have uncovered these early breads, or unleavened cakes, in Stone Age dwellings, attesting to their antiquity. No one knows for sure what these breads may have signified to Stone Age people, but in later antiquity and in Christian times bread was eaten as a sacrament. Bread was, and still is, eaten as the body of a god.

For many centuries the consumption of bread has signified the partaking of the divine. Aztec priests ritually consecrated their bread, an act that they believed transformed the loaves into the actual body of the divinity. The magical conversion of bread into flesh,

Bread was perhaps the most important food to all cultures that baked. Because bread making involved grain, which died and was resurrected with the seasons, bread came to symbolize life, regeneration, and the cyclical nature of existence. (Library of Congress)

or of one substance into another, is known as transubstantiation. The consumption of consecrated bread allows a communion with the divine. In the Christian Eucharist, bread and wine become the body and blood of Christ. The ancient Aryans of India performed similar rituals with rice cakes. The Aztecs ate a representation of their war god Huitzilopochtli, made from maize or from a grain called amaranth. Many cultures, before and since the advent of Christian communion, practiced similar rites with bread. Long ago, people baked sacramental loaves in human form, which may have reinforced a belief in transubstantiation.

The doctrine of transubstantiation may be rooted in the ancient belief that by eating the flesh of a human or animal, the consumer gained the dead animal's attributes. One who ate a deer gained swiftness; one who ate a lion gained courage; one who ate a bear gained strength. By analogy, one who ate a god gained divinity, so people ate consecrated bread that magically became divine flesh. Some groups that practiced cannibalism reasoned in this same manner. They believed a that person who ate a brave chief became brave, for instance, and that in general, a person gained whatever exceptional qualities the person he ate possessed.

The ancients connected bread with both flesh and spirit. Bread could become both body and immortal spirit because the ancients invested grain with soul. They had to kill the grain when they harvested it, but its soul lived on in the bread. Bread symbolized the rebirth of the grain; in other words, the grain was renewed in the baking process. Russian tales often deal with the symbolism of baking. They feature a female, symbolic of the stove, who rewards children by protecting them and offering them bread. The ancient Slavs performed a curious ritual that they called "baking the child," in which they put a child inside a warm stove to undergo a transformation similar to the transformation from dough to bread. This was a healing ritual; the child metaphorically returned to the mother's womb to be born again healthy, transformed, and reformed by healing fire. The Slavs performed this ritual to heal through fire, to change the unacceptable to the acceptable, just as the baking process turned raw food into cooked. But legends and folktales often twisted the ritual into something evil. In one Slavic folktale, the witch Baba-Yaga roasts children; and the witch in the German folktale of Hansel and Gretel bakes children into bread and cakes of all sorts.

The ancient Greeks felt that they had to appease the soul of the grain to obtain bread, and that by honoring the grain, they honored the living soul. Both were goals in the worship of the earth goddess Demeter, who controlled the birth and death of grain. Demeter's grain died during the reaping but was regenerated in the symbolic womb of the warm oven. The soul of the grain survived. In many cultures bread symbolized fertility and life as well as death and divine resurrection, including that of Jesus Christ and of the Egyptian god Osiris. Bread attested to the immortality of moon, sun, god, and grain. (Darby et al. 1977; Frazer 1950; Jacob 1944; Kahn 1985; Norman 1972; Toussaint-Samat 1992)

See also Amaranth; Barley; Blood and Flesh; Cake; Corn; Grain; Millet; Oats; Quinoa; Rice; Rye; Sorghum; Wheat

BREADFRUIT

Breadfruit is a staple food of the Pacific islands, where people have cultivated the tree since antiquity. This tree likely originated on the Malay Peninsula, then long ago spread, from island to island, throughout the Pacific region. The people of the Pacific relied on breadfruit for food, but they also utilized every part of the tree. They used the young branches and shoots to make bark cloth or tapa; the wood, to make furniture and canoes; and the milky sap, to make caulking material. The round, pulpy fruit they boiled, roasted, baked, or fried and ate as a primary source of carbohydrates, or ground into a paste and stored in food pits buried in the ground.

People knew they could depend on this valuable tree for survival even during times of famine and drought.

Numerous legends surrounding the breadfruit attest to its importance in Oceanic culture. Mythmakers typically assigned their food plants magical properties, and early islanders searched for explanations of how this useful tree originated and spread from island to island. Most legends of the breadfruit deal with its origin. In some stories, the breadfruit tree grew first on a mythical island; then gods or goddesses or people with magic powers carried the seeds from place to place. In a Hawaiian legend, the breadfruit tree grew from the body of the god Ku, and its fruit had magical power because Ku himself had magical power. Because food appears to sprout miraculously from the earth and enables people to survive, mythmakers typically assigned their food plants magical properties.

The supernatural origins of food plants, as described in myths from around the world, often involved the production of food from someone's body. In another Hawaiian legend, breadfruit grew from the testicles of a man, then spread from the vomit of the gods. A group of gods saw the breadfruit and began eating it; but when the higher gods Kane and Kanaloa told them they were eating a dead man's testicles, they vomited all over Hawaii. Breadfruit trees sprang up everywhere.

Breadfruit grew in many places, but people greatly feared what would happen should it disappear. In the Marquesas Islands, warfare was commonplace, and legends described the destruction of the precious breadfruit during war. In one myth, a man had a vision that his grandfather was killed and all his fruit trees destroyed. Then the man discovered that his vision was true. The only plants left after the rampage were one breadfruit and one banana, each hidden in one of his grandfather's ears.

At the time these myths were created, warriors in these areas typically cut down trees and destroyed the breadfruit and the coconuts on their rampages. Famine was a problem, not only during war but because of frequent drought. Breadfruit crops frequently dwindled, but people stored them in food pits where the fermented pulp remained edible for years. The Polynesians say that the felling of a breadfruit tree is a harbinger of death—perhaps because they recognize how important this tree once was in saving lives. In one Hawaiian myth, breadfruit arose from the head of a man who wanted to feed his family. According to this myth, long ago, the people had only red clay and ferns to eat. When a man named Ulu died of starvation, his family buried him near a spring by their house. During the night they heard the sounds of heavy fruit falling to the ground; and when they awoke, they found a breadfruit tree growing outside their door. The famine ended. Ulu had died to feed his family, and the breadfruit grew miraculously from his head.

In other myths of Oceania, coconuts grew from the heads of other people, because coconuts, like breadfruit, resemble human heads in shape. In the breadfruit myth, the man's wife, in gratitude, called the breadfruit tree Ulu, after her husband. In some versions of this myth, sugarcane also grew from Ulu, as did bananas and yams. Food myths that describe the growth of crops from dead bodies arose in recognition of the cyclical nature of the universe and the reciprocity between life and death. (Beckwith 1970; Cox and Banack 1991)

See also Coconuts; Taro

BUFFALO
Buffalo meat was a staple food for many groups in early America as well as for some people in India and Southeast Asia. The buffalo provides a lot of meat: A mature American bison typically weighs about 2,000 pounds, so it often supplied enough food to distribute throughout a tribe. The indigenous peoples of Indochina also traditionally slaughtered buffaloes and consumed them in great feasts. In India, people primarily consumed their milk. The only buffalo species in India is a water buffalo—a very

The Plains Indians relied on buffalo for survival and considered the meat of these animals sacred. Food seemed magical because it gave life, and game animals seemed to appear on the hunting grounds as a gift from the creator. (Library of Congress)

different animal from the bison that roamed the American Great Plains. Hindus today use buffalo milk to make ghee, or clarified butter, but never eat its flesh. They consider water buffalo unclean and associate it with death and demonic forces.

Hindus believe that the consumption of animal flesh violates the principle of ahimsa, or noninjury to living things. Eating beef also violates their concept of the sacred cow. But though the buffalo is similar to the cow, they appear to have opposite connotations to Hindus, who don't eat either animal, but for different reasons. The Hindus consider the cow a symbol of goodness, but the buffalo they associate with evil, death, and disease. They consider buffaloes unclean and unlucky, and they equate the blackness of their bodies with the blackness of their souls.

Sometime between 2000 and 1500 B.C., dark-skinned races of people called Dravidians

settled in southern India. They revered the water buffalo and sacrificed it to their deities. After the sacrifices, they would eat the buffalo flesh. Early Hindus regarded the Dravidians much as they did the water buffalo, as dark and foreboding. Brahmans and priests did not eat the buffalo, but commoners did. In Hindu myth, Yama, the god of death, rode on a water buffalo, which further contributed to Hindus' rejection of the animal. The Dravidians and other Indian meat-eating tribal groups prized the water buffalo for the food it provided. Like the Dravidians, other meat-eating tribes used the buffalo as their major sacrificial offering, particularly to mother goddesses, and considered buffalo meat the most desirable food for religious feasts.

Many groups in North America accorded similarly high status to their buffalo, correctly called the bison. Native Americans greatly respected the animal for its size and strength.

Not only did they rely on the buffalo for food but they considered both the animal and the meat it provided sacred. The Plains Indians considered buffalo and maize their primary foodstuffs; they paired them as God-given sustenance, and they paired them in myths as well. One Cheyenne myth traced both buffalo and maize to a magic mountain and to Old Woman, who lived inside the mountain, where she raised herds of buffalo and fields of maize. When two men set out in search of food and managed to enter the magic mountain, Old Woman let them taste the buffalo meat she had been cooking in magic pots. She then sent the men home with her precious corn seeds, and sent the herds out of her mountain cave to the open plains and the tribal hunting grounds.

The Plains Indians considered buffalo meat sacred and assigned it a magic origin. Food was magic because it gave life, and game animals appeared on the hunting grounds as a gift from the creator. When no buffaloes roamed the plains, famine resulted. Just as the hunters believed benevolent deities sent the buffalo to them when the animals were abundant, they believed that demons took them away when they disappeared. A Blackfoot legend tells of a buffalo stealer who had taken all the buffalo herds away and was hoarding them in a cavern for his own use. The creator god Napi succeeded in locating the thief, and returned the buffalo to the prairie. As in the Cheyenne legend, the buffalo in this Blackfoot tale were confined in a mountain cave.

The same motif recurs in many hunting myths of North America. Many of these myths recount how long ago in a mythical era, game animals remained captive, so hunting was unnecessary. But then the people released them, either by accident or out of curiosity, and the animals scattered. Thereafter the people had to hunt animals for their food.

The buffalo hunt was of crucial significance to the Plains tribes because these people relied on the buffalo for survival. Not only did they subsist on buffalo meat but they also utilized the hides for clothing and shelter and the bones for weapons and tools. The buffalo migrated seasonally, and when they returned to the hunting grounds, the people considered it a time for celebration. The Mandan tribe of the northern Great Plains held a buffalo festival each year to mark the return of their primary game animal and to honor it for his role in supplying food. The Mandan dressed in buffalo hides and imitated the animal. They performed a buffalo dance that culminated in the successful banishment of the demon of famine, impersonated by one of the tribe members.

Tribes of the American plains performed the ritual Buffalo Dance as a sort of prayer to increase the number of buffalo available for food. The Hopi perform it still, and their Buffalo Dance involves a dancing kachina spirit. The Blackfoot dance involves a select group of tribal men. These people perform the Buffalo Dance as a sacred ritual, and tell myths to explain the origin of the dance as well as that of the buffalo. In a myth from Taos, the trickster Coyote brought buffalo to the people after discovering a herd roaming the plains. Coyote sang as he drove the animals to the hunting grounds, and as he did, the buffalo danced. The people of Taos saw them coming and witnessed their dancing. Ever since, the people have performed the dance to draw the buffalo nearer to their hunting grounds.

In Blackfoot legend, the Buffalo Dance originated after an impressive display of magic convinced the buffalo to reveal an important secret—the ability to return their dead to life. The Blackfoot obtained their meat by dressing up in buffalo costumes and tricking the buffalo into falling over steep cliffs, where the men could easily slaughter them on the rocks below. But according to legend, one time this trick failed to work, and a young woman, longing to save her people from starvation, promised to marry one of the buffalo if they would all agree to jump off the cliff themselves. To her surprise, the buffalo began jumping off the cliff in great numbers. Then one large buffalo bull carried the woman off to live with him as his wife. The woman's father went to search for his daughter but was tragically trampled to death by the herd. When the daughter miraculously returned him to life with a magic song, the buffalo agreed to share their magic with the tribe. The buffalo taught the man and his daughter the Buffalo Dance, actually a magical ritual that returned the slaughtered buffalo to life just as the woman's magic song had done for her father. From then on, select men in the tribe performed the Buffalo Dance each time they hunted buffalo.

The Buffalo Dance served a purpose similar to that of rituals performed elsewhere in the world to increase food supplies: for example, the Ainu bear ritual, or the First Salmon rites of the Inuit. These rituals rely on the certainty of resurrection. Hunters who believe they can appease the animal spirits count on the willingness of these spirits to return to life in the bodies of other animals, and to once again sacrifice themselves for the people's benefit. (Edmonds and Clark 1989; Hoffpauir 1982; Simoons 1994)

See also Corn; Deer; Meat; Reindeer and Caribou; Salmon

BUTTER

In myths of many ancient cultures, butter symbolized fertility as well as purity. The churned butter symbolized semen; the churning, the sexual act; and the solidification of the butter, the baby inside the womb. Thus butter assumed a sacred quality. Furthermore, butter is gold in color, like honey—a product so pure and unadulterated that the ancients perceived it as food for the gods.

Myths of Hindu India attest to the purity of butter, particularly of clarified butter or ghee, a golden liquid produced by melting the butter and then removing from it the whey products that rise to the top and the salt that sinks to the bottom. To the Hindus, ghee is a sacred substance, a product of the sacred cow; in myth, ghee arose at the beginning of the world, as the gods and demons churned the

ocean of milk. During the Deluge, soma (or *amrita*), the elixir of life, had gotten submerged in this ocean, and the gods had to retrieve it to regain their strength. They used the snake deity Vasuki as a rope and Mount Mandara as a churning pole to churn the ocean until high gods and sacred objects arose from its depths, solidifying like butter from milk. Soma, the elixir of life, finally emerged.

In another ancient Indian myth, Prajapati, also known as Brahma, rubbed or churned his hands together to create butter, or the sacred ghee. He then poured the ghee into the fire to produce offspring. Vedic rituals commonly involved pouring ghee into fire, particularly in the worship of Agni, the fire god. Butter was golden, like fire, and a source of magic and sacred energy. It also had regenerative powers: When thrown onto a fire, it nourished and renewed the flames. In myth, the pouring of butter on fire was an engendering act; in ritual, it served as a reenactment of creation. Hymns in the Rig Veda praise ghee as the fertilizing seed, as energy and inspiration. It fortified Agni, who himself was the embodiment of fire, and acted as a purifier of sacrificial offerings.

Hindu rituals today often involve the use of both fire and ghee as purifiers. Worshipers anoint images of gods such as Vishnu and Krishna with ghee; they also wash them with milk, or with a mixture of milk, curd, butter, honey, and sugar. The effectiveness of this purification stems from the belief in cows themselves as purifiers. Although Hindus eschew the flesh of the cow, they greatly prize dairy products, including milk, butter, curd, and even use the cow's dung and urine. The cow imparts its sacredness and purity through these products. Because the milk of the cow is pure, milk acts as a purifying food. Because butter comes from milk, it too becomes a purifier, working to counteract pollutants and, some say, even to eradicate evil.

Hindus who consider cows sacred liken them to mothers, great providers who give sustenance in the form of milk and butter. In

Hindu myth, Krishna received his nourishment from butter and milk provided by the milkmaids' cows, often stealing butter from them as a prank. Tales from England and Ireland also speak of stolen butter; if butter did not arise during the churning process, it was commonly believed that either witches or fairies had stolen it. Butter was, after all, a highly valued commodity. The fact that magic people and even Krishna himself coveted it attested to the desirability of the golden and somewhat magical substance.

Indian cooks today frequently incorporate butter, or ghee, into recipes. It has become a cooking staple, and some pious Hindus continue to believe in its sanctity. Buffalo milk has almost double the amount of butterfat as the milk of the dairy cow, so Indian cooks often use this product to make ghee, though the buffalo never achieved the sanctity of the cow and thus its products never gained ritual value. But products of the cow constituted fitting foods for the deities. The Indian people have used butter from cows as an offering since Vedic times.

Hindu sacrifices to the fire god Agni prevailed in Vedic times. Fire and butter not only acted as purifiers but also symbolized gold, and thus they were auspicious objects highly valued by the gods. Ghee probably gained significance as an elixir of life in the later Vedic period, after milk and other cow products replaced the earlier beef offerings to the deities. Hindus today use ghee to light temple lamps, a rite that may have its beginnings in ancient sacrificial libations. In myth, when worshipers poured their libations on the sacrificial fires, Agni licked up the butter. That's what fed him, just as soma, the elixir of immortality, fed the high god Indra. So Agni had seven tongues for this purpose, each of them important enough in Agni's myth to warrant a special name. Today's Hindus continue to worship Agni, using ghee and fire, and they adhere to the belief in the ritual value of butter as purifier.

The ancient people of Iceland also linked fire with butter: Farmers' wives traditionally appealed to Gobhin, the smith god, to watch over their butter. Butter had links to fire and purity but also to fertility and abundance. The Masai, a pastoral people of East Africa, consider butter an agent of blessing and use it as an ointment in all life-cycle rituals. The Masai consider milk the ultimate food and consider butter refined milk; they say that it provides sustenance and ensures growth and fertility. Tibetan pastoralists, who rely on the yak, assign special significance to yak butter as well, and Tibetan lamas spend months every year carving statues of the deities from the butter. To Tibetans, yaks represent prosperity, as do cows to the Masai and other peoples whose culture derives sustenance from these animals.

In Ireland, Saint Brigit took over the functions of the earlier Celtic goddess Brigit, a mother goddess and guardian of cows and ewes. Brigit and her cows embodied female abundance. Brigit had closer ties to milk than to butter, but her ewes gave both products freely. The goddess, in her role as nurturer and provider, not only supplied her people with sustenance from her lake of milk but also appears to have had a magic store of butter, and fed the people from its inexhaustible supply. (Mahias 1988; Simoons 1974b; Toussaint-Samat 1992; Visser 1986)

See also Beef; Cheese; Milk; Yogurt

CABBAGE

Cabbage is one of the oldest-known vegetables, one that people have consumed for more than 4,000 years. It originated as sea cabbage growing along the Mediterranean rivers and northern coastlines, and because it served as a staple food for peasants in much of northern Europe, it figured in the legends of the European peoples long before it spread to the rest of the world. In one of these legends, a man desired cabbage so desperately that he stole it from his neighbor, then was sent to the moon, where no cabbages grew, as punishment. In this legend, the "man in the moon" many people recognize when they look at the lunar surface today is none other than this cabbage thief, who remains there as a warning to young children not to steal anything, even if they desire it desperately.

Cabbages were prized as food in ancient Europe. The Egyptians erected altars to the plant and worshiped it as a god. The ancient Romans considered cabbage the perfect medicinal plant, and prescribed large amounts of it for ailments of all sorts, ranging from common warts to deafness to intoxication. Cabbage does, in fact, contain B vitamins, which work to oxygenate the blood and thus lessen the adverse effects of alcohol. Perhaps for this reason, the Greeks, Romans, and Egyptians viewed cabbage as a natural enemy to the grapevine. In Greek mythology, Lycurgus, the king of Thrace, opposed the worship of Dionysus, the god of the vine. When Dionysus and his jovial roving band of satyrs and maenads wandered into Thrace, Lycurgus captured everyone except Dionysus, who escaped to an undersea cave. In one version of the myth, the god later punished Lycurgus by binding him to the vine. In another version, the earth goddess Rhea punished Lycurgus by driving him mad. In his maddened state, Lycurgus destroyed the vines in Dionysus's vineyard, mistakenly also cutting his son Dryas to pieces, thinking he was a vine stock. Cabbages grew from the sand where Lycurgus's tears fell.

In the myth of Lycurgus and Dionysus, cabbage proved a formidable enemy to the grapevine. In nature, cabbage acts inimically to other plants as well, because it takes up so much room in the ground and tends to rob neighboring plants of nourishment. Different kinds of cabbage exist, some of them extremely large. In Britain and France, for instance, certain varieties of cabbages grow up to sixteen feet high. These tall cabbages likely impressed early people and led them to create legends of people climbing to the sky on cabbages, much like Jack on his bean stalk. In the British Isles, young girls often used cabbages to divine the future; they believed, for instance, that whoever picked a tall cabbage was destined to marry a tall man. In Ireland, children flocked to cabbage patches at Halloween, and they believed that the general shape of the first cabbage they picked indicated the shape of their future spouse. In early times, people assigned symbolic significance to cabbages and other plants based on their physical characteristics. A Greek myth explained how cabbage got its firm, round head: It grew from droplets of sweat shed by Zeus, the sky god, as he puzzled over which of two oracles' prophecies was the correct one. (*Oxford Dictionary of Plant-Lore* 1995; Skinner n.d.; Toussaint-Samat 1992)

CACAO
See Chocolate

CACTUS

Cactus plants dominate much of the landscape in Mexico and the American Southwest, and many types of these cacti have consumable fruits. The people living in these regions long ago lived off the land and respected it; they learned how to use the gifts of the earth goddess for food and medicine. Cacti provided a reliable source of food for desert peoples, often the only available vegetable food. They stored water, and the Pueblo, for instance, lived on cactus plants in times of drought. Furthermore, people throughout Mexico and far up into North America learned that certain kinds of cactus had hallucinogenic powers, and people all over the world worshiped hallucinogenic plants as gods.

Native Americans have a rich plant lore, considering themselves of the same spiritual essence as the land and the plant forms that arise from it. They believe that plants have souls and that human beings must adhere to strict rituals in order to show the plants proper respect. In Navajo legend, when people gather the fruits of the prickly pear cactus, they must pluck a hair from their heads to keep from destroying the plant when they take its fruits. This type of legend typifies many of the beliefs surrounding wild plant foods. Native Americans so depended on the food they gathered that they took care not to harm the plants or offend the spirits that ruled them. The Zuni consider plants a part of themselves. They believe that some plants existed as human beings before they became plants, and others were dropped to earth by the Star People. Some plants clearly belong to the gods.

Native Americans of the Southwest, in past times particularly, venerated their food plants, and cacti were prominent among them. The cacti bearing edible fruit include the prickly pear cactus, the hedgehog cactus or Mexican strawberry, the melon cactus or melon thistle, and the tree cactus. Saguaro is the fruit of the tree cactus, and centuries ago, early Americans learned to use this fruit to make jellies and syrups. The Pima and Papago tribes of southern Arizona depended on the fruits of the saguaro cactus, and believed that the ritual consumption of saguaro wine would bring relief from drought. The tribes of the Southwest typically made wine from their cactus juice, cooked the leaves in soups, and ate the fruits raw, baked, boiled, or ground into meal. The cactus fruit *(nochtli)* used by the Aztecs was sweet, crimson in color, and shaped almost like a heart. Aztecs venerated it, believing that it represented the human hearts the gods so desired as sacrifices.

The Aztecs' beliefs and rituals surrounding cactus plants were a central part of their mythology. They venerated cacti as a source of nourishment, but they considered the hallucinogenic powers of these plants even more miraculous. Peyote is the best known of the hallucinogenic cacti; Mesoamericans have used this small, carrot-shaped cactus for magico-religious purposes since pre-Columbian times. Like the magic mushrooms and the mysterious soma of India, the Aztecs believed their peyote to be a mediator between human beings and the supernatural, allowing people to see deities and to learn their wishes and understand their motives. The peyote cactus held powerful magic; shamans used it in healing ceremonies, and many people believed it could bestow the gift of prophecy. The rounded tops of the peyote plants, called peyote buttons, were eaten raw or dried, or made into a mash or tea. The Aztecs gave peyote drinks to persons before they sacrificed them; Aztec physicians used peyote medicinally, particularly for fever and headaches; and Aztec warriors wore the buttons as amulets to give them Herculean strength and protect them against sorcery. Others used them as charms to ward off evil influences of other sorts.

Toward the end of the nineteenth century, peyote moved northward from Mexico, as several tribes of the southwestern United States

Woman harvesting cactus fruit. Long ago, the people living in the American Southwest learned how to derive food and medicines from cactus and other gifts from the earth goddess. (Library of Congress)

began to practice the ritual consumption of peyote. Like their southern neighbors, these tribes venerated the miraculous cactus and consumed it as a religious sacrament. They established a widely known peyote cult involving the worship of peyote buttons. Tribes that make ceremonial use of the peyote cactus have tutelary deities of peyote—gods and goddesses who protect both the plant and its magical powers—and have created myths and legends about the miracle cactus. In some of these legends, the peyote plants have the ability to talk and sing, and can alert people searching for the cactus to their exact location in the ground. (Niethammer 1974; Ratsch 1992; Schultes and Hofmann 1979)

See also Ayahuasca; Balche; Coca; Frogs and Toads; Mushrooms; Nightshades; Ololiuqui; Soma

CAKE

People have consumed cakes of all kinds throughout history and at all sorts of ceremonial occasions. In today's world, people traditionally serve cakes at holidays, birthdays, weddings, funerals, and baptisms—in short, at all significant times in the cycle of life. The tradition of eating cake on ceremonial occasions has its basis in ancient ritual. Cakes, in the ancient world, had ties with the annual cycle, and people used them as offerings to the gods and spirits who exercised their powers at particular times of the year.

At Thesmophoria, the harvest festival of the ancient Greeks, worshipers made harvest cakes for Demeter, the earth goddess, who they believed controlled the fruitfulness of the land. Harvest was a critical time for early agriculturists; in much of the ancient world, it was a time when cakes were offered to the deities who influenced the crops. The Chinese made cakes at harvest time to honor their moon goddess, Heng O. They recognized that the moon played a crucial role in the seasonal cycle, so they made round cakes shaped like the moon to reward the lunar goddess, with

an image of the illustrious Heng O stamped on top. The Chinese today continue to make moon cakes; they make them out of rice and eat them at the Harvest Moon festival called Yue Ping, which they hold every 15 August. According to legend, Heng O ascended to the moon after swallowing a pill of immortality, and she remains there today, along with a lunar rabbit who continually pounds out rice. The lunar goddess appears most accessible in mid-August, at harvesttime, when the moon is particularly bright and beautiful.

Ancient peoples engaged in the ritual eating of cakes at harvesttime as an attempt to control their fate. Cake, they believed, propitiated the deities, so they made cake to thank these gods for the past year's harvest and to influence them to continue to provide food in the future. People consumed cakes and offered them to their deities at significant times in the agricultural cycle because early people knew the importance of cyclical order. They knew that powerful gods controlled that order, and that through the ritual consumption of cake offerings, people could enter into communion with those gods and pay them proper respect.

The Russians traditionally pay their respects in spring to a deity named Maslenitsa by making *bliny,* thin pancakes they call sun cakes. In Slavic legend, Maslenitsa was the daughter of Father Frost, and long ago, a peasant encountered the beautiful maiden and was delighted to discover that unlike her father, this goddess brought warmth to their villages. Maslenitsa stayed a while in the peasant village and kept the people warm and happy. When it was time for her to leave, the people once again feared the icy grip of Father Frost; so before Maslenitsa left, she told them to make little suns out of batter and to eat them, saying that this would keep the spring sun in their lives forever. So Russians today continue to honor Maslenitsa and the sun by making bliny. They eat the sun cakes at a festival they call Maslenitsa, which celebrates the end of winter and the return of the spring sun.

A baker in Hong Kong makes moon cakes for the autumn Harvest Moon festival, a harvest celebration held to thank the moon goddess for her role in securing the seasonal cycle and providing an abundant supply of food. (Earl and Nazima Kowall/Corbis)

The pagan Slavs were not the only people to make round cakes to celebrate the spring sun. The ancient Celts, who celebrated Beltane on the first day of spring, baked and ate Beltane cakes as an important part of their celebration. Long ago they may have offered these cakes to the solar deity Belenus, who ensured that the sun continued to move in its proper path. At the Beltane festival, the ancient Celts also rolled the cakes down a hill to imitate solar movement. Rolling the cakes, they hoped, would ensure the continued motion of the sun. This activity also served as a form of divination: If the cake broke when it reached the bottom of the hill, the Celts believed that whoever rolled it would die within a year's time; but if the cake remained intact, they believed that person would reap a year's good fortune.

Divining with Beltane cakes was common practice in later times, but it appears that the cakes may have originally been used to select victims for sacrifice. The people who prepared these cakes blackened one small part with charcoal, and whoever got the blackened piece became the victim. In later years, the person who received the blackened cake was symbolically sacrificed.

It has been said that cake customs around the world originated from ancient rituals of propitiation and sacrifice. People used cakes to thank the kind gods for their benevolence and to propitiate gods with a propensity toward evil. The ancient Greeks left cakes at crossroads to appease the evil goddess Hecate, and the Estonians threw cake into the waters to appease Nakk, a dangerous Estonian water spirit. People often made cake offerings to deities to remove their evil influence. They also offered cake to spirits of the dead, believing that the cakes would nourish them during their long journey to the otherworld.

One of the best-known examples of cakes for the dead are soul cakes, made on 28 October, in connection with All Souls' Day. For many pagan peoples—the early Celts, for instance—this was the day the dead got up and walked around on earth, and unless they were fed, people believed, the spirits might harm the living. In some areas of Germany, soul cakes are black in color, suggesting death. The Ainu of Japan also made cakes for their dead. The people of Germany and Austria left cakes on graves, and the ancient Egyptians placed them inside tombs. Throughout Europe, people offered soul cakes to the dead to nourish them on their journey to the otherworld, or used cakes as offerings during funeral rites and feasts. Eating cakes on All Souls' Day became common practice. In Belgium, people believed that on this day, one soul was released from purgatory for every cake consumed.

Agricultural peoples around the globe made offerings of cakes prepared from the grains and fruits that arose from their soil. The types of ingredients used to make these cakes contributed to their symbolism. The Hindus, for instance, offered sesame cakes to the dead because they connected the sesame plant with death. The cake's size and shape were equally symbolic of its ritual purpose: The ancient Greeks, like the Hindus, connected sesame with death, but they also connected it with fertility. So they made harvest cakes for Demeter out of sesame, but also made them phallic in shape. Phallic-shaped cakes symbolized fertility, round cakes symbolized the sun or the moon, and cakes made to resemble humans or animals often served as substitutes for sacrificial victims.

All of these cakes had definitive links to the myths the people embraced. Similarly, many Hindu Indian rites involve offering a cake in the shape of a tortoise, possibly because of the role the tortoise played in Hindu myth. Because Vishnu appeared in the form of a tortoise to support the world when the gods and demons churned the ocean of milk, it is quite possible that the Hindus considered tortoise-shaped cakes a firm and solid sacrifice. Concerns with size, shape, and the type of grain used in the baking process applied to dough images of any kind. Grains were often deified in myths, and cakes, especially in folktales, had magical power. Cake developed as a variation of bread, and as such it took on similar symbolic and ritual significance. (*Funk and Wagnall's* 1972; Hu 1996; Simoons 1998; Toussaint-Samat 1992)

See also Beans; Bread; Grain; Sesame; Turtle

CANDY

Candy today is one of the world's delectable treats. The history of candy dates to at least 2000 B.C. in Egypt, where archaeologists discovered tomb drawings of candies molded in the shapes of bulls and geese and sweetened with honey. The Egyptians probably prepared these treats as offerings for the gods. In the myths of Egypt and other lands, the gods loved sweets. They feasted on fruits, nectar and ambrosia, and sweet spices that could sustain life by their smell alone. Sweet foods pleased deities in both the Old World and the Americas. The gods and spirits of North America loved maple syrup. The Aztec god Quetzalcoatl loved chocolate, and Aztecs fed him a sacred sweetened beverage, the first chocolate, made from cacao beans, chili peppers, and honey.

Myths all over the world have linked honey with the gods. The Promised Land of the Bible flowed with milk and honey, and Zeus and the high gods of other lands possessed the golden substance in paradise. Once people mastered the art of apiculture, they quickly put honey to use. They used it for libations and offerings, and made candy with it long before they used sugar. The Egyptians made candy using honey, nuts, spices, and seeds. The Greeks and Romans used honey to coat fruits and flowers of all sorts. Honey had as much appeal as liquid gold.

But the people of the Americas used liquid gold of another sort—maple tree sap—to make candy. In legend, a benevolent tree spirit told an Ojibwa man how to cut the maple tree, extract the sap, boil it to make syrup, then stir the syrup until the substance hardened. The Ojibwa and other tribes of North America learned that if they stirred the thick syrup long enough, they got sugar, but if they stopped stirring just before the sugar formed, they could make candy. They learned to pour the precious liquid onto the snow, where it would cool into sugary, hard, delectable treats.

Sugarcane did not come to North America until the first European explorers arrived, and bees were not imported until the 1630s, so the boiling of maple sap was the only process by which early Americans could make candy. Candy makers today make their treats by boiling sugar, water, and corn syrup; the temperature the mixture reaches and the length of time it cools determines the texture of the resulting candy.

Some of the earliest candies were made with honey, fruits, and nuts, which were then flavored with herbs and spices. People learned that making candies this way not only satisfied their desire for sweets but also preserved their fruits. Sugared almonds, most likely from ancient Rome, were some of the oldest candies in history, as were candies made from barley grains, which the Greeks and Romans ate unsweetened. The Chinese also boiled barley and water and made barley sticks, which they rolled in sesame seeds and allowed to harden.

The ancients apparently offered candy to the gods to win their favor. In Chinese legend, however, people offered a taffy candy shaped like melons to Tsao-wang, the Kitchen God, for other reasons. A Chinese legend recounts how long ago, the Jade Emperor sent Tsao-wang to earth to ensure that the people would respect their foods and never waste them. Tsao-wang had to supervise the affairs of each household, then report back to the Jade Emperor every year and inform him whether or not the people were behaving properly. Tsao-wang was a fat and lazy god, however, and he neglected to keep a watchful

eye on the people. As a result, he had to fabricate his report to the Jade Emperor. He reported that the people had made food and then stepped on it. The Jade Emperor became outraged when he heard this, and sent floods and droughts to punish the people on earth. Soon, famine spread throughout the land, and many people starved. All this time, however, the star god was watching this brutality, and he finally told the people that the Kitchen God was responsible for their misery. The people revolted against him. They made him miserable all year, placing his altar where it would be inundated by smoke, fumes, and grease. They gave him no food offerings at all. When it was time for his next visit to the Jade Emperor, the people fed him taffy before he left, and the taffy stuck to his teeth. Tsao-wang could say nothing at all to the Jade Emperor. (Hu 1991; Toussaint-Samat 1992)

See also Chocolate; Honey; Maple Syrup; Sugar and Sugarcane

CARIBOU
See Reindeer and Caribou

CAROB
The carob tree is native to the eastern Mediterranean and grows extensively in this area as well as in warm areas of North and South America, where people learned to cultivate the tree long ago. The carob tree is an evergreen, so in ancient Mesopotamian myths it served as a Tree of Life; it symbolized to ancient people of the area the immortality of the natural world. The fruit of the carob tree, which grows in the form of large, flat pods, is so nutritious and substantial that ancient goldsmiths used it as the original "carat" or "carob" weight to measure gold. Carob seeds are typically called husks or locusts, or sometimes Saint John's bread.

According to the gospels, John the Baptist subsisted on locusts during his forty days in the desert. Locusts frequently swarm in desert

Carob seeds are typically called husks or locusts, or sometimes Saint John's bread. Many scholars believe that John the Baptist survived solely on carob beans for forty days in the desert. (Scala/Art Resource, NY)

areas, and the people of the region often consumed them, as well as bugs of other sorts. But the term "locusts" may in fact refer to carob beans rather than the insects. According to the New Testament, the husks or "locusts" served primarily as fodder for cattle, but humans ate them in extreme circumstances. Nutritionists today know that carob beans have high concentrations of calcium and B vitamins, so the beans alone may well have been enough to enable John the Baptist, or anyone, to survive for long periods of time.

Carob beans may have made ideal food for animals, but people found other uses for them

too, and not just in emergencies. They used the pulp for making candy and the fermented seeds to make alcoholic drinks. A legend from the Talmud tells of a young rabbi who saw a man planting a carob tree by the road, and he made fun of the man, for he knew that these trees took thirty or more years to produce fruit. The man replied that he was planting the tree not for his own benefit but for people to enjoy in the future, just as people in past times had planted carob trees long ago for him to enjoy. Carob beans have long had associations with magic, particularly when fermented and made into reputedly magical mead. The magic of the carob beans must have affected the rabbi: He fell asleep, and when he finally awoke, seventy years had passed, and the carob tree the man had planted was fully grown and full of fruit. This tale gained fame centuries later when Washington Irving wrote the story of Rip Van Winkle. Perhaps the Hebrews carried this tale with them as they traveled, for similar tales emerged in many parts of the ancient world.

People long ago learned to make fermented drinks from fruits and seeds of all kinds of plants, including bananas, dates, figs, pineapples, sugarcane, and sweet potatoes; the Talmudic legend suggests that the Israelites made such a drink from carob as well. The Chaco tribes of South America make algaroba beer from carob beans to this day. The intoxication a person feels after consuming alcohol makes people of many cultures feel the presence of magic. An Argentinean legend tells of a magic carob tree that revealed the secret of releasing the rains to a young boy. When a terrible drought plagued the land, the young boy set his sights on bringing back the rain. The carob tree told the boy that in order to do this, he had to scare away the bird of the underworld that slept in the tree's highest branches and blocked the people's prayers to the gods. The boy succeeded in scaring away the evil bird with the help of the entire village. Rain poured down from the heavens. As a reward to the boy and the villagers who helped release the rains, the carob tree dropped its red beans all over the land so that more carob trees could grow. (Goor and Nurock 1968; Moldenke and Moldenke 1952; Van Laan 1998)

See also Alcoholic Beverages; Insects; Mead; Mesquite; Pine and Pine Nuts

CARROTS

Most wild carrots grow in the Mediterranean region and in southwest Asia, and the people of these areas have eaten them since antiquity. These varieties of carrots differ from the orange carrots familiar to most Americans to-day; they're much darker in color—some are bloodred—and ancient mythmakers tended to lump them into the same category with other root crops, as plants that originated underground, and believed that they had connections to the powers under the earth. Carrots have much in common with other root crops, especially with radishes. In fact, the Asian varieties of carrots and radishes look alike; not only are the carrots red or purplish red in color but the radishes also grow in elongated forms.

While most people in Europe and the Americas have no familiarity with the Asian varieties of carrots and radishes, their similar appearance led to confusion in the myths. The Buddhists applied the myth of Mu-lien, for instance, to both vegetables, the red carrot and the red radish, called the *lo-phu*. Mu-lien was a compassionate young man with a mother as mean and ungrateful as he was kind. While Mu-lien dedicated his life to serving God, his mother thought of nothing but herself and her desire to eat food, and she continually killed animals to satisfy her hunger, piling up their bones and skins in her garden. Mulien adhered strictly to Buddhist doctrine, and he believed that his mother would suffer severe punishment for taking the animals' lives. He tried to warn her, but she paid him no heed, and continued to kill animals until she neared death.

Finally, on her deathbed, Mu-lien's mother began to realize that she indeed would suffer for her evils, and she begged Mu-lien to save her from damnation. So he spent his life's savings on Buddhist and Taoist priests to pray for his mother; but nevertheless, his mother did go to hell, where she suffered eternal starvation. Mu-lien continued praying for his mother, however, until finally he became a Buddha and gained the power to descend into hell to retrieve his mother. When he pulled her up to the surface, however, she immediately sought personal satisfaction. She spied some carrots growing in a field and plucked one from the ground and ate it. Mu-lien was terribly upset by this, knowing that if the gods found out, they would return his mother to hell forever. So he cut off his finger and put it in the ground where the carrot had grown. A carrot, red with Mu-lien's blood, sprouted on the spot.

Some myths call the vegetable in the myth of Mu-lien the red radish or lo-phu, and they explain that Mu-lien was also known as the Buddhist teacher Maudgalyayana, or Lo Pu, for the radish he created. Whether it refers to a carrot or a radish, the myth embraced the same themes. The body parts of humans or animals were often transformed into plants in myths, conveying the ancient belief that the life, the spirit or soul, existed in all forms of life, including plants, making the blood of Mu-lien interchangeable with the blood, or the red color, of the carrot or radish. Legends of root plants often emphasize the consequences of pulling these plants out of the ground, and the myth of Mu-lien had the additional consequence of violating the sanctity of life espoused in Buddhist doctrine. The Buddhists may have assigned carrots and radishes a place in their myths in part because they grew underground. Root crops that thrived in the dark, cold soil seemed to have some mysterious connection with the underworld, and they often crop up in death myths. One bit of American folklore holds that for each carrot plant that goes to seed, someone will die in the coming year. (Dorson 1963; Simoons 1994)

See also Radishes; Turnips

CASSAVA
See Manioc

CELERY
See Parsley and Celery

CEREALS
See Grain

CHEESE

Cheese was the first dairy product made: It was produced in Europe and the Middle East at least 4,000 years ago, long before butter. People likely made the first cheeses from the milk of sheep and goats; later, cheese was made from the milk of many other mammals, including donkeys and zebus. Wandering nomads carried the milk in pouches they made from the stomachs and bladders of slaughtered animals. Over long distances, the heat and the motion quickly churned and curdled the milk. Long before pottery, these makeshift containers worked well: The curdled milk, combined with an enzyme called rennin, secreted by the lining of the animal's stomach, produced cheese.

The Hebrews made cheese in this same manner until, according to the Bible, Moses revealed a dietary law that prohibited mixing milk with animal products. But there were other methods of making cheese. According to Marco Polo, the Mongols skimmed the cream off their milk to be churned into butter, then left the skimmed milk out in the sun. Even without rennin the milk curdled, after which it was boiled, and the curds were compressed into cheese.

The ancients quickly recognized the value of cheese. It came from milk, after all, and even in antiquity people knew milk as a perfect form of nourishment. The ancients domesticated various animals for milking, and pastoral people such as the Khoi of Africa, the Lapps of Europe, and the Todas of India continue to rely on milk and its products as a primary source of food. In Greek myth, the god Aristaeus gave humans the gift of cheese. Aristaeus was a guardian of herds, and thus a likely cheese maker, as well as a beekeeper and a protector of grapevines and olive trees. In Homer's *Odyssey,* the Cyclops Polyphemus made cheese. Like Aristaeus, Polyphemus had herds of ewes and goats, and he milked these animals, let the milk curdle, and drained the curdled milk in wicker baskets. Polyphemus and his herds lived in a cave; Odysseus and his men entered the cave, discovered the cheese, and ate it. This nourishing food provided Odysseus and his men with the sustenance they needed. They killed the Cyclops and continued on their journey.

Cheese was strengthening food, like milk. It was a staple food of the Athenian army, and it gave Olympic athletes the strength they needed to perform. According to the Roman scholar Pliny the Elder, Zarathustra or Zoroaster, the great prophet of ancient Persia, lived entirely on cheese for twenty years, from which he acquired the great eloquence that made him a leader. The Greeks and Romans alluded to the fortifying properties of cheese several times in myth. In addition to feeding Odysseus and his men, cheese revived Machaon, a surgeon who fought in the Trojan War and suffered serious wounds. Nestor, the elder

statesman renowned for his wisdom, decided that goat cheese would help heal Machaon's wounds, so his woman Hecamede made a special potion with the cheese and gave it to Machaon.

Greek epicures hailed the properties of cheese as well as cheesecakes. Cheese was a common ingredient in ancient pastries, and Athenaeus, the noted epicure of the third century, devoted an entire section of his fifteen-volume work, *The Deipnosophists,* to cheesecakes, a Greek and Roman favorite. The ancient Greeks served cheese-filled pastries as appetizers as well as cream cheese dessert cakes similar to today's cheesecake. Early Greek cheesecakes were made of molded cream cheese and chilled in snow, and were likely predecessors of traditional wedding cakes and of dessert cakes popular throughout Europe and North America today. (Mahias 1988; Norman 1972; Tannahill 1973; Toussaint-Samat 1992; Visser 1986)

See also Beef; Butter; Milk; Yogurt

CHERRIES

In Japan, the cherry tree has long been a symbol of beauty as well as of courtesy, gentility, and even virginity. Many species of the cherry tree grow in Asia, and the Japanese revere them. The cherries that grow in Japan have no food value except as fodder for pigs, but the trees are exceptionally beautiful. The Japanese have created many myths about the cherry tree, particularly about its lovely blossoms.

In parts of northern Europe, evil spirits were believed to inhabit cherry trees. But most European myths about cherries stressed their connection with fortune and fertility. In many cases, the trees themselves brought good luck to lovers who met under their branches or to people who planted them near their homes. The story behind the German festival called Feast of the Cherries reveals the cherry's connection to good fortune. In 1432, the Hussites threatened to destroy Hamburg, so the Germans sent their children out in the streets

In the Asian lands, the beauty of the cherry tree, with its blossoms white as the snow and its berries bright as the sun, inspired love, admiration, and reverence in the Asian people. (The Newark Museum, Art Resource, NY)

carrying cherries. This touched the Hussite leader deeply, and he spared the city and feasted on cherries with the children.

In Lithuanian legend, Kirnis was both the guardian of cherry trees and the spirit of the cherry tree itself. The Japanese continue to believe today that blossoming trees are inhabited by a spirit, or *kami,* that exists throughout the natural world. In Japanese myth, the god of love, Musubi-no-kami, lived in a cherry tree. One Japanese legend tells of a man who had the power to make cherry trees bloom. He believed the spirit of his dead dog lived in the cherry tree, and the dog's spirit helped him perform this miraculous feat. Another legend told of the spirit of a wet nurse who had died. The nurse prayed that the disease that was killing a young baby in her charge be transferred to her instead. Her spirit also made the trees bloom, and every year on the anniversary of her death, the tree filled with the most beautiful cherry blossoms.

The beauty of the cherry tree, with its snow-white blossoms and bright berries, aroused love and admiration in the people; and in legend, it aroused love and admiration also in other plants. One Japanese legend tells of a particularly beautiful cherry tree named Lady Yaye-zakura. A grass prince named Susuki fell in love with Lady Yaye-zakura, but she resisted him. She could resist him, however, only when she was in full bloom. When her petals began to fall, she submitted. But a plum tree also fell in love with the Lady Yaye-zakura, and this plum tree was overcome with jealousy, and distressed that the cherry, the loveliest of all trees, had given her love to one of the inferior grass folk. The plum tree got all the other trees to battle the grass folk. The trees won the battle, and Susuki, the grass prince, died. Lady Yaye-zakura, in mourning, donned dark robes. This explained the dark color of the flowers and why from then on, Lady Yaye-zakura was known as Sumi-zome-zakura, which meant "a cherry tree in black robes."

Cherry trees played a large role in legendary lore. They brought fertility in Finnish myth, and in Chinese myth, they even bestowed immortality. The Chinese usually referred to peaches as the fruit of immortality, but in one variation of the myth, cherries take the place of peaches. The goddess Hsi Wang Mu had a garden in which the cherries (or peaches) of immortality ripened every 3,000 years, and the gods feasted on them to maintain their immortal status. In a Finnish myth, Marjatta, the maiden of the air, became pregnant after swallowing a cherry. She bore her child in a manger, and he grew up to be king.

Similarly, the cherry entered into the Buddhist myth of Maya and the birth of Buddha and the Christian myth of the Virgin Mary and the birth of Jesus. In Buddhist myth, Maya clung to a cherry tree as she gave birth to the Buddha, and the tree bent down and offered her the fruit. In Christian legend, the cherry tree bent down to offer Mary the fruit. Mary had longed for these cherries, but they hung from a tree high over her head, and Joseph wouldn't pick them for her, saying that the true father of her child should provide them. Cherries were dedicated to Mary after that, and the cherry blossoms represented her purity. (Folkard 1892; Greimas 1992; Piggott 1997; Reed 1992; Skinner n.d.; Toussaint-Samat 1992)

See also Peaches; Plums

CHESTNUTS

Mythmakers around the world endowed nuts of all sorts with magical properties. People thought chestnuts, in particular, possessed healing powers, and they used these nuts as charms and remedies against various ailments, including backaches, rheumatism, and asthma. Chestnuts have food value as well as medicinal value, and people relied on them for centuries as a substitute for cereals in areas where grains did not grow. In the mountainous regions of the Mediterranean, for instance, chestnuts were a staple food, eaten in the form of porridge and flat bread. Chestnut bread provided the Thracians and Spartans with a necessary source of nourishment—often the only source available for long periods of time.

Chestnut trees grew wild in Europe, China, Japan, and in the eastern North American forests. Early American hunter-gatherers relied on chestnuts as well as acorns, pine nuts, and seeds and nuts of other kinds. North America and South America both have rich supplies of native nuts, and before a fungal disease imported from Europe destroyed most of them in the 1930s, chestnuts were one of the most common trees in the eastern woodlands. Legends commonly tell of the nuts saving people from starvation.

Chestnut trees typically produce so many nuts that they became fertility symbols in ancient times. In Europe, the nuts assumed such importance that the people of France viewed the chestnut as the Tree of Life, a source of life and sustenance. In an Asian legend, chestnuts provided food for the Buddhist priest Kobo-Daishi; and because it sustained him in the lack of available other food, the priest bestowed on the chestnut tree the ability to bear nuts two or three times a year. In China, chestnuts represent the easy birth of sons; in some areas of the country, chestnuts are placed in the bedrooms of newly married couples, sometimes sewn into the marriage bed. (Reed 1992; Simoons 1991; Toussaint-Samat 1992)

See also Acorns; Almonds; Hazelnuts; Peanuts; Pine and Pine Nuts; Walnuts

CHICHA

Chicha is an alcoholic beverage consumed by people of South America, particularly tribes of the Andes, where the Inca ritualized its brewing and consumption long ago. Chicha was the favorite Inca drink, most commonly made from maize, the primary crop and the lifeblood of the Inca society; less frequently, it was made from quinoa or from fermented seeds and fruits. The Inca consumed chicha ceremonially and offered it to their gods. They venerated the drink, as they did the corn, surrounding the brewing and consumption of chicha with magical beliefs.

Most people who drink chicha today do so casually, as one would any other type of beer. Chicha is considered both healthful and sustaining: It not only quenches the thirst but is also believed to contain great nutritional and medicinal value. Furthermore, the drink has a long history in myth and ritual. One Incan ritual of note involved the daily offering of chicha to the sun. Long ago, chosen women lived in cloisters called *acllaguaci,* located next to temples dedicated to the sun, and these women performed services for the highest gods. These chosen women were virgins, much like Catholic nuns or the vestal virgins of ancient Rome; but these Incan virgins had the duty of making large quantities of chicha and serving it to the sun in a golden cup each morning as he rose above the horizon. They also served chicha to the priests of the sun and to other attendants of the temple. This powerful drink seemed a worthy offering. In other religious ceremonies, the Inca poured chicha on the ground and offered it to Pachamama, or Mother Earth. When consuming chicha, they often spat out the first sip as an offering to Mother Earth, or dipped their fingers in the chicha and sprinkled the liquid on the earth or toward the sun in prayer.

The preparation and consumption of chicha played a large role in the ceremonial life of the Inca. They offered the beverage not only to the sun and the earth but also to the dead, believing that a person had the same physical requirements in death as in life. The dead enjoyed chicha, the Inca presumed, because they themselves enjoyed the drink at numerous festivals and religious ceremonies. Inca women made chicha by chewing the corn, mashing it to a pulp with their teeth, then spitting it out. Enzymes in the women's saliva helped the grain to ferment. Because of chicha's role in their ritual life, the Inca surrounded its preparation in magical beliefs. Sometimes sacrifices accompanied the making of chicha; the sacrifice of sheep, for instance, ensured a good batch of brew, or a good harvest of corn with which to make the brew. The women's saliva made the brew particularly potent, and the older the woman, the Inca said, the tastier and more potent the chicha.

In modern-day Peru, women still brew chicha, using yeast and sugar to make it ferment. They brew it from purple or yellow light corn, and vary the taste by adding a variety of different spices. Some kinds of chicha are unfermented and sweetened with cinnamon and cloves—more of a soda pop than a beer—and some are flavored with lemon and hot pepper sauce, or strawberries and other fruits. The Peruvians have held the brewing of beer sacred for centuries. Even today many Peruvians consider the drinking of chicha a sacrament, and everyone, young and old, consumes the drink. Some put a jar of chicha on the roofs of newly built houses for good luck, and most pour a few drops of the chicha on the ground before they drink it themselves. They consider this an offering of thanks to the corn goddess, Mama Sara, who provided them with the sacred corn, the essence of both food and wine. (Cobo 1990; Coe 1994; Fussell 1992)

See also Alcoholic Beverages; Ayahuasca; Balche; Beer; Kava; Mead; Pulque; Sake; Soma; Wine

CHICKEN

Chicken, one of the most popular flesh foods of America today, has a colorful past in the myths and rituals of early cultures. Chickens were first domesticated in Southeast Asia, yet many people of this region refused to eat them; they assigned such a significant symbolic role to these birds that consuming them would have violated their respect for the divine.

Though many early people ate chicken, many others strictly avoided it. Some did so because they considered chickens sacred; others, because they believed that eating chickens interfered with fertility. Many bans applied to the eating of cocks, in particular. In China,

the cock embodies yang, the male principle. Some people of ancient China believed the cock had the ability to transform itself into human form. They believed it had knowledge of good and evil, and could inflict either goodness or harm on human beings.

Much of the disdain for eating chicken had to do with the role this bird played in myth and legend. People in many lands considered the cock a sacred bird, a living link between heaven and earth. In myths and legends, birds often served as messengers between the two worlds. They could fly to the sky and back, and therefore had the ability to commune with the sky powers. The cock had a particular advantage—he crowed at dawn. To early people, this in itself revealed his powers. If the cock crowed at dawn, they reasoned, he must have a knowledge of the distinction between light and dark, heaven and earth, good and evil. The crowing cock appeared to be chasing away evil, ushering in the light and thereby dispelling the darkness and the night demons that went with it.

Placing the cock in this important role discouraged people of many lands from killing and eating chickens. Perhaps they feared that the bird would tell the high gods of its poor treatment, or perhaps they believed that the flesh of such a sacred animal was reserved only for the gods.

In myth, ancient people associated the cock with gods of light, so they sacrificed the animal to these deities in particular. The Persians, for instance, sacrificed the cock to Mithra. They offered him white cocks, a fitting symbol for the white light this great god embodied. The Persians venerated the cock because they revered the light. Because they associated this bird with the battle between light and darkness, they endowed it with the knowledge of good and evil—the fundamental dichotomy of the Zoroastrian religion. These ideas influenced the Greeks, who also came to associate the cock with light and the sun. The ancient Iranians ate chicken, but they generally used the cocks for sacrifice rather than for common food. The worshipers of Mithra, however, ate cocks during religious rituals.

The perception of the cock as a sacred animal and as a messenger between humans and gods led to the practice of chicken divination. Pacific Islanders and many Asians used the bones, intestines, and eggs of chickens to augur the future. Chicken divination was common in Southeast Asia, southern China, Uganda, Sudan, Ethiopia, among some groups in the Americas, and in ancient Greece and Rome. Many ancient peoples also used chickens for sacrifice. Some scholars believe the early Southeast Asians who first domesticated the chicken did so for the purposes of divination and sacrifice rather than for food. But not everyone who used chickens for these purposes refused to eat them.

Those who did refuse to eat chicken did so for a variety of reasons. Many pious Buddhists and Hindus considered the killing and eating of any animal contrary to their beliefs. Even today, many groups refuse to eat chicken and eggs, either because of taboos against consuming any flesh or because they associate chickens with fertility. Some groups in Africa believe that eating chicken and eggs causes sterility or difficulty in bearing children, and for this reason, they punish women of childbearing age who break the ban on eating these birds. The ancient Egyptians, however, took a different view. Though they too connected the chicken and its eggs with fertility and childbirth, many believed that a woman should eat chicken before delivering a child. The chicken was said to give the woman strength. (Simoons 1994; Visser 1986)

See also Eggs; Goose and Turkey

CHICORY AND ENDIVE

People today cultivate chicory for its roots and tender young leaves, which are called endive. This plant grew wild in Egypt and western Asia long ago, and the people of biblical times likely consumed it along with other weedy plants, in ancient equivalents to today's salads. Chicory grew abundantly in the Old World, and the wild varieties were bitter to the taste.

Since the second century A.D., many Jews have used chicory and endive as the "bitter herbs" called for in the Passover meal. Passover celebrates the time God passed over the houses of the Israelites when he destroyed the firstborn sons of the Egyptians. Before fleeing their bondage in Egypt, the Israelites ate bitter herbs with a sacrificial lamb and unleavened bread; the bitter herbs symbolized their suffering during captivity in Egypt. Some scholars agree with this choice of greens, noting that the Egyptians grew and consumed chicory, and believing it likely that the Israelites learned to eat its leaves during their enslavement. But other scholars disagree. Endive refers either to Indian endive or to the young leaves of the chicory plant, and these scholars place the origin of chicory endive in India, and think it doubtful that the plant reached Egypt by the time of Moses. These scholars identify other plants as the bitter herbs, including lettuce, watercress, sorrel, and dandelion.[*]

In Europe, chicory was used as an aphrodisiac for centuries, and its seeds were used in love potions. Legends explained the appearance of the plant with the lovely blue flowers blossoming by roadsides. In a German tale, a young girl waited for her lover by the roadside for months, and finally took root and turned into a chicory plant—or an endive. In another German legend, endive was once human—the plants with blue flowers were the good people and the plants with white flowers were the evil ones. Fortunately, endive with blue flowers grew far more frequently! In one variation of the endive legend, a Bavarian princess abandoned by her prince grieved so desperately for him that God changed her and her handmaidens into endive plants, and the prince had to look upon the blue flowers everywhere he went and

---

[*]Jews who celebrate Passover today often use horseradish for bitter herbs, though people of biblical times knew nothing of horseradish.

remember his princess. A Romanian legend of chicory also recounts a story of lost love: The sun god fell in love with a woman named Florilor, but Florilor resisted his love, for she felt unworthy of marrying the sun god. The sun god became angry and turned her into the chicory flower. The chicory flower always turned toward the sun, following the sun god every day on his path. (Folkard 1892; Moldenke and Moldenke 1952; Skinner n.d.)

See also Goat, Lamb, and Ram; Herbs

CHOCOLATE

Chocolate comes from the cacao tree—specifically, from cacao beans—which was discovered by people living in the tropical forests of ancient Mesoamerica about three or four millennia ago.★ The chocolate of today differs from the chocolate of early days. Until the end of the seventeenth century, chocolate referred to a drink made of water, ground and roasted cacao beans, honey, chili peppers, and a number of other spices. This first chocolate was a stimulating and highly prized drink, called *cacaoatl* by the Aztecs, who used the cacao beans not only for food and drink but also as currency and as a symbol of wealth and self-indulgence. The Aztecs considered the chocolate liquid symbolic of the blood associated with the sacrifice and extraction of the human heart.

Chocolate originated in the Amazon or Orinoco basin, and Christopher Columbus reputedly saw the beans and ignored them; but just twenty years later, Spanish conquistador Hernán Cortés did not. The Spanish did not discover chocolate but appropriated it from the Aztecs, and by the 1700s were manufacturing chocolate candies (similar to ours today) back home in Spain.

★Chocolate is the same as cacao and cocoa and was first consumed by the Olmec, the Maya, and then the Aztecs. Coca is a different plant entirely, and not related to chocolate at all. Coca is native to the Andes and it yields cocaine. The Inca did not consume the cacao known to the Mesoamericans. *See* Coca.

The Aztecs also inherited their knowledge of cacao, which had been discovered by the Olmec, known as the "mother culture of Mesoamerica," and handed down to the Maya. In Aztec myth, the god Quetzalcoatl brought cacao beans from heaven and taught the people how to roast and grind them and make them into a precious drink. The consumption of the original chocolate was key to Aztec rituals. Perhaps in part because of its rarity and in part because of its stimulating effects, the Aztecs were passionate about chocolate and reserved its consumption for the priesthood and nobility. Montezuma consumed the drink in great quantities—as legend has it, fifty glasses a day. He kept his stores of cacao in golden jars, and drank it from golden goblets. People of the time believed it acted as an aphrodisiac. Montezuma was said to have considered his chocolate so precious that he threw away each goblet after only one use, and the people of Montezuma's time considered their chocolate so valuable that they used the beans as money, as apparently the Maya had before them. The Aztecs also used the beans in sacred rituals involving human sacrifice.

Scholars have found the connection the Aztecs made between cacao and human blood difficult to interpret. Eric Thompson, in his study of cacao among the Aztecs and Maya, suggested that both blood and the chocolate drink were invaluable liquids, and both the human heart and the cacao bean contained them. The Aztecs and the Maya both seemed to attach value to the cacao liquid, in part because they believed it had inebriating qualities. The early Mesoamericans had an extensive knowledge of intoxicating plants, which they used in a sacred or divine context. The Maya may have connected cacao with a male deity they knew as Seven Flower, and the Aztecs with his equivalent, Xochipilli. Seven Flower and Xochipilli controlled stimulants and hallucinogens—sacred mushrooms, tobacco, pulque (an intoxicating drink made from the maguay, the agave plant), and quite likely, chocolate as well. Because the early

Mesoamericans apparently considered the precious liquid an intoxicant, and intoxicants were often associated with the divine, chocolate held its place in myth.

The people of pre-Conquest Mexico viewed alcoholic beverages with mixed emotions, and the chocolate drink they consumed appeared to have contradictory properties. On one hand, it caused intoxication, which the ancients believed elevated human beings to a divine state; on the other hand, it had earthly, nutritional value. The Mesoamericans assigned all things on earth, and even the gods, a dual nature, believing them composed of both the light and invisible matter they associated with spirit and the heavy and visible matter they associated with death. They also assigned these properties to chocolate.

The Aztecs expressed the ambiguous nature of chocolate in a legend of the emperor Montezuma I (not to be confused with Montezuma II, the best known of the two, who ruled until the Conquest). Montezuma I sent a delegation of sixty old magicians to search for Culhuacan, a legendary city and the place of origin of the Mexican people and of Huitzilopochtli, their primary deity. The magicians went to present gifts (including chocolate) to the earth goddess Coatlicue, Huitzilopochtli's mother. The path to Culhuacan was difficult; the magicians had to transform themselves into birds and beasts in order to reach the environs of the city, then transform themselves back into human form to canoe across the gigantic lake surrounding it. The city itself was situated on a hill, in the middle of the lake. When the magicians finally reached the city, a servant of Coatlicue met them and attempted to lead them up the hill to their goddess. But the magicians kept slipping down into the sand; the earthly food and chocolate they had consumed had made their bodies heavy. Eventually, the servant of Coatlicue succeeded in helping the magicians up the mountain, and there the goddess warned them against consuming chocolate. Though people had no choice but to con-

sume the foods available to them on earth, those foods contained heavy matter that led to death. Chocolate, it appeared, was the heaviest of all. (Coe and Coe 1996; Foster and Cordell 1992; Fuller 1994; Toussaint-Samat 1992; Young 1994)

See also Alcoholic Beverages; Candy; Vanilla

CINNAMON

Aromatic and alluring, cinnamon appeared in ancient myths as a celestial seasoning, a spice that grew in the sky, sometimes associated with the sun and other times associated with the moon. Cinnamon, the ancients knew, came from the bark of several kinds of trees—one of them the cassia tree, which surfaced in some Chinese myths as the tree of immortality. People of the ancient world considered cassia cinnamon a variant of true cinnamon. Cinnamon from the cassia tree was likely the first type cultivated, and it yielded a particularly strong and fragrant spice.

The cassia tree of Chinese myths grew in the middle of the moon—or in some variants, such trees grew all over the moon. The moon goddess Heng O built her lunar palace out of cinnamon bark when she ascended to the moon and took up residence there after swallowing a pill of immortality. In one myth, a man named Kang Wou stood at the foot of the cassia tree in the middle of the moon and continually attempted to chop it down. According to this myth, Kang Wou offended a powerful genie, and the genie condemned him to forever cut down the lunar cassia tree.

The ancient Chinese called the moon Kueilan, or the disk of the cassia, and Chinese myths frequently mention the gigantic lunar cassia tree, 10,000 feet high, which had the ability to bestow immortality. The lunar cassia tree appears to have replaced the peach tree of earlier myths as the Tree of Life and immortality.

The ancients used aromatic spices for incense, and in ancient thought, incense was a potent, animating force and a divine substance that had the power to resurrect the dead. In legend, a man named Chang Ki'en traveled up the Yellow River, the most sacred river in China, which reputedly originated in the sky. Chang Ki'en followed the river to the sky and reached the gigantic cassia. There he found immortal animals, among them a toad and the lunar rabbit, whom the Chinese worshiped as the giver of rice. In Chinese moon lore, the rabbit in the moon continually pounds out rice, and people recognized his image in the pattern of light and dark areas on the lunar surface.

Other ancient peoples, among them the Greeks, tended to associate cinnamon and other spices with the fiery power of the sun. In Greek legend, spice collectors gathered cinnamon from the nests of the gigantic spice bird or phoenix, the legendary bird that burned itself up, then arose, renewed, from its ashes. To those who connected cinnamon and other spices with the sun, the phoenix was a fitting character to possess cinnamon, as its storied death and rebirth symbolized the setting and rising of the celestial fire. In another legend, the Sun himself came and carried off a portion of the cinnamon that people collected. The Greek philosopher and botanist Theophrastus and other ancient Greeks thought that cinnamon and aromatic spices came from southern Arabia, a place they referred to as the Land of Spices (although in fact cinnamon came from the East Indies and Southeast Asia). The Greek historian Herodotus, who also believed that cinnamon came from Arabia, said that because that land was so hot and so dry, so exposed to the fiery summer sun in the heat of midday, a sweet, pungent aroma permeated the entire peninsula.

Herodotus also explained how the Arabs acquired cinnamon bark by stealing it from the spice birds. These gigantic birds carried the cinnamon sticks off to their nests, which they built in areas completely inaccessible to human beings. But the clever Arabs tricked the spice birds by setting out chunks of animal flesh so large that when the birds brought them to their nests, the nests and the cinnamon fell to the ground. The Arabs then gathered up the precious spice.

Spices must be harvested carefully, for they lose their potency if they are crushed in the process. Perhaps this led to myths describing the perils involved in the collection of cinnamon. The cinnamon the Arabs collected from the spice birds was often identified as true cinnamon rather than cassia cinnamon. In Greek myth, cassia grew in a lake and cinnamon in the sky, but both of them posed problems for spice collectors.

The collection of true cinnamon involved retrieving it from a precarious location above the earth; and the collection of cassia cinnamon involved gathering it from a location underground, where it grew either in a shallow lake inhabited by ominous batlike creatures or in ravines filled with venomous snakes. Either way, retrieving the cinnamon was risky business, and a process the Greeks reserved for priests. When the priests succeeded in collecting the cinnamon, they divided their precious spice into three portions and left one on an altar for the sun god. As soon as the collectors left the spot, it was said, the sun god ignited the cinnamon and burned it to ashes. (Detienne 1977; Mackenzie 1994; Simoons 1991)

See also Ginger; Saffron; Spices; Turmeric

CITRONS
See Lemons and Citrons

COCA
Coca is probably one of the oldest domesticated plants of the Americas. It was discovered and used by native peoples of the Andean region in South America. These pre-Columbian Americans thought the coca plant of divine origin because of its invigorating effects. In a technical sense coca is not food, yet early people considered it such. People of

the Andes used the coca plant for centuries to allay hunger and fatigue, and relied on coca as a source of nutrients. Coca leaves contain a variety of vitamins and minerals including calcium, iron, phosphorus, and vitamins A, B-2, and E, which filled a nutritional gap in a diet high in carbohydrates and low in green vegetables.

The energy gained by chewing coca leaves seemed nothing short of magical. Coca enabled the body to withstand prolonged physical exertion, especially at high altitudes, because it prevented the rapid breathing and exhaustion typically experienced when climbing mountains. Fortunately, coca thrived in the tropical Andes; unlike other greens, it grew abundantly on the mountain slopes despite the high rainfall and eroded soil. Pre-Columbian peoples drank it as tea, or ground the leaves into fine powder and mixed it with cassava flour, potato flour, or ash from burnt quinoa stems. Often, they chewed the dried leaves with mineral lime, a substance that aided the absorption of alkaloids within the leaves. Once the coca went to work, the consumers of this miraculous plant knew no hunger or thirst, and they gained strength. In the absence of other foods, coca served as a source of energy, a preserver of health, and a valuable emergency resource that had the ability to prolong life until other foods became available.

A legend from the Yungas Valley recounts the discovery of coca by the natives who settled the area and set fire to the forests to clear the land for cultivation. These fires angered Khuno, the storm god, who then flooded the land and destroyed the Yungas civilization. After the flood the people had no food to eat, but they discovered a green shrub that miraculously stayed their hunger and renewed their energy. They spread the news of this plant to the elders of Tiahuanaco, and soon knowledge of the plant's powers spread across the land. Given the stimulating effects of coca, the people in pre-Inca times certainly appreciated their sacred plant for more than its nutritional value.

Though they used coca as both a stimulant and a narcotic, early peoples consumed the plant primarily for religious reasons. People today make cocaine by treating coca leaves with chemicals; in most cases, they consume it for pleasure rather than for religious or ceremonial reasons. But in the past people tapped into coca for its supernatural power, often restricting its use to the higher classes or to shamans and others who understood plant magic. Some South American peoples today continue to use coca in a religious context. They consider coca powder magic, believing that it protects and revitalizes the body and spirit. Some South American shamans consume coca leaves to transcend the earthly realm and commune with the spirits. Some of them believe they can use coca to activate the powers of the spirits to protect their people against evil and witchcraft and to ensure good fortune.

Natives of the Andes in particular attributed all sorts of powers to coca. They used it to contact the supernatural, to forecast the future, and to cure certain ailments. Because they considered the plant sacred, they made offerings of coca to their deities, particularly to deities with control over the earth and fertility. Andean peoples offered coca during natural disasters such as drought, flood, frost, and hail, and also at critical times in the seasonal cycle. In the Andean pantheon, Pachamama was Mother Earth, and the participants in coca rituals believed that chewing the sacred, magical leaves of the plant would help them understand the motives of Pachamama as well as the punishments inflicted by her and the other nature gods. They also used coca in fertility rites, as a symbol of abundance. The Andean people personified coca as a benevolent goddess, Mama Coca, who controlled fertility and blessed human beings with her power. In myth, people began consuming coca long ago, when Mama Coca lived as a beautiful young woman. This woman was so promiscuous, however, that the people killed her for her indiscretion. Coca grew from her body. In some versions of the myth, a man had to rub a concoction of coca on his penis and have intercourse with a woman before he could harvest the coca. This pleased Mama Coca, and she then gave her blessings to the harvest.

Some Andean peoples still consider the coca plant magic, use it to foretell the future and to diagnose disease, and make offerings of it to ensure fruitful crops and good luck when building new homes. In a myth recounting the divine origin of coca, the children of the sun presented the coca leaf to the Incas when the formation of their empire was complete, to satisfy their hunger and to rejuvenate them after their hard work. In order to thank the gods, the Incas worshiped the miraculous leaf as the divine Mama Coca; and when designing idols of their gods, they gave them fat cheeks—implicitly, stuffed with coca leaves to denote divinity. (Mortimer 1974; Osborne 1983; Ratsch 1992; Ricciuti 1978)

See also Betel Nuts; Coffee; Cola Nuts; Herbs; Tobacco

COCONUTS

The coconut palm had significant value as a food plant for much of the ancient world. It entered into the myths of India, where it was a symbol of fertility and an emblem of Lakshmi, the goddess of fortune and prosperity. In Africa it was revered as a sacred tree and likened to a mother goddess who gave her people the gift of milk. Pre-Columbian Americans also cultivated the coconut palm, and it served as a staple food for most of the Oceanian world.

In many Oceanian myths, the coconut palm and its unusual fruit originated from a head, either human or divine. One of the best-known myths comes from Polynesia and centers around the goddess Hina and her husband, Te Tuna, the Monster Eel. Hina and Te Tuna lived together in the sea, until one day Hina left her eel husband and set out in search of a new lover. She settled on the trickster Maui, a frequently recurring figure in Polynesian myth

who often performed miraculous feats to help humankind. When Te Tuna came after Maui, Maui challenged him to a duel. Maui again proved himself a clever master of magic: Each of the rivals, he said, must enter into the body of the other. The Monster Eel entered into Maui first, but did not disturb him the slightest bit. Then Maui entered Te Tuna and split him apart. He then cut off Te Tuna's head and buried it. Soon afterward, shoots sprouted from the ground, and a coconut tree grew that provided enough food for all the people of Polynesia.

Varying myths of coconuts springing from heads circulated throughout Oceania and beyond. In Kiribati, in the Pacific Islands, the coconut reportedly sprang from the head of Neititua Abinem, the goddess of vegetation. In Ceylon, the fruit grew from the head of an astrologer, planted in the ground by the king. Like the Polynesian myth of Te Tuna, a Tahitian myth told of the coconut springing from the head of an eel, sealed within a calabash and intended as a gift from the gods. These stories illustrate a common theme in world mythology—the notion of food plants arising from a murdered body, usually that of an immortal. Yet in a story from New Guinea, the coconut sprang from the head of a young boy who had fallen into a fire during a picnic with his mother; and in another myth from New Guinea, from the head of a man who used to fish in the sea by removing his head and allowing the fish to swim directly into his stomach. In this story, some men followed this fisherman, jealous that he brought home so many large fish. When they saw him take off his head and wade into the ocean, they stole the head and buried it. From that spot the coconut tree grew.

In Indonesia, an origin myth of the coconut also recounts its birth from a human head, this time after a feud between two kings, the king of Yueh and the king of Champa. The king of Champa sent an assassin to kill the king of Yueh and hang his head on a tree. His head became a coconut, and the king of Champa used the coconut shell as a cup for his wine. The Li of modern Hainan have a similar story that involves the buried heads of decapitated prisoners—from which coconut trees sprang up, with head-sized fruits. The Li, too, used the coconut shells to hold their wine.

The resemblance between coconuts and human heads impressed the ancients, and in many instances they offered coconuts as sacrifices to the gods instead of human heads. With its headlike shape, two dark spots that resemble eyes, and coarse, hairlike fibers, the coconut shell served as a substitute for human sacrifice in Hindu religious rites; and coconuts were thrown into the sea as an offering and propitiation to Varuna, the Hindu god of the waters. The Hindus used coconuts as offerings in many kinds of ceremonies, particularly those performed to ensure fertility or to ward off evil spirits.

The Hindu origin myth of the coconut placed this food in paradise, a place that existed temporarily between heaven and earth. A great sage with supernatural powers sent a man named Satyavrata to heaven in his body to reward him for taking care of the sage's family. But because only souls belong in heaven, the sage's act angered Indra, and when Satyavrata arrived in heaven, Indra threw the man out. The sage used his supernatural powers once again to help Satyavrata, this time to catch the man's fall and establish a place for him with eternal nourishment. The sage suspended Satyavrata in the air, then held him there with a pole, which later became the coconut palm.

The coconut was an important food plant of antiquity, and revered by many people because it produced milk and provided nourishment. In this sense, they likened it to a generous mother goddess. Some people of India believed coconut trees felt pain when they were injured, and in parts of Africa the destruction of a coconut tree was considered a crime similar to matricide. Many people of Africa even today consider coconut milk a sacred substance. Monks in Thailand and other Buddhists hold similar beliefs. (Beckwith 1970;

Gupta 1991; Hu 1996; Knappert 1995c; Poignant 1967; Reed 1992; Visser 1986)

See also Breadfruit; Coffee; Milk; Sugar and Sugarcane; Taro

COFFEE

Coffee beans are native to Africa, particularly to the Abyssinian province of Caffa, from which coffee got its name. In Abyssinia (modern Ethiopia), coffee beans grew abundantly, and African people have consumed them, both in bean form and as a beverage, since antiquity. Coffee beans are small and green, and they grow on jasmine-scented evergreen shrubs in lands close to the equator. The shrubs have flowers and fruits similar to cherries, and the coffee beans are actually the pits of these fruits. People consumed these pits, or berries, then discovered they could boil both the berries and the leaves to make a stimulating drink. According to legend, Ethiopian goatherds first noticed the stimulating powers of the coffee bush when their goats nibbled on the berries and remained awake and unusually frisky at night.

The most popular legend surrounding coffee beans centers around Kaldi, an Ethiopian goatherd who tasted the berries himself after he noticed the remarkable effect they had on his herd. Kaldi, too, became exhilarated. The goatherd then took some of the berries to the chief mullah, and the chief decided the berries could help keep people awake during lengthy religious services. The Ethiopians soon began to use coffee as a stimulant. Later, they discovered the technique of roasting the beans and preparing a drink from them. They also made coffee bean balls by grinding up the berries and mixing them with animal fat. This food proved to be a good form of sustenance for warriors during raids against hostile tribes.

Since these early times, coffee has revolutionized the world; certainly it has molded people's morning rituals. Some Africans continue to use spiced coffee in mystical rituals, and some believe the beans themselves house healing spirits. African Sufis believe that coffee not only keeps them alert but enables them to enter into ecstatic states. Universal consumption of coffee began after Arab traders transported the plant across the Red Sea to Yemen, the southernmost port of Arabia, and cultivated it on their plantations, around 1000 A.D. From there it moved to Europe, where people eventually consumed it in great quantities.

The Ethiopian legend of Kaldi has parallels in an Arabian legend of coffee. In the latter, Sheik Omar discovered coffee by chance while he was in the Arabian desert, exiled from Yemen over morality issues. Sheik Omar was starving in the Arabian desert, and his people clearly expected him to die. But he discovered coffee berries growing wild and ate some. Then he roasted them to improve their bitter taste. Finally he boiled them and discovered that the water was not bitter at all, but tasteful, and that drinking it worked to suppress his appetite. When he returned to Mocha, Yemen's port, the people considered his survival a miracle. They made their formerly exiled sheik a saint, and from then on considered coffee a highly prized commodity.

When coffee first arrived in Europe, people viewed the product much as they had other products that arrived from Arabia. Like spices, coffee seemed exotic, even magical. Some people considered it an aphrodisiac, others a panacea. Still others believed the black beans held the power of black magic. Arabia was a mystical land, little understood and full of surprises. Not until the seventeenth century did Europeans fully accept coffee.

In Europe, as in Arabia, an interesting perception arose about this exotic beverage. Coffee became a kind of "wholesome liquor," an acceptable indulgence, yet in many ways the inverse of alcohol. Beer was a staple in Old Europe, and coffee was a beverage of sobriety. It affected the mind but did not cause drunkenness. It even appeared to combat drunkenness—drinking coffee clearly made drunk people sober. It has been said that the Arabian

mullahs who used coffee to stay awake during prayers thought Mohammed gave them coffee to send them a message, and that the angel Gabriel gave the coffee to Mohammed. This product enhanced the mind and helped them stay alert and focused. Mohammed had commanded them to abstain from wine and gave them magical coffee beans instead.

The Arabic name for coffee was *qahwah,* a word that also means "that which excites and causes the spirits to rise." Qahwah referred to wine, as well as to a Persian king, who according to legend could ascend into heaven simply by power of thought. In these early times, before the beans were roasted, coffee indeed had qualities similar to those of wine, and therefore produced similar effects. These early people made coffee not simply with the beans but with the hull and the pulp surrounding them. This pulp, or coffee fruit, fermented quickly, as did the grape and other fruits from which early peoples derived intoxicating drinks. (Dodge 1979; Norman 1972; Ratsch 1992; Schivelbusch 1992; Toussaint-Samat 1992; Wellman 1961)

See also Alcoholic Beverages; Betel Nuts; Chocolate; Coca; Cola Nuts; Tea

COLA NUTS

The cola nut is not a food exactly, but a masticatory. West Africans chew cola nuts like Hindu Indians chew betel nuts; they chew them for their caffeine stimulants, to sharpen their minds, reduce fatigue, slake the appetite, and counter intoxication. Cola nuts grew wild in the tropical rain forests of West Africa long ago, and were later domesticated there. Cultivation of the nuts continues on a large scale in West Africa today. Muslims in northern Nigeria knew of cola nuts at least 800 years ago, and because these nuts had seemingly magical properties, they considered them sacred.

The passion for cola nuts remains high in many West African societies today, like the passion for betel nuts in India and in much of the Asian world. The Hindu Indians consider betel nuts divine sustenance, and the Muslims in Africa view cola nuts in much the same way. Some Hindu Indians believe a snake god—the brother of Vasuki, king of all the snakes—gave them betel nuts; West African Muslims believe the prophet Mohammed gave them cola nuts. The power these nuts had to invigorate and heighten the senses led people to recognize in them a connection to the celestial realm. In one West African myth, the creator god Nzambi possessed cola nuts in heaven, and human beings knew nothing of their existence until they witnessed Nzambi eating one when he descended to earth once to visit the people. The man who saw Nzambi's cola nut managed to get hold of it while the creator god wasn't looking; but when Nzambi saw him, he quickly snatched it back. Food myths all over the world emphasized the division between food for humans and food for gods. If the food of the gods penetrated the human sphere at all, people often felt obligated to reserve these foods for ritual use.

The West Africans found a number of uses for cola nuts, including uses in ritual contexts. They attributed miraculous properties to the nuts, including the ability to protect the possessor from sin. West Africans chew cola nuts fresh and make stimulating beverages from them; they use them as charms and amulets, as medicines and as aphrodisiacs. At one time, they also used the dried nuts as currency and as divining tools. Because the West Africans value cola nuts, they still give them as tokens of friendship and goodwill during social ceremonies such as birth, child naming, marriage, death, and the installation of tribal chiefs. Some tribal groups in Nigeria still consider cola nuts symbolic of hospitality.

The people of West Africa were no strangers to stimulating plants, as they too discovered wild coffee plants in Ethiopia. But cola nuts have stronger power than coffee beans; in small doses they stimulate, but in larger doses they inebriate. The seemingly magical properties of cola nuts led West Africans and other users to consider them necessities for human beings and gifts from the gods. (Ratsch 1992; Rosengarten 1984)

See also Betel Nuts; Coca; Coffee; Tobacco

CORN

In the language of myth, the word *corn* often referred to any grain or to any food crop in general. The Greek Demeter, for instance, was not simply the mother of corn, as she was often called, but the mother of all grains, particularly of barley and wheat, as well as the mother of agriculture. The Chinese recognized a special constellation of eight stars, one for each of the eight varieties of corn: rice, millet, barley, wheat, beans, peas, maize, and hemp. Myths about maize arose primarily in the Americas, where in agricultural societies, the golden grain formed the basis of life.

Some Native American tribes considered maize the embodiment of all life, and they incorporated myths of its origin and cultivation into their entire system of cosmological belief. Corn originated in Mesoamerica with the yellow maize the Aztecs, the Maya, the Inca, and other peoples of the area revered. In ancient times, these people considered their maize god a primary deity, and the maize kernels themselves a part of the god. All maize-growing cultures in the Americas had corn gods; some had corn mothers or corn maidens, and others, male deities who controlled the fertility of the earth and distribution of the grain. Because these people depended on the production of maize for survival, myths of its origin and life cycle permeated their personal, social, and ceremonial lives.

The Inca and the Aztecs considered maize the lifeblood of their culture and a sacred symbol of the life-giving sun. The yellow grain that covered their fields they labeled the sun's gold, and they considered their precious maize the plant with the greatest life energy. Both the Inca and the Aztecs viewed the sun as the driving life force of their civilizations, and they knew that the sun influenced the production of food. In Aztec myth, the maize

The Aztecs offering their precious maize to the gods. (Library of Congress)

god, Tlazopilli, was born from the union of the sun god and the Great Mother. In Peruvian myth, the first human beings died because the high god Pachacamac, who had created them, created no food to sustain them. The sun helped one woman survive by allowing her to live on fruits and to have a son. Pachacamac killed the son, and from his body grew cultivated plants and maize.

Though in Incan myth the first mortals lived without maize, in Aztec and Mayan myth, maize preceded mortals on the earth. The Maya said that the first humans were formed from maize. The Popul Vuh, the epic mythology of the Quiche Maya, recounts how the gods tried three times to make human beings and failed: They made them from mud, but the rains destroyed them; they made them from wood, but they were too stiff; they made them from flesh, but they were too easily corrupted. Finally, they made them from corn and declared them perfect. The Pueblo peoples of North America considered corn a fifth element of nature, along with earth, air, fire, and water. In cultures of southwestern North America, the mythology of corn in large part reveals the sanctity of nature. Corn was not simply a staple food for these people; it was a staple of life in every respect. Natives built shelters from corn, they adorned themselves with it, and certainly they revered it as a god.

The Corn Mother of North America often took on the role of great goddess, the deity who guaranteed the fertility and immortality of the earth. In fact, many European peoples past and present personified corn as a mother goddess. So did the people of the East Indies and other parts of the world, who assigned similar characteristics to their rice mothers and barley mothers. In North America, the Corn Mother served as a female symbol, the giver of life, the womb and tomb of their sacred foodstuffs. Along with the rice mothers and barley mothers and the mother goddesses of many lands, the Corn Mother was as sacred as the earth itself. The sanctity of the earth derived largely from the fact that it harbored this miraculous grain in its womb and delivered it to the people.

Though all cultures believed corn deities controlled fertility, some cultures made these deities male instead of female. The Hindu god Indra and the Norse god Thor both presided over corn. They controlled the heavens, but they energized the earth with storm power and thus fertilized the seed within it. In Egypt, Osiris personified the corn. Corn grew after the inundation of the earth by water from the Nile, and because Osiris embodied the Nile, corn sprouted from his body. Like the Corn Mother of North America, Osiris actually produced the grain from his body—that was what the myths said. He died, but was resurrected, like the corn; so in essence, he died to feed the people.

In Egyptian myth, the evil god Seth dismembered the body of Osiris and then scattered the pieces over the land, burying them in different places. In this manner, the myths expressed the sowing of corn seed. Myths of Osiris and Demeter and the Corn Mother clearly attested to the fact that early people believed corn had spirit. People all over the world who recognized a corn spirit, whether it be a spirit of corn alone or of grain in gen-

eral, found the need to represent this spirit in either human or animal form. Sometimes the corn spirit manifested itself as a young maiden, a temporary embodiment of the first harvest, or as an old woman, a temporary embodiment of the last sheaf. The last sheaf, in many myths, took primary significance. Because some people believed the spirit resided in the last sheaf, consuming it meant partaking of the god or the spirit itself. Those who invoked the corn spirit sometimes felt they had to either render the spirit inactive or transfer the spirit to a new crop.

This philosophy at times led to the killing of the human or animal representative of the corn. In Aztec and Mayan cultures, in particular, sacrifice became an integral part of harvest rituals. Because early planting cultures often adhered to the notion of the universe forming from the body of a primal being, early myths and ceremonies of agricultural societies (e.g., the Egyptian myth of Osiris) emphasized the dependence of life upon death. Death of the god or primal being, and of the corn seed, generated new life. The planting and reaping of corn, and the reliable pattern this entailed, connected creation to sacrifice. Each year the corn had to die before it could be reborn.

A myth in the Popul Vuh provided a metaphor for the planting, growth, and fruition of maize. It also emphasized the dependence of life upon death. The first pair of divine twins descended to the underworld, Xibalba, and were defeated by the Lords of the Night. The severed head of one of these twins was then hung in a tree, and miraculously, the disembodied head impregnated the daughter of a Xibalban ruler. The woman gave birth to the second pair of divine twins, Hunahpu and Xbalanque, and these twins also battled the Lords of the Night to avenge their father's death. The story of Hunahpu and Xbalanque made up a large part of the Popul Vuh, and it involved the twins resurrecting their slain father, who became the Maize God.

In the story of Hunahpu and Xbalanque, the Maya recounted the death and rebirth of corn. The Aztecs also recognized the corn's association with death and rebirth, and likewise connected fertility with sacrifice. In a sense, the Aztec vegetation god Xipe Totec (the flayed lord) embodied this connection. In a festival held in his honor, the Aztecs chose victims for sacrifice, flayed them, and then adorned Xipe Totec's priests with their skins. This act symbolized the regeneration of plant life, and the skins represented the husk of the maize, which enclosed its living spirit. In another maize ritual, the Aztecs sacrificed young virgins, first painting them in the colors of the corn plant and then tearing out their hearts. Tearing out the heart represented the husking of the corn; and the virgin represented the young, tender ear of corn that the people worshiped.

A North American legend of the Ojibwa also integrated the theme of life springing from death into an explanation of corn's origins. The Ojibwa, as the story goes, lived by hunting and fishing, until an Ojibwa shaman named Wunzh introduced them to agriculture. In response to his people's hunger, Wunzh sought spiritual guidance. He found help in the form of a young spirit-man dressed in yellow and green clothing and a headdress made of green feathers. Though famished and weak, Wunzh wrestled with the spirit and held his ground. The Great Spirit rewarded him for his strength and persistence by enabling the Ojibwa to move from a hunting to an agricultural existence. Wunzh defeated the spirit, stripped him of his clothes, and threw the dead body onto the ground. When tips of the spirit's feather headdress sprouted up from the earth, corn came into existence.

Early agriculturists told numerous myths to explain the origin of corn. In many North American native myths, animals gave the precious grain to human beings as a gift. In Narragansett legend, a crow brought it, carrying a kernel of corn in one ear and a bean in the other. In Navajo legend a turkey brought it; while flying to earth from the Morning Star, the turkey shook an ear of corn out from un-

der its feathers. Early people needed to explain the origin of corn before they tackled the miracle of sowing and reaping, and they almost always attributed corn to supernatural or divine intervention. The Aztecs credited the discovery of maize to Quetzalcoatl, who followed a red ant into the Mountain of Sustenance, where he found maize kernels and the seeds of beans and other edible food plants. With the help of Nanahuatzin, who split open the mountain, Quetzalcoatl brought the foodstuffs to his people. Then the Tlaloques, the gods of rain and storm, scattered the seeds over the land.

The movement from hunting and gathering to agriculture was an evolutionary leap. Once people learned how to cultivate grain, they no longer had to constantly search for food, and they felt eternally grateful for this revelation. The Eleusinian Mysteries of ancient Greece constituted an entire religion based on the mystery of corn, or on the mystery of agriculture in general. Demeter, the earth goddess, transformed the barren land into a cornfield and taught the prince Triptolemus how to cultivate it. After people learned the art of cultivation, they flourished. So people worshiped the corn and the goddesses who provided it. In the cult of Eleusinian Mysteries, the harvested ear of corn was the central mystery. People all over the world felt awed by the miracle of growth and the ability of the earth to produce food. The many different myths of corn reveal that early peoples recognized their earth, and their staple grain, as a mysterious and miraculous life-giving force. (Campbell 1988; Frazer 1950; Fussell 1992; Kahn 1985; Toussaint-Samat 1992; Visser 1986)

See also Amaranth; Barley; Bread; Cake; Grain; Millet; Oats; Quinoa; Rice; Rye; Sorghum; Wheat

CRANBERRIES

The fruit commonly known today as the cranberry was known long ago to the ancient Druids. The Druids called the berries Samolus. Later peoples of Great Britain called these same fruits marsh worts or fen berries because they grew in swamps and marshes. In America, cranberries also grew in bogs. Early European settlers named the fruit kraneberries or cranberries, perhaps because the scarlet berries attracted cranes, who built their nests near this favorite food source.

Native Americans knew that cranes and other birds ate cranberries, and along the Northwest coast, they commonly believed that birds also had the power to ripen the berries. In a Squamish legend, a man sent the husband of his newly married daughter to search for cranberries in winter. The man magically produced them, but they were still green, so he called the birds to sing them into ripening.

The quest for berries in winter permeated the folklore traditions of both Europe and America, some tales involving cranberries, and others, strawberries, blueberries, or berries of other sorts. In Europe, cruel stepmothers often sent children on this quest, hoping they would die before they completed the seemingly impossible task. Along the Northwest coast of America, similar tales featured jealous fathers rather than cruel stepmothers, and young sons-in-law rather than frightened children. In the Comox version of the tale, an old grandfather with supernatural powers helped the young husband by whistling the cranberries into existence. The grandfather's whistling served the same purpose in this tale as the singing of birds did in others.

Hunter-gatherers in early America relied on cranberries to survive, as they did on nuts and berries of other sorts. The Native Americans introduced cranberries to the Pilgrims, who incorporated them into their Thanksgiving feasts as a symbol of the earth's abundance. The Native Americans also told legends

The Native Americans introduced cranberries to the Pilgrims, who incorporated them into their Thanksgiving feasts as a symbol of the earth's abundance. (Library of Congress)

of this important food. In a Chippewa legend, for example, three sister cranberries—one white, one red, and one green—were living together in a lodge. It was winter, and snow covered the ground, and the three cranberries were afraid that a wolf would come and eat them. When a wolf did come to eat them, the three cranberries quickly went into hiding. The white one hid in a kettle of white hominy, but the wolf devoured the entire pot. The red one burrowed under the snow, but the wolf trampled her to pieces. The green one climbed up into the spruce tree and was saved.

Though numerous varieties of the cranberry grow throughout North America, true cranberries are difficult to cultivate, so hybrid varieties have been developed, such as the highbush cranberry, which grows as tall as eight to twelve feet and has a much higher survival rate. The fruit of the highbush cranberry looks luscious but often tastes sour—it's good when sweetened with honey, as the Pilgrims discovered, but not when eaten raw. According to Cree legend, a man perceived to be a magician cursed the berries and made them sour. This hungry man was sitting on a riverbank one day when suddenly he saw bunches of ripe, red cranberries floating in the water. He jumped into the water and tried to reach them, but they vanished just as quickly as they had appeared. The magician dove deep into the water, over and over again, but never found the cranberries. Then he realized that it was only the reflection of the cranberries he saw in the water; the real fruit hung from a tree overhead. The cranberry bush, which had a mind of its own, decided to trick the foolish magician by moving up higher and higher and staying just out of the magician's reach. This so frustrated the man that he cursed the cranberries. From then on, this highbush cranberry produced only berries that were bitter to the taste. (*Funk and Wagnall's* 1972; MacFarlan 1968; Reed 1992)

See also Blackberries; Blueberries; Elderberries; Gooseberries; Mulberries; Raspberries; Strawberries

CUCUMBERS

Cucumbers were mentioned in the first written legend, the Sumerian *Epic of Gilgamesh,* recorded on cuneiform tablets around 3000 B.C. They were a favored fruit of past times, and were cultivated extensively in Greece, Rome, China, Egypt, and Southeast Asia from antiquity. The Chinese call cucumbers *kua,* along with pumpkins, gourds, melons, and squash, and Chinese folklore places them under the patronage of Kua Hsien, the Melon Fairy. Cucumbers are botanical relatives of melons and gourds, and they share much of the same symbolism. They have hard rinds, and when hollowed out they make convenient vessels. Their many seeds make them symbols of fertility and abundance.

Both the seeds and the shape of the cucumber connect it with fertility. The fruits are phallic in shape, and can become extremely large, like snakes, giving them obvious links to the fecundity of both earth and water. Buddhists connected the cucumber with fertility, and in one variant of their legend of Sagara, the sea god, Sagara's wife had 60,000 sons, the first of which was a cucumber. This firstborn son of Sagara was named Ikshvaku, and either Ikshvaku himself or one of his descendants climbed to heaven on his own vine. In another myth, Ikshvaku became the father of a solar dynasty, a mythical race of kings in India. Ikshvaku himself descended from the son of Manu, the father of humankind. In this myth, Ikshvaku was born of the sneeze of Manu, and his descendants from the cucumber seeds.

Although the cucumber was a fertility symbol, it was also linked to coldness, and therefore to death. Some believed that cucumbers, because they were inherently cold, had the power to kill. In England, a superstition that cucumbers could bring death kept the vegetable out of people's diets for hundreds of years. In China, too, people refused to eat cucumbers. The plant grew abundantly in China, but many believed that cold foods caused illness.

In Japanese mythology, the evil Kappa rode on a cucumber. (Victoria & Albert Museum, London/Art Resource, NY)

It appears that long ago many Japanese people also avoided cucumbers. According to legend, one Japanese family believed that a cucumber spirit had been protecting their family for centuries because their ancestors had vowed long before never to eat them. The Japanese believed that everything in the natural world had kami, or spirit, so cucumbers had kami too. In another legend, a cucumber spirit foiled the attempts of a doctor to evade his pursuers. In trying to escape, the man tripped over the stalk of a cucumber plant, fell, and was captured and killed.

Japanese artists sometimes depicted the Kappa, an evil water spirit, riding on a cucumber. The Japanese believed cucumbers protected them from the Kappa. These demons looked like hairless monkeys, but they sometimes had the scales of fish or the shells of tortoises. They inhabited rivers and ponds, and they pulled people under the water and drowned them, then drank the blood of their victims. Kappa, however, loved cucumbers, so people placated the Kappa by throwing cucumbers into the water. Sometimes people put the names of their loved ones on the cucumbers to ensure that the Kappa wouldn't pull them into the water either. (Deerr 1949; Piggott 1997)

See also Pumpkins and Gourds; Squash; Watermelons

DATES

Dates held significance in many Old World myths and were considered sacred or of divine origin by many cultures. In Mesopotamia, where people have venerated the date palm for at least 8,000 years, the tree is said to have originated in heaven. It served as the Mesopotamian Tree of Life (a symbol of immortality)—a role it also fulfilled for the Egyptians and Chinese Taoists. These people made various foodstuffs from the date palm; they made the seeds into coffee or oil, they ate the fruit dried or made it into cakes, and they used the date juice to make a potent wine, which was particularly popular among ancient Egyptians.

Date palms grew in many parts of the Old World. Some legends say Mohammed created them, and others say they arose when St. Christopher put his staff in the ground. One myth says the date palm was formed from the earth that remained after the creation of Adam. Some scholars have suggested that it is dates, not the honey of bees, that is meant in the biblical description of the Promised Land as the "land of milk and honey." The desert areas of Persia, Arabia, and North Africa have been called the Land of Dates because the palms grew there in abundance. These trees provided a large crop of fruit each year, which served as a staple food and a principal source of wealth.

The date palm signified riches as well as immortality. Because the date palm was supposed to grow a new branch every lunar month, the Egyptians associated the tree with time and control of the life span, and called it the Tree of the Year. The Egyptians also called the date palm the Tree of Life *(bnr* or *bni)* and related it to the *bennu,* the phoenix. This stemmed from the belief that even if fire destroyed the date palm it would regenerate as had the phoenix, the mythical bird that burned up and then arose again from the ashes. The Egyptians used date products in a number of sacred rituals: Egyptian magicians used date seeds as magical instruments, and they also washed the bodies of the dead with date wine during mummification. Egyptian lore connected the milky juice produced by the date palm with the milk of Hathor, the mother goddess, and with Isis.

The Greeks associated the date palm with Artemis, the Greek equivalent to Isis, and with her brother Apollo, the sun god. In Greek myth, when Leto became pregnant with Apollo and Artemis by Zeus, Zeus's wife Hera became enraged and decreed that Leto could not give birth in any place where sunlight had fallen. Poseidon, the sea god, helped Leto by creating an island and holding a wave over it to block out the sun, allowing her to give birth, which she did while clinging to a date palm. The Greeks dedicated the date palm to Apollo, in part because the tree symbolized light as well as worldly riches, victory, and procreation. The tree also represented Artemis, or the Roman Diana, perhaps for her identification as a mother goddess. A famous statue of Diana portrays her covered with dates, which may symbolize breasts exuding milky juice. The Tree of Life, like a great mother, served as a provider of sustenance and eternal life.

Because the date palm held such a revered place in early belief systems, many cultures identified it with high gods and used the sacred fruits of this tree as offerings to them. Hindus offered dates to many important deities, among them Krishna and Radha. They believed the plant arose from the chest of Shiva,

DEER

A statue of Artemis (Diana) of Ephesus, portraying the goddess covered with dates. Like a mother goddess, the date tree served as a provider of life and sustenance. (Scala/Art Resource, NY)

Most people today don't consider deer hunting a mysterious endeavor, but Native Americans, in past times particularly, infused the hunt with magic. Many Native Americans believe in the unity of life and in the interconnectedness of all that exists in the physical and spiritual worlds; this lay at the root of hunting magic in general and of deer magic in particular. Deer were a major source of food for many Native American peoples, yet those who hunted and killed deer felt a deep spiritual bond with the animals. This bond, they believed, enabled them to magically control the animals and to communicate with them, and thus to see the animals' whereabouts in clairvoyant visions.

Hunting magic was of primary importance to ancient hunting peoples. It permeated their cultures and defined the people's relationship to the natural world. The Celts considered the stag a symbol of abundance and prosperity and a guardian of nature. They revered the stag and they made their powerful stag god Cernunnos Lord of the Animals. Respect for the animals was essential to making the magic work.

The Celts and the Native Americans both hunted deer and held them sacred, and knew that a successful hunt depended on the hunters' harmonious relationship with their prey. A widespread practice among Native American hunters involved their apologizing to the animal's spirit, even offering the dead deer libations. Hunting peoples in North America and elsewhere believed that placating the animals' spirits encouraged them to give themselves willingly in sacrifice. They believed that placation and an appropriate show of respect ensured that the dead animal's spirit would return to the people again, in another animal, which would also give its life willingly.

Ancient peoples placated animals and performed various magic rituals primarily to increase their supply of game. The Pueblo, for instance, used dance and song as forms of deer

one of the three manifestations of the Supreme Deity. The Hindus considered the date tree highly intelligent, just one step away from the animal kingdom. Those who considered it the Tree of Life thought it produced immortal fruit, and they thus connected it to fertility and regeneration. (Ratsch 1992; Reed 1992; Tannahill 1973; Toussaint-Samat 1992)

See also Figs; Milk

magic. Often in these rituals, they would make themselves look like the deer they intended to kill. During deer dances, the dancers would wear antlers on their heads, and in some cases, would wrap their entire bodies in deerskins. By imitating the deer, they believed they could commune with the deer spirits and telepathically guide them out of the forests and into their villages.

Some Native American deer hunters today perform rituals just as their ancestors did in ancient times. They stage elaborate dances, use good-luck charms, and embrace traditional rituals of magic at every stage of the hunt, even after the animal dies. For example, the Zuni sometimes inhale the last breath of the deer, believing that in doing so they inhale the mystery of life.

Belief systems in any culture interweave ritual with myth. Hunting magic was endemic in nonagricultural societies; but the Pueblo were farmers, so they likely felt the need to explain, through myth, how deer hunting arose and why eating deer meat became necessary. Hunting myths of North America reveal a general belief that supernatural beings held game animals captive long ago, trapped in storehouses or caves to make them constantly available to feed the people. No one had to hunt at all until someone released these animals, either by accident or out of curiosity, and the animals scattered throughout the land. Hunting origin myths of the Pueblo build on this theme by relating deer to agriculture. In Zuni myth, for instance, the deer provide not only meat but also water for the fields. When

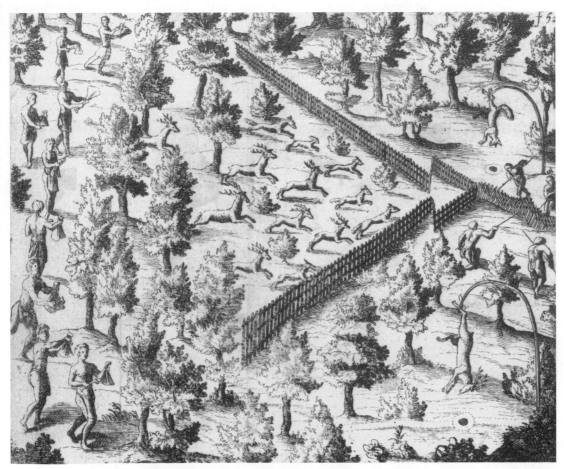

A Native American deer hunt. (Library of Congress)

the deer remained trapped in their original caves, the Zuni say, the land suffered a great drought, but after their release the rains came. In another Pueblo myth, the kachina Heluta, the father of deer, planted the dewclaws of deer in the earth like seeds and grew these game animals as one grows corn.

Pueblo myths often tell of spirits bringing deer to the people, particularly kachina spirits who were believed to live with the deer spirits in the mountains and to become deer themselves upon their death. The connection between kachinas and deer again reflects the Pueblo reliance on agriculture, since both the kachinas and the deer spirits were thought to control the release of rain. When the Zuni would bring the deer to their villages, they also brought the clouds, and the clouds in turn brought the rain that nourished the crops. One Zuni myth explains that the Zuni people lived primarily on corn and rabbits until the Long Horn kachina, Saiyatasha, convinced the Great Spirit that the people needed deer meat to add substance to their diet. In response to this request, the Great Spirit made the Zuni think and sing about deer. He made them create an image of a deer in song. Then he sent the little deer kachina, Natsiko, to the people. Natsiko shed his skin and appeared to the Zuni in human form.

Pueblo myths commonly involve kachinas becoming deer, and they stress the interconnectedness between the two. Natsiko made this transformation, and enabled the Zuni to be successful in hunting deer from then on, and to reap the benefits from eating deer flesh. The belief in the interconnectedness of deer and humans, however, involved another conflicting concept. One element of Pueblo belief involves the fear that a person who eats a deer may actually be eating a person, perhaps even a dead relative. Pueblo myths express this fear in stories of humans being transformed into deer and back again. (Campbell 1988; Tyler 1975)

See also Bear; Buffalo; Meat; Reindeer and Caribou; Salmon; Whale

DOG

Most people of the Western world recoil at the notion of eating dogs, which they consider pets and companions, not animals reared to be eaten. But in large areas of the ancient world, people did consume dogs, and some groups continue to do so today. People who ate dogs did so for a variety of reasons, some grounded in myth; those who refused to eat dogs often associated them with ancestors or important deities, and so considered killing and eating them a violation of the sacred.

Despite widespread taboos against the eating of dog flesh, dog-eating rituals occurred among people in much of the world. In ancient Mexico and pre-Incan Peru, dog flesh was a common food. The Maya typically sacrificed dogs twice a year, once at the New Year and again in May, when they sacrificed them to the cacao plantations. The Ainu of Japan and certain peoples of Siberia often ate dog meat, along with bear meat, as part of their bear festival. Natives of the Pacific Northwest coast tore dogs to pieces and devoured them. The ceremonial eating of dog flesh occurred among all tribes of the northeastern woodlands, typically among warriors who ate the meat to gain courage. In the ceremonial war feast of the Natchez Indians, the people roasted a dog whole and ate the flesh to gain the doglike tenacity expected of warriors. The Yoruba of Nigeria worshiped a god named Oro, who once lived on earth and ate humans because the people did not know what to offer him. When they finally offered him dogs, Oro was happy and did not eat humans anymore.

The Chinese are perhaps the best-known dog eaters. Although today the Chinese consume dogs simply as a protein source and not for any ritual purpose, in ancient times they considered dog flesh fitting food for deities. The Hawaiians offered dogs to their gods and high chiefs; the Romans sacrificed nursing puppies to their gods; and the Greeks offered dogs, usually black female puppies, to Hecate, the moon goddess. Before the Aryan invasion, early Europeans associated the dog with the night and the moon goddess, probably because dogs howled at the moon. The moon goddess (Hecate) was believed to subsist on cooked dog flesh and to possess powers of black magic; due to these beliefs, people in much of the ancient world consumed dog flesh for magical purposes. Ancient diviners in Ireland even chewed dog flesh in order to prophesy the future.

Many peoples of Africa, Greece and Rome, Ireland, North America, Siberia, and the South Pacific considered dog flesh magical. Dogs' association with various deities was believed to give them special powers, and in some cases it ensured their sanctity as well. The Hindus associated dogs with the deity Bhairava, one of the many names for Shiva, and they worshiped Bhairava as an incarnation of Shiva in the form of a black dog. These worshipers did not eat dogs but instead fed them in order to appease Bhairava. The Polynesians believed dogs descended from Irawaru, the husband of Hina, the moon goddess, and this made eating their flesh taboo to women. The Zoroastrians of ancient Persia associated the dog with their god of light, Ahura Mazda, and therefore regarded the dog as the holiest animal of all. Not only did they refuse to kill or eat dogs but they made it an offense to mistreat them in any way. The people of Dahomey also refused to kill and eat dogs, associating them with Legba, their divine trickster. In local myth, the first dog was created by Legba to solve a dispute, and its success made it blessed as a great guardian.

In addition to these associations between dogs and deities, scholars identify several reasons why people might have refused to eat dog flesh. The fact that dogs served as pets, guardians, and hunting companions certainly played a part, but so did the widespread perception of dogs as impure and unclean scavengers who feasted on corpses. Muslims and Jews traditionally considered dogs unclean, as did the Vedic Indians. This concept of uncleanness also had its basis in myth. The Vedic Indians associated dogs with death and with Yama, the Lord of the Dead. Yama had two dogs, Syama and Sabala, each of which had four eyes and was terribly fierce. Syama and Sabala guarded the way to the underworld, where Yama ruled, and dead souls feared encountering these dogs along their path, even though the animals were supposed to protect them. In Hindu myth, Bhairava also had connections to death; and in Greek myth, the dog Cerberus guarded the entrance to the underworld. Scholars have suggested that the association between death and these mythological dogs led to the belief in the dog's impurity, and to the notion that by eating dog flesh people would become impure themselves.

The notion that dogs devoured the dead may have made their flesh impure, but in much of the Asian world it also made them objects of veneration. Much of tribal India considered dogs repositories of departed souls, and thus the people worshiped dogs as guardians and protectors, sometimes against smallpox. The ancient Greeks, as a rule, did not eat dogs; because dogs ate corpses, the Greeks associated them with death and disease. But they also assigned them significant roles in healing cults. Gula, an Akkadian healing goddess, and Asclepius, the Greek god of medicine, both had dogs that effected cures. In the cult of Gula, the dog assumed a protective role, both as healer and as guardian. In temples dedicated to the cult of Asclepius, dogs roamed freely, in great numbers. People who worshiped in both of these cults believed that the dogs aided their deities by licking the wounds of the sick. That the licking of dogs cleansed and healed has been recognized since ancient times. These dogs were sacred, yet their flesh remained impure.

In many parts of the world people avoid eating dog flesh because they believe dogs are their ancestors. This belief emerged among early peoples of China, Indochina, and North America, whose myths typically featured dogs as fathers of individual persons or as founders of entire tribes. The Buriat of Siberia have a myth of a country where all human beings were born first as extremely large dogs, and the Aleuts say that they descended from a dog who fell from the sky. People in Southeast Asia also tell legends of their descent from dogs who married human princesses long ago. A legend from Indochina tells of a Yao king who was attacked by an invading army. He offered half his kingdom and his daughter's hand in marriage to anyone who could kill the enemy leader. A dog named P'an Hu killed the leader. The dog then married the king's daughter, and their children became the ancestors of the Yao people. (Darby et al. 1977; Leach 1961; Simoons 1994)

See also Blood and Flesh; Meat

destroyed, and while the eggplants of Sodom appeared plump and ripe on the outside, an insect invaded the inside, causing the pulp to decay and create a powdery substance inside the seemingly perfect skin. Farmers later learned what destroyed these fruits and how to combat the insect infestations; but early on, people could only speculate on the cause. They knew that God reduced the evil city of Sodom to ashes, so they easily attributed a similar evil to the ash-producing fruits they found growing there. The ancient Jewish historian Josephus called the eggplant the "apple of Sodom," and people believed the food unfit to eat. Josephus interpreted the presence of the fruit along the Dead Sea as evidence of the corruption of Sodom's inhabitants.

Today, however, eggplant is common fare throughout the Middle East, as well as in India, where it is called *brinjal* and incorporated into many dishes. Though Hindus today use eggplant readily, in past times they too banned its use. They likened eggplants, along with potatoes, onions, and garlic, to flesh foods. In fact, they believed that eggplants turned into meat: They had a reddish color, like blood; a shape resembling a human head; and perhaps most importantly, a fleshy consistency when cooked. This made such foods unsuitable to Vaishnavas (devotees of Vishnu) or to anyone dedicated to vegetarianism and the concept of ahimsa, or noninjury to living creatures; and certainly to anyone who believed, as did Pythagoras and his followers, that vegetables had souls. It also made eggplants unsuitable offerings to the gods.

Eggplants were unacceptable foods for peoples of the Jain religion, who avoided not only eggplant but all foods that grew in bulbous forms, including roots, mushrooms, and onions. The Jains believe that plants that produce fruit having a bulbous form contain living organisms, so they never intentionally destroy such plants. They also see a similarity between such fruits and human heads. They

EGGPLANT

The eggplant belongs to the nightshade family, and although most foods in the nightshade family (such as potatoes and tomatoes) originated in the Americas, the eggplant comes from India and Southeast Asia, where it grew in a variety of forms and colors. The eggplants that first reached northern Europe had fruits that resembled eggs, and were not purple like the common eggplants today, but white or yellow, somewhat like swans' eggs. Because eggplants were nightshades and because people believed the purple bulbous kind resembled mandrakes more closely than eggs, these foods suffered a lack of respect for a long time. Mandrakes, like most nightshades, were poisonous, so at one time, people thought eggplants were too. They became known as mad apples because people believed that eggplants made those who ate them insane.

The myths and legends surrounding eggplant substantiated the fears people had of eating them. Some scholars have identified eggplants as the Dead Sea fruit of the Bible and of John Milton's *Paradise Lost,* in which fallen angels wandered by the Dead Sea in hunger and found purple fruits that looked delicious, but upon eating them discovered that the pulp of the fruit turned to ashes. This strange legend may have a factual basis. Eggplants indeed grew along the Dead Sea near Sodom, the biblical city of sinners that God therefore consider the consumption of bulbous fruits tantamount to blood sacrifice. One Hindu sect has been known to ban eggplant not because the vegetable resembles a head but the scrotum of a water buffalo. These people, the Satnami of central India, regard the water buffalo as an impure animal, a dark being connected with death and the forces of the underworld. (Heiser 1969; McDonald 1971; Simoons 1998)

See also Garlic; Mandrakes; Meat; Nightshades; Onions and Leeks; Potatoes; Tomatoes

EGGS

Because eggs embody the essence of life, people from ancient times to the modern day have surrounded them with magical beliefs, endowing them with the power not only to create life but to prophesy the future. Eggs symbolize birth and are believed to ensure fertility. They also symbolize rebirth, and thus long life and even immortality. Eggs represent life in its various stages of development, encompassing the mystery and magic of creation.

Creation myths commonly describe how the universe hatched from an egg, often laid by some mythical water bird swimming in the primordial waters. In Hindu myth, Prajapati fertilized the primordial waters and created a golden egg with Brahma inside. In Oceanian myth, humans emerged from eggs, as did P'an Ku of Chinese myth—the primordial giant whose body parts formed the world. In Egyptian myth, the Nile goose laid the cosmic egg, and Ra, the sun god, hatched from it. Early mythmakers viewed both the sun and the egg as the source of all life; the round, yellow yolk even symbolized the sun. Clearly, eggs had great symbolic potential. From cosmic eggs miracles arose—the sun, human beings, gods, the earth, the sea, and the sky. In the Egyptian myth, Ra arose from the cosmic egg, in turn creating Geb the earth god and Nut the sky goddess. In Europe of pagan and Christian times, eggs symbolized life and resurrection.

Human beings have long consumed eggs of all sorts—of hens, ducks, geese, partridges, pigeons, pheasants, ostriches, peacocks, and other bird species. In legends, fairies consumed eggs of mythical birds such as the phoenix. People ate eggs for a variety of reasons. Some sought to absorb their magical properties by eating them. Others ate them to ensure fertility. In the Slavonic and Germanic lands, people also smeared their hoes with eggs, in the hope of transferring the eggs' fertility to the soil. Some marriage and fertility rites even today involve the use of eggs in some manner. In Iran, brides and grooms exchange eggs. In seventeenth-century France, a bride broke an egg when she first entered her new home. In China, people give mothers of new babies eggs so that they will continue to produce—they believe eggs have that kind of magic.

Sometimes, however, fertility magic imposed a taboo on eating eggs. In fact, the earliest reason for rejecting eggs as food stemmed from the belief that injury would befall people who ate fertility symbols. In legends of the Ibibo of Nigeria, the first women on earth were barren, and the goddess of heaven gave them eggs to make them fertile. But they couldn't eat these eggs. If they did, their goddess would take back her gift, and the women would lose their fertility.

The perception of eggs as symbols of fertility and embodiments of life force compelled people of certain cultures not only to shun them as food but to avoid destroying them at all costs. The Druids believed that eating eggs destroyed their vital principle; and Orpheus and Pythagoras listed eggs as forbidden foods for this same reason. Some people avoided eating eggs laid by their tribal totems; certain groups of aborigines in Australia, for instance, believed they descended from the emu, so they placed strict taboos on eating the eggs of these ancestral birds. To these people, emu eggs were even more taboo than emu flesh, due to their belief that the totem's life force resided in the eggs. Other groups of people based their egg avoidance on beliefs of other sorts. Inhabitants of the Mackenzie Delta in Canada believed that eggs caused disease. Many Africans, including the Ibibo of Nigeria, believe that eating eggs condemns a woman to barrenness.

Though people frequently forbade the eating of eggs, eggs were often used for divining purposes. Their widespread use in divination likely stemmed from the belief that they symbolized life—particularly, potential life in the future. The Chinese and certain tribal groups in southern Asia used the eggs of chickens or ducks to divine the future. One method involved painting the eggs, boiling them, and reading the patterns in the cracks. Another method involved tossing the eggs, and divining the future based on whether or not the eggs broke. Europeans frequently divined the future with eggs, a process known as oomancy. These early diviners knew that within the egg lay the potential for life and even magic but that they themselves had to learn to use that magic and to interpret the signs revealed to them in this mysterious object.

The concept of eggs as life symbols went hand in hand with the concept of eggs as emblems of immortality. Easter eggs, in fact, symbolize immortality, and particularly the resurrection of Christ, who rose from a sealed tomb just as a bird breaks through an eggshell. The connection between eggs, life, and immortality led people to offer eggs to the dead, who were thought to desire to return to life. The early Russians and Swedes left eggs in tombs for similar reasons, as an emblem of immortality and a symbol of new life. Jewish tradition also contains similar usages. The Jews traditionally served eggs at Passover as a symbol of sacrifice and rebirth. (*Funk and Wagnall's* 1972; Jones 1995; Newall 1971; Simoons 1994, 1998; Toussaint-Samat 1992)

See also Chicken

ELDERBERRIES

The elder tree and its berries have suffered a poor reputation in myths and as symbols, particularly in Great Britain. Spirits inhabited el-

der trees, the people said, and those spirits were particularly vengeful. To those who believed in evil spirits, the elder spirits posed such a threat that the people dared not chop down the elder tree or burn its wood for fear of the spirits' revenge. The traditional belief that Judas hanged himself on an elder tree (though some scholars maintain that it was a fig tree) added to that fear. Such legends might well explain why the quality of elderberries has diminished over the centuries: The popular neglect of and disregard for the species seems to have resulted in a decline both in the flavor and in the size of the berries.

People in much of western Europe embraced various folk beliefs about the elder tree. West Europeans have long considered the tree a plant of ill fortune, the abode of witches and fairies, or of evil spirits of other sorts. People hesitated to bring elder wood into the house for fear that ghosts would come in with it, and they hesitated to burn elder logs for fear the devil would come and perch on their chimneys. Some people believed that burning elder wood would bewitch them, or that sleeping under an elder tree would cause them to dream of death. Elderberries are dark red or deep purple in color, and in Scottish legend, the dwarf elder only grew on ground that had been saturated with blood.

People clung to all sorts of beliefs about the berries and the wood. They believed that picking the berries would turn them to stone, or that in order to pick them, a person had to first ask the tree's permission. Because Christians linked the elder tree with Jesus, elderberries symbolized sorrow, for not only did Judas hang himself on the tree but Christ's cross was said to have been made of elder wood. Some people believed that this made the wood smell bad, and they feared that if they slept under the elder tree, the smell would poison them.

The elder tree held a curious place in the folk traditions of Europe; it was both feared for its connections to malevolent beings and prized for its protective powers. In much of England people thought the elder tree attracted

In Christian legend, Judas was said to have hung himself on an elderberry tree. This may have been one reason people came to view the tree as a symbol of misfortune. (The Pierpont Morgan Library / Art Resource, NY)

evil spirits; but in much of Scotland, people thought the tree drove evil spirits away. Some believed the tree could alert people to the activities of witches. Many considered elderberries a curative and used them medicinally, or made wine from their juice. In Danish folklore, the elder tree was said to be inhabited by Elle Woman, or Hylde Moer, a dryad or wood nymph; and people had to apologize to Elle Woman before they cut even one twig of her wood. People attached these twigs to cattle sheds to keep evil away from the animals. They also gathered elder leaves and attached them to doors and windows to keep witches out of their houses.

Elderberries grow in much of North America as well as in Europe, and in North America too people incorporated the "magic" of these fruits into their lore and legends. The Tsimschian of the American Northwest assigned the shrub a crucial role in their myth of creation. The Tsimschian said that in the beginning of the world, the elderberry argued with a boulder over who would give birth to the human race. Raven instructed the elderberry to give birth first, so it was the elderberry from which human beings arose. The Tsimschian apparently felt it necessary to explain why people did not live very long, and they understood that elderberries did not live long either. In contrast, boulders did. If the boulder had won the battle, people would live a long time; but as it was, the elderberry won, so the Tsimschian people die. Not only did this legend explain the reason for the short life span of human beings but it also explained why the elderberry grows on graves. (Daniels 1971; *Funk and Wagnall's* 1972; *Oxford Dictionary of Plant-Lore* 1995; Reed 1992)

See also Blackberries; Blueberries; Cranberries; Figs; Gooseberries; Mulberries; Raspberries; Strawberries

FIGS

Magic figs and fig trees abound in myths, legends, and folktales. Fig trees provided a staple food to many ancient peoples, and the sap these trees produced seemed to them as miraculous a substance as the milk of holy goddesses. Both the fig tree and its fruits were revered in all countries of southwestern Asia, Egypt, Greece, and Italy, but not always for their ability to provide food. Fig trees fed the deities and housed their spirits. The trees symbolized peace, abundance, fertility, and enlightenment. Muslims considered the fig tree the most intelligent tree of all, and throughout the ancient world, people revered it as the Tree of Life and Knowledge.

Because the fig tree grew abundantly in much of the Old World, the fig was one of the most widely revered fruits. The tree was considered a great provider, and in many cultures it was viewed as a manifestation of the mother goddess. Hindus considered the pipal fig tree the mother of Lord Krishna; and the ancient Persians considered the udumbara fig tree the mother of their sun god, Mithra, who fed on its fruits and clothed himself in its leaves. The Romans worshiped their fig tree as a mother goddess and named the tree after Rumina, the goddess of nursing, because of the tree's milky sap. The Egyptians considered the sycamore fig the tree of their goddesses Hathor and Nut and the mother of Horus.

Ancient Egyptian paintings show Hathor and Nut as sycamores suckling the king with their sacred milk. The Egyptian pyramid texts describe figs as divine foods and as incarnations of Hathor and Nut. Figs were among the fruits most commonly buried in Egyptian tombs and depicted in tomb reliefs and paintings, because they were considered a desirable food to carry into the afterlife.

Some of the Egyptian tomb reliefs show monkeys in the branches of fig trees, throwing figs into the baskets of peasants and eating some of the fruit themselves. The sycamore fig of Egypt, also known as the Egyptian mulberry, produced a lot of fruit, and nearly year-round, so most likely these reliefs showed monkeys feeding peasants because these trees provided a valuable source of food for the poor.

The Greeks and Romans valued their fig trees as much as did the Egyptians. One Greek myth credits the introduction of the fig to Dionysus (in Roman myth, this role is attributed to Bacchus). The Greeks offered the first figs of the season to Dionysus, and the images they created of the god often showed him crowned in fig leaves. Another Greek myth credits the introduction of the fig to Demeter, the goddess of agriculture. King Phytalus treated the goddess so kindly and so hospitably that she rewarded him with a fig tree, the first in ancient Athens, and she taught him how to cultivate it. The ancient Greeks said that this first fig tree marked the sacred road to Eleusis and served as the parent tree of Athens. The Greeks feasted on figs at banquets, stuffed them inside sacrificial animals, and commonly offered them to the gods. Athenaeus, a Greek epicurean of the second and third centuries, thought the fig tree native to Greece, but most likely it came from farther east, where the fruit grew in abundance.

Two of the most sacred fig trees of the world continue to hold prominent places in the myths and rituals of India. Hindus traditionally

The Tree of Bodhi, one of the most sacred fig trees of the world. Pious Hindus and Buddhists revere the tree, believing that it housed their most venerated gods. (Alinari / Art Resource, NY)

revered both the pipal tree (*pipal* to the Hindus, but *bo* or *bodhi* to the Buddhists)★ and the banyan as immortal incarnations of their most powerful gods. The pipal and the banyan tree received reverence not for their food value but because in myth they housed the gods, and in Vedic times, the gods assembled beneath their branches. Brahma took up residence under the banyan tree, and Vishnu was born beneath the pipal. Lakshmi, Vishnu's wife, and Lord Krishna, his best-known avatar or incarnation, took up residence beneath the pipal tree as well. In Buddhist myth, the Buddha himself achieved enlightenment under the banyan fig, and the tree sheltered and provided for him all the while.

After the Buddha became enlightened, the fig tree itself became the tree of enlightenment and a symbol of Buddha's divine gift of wisdom. Such important mythological events obviously elevated fig trees to high status. In India, the trees grow tall and their branches spread out wide and provide shelter from the brutal heat of the sun. Not only did the fig tree shelter Buddha, but in Estonian legend it sheltered Jesus, and some Christians say this is why the tree became an evergreen. In Roman myth, the fig tree sheltered the first princes, Romulus and Remus, who washed ashore on the banks of the Tiber River. When in Hindu myth the Deluge destroyed the world, Krishna remained at the top of a fig tree, which reached high above the flood waters. Because the fig tree sheltered Vishnu and protected him, Hindus today perform ceremonies un-

---

★In Sanskrit literature, the pipal or bodhi tree is often called the *asvattha*.

der its branches, just as their ancestors did. Those who worship Vishnu in the form of a fig tree believe they can invoke their great god, who then manifests himself during their rituals.

In folktales, fig trees housed other kinds of supernaturals as well, including gods of lesser power, spirits of the dead, genies, and demons. In the lore of Central Africa ancestral spirits lived in fig trees, and in the lore of Australia the Yara-ma-yha-who, an odd little red man who lived in the fig tree, pounced on children and swallowed them whole. People of many cultures considered their fig trees wishing trees. The ancients used to pray under fig trees for protection against disease and for deliverance from evil, as well as for health, wealth, happiness, and fertility. The connection between fig trees and fertility should not be underestimated. The white sap conveyed procreative energy, and the ancients connected it to both milk and semen. The Hindus identified their fertility goddess Lakshmi with the sacred fig; they believed she inhabited the tree, as did Shashthi, a goddess of childbirth whom Hindus worship as a banyan branch laden with fruit. They therefore appeal to the banyan to help them conceive and bear children. People in parts of Africa use the sap of their fig trees in ointments they believe protect them against barrenness and stimulate their breasts to produce milk. People throughout the world held fig trees sacred, both for their fertilizing powers and for their connection to knowledge. Just as the Buddha gained knowledge under the tree, people in other parts of the world did as well. In a myth from Australia, for instance, a man fell asleep under a fig tree and dreamed of an important song and dance, which he then taught his sons and they in turn taught to other tribes.

The fig and fig tree were hallowed as universal trees of life and knowledge in many ancient religions. In ancient Babylon, the fig goddess was often depicted as the pivot of the world, a tree with roots in the underworld and branches in heaven. In Polynesian myth, the first banyan tree existed on the moon, and

Hina, the moon goddess, took bark from this tree to make tapa cloth for the gods. She had a parrot who lived in the tree and ate the figs. Once Hina accidentally broke a branch off the tree, and it drifted through the air and down to earth, where it took root. This became the first banyan tree on earth, and the Tree of Life for many Oceanian peoples. (Condit 1947; Darby et al. 1977; Goor and Nurock 1968; Gupta 1991; Hewett 1907; Simoons 1998; Toussaint-Samat 1992)

See also Dates; Milk

FISH

Fish is one of the oldest foods, but not all ancient peoples with fish available to them chose to eat these creatures. Many, in fact, strictly avoided them. Mythical associations with fish ranged from evil water snake to lovely goddess of fertility and abundance. Some cultures shunned fish because fish were believed to harbor impurities; others revered them as emblems of immortality and regeneration.

In times past, people who avoided eating fish appeared to have reasons largely grounded in myth. Many of the myths centered around the notion of sacred water and the notion that the fish who swam in sacred waters were sacred too, so eating them would certainly violate their sanctity. People of ancient Greece refused the fish in their sacred waters. Hindus living long ago in India refused to eat fish from their sacred rivers and ponds. In India today, the taboo against eating fish has more to do with ahimsa, the Hindu doctrine of nonviolence and the respect for life. But in some cultures, people still believe that fish embody water's supernatural force. Some Africans believe that their ancestors live within fish bodies. Fish totems are venerated also among Native Americans of the Pacific Northwest. In the Americas, certain tribes banned fish eating for other reasons as well. The Zuni and the Hopi refused to eat fish because they considered their waters sacred. The Navajo considered the waters the property of a great water monster who would punish people severely if they killed and ate any of his children.

The ban on fish eating in ancient Egypt also was based in the mythology of water. Creatures of the deep were eerie, if not inherently evil. Some people in other parts of the African continent as well as in India saw fish as impure and associated them with evil snakes and serpents that slithered through the waters. The early Egyptians ate fish, but over time these creatures gradually lost favor as food. Commoners continued to eat them, but priests and kings abstained. The priestly avoidance of fish has been attributed, at least in part, to the identification of the fish with the evil god Seth, and the battles this god fought with Osiris and his son Horus. When Osiris inherited the throne of Egypt, Seth went into a jealous rage, killed Osiris, and threw him into the Nile. Three fish—the Oxyrhynchus, the Phagrus, and the Lepidotus, or Nile perch—are said to have devoured Osiris's penis. It was said that Seth's companions had turned themselves into fish to avoid Horus's wrath. This mythological incident led to a dual perception of fish in Egyptian thought. On one hand, the fish gained sanctity because by eating Osiris it absorbed the god's powers. But on the other hand, the fish emasculated the fertility god and was thus considered an abomination. Viewing fish both as sacred and as an abomination, the priests and followers of Osiris never ate them. The followers of Seth worshiped fish, erecting bronze statues of them in their centers of worship. Modern-day archaeologists who have discovered mummified bodies of Nile perch believe that these mummies, along with fishing scenes depicted on ancient artifacts, indicate a prevalent fishing culture: The sanctity of fish to some early Egyptians is certain, but fish clearly provided food for many others.

Fishing cultures around the globe that relied on the sea to provide food associated the sea, and the fish, with abundance. Numerous fish gods populate the pantheons of the Oceanian lands. One of the highest of these gods is Ku-ula-kai, the god of the sea's abundance. Ku-ula-kai once lived on earth as a man in Maui, and it was there that he built the world's first fish pond and taught his son Aiai how to control the fish and set up altars to the fish gods. In Maori thought, fish were intended to be caught and eaten. In myth, the Pacific Islands themselves had once existed as fish, before Maui, the culture hero, fished them up from the depths of the ocean. While people of other lands certainly recognized the fertility of the sea, the land-from-fish myth was a particularly overt reference. Furthermore, Tangaroa, the Maori sea god, served not only as the father of fish but in some areas as the primary creator god. He emerged when earth and sky separated, and all landforms and living things were formed from his body.

Polynesian food myths often center on Hawaiki, a mythical land of ancestors that existed in the East, where the sun rose. The Polynesians envisioned this land as the source of life and fertility. In myth, human life originated in Hawaiki, and many foodstuffs did as well; the ancestors brought food plants from this land to give to the people. Some of the most valued food plants grew wild on Hawaiki before people learned to cultivate them, including taro, gourds, and kumara, or yams, the most valued food plant of all. Even fish had their mythical origin in Hawaiki. Some Polynesian food myths explained that the fish that filled the oceans originated in an undersea spring near Hawaiki. Tangaroa continues to send them from this spring into the other waters and into the nets of fishermen, to provide food.

People connected fish with fertility not only because they came from the waters but because they reproduced prolifically. The symbolism of fish therefore went hand in hand with the symbolism of water, as both water and fish represented fecundity and abundance. To the Dogon of West Africa, the fish is a phallic symbol, and is therefore connected with love and sex. Some consumed it to ensure fertility, and others simply as an aphrodisiac. In

Rome, the worshipers of Venus ate fish as an aphrodisiac every Friday on her worship day; Venus was the Roman goddess of love and sex, and fish were sacred to her.* Venus, like the Hindu love goddess Lakshmi, rose from the sea water.

The people of Assyria, in worshiping their fertility goddess Atargatis, never ate fish, though they did sacrifice them to her. They believed that long ago a fish from the Euphrates River pushed an egg ashore that contained Atargatis, who then hatched from the egg. The emergence of Atargatis legitimated the connections between water, fish, life, birth, and immortality. In India, fish symbolized spiritual rebirth, a metaphorical emergence from the dark waters, and in Christian symbolism, the fish represents the soul. This idea apparently stemmed, once again, from the connection of fish with its waters. Fish emerged from the rivers and seas just as the Christian soul arose from the baptismal waters—and as Jesus himself arose from the dead. Furthermore, fish was the first food Jesus is said to have eaten after his resurrection, and thus it became one of the symbols of the Eucharistic meal. (Darby et al. 1977; Norman 1972; Simoons 1994; Soyer 1977; Toussaint-Samat 1992; Wilkins et al. 1995)

See also Salmon; Water; Whale

FLOWERS

Edible flowers of all sorts have made their appearances in myths and legends. In the past, people consumed many types of flowers—candied, or in salads, teas, and wines—and they often used them as people use herbs and spices today. For centuries, flowers flavored puddings, custards, tarts, liqueurs, candies, syrups, and stuffings for fowl. People ate them both raw and cooked. People today don't think of flowers as food, yet they eat flowers regularly without

realizing it. Broccoli and cauliflower, for instance, are flower buds; the exotic spice saffron comes from a crocus; and the popular vanilla flavoring comes from a species of orchid.

One of the most common culinary uses of flowers in general and roses in particular was in brewing tea. Bitter root-bark tea made from roses was popular, as were teas made from peonies, carnations, marigolds, jasmine, and chamomile flowers. The English and the Irish made both tea and wine from dandelions. They considered the flowers medicinal, and magic as well, particularly those dandelions gathered on St. John's Day, which reputedly had the power to keep away witches. Wildflowers have always seemed mysterious and magic, so people frequently associated them with sorcery and witchcraft, and with mysterious beings like fairies and nymphs who inhabited forests and lived among the flowers. In Teutonic myths, fairies or dwarves had custody of roses, and people knew they had to ask the little people for permission before they picked them. In the Middle Ages, an inebriating drink brewed with flowers as a main ingredient made people believe they could actually see fairies. In Homer's *Odyssey,* the Lotophagi Odysseus encountered on the African coast ate from the lotus trees, the flowers of which had seemingly magic properties. When Odysseus's companions ate of the lotus, they entered a state of euphoria and lost their memories. In Greek myth, these two lotus trees from which the travelers ate were at one time nymphs—one named Lotis, and the other, Dryope.

The association of flowers with magic led to their use in charms and amulets. Some flowers used for charms worked to avert evil, and others worked to incite the powers of love. People consistently used orchids in amulets, and people of the British Isles used marigolds in love charms. The Aztecs believed marigolds had particularly strong magical powers, and they connected them to Xochequetzal, their love goddess and goddess of the dead. The Aztecs connected marigolds with death, because according to legend, they arose from the blood of their

---

*Christians, on the other hand, ate fish on Friday for the opposite reason. They believed that meat incited passion but that fish quelled it.

A London chef plucks petals from a large flower head. The petals will be boiled with milk, butter, cornflower, and seasonings to make chrysanthemum soup. (Hulton Deutsch Collection/Corbis)

people who were killed by the Spanish invaders. Aztecs offered marigolds to their dead, a practice that people continue to perform on the Day of the Dead, or All Souls' Day. Other people connected marigolds to love because they believed them to be potent aphrodisiacs.

People in many parts of the world considered flowers aphrodisiacs—primroses, violets, and hawthorn, for instance—which they commonly ate candied. Some people consumed periwinkles to evoke the love powers, and some consumed them with powdered earthworms and meat to intensify their powers. The Japanese considered chrysanthemums life prolongers because they were connected with the sun; they customarily soaked the petals of the flower in sake, another life prolonger, and ate them at the chrysanthemum festival. Other people considered certain types of flowers particularly effective for warding off evil—like the lavender, a flower of the mythological witches Hecate, Medea, and Circe, and the peony, which the Greeks named after Paeon, the physician to the gods. The Greeks thought the peony of divine origin, and believed it warded off storms and other harmful occurrences.

Roses and orchids enjoyed popularity in myths and legends, and both have served as food and medicine since ancient times. The rose has been consumed consistently since these early days. The fruit of the rose, called hips, contains twenty times the vitamin C of oranges. The fruit, the roots, the leaves and petals, and the bark of the rosebush have been used to make all kinds of foods, from soups and salads to teas and desserts. Many folktales tell of people who were placed under magic spells and turned into animals, then returned to their human forms after consuming roses.

The rose, originally from Persia, symbolized joy, and the ancient Greeks and Romans associated it with the love goddesses Aphrodite and Venus. The ancients considered both roses and orchids aphrodisiacs. There are more than 30,000 species of orchids in the world, and many of them were considered magic. Satyrion

is the best-known species of orchid and traditionally was thought to be an aphrodisiac food of the satyrs, the sex-starved companions of Dionysus. Some people believed that anyone who ate this species of orchid would become a satyr. The belief in the orchid's aphrodisiac powers likely stemmed from the knowledge that certain species of the flower have a pair of tubers that the ancients connected with testicles. The name orchid comes from the Greek word orchis, which means testicle; and the symbolism and beliefs surrounding the flower stemmed from its physical appearance. Perhaps the belief in the rose's aphrodisiac powers stemmed from its association with Venus. Legends say that the rose sprang from the tears of Venus as a divine gift in celebration of her rising from the sea foam. (Baumann 1993; Cavendish 1994; Elkhort 1991; Norman 1972; Skinner n.d.)

See also Herbs; Lotus; Ololiuqui; Saffron; Sunflower Seeds; Tea; Vanilla

FROGS AND TOADS

Frogs and toads had deep mythological significance to peoples of the ancient world. For example, the ancient Maya and their predecessors in the South American rain forests revered toads, probably valuing them more for their hallucinogenic properties than for their usefulness as food. Certain toads secrete a poisonous substance from parotid glands under the skin around their necks, which when ingested by people commonly causes convulsions, breathing difficulty, fainting, cold sweats, paralysis, and eventual death. Early people discovered this poison long ago, and they quickly put toads to use in creating deadly potions and poison for their arrows.

The poisonous substance secreted by toads is an alkaloid called bufotenine, and today scientists know that it occurs in other plants and animals as well as in toads. In large doses bufotenine can kill people; but in small doses it causes hallucinations, altering brain function in ways that ancient peoples readily perceived as magic. The ancient Maya probably experienced this magic. Archaeologists have unearthed the bones of toads at human burial sites and discovered frequently recurring frog and toad motifs in ancient Mayan art relics, generally in religious or ceremonial contexts. Many of the relics depict the toads with enlarged parotid glands and with scrolls swirling from the glands, apparently portraying the emission of the potent, magical substance.

Many scholars believe that the Maya frequently engaged in magico-religious inebriation, and that they likely used toads and their bufotenine secretions to achieve the otherworldly state that they thought enabled them to commune with the gods and spirits. Some scholars who have researched the psychotropic drug use of the ancient Maya believe that they added toad poison to their maize beer, and that they steeped the toads in the fermented beverage to make it particularly potent. The toad is a common religious symbol in both North and South America, revered as a manifestation of the earth goddess, the creator and destroyer of life. In some myths, the toad serves as the earth itself, and the first food plants sprouted from her body. In Mexico, maize sprouted from the body of the toad; and interestingly, the early people of Mexico worshiped toads in connection with Chac, the rain god who controlled the growth of maize. The Maya considered the toad the messenger of Chac, in fact. Some scholars believe it possible that shamans consumed a potion made from the bufotenine secretions of these toad messengers in order to communicate with Chac and to influence him to release the rains and water the maize fields. Aztec priests may have had similar intentions when they entered a lake and swallowed live frogs, animals they appear to have connected to Chalchihuitlicue, their water goddess. (Dobkin De Rios 1974, 1976; Hamblin 1984; Miller and Taube 1993)

See also Mandrakes; Mushrooms; Nightshades; Thornapples

GARLIC

Garlic suffered a poor reputation in ancient legends because both the vegetables themselves and the people who eat them give off offensive odors. People believed that strong odors like that of garlic deeply offended the gods. In myth, fragrant perfumes and spices characterized the gods, and repugnant odors characterized demons. In Zoroastrian myth, for instance, Ahura Mazda, the god of light, smelled wonderful, but the evil Ahriman, his opponent, smelled putrid and rotten. It has long been believed that gods, like people, enjoy pleasant aromas. For this reason, people offered them frankincense and myrrh and fragrant foods of all sorts, and they burned aromatic oils and incense in sacred rituals.

People today may not consider the smell of garlic putrid or rotten, but some people of the past considered it so for several reasons. In the religions of India, people likened garlic and onions to flesh foods because they resembled human heads and because they contained lines that looked like veins. In India, this likeness, together with the pungent smell, led to the belief that demons desired garlic and onions just as they desired blood sacrifice. But the gods found them terribly offensive—they likened the odor of garlic to that of rotting meat. Because some people believed that meat—and by extension garlic—represented decay, they associated garlic with spirits of the

underworld and they believed that it smelled like death. In parts of India, people believed that when they smelled garlic, demons were rising from the underworld and invading their realm.

Throughout history, people of many cultures shunned onions because they associated them with evil. In Indian legends, garlic originated from the body of a demon. In Buddhist myth, garlic arose from the blood of a demonic spirit killed by the god Vishnu. In Islamic myth, garlic arose from the left foot of Satan when he left the Garden of Eden following the fall of man. The connection of garlic and onions with demons and devils made these foods suitable offerings to underworld spirits. It also created a particular concern with keeping them away from the gods. Higher-caste Hindus as well as Jains, Taoists, and Chinese Buddhists had concerns about garlic because adherents to these religions strove to attain the ritual purity they believed necessary to reach heaven. Polluting foods, they believed, kept them out of heaven, because decay and stench had no place in the realm of the gods. In Hindu India even today some people consider garlic, or even foods prepared with garlic, inappropriate foods, and certainly inappropriate offerings for their deities. Since antiquity, people concerned with pleasing the gods took care to keep anything malodorous out of their offerings and their temples. The pungency of garlic attested to its power, and its offensive smell revealed that the power it had contrasted with the will of the gods.

Ancient people used the power of garlic for myriad purposes, most aimed at removing evil influence. The ancient Persians fed garlic to the devil to drive him away. Ancient Italians wore garlic cloves as charms against the evil eye. Similar customs in practice today among the Greeks, Romanians, Arabs, and Turks indicate that people continue to adhere to the belief in garlic's power. Some believe it repels witches, vampires, and demons of all sorts. Long ago, people in India and England used garlic in exorcism rites, believing that people possessed by the devil could consume garlic to remove the demon from their bodies. This likely led to the use of garlic for medicinal purposes. Surely if garlic had the power to drive out demons, it had the power to cure diseases. After all, in ancient thought, demons brought disease. In Greek myth, the evil goddess Hecate had the power either to cure or to cause disease. The Greeks offered her garlic to rouse her powers, and because Hecate resided at crossroads, travelers often carried garlic to protect themselves from her evil influence.

The pungency of garlic and its association with death and decay made it both a powerful weapon and an impure food. People concerned with ritual purity understood garlic to violate their desired condition. They also knew that garlic had a reputation for arousing sexual desire—and sexual desire interfered with purity. Most people recognized stimulating properties in garlic, but many considered these powers a benefit rather than a vice. In classical Greece, athletes consumed garlic before competitions and warriors consumed it before battles. Even the warrior castes of Hindus consumed it, believing that it not only roused the senses but stimulated anger, encouraged combativeness, and promoted strength and bravery. Clearly these properties offered advantages. The stimulating powers of garlic led ancient peoples to employ it to instill vigor and fierceness not only in warriors but in their horses as well. This perception no doubt influenced the Romans to consecrate garlic to Mars, their war god. (Simoons 1998; Skinner n.d.)

See also Eggplant; Onions and Leeks; Spices

GINGER

Ginger, like cinnamon, cloves, and other aromatic spices, conjures up images of paradise. Fragrant smells help define the gods' nature; and ginger, fiery and pungent, evoked images of the mysterious Orient, the land of the East that the ancients called the Land of Spices and associated with the otherworld. People cultivated ginger in the East far back in antiquity; and in India, Southeast Asia, and China they consumed it in numerous forms, using it to flavor meats and oils and to make tea and wine. They also used it as a spice, a perfume, a medicine, and an aphrodisiac. Along with ginger's pungent aroma, its golden color and "hot" flavor added to its allure and prompted ancient people to link it with solar fire.

The ancients typically linked many spices with fire. In Greek mythology, the legendary phoenix built his nest and his funeral pyre out of spices; he burned himself up in the resulting flames and then arose anew, like the sun, from the ashes. The ancient Greeks knew the phoenix as the spice bird and believed that cinnamon came from phoenix nests, but they also connected ginger and other spices with the fiery power of the sun. Early people of India believed that ginger ignited Agni—the divine, creative fire that was linked to both earth and sky. The Mesopotamians appear to have connected ginger with dragons because of their legendary tempestuous nature and fiery breath.

Ginger carries a symbolism similar to that of cinnamon, cloves, turmeric, and saffron. Ancient people associated these spices with magic, and they credited magicians and shamans with controlling these spices and tapping into their powers. People in the South Pacific used ginger as a food, but they also used it prolifically in magical ceremonies. Healers on some South Pacific islands used ginger to cure disease; they chewed the gingerroot and then spat it out onto their patients. Shamans and magicians also frequently used ginger to drive out evil spirits. The South Pacific islanders knew of ginger's powers but believed that only experienced magicians could activate them. Sometime these magicians used ginger to effect love magic, as the golden color of ginger, combined with its fiery nature, connected it with heat and passion.

The phoenix of classical myths, who burned himself up in his own ashes, was similarly labeled the spice bird, a representation of ginger and other fiery spices. (Erich Lessing/Art Resource, NY)

Melanesians traditionally used ginger as a love charm, and the Chinese used it to arouse the passions and increase fertility. Since antiquity the Chinese have considered ginger a strengthening food, believing that it acts as a stimulant and increases sexual desire. (Chang 1978; Ratsch 1992; Simoons 1991)

See also Cinnamon; Saffron; Spices; Turmeric

GINSENG

Ginseng is indigenous to north China and adjacent lands. The peoples of this region since ancient times have assigned the ginseng root magical properties. The ginseng plant attracted attention in part because of the red color of its stem and berries, which symbolized blood and life force, and even more so because of the humanlike shape of its root. Ginseng has been credited with all kinds of magic, including the ability to cure impotence and sterility, heal the sick, promote longevity, and even revive the dead. In Chinese belief, the ginseng root contains part of the Great Spirit, so it possesses godly properties. Some legends say that it grows in paradise, on the Islands of the Blessed, and that the gods themselves first cultivated the magic herb and then brought it to earth to help relieve human suffering.

Perhaps no one assigns more significance to ginseng than do the Chinese. They consider this herb the material manifestation of the spiritual part of nature, and a panacea for all the ills that plague humankind. The plant's name comes from *gin,* which means man, and *seng,* which means essence, and derives from the Chinese belief that the root of the ginseng contains the essence of life, the yin and the yang, the forces of heaven and earth. Sometimes, the Chinese call ginseng the "root of lightning" because in legend, ginseng forms when lightning strikes a mountain stream and the stream disappears into the earth. The plant grows up on the spot, and thus contains the power of both fire and water. Whoever consumes the ginseng root, the Chinese say, absorbs the power of fire and water within his body, and that power is strong enough to cure physical ills, ensure long life, and even guarantee eternal life. Taoist magicians believed in this power and often used ginseng root in preparing elixirs of immortality.

Much of the power attributed to ginseng had to do with the humanlike shape of its root. The Chinese called it the "root of lightning" and the "man root," and they recounted legends of the plant's powers of transformation, its ability to leave the ground and assume either human or animal form. People who spotted animals or birds in the forest and then lost sight of them often believed they had seen a transformed ginseng plant; and in legend, beautiful young women who materialized in the forest often turned out to be ginseng in disguise. In one Chinese legend, the ginseng root grows more and more human in the course of 300 years, and eventually emerges from the ground in human form but with superhuman, white blood. Just a few drops of this blood can bring the dead back to life. But this ginseng spirit is difficult to capture, and his blood nearly impossible to obtain. Supernatural forces guard and protect the ginseng, and the spirit of the ginseng, whatever his form, does not want to be captured.

Many ginseng legends involve mountain spirits or other divinities of nature who guard and protect the herb and who use the root to benefit only the people who are worthy and pure of mind. In Korean legend, a young boy discovered the plant's healing powers when he prayed to the Mountain Spirit to save his dying father. The Mountain Spirit told the boy to go to a certain place in the mountains to harvest ginseng, and then use the root to make an elixir for his father to drink. The boy found the herb and made the elixir, and his father recovered. But because ginseng did have such powers, the spirits made sure that the wicked and greedy never received its benefits. In legend, ill-intentioned ginseng hunters wishing to sell the precious herb at outlandish prices never got their prize. In southern Manchuria particularly, ginseng hunters took to the mountains because wild ginseng from these parts did fetch outlandish prices on the market, and these people made it their mission to search for and procure the largest and most valuable roots. In legend, not only do the spirits of mountains and rivers protect the ginseng from the hunters, but tigers do as well—and the tigers often devour greedy people. The desire for wild ginseng permeated Asian cultures: The people were constantly searching for miraculous cures, and the legends indicated that ginseng could provide them. Once people learned of ginseng's powers, they cultivated the plant extensively, but found the cultivated plants not nearly so powerful as the wild variety that grew in the mountains. Only wild ginseng brought about miraculous cures, and only wild ginseng warranted the protection of tutelary deities.

Scores of ginseng hunters frequented the forests of Manchuria, and these people lived hard lives and faced dangers at every turn. Not all ginseng hunters were wicked; many were simply trying to make a living and were constantly exploited by collectors and retailers. The ginseng hunters were real, their stories legendary, and the legends they told revealed the dangers of their work and the difficulty they had in locating the precious herb. The legends also revealed a belief in the plant's magic. In Chinese legend, a sage named Lao-tse first discovered ginseng growing in southern China, but after he told his people about it, the plant disappeared from the south and re-appeared in the north. No one could locate the ginseng for a long time. Eventually, a young prince named Lao Khan-van found it again. But once again ginseng fled even farther north, into the inaccessible parts of the mountains. Ginseng spirits habitually retreated from their captors, just as ginseng roots often hid deep within the earth. In another legend, a boy named Ma-lin lived with his uncle, a particu-larly wicked ginseng hunter who treated the boy with merciless cruelty. A ginseng spirit, in the form of a young girl, revealed herself to Ma-lin, and when his wicked uncle learned of this, he forced Ma-lin to capture her. When the ginseng spirit ran away, the uncle killed the boy; but the ginseng spirit revived him with her healing powers and turned him into a ginseng spirit as well. The two ginseng spir-its then retreated together, farther and farther into the forest, until the wicked uncle, bent on capturing them, died of exhaustion. (Heffern 1974; Kimmins 1977; Ratsch 1992; Ricciuti 1978)

See also Herbs; Mandrakes; Turnips

GOAT, LAMB, AND RAM

People of many cultures traditionally per-formed animal sacrifice as a pious religious act. In much of the ancient world—particu-larly in the Middle East—goats, lambs, and rams were considered the most appropriate animals for sacrifice. Wandering herdsmen of the region tended large flocks of these ani-mals, and the people valued them highly as sources of food. The lambs, or young, of these animals became the most common sacrifice to the gods. Later, the sacrificial lamb became a symbol of the crucified Christ.

The goat may have been the earliest do-mesticated food animal. It also has been asso-ciated with magico-religious rites from prehistoric times. Scholars have discovered the bones of goats and sheep in Neolithic graves, indicating their use as burial offerings. In later times, the Greeks, Hebrews, Egyptians, and Africans all offered goats and sheep to the deities. The people of ancient Rome sacrificed goats at the Lupercalia, a fertility festival re-putedly established by Romulus and Remus. Lupercal was said to be the site where the she-wolf had suckled the legendary princes, and the sacrifice of goats on this site was believed to promote the fertility of the land and of women. Pagan rituals throughout Greece and Rome featured goat sacrifice, among them the festivals honoring Hera and Dionysus. The reason for this appears in the myths. Worship-ers of Hera sacrificed goats because in one myth, when Hera fled into the forest to es-cape the wrath of Zeus, the goat revealed her hiding place. Hera sacrificed the goat to pun-ish him. The followers of Dionysus sacrificed goats because in another myth Zeus turned Dionysus into a goat to protect him from the wrath of Hera. Hera attempted to kill the young god to avenge her husband Zeus for fathering Dionysus with Semele. The follow-ers of Dionysus considered the goat an ac-ceptable sacrifice because they sanctified it to their god. They tore live goats to pieces and devoured the raw flesh, and by doing so, sym-bolically assimilated the god's powers. The Pythagoreans considered the goat an accept-able sacrifice because it ate the vines of Dionysus and spoiled his grapes. Like the pig, which uprooted young seedlings and trampled plants, the goat destroyed the harvest and thus acted as an adversary to the gods.

The Hebrews as well as the Greeks con-sidered the goat an acceptable sacrifice. He-brew myths connect this animal with Azazel, the Hebrew equivalent of Pan, the Greek for-est god who had the legs, horns, and beard of a goat. Azazel acted wild and untamed; but whereas Pan inhabited the forest, Azazel in-habited the desert. In Hebrew tradition, on the Day of Atonement (Yom Kippur) a priest cast lots between two goats. One would be sacrificed to Yahweh and the other would be taken to the desert and released. The surviv-ing goat, Azazel, took on an important sym-bolic role. It became the proverbial scapegoat, carrying the sins of the people with it into the desert. The lamb sacrificed to Yahweh enjoyed a more far-reaching symbolism, however, especially when the Christians adopted it as a symbol of Christ. God sacrificed this "lamb" for the lives of his followers. The life of a lamb for the life of a human being. In Hebrew belief, on the Day of Atonement God decides who shall live and who shall die in the coming year, their lots symbolically intertwined with that of the two goats. The Old Testament indicates that God intended goats and rams for sacrifice. In the book of Genesis, Yahweh provided a ram for Abraham to sacrifice in place of his son Isaac; and in Jewish folklore, the ram had been caught in the thicket since the sixth day of creation, waiting for Abraham all that time. The Semitic peoples appear to have substituted animal for human sacrifice. They sacrificed a lamb every year at Passover, in commemoration of God's passing over the houses of the Israelites and sparing them while destroying the firstborn in each Egyptian family.

The Jewish celebration of Passover perhaps best illustrates a modern-day religious rite based on the symbolism of the sacrificial lamb. Most modern Jews don't sacrifice lambs as did the ancient Hebrews, but they incorporate a lamb bone or some kind of meat into their feast as a remembrance of the lamb their ancestors sacrificed before their exodus from Egypt. The Passover lamb, or Paschal Lamb, belongs to Yahweh, as Yahweh, the Lord, ordained its sacrifice in the Old Testament. He told the Israelites to take the lamb of either a sheep or a goat and slaughter and eat it. The Israelites consumed the lamb, and then began their exodus. At the time of this first Passover, most Jews had goats and sheep at ready disposal. The Israelites were desert shepherds during these times, and their families typically celebrated the advent of spring by offering one of their herd animals for sacrifice. In rites throughout the world, sacrifice always involved the surrendering of something of value—domesticated animals rather than wild ones, cul-

tivated plants rather than those given freely as nature's gifts.

Biblical myths often have parallels in pagan beliefs and practices, and many Hebrew traditions were preceded by more ancient Middle Eastern variants. For example, the sacrifice of lambs was practiced long before Passover, with these offerings being made to ancient sun gods. Later, the identification of Christ as the sacrificial lamb served this same purpose. Passover occurred in the spring, a time of renewal of light and life, a time to celebrate the sun's power of resurrection. In pagan mythology, the goat and the ram symbolized the reproductive powers of the sun. The ancient Egyptians sacrificed rams to Ra, their ram-headed sun god. The ram with the golden fleece in the Greek myth of Jason and the Argonauts symbolized renewal—specifically, the renewal of solar energy. It was this ram, this golden solar ram, that the Christians identified with Jesus. The resurrection of Jesus recalled the return of the sun god. Biblical references frequently refer to Jesus as the Lamb of God, the sacrificial lamb who died in the name of the Lord to take away the sins of the world. This recalls the Hebrew scapegoat turned out into the woods, the innocent that carried the sins of others. It also recalls the lamb that the Hebrews sacrificed before their exodus from Egypt.

The lamb symbolizes martyrdom, innocence, and purity: It trusts the shepherd that watches over it, even as it walks to the slaughter. In Hebrew myth, God was the shepherd and Israel was the lamb. The Israelites walked trustingly to the Promised Land. In legend, the Egyptian pharaoh dreamed that he put all the powerful princes and warriors of Egypt on one side of a scale, and one fatted lamb on the other side to balance it. Israel, the lamb, had more power than Egypt. So the Hebrews sacrificed the lamb to save Israel from bondage. They spilled the lamb's blood at Passover to signify their obedience to God. In Christian myth, God was the shepherd and Jesus was the lamb. Jesus was slaughtered and then resurrected to become the symbol of life, renewal, and the eternal light of the sun god.

The theme of resurrection appears time and time again in myths of slaughtered animals. In Norse myth, Thor, the thunder god, resurrected them directly. Thor drove his chariot from the celestial realm to earth, and stopped at a farmhouse for the night. Two goats led Thor's chariot, and at the farmhouse, Thor slaughtered the goats for dinner, indispensable to him as they were. But then the great thunder god returned the goats to life. The farmer and his family feasted on the goats, but at Thor's instructions, left the bone marrow untouched. Then Thor dressed the bone marrow in goat skins, waved his hammer over them like a magic wand, and resurrected his goats.

The Otherworld Cauldron that appeared in Norse myths has similar associations with resurrection. At Viking feasts, there were generally two cauldrons—one for mead and one for meat, and the contents of both were never exhausted. In Irish legends, pigs frequently filled the cauldrons, and the pigs of Manannan returned to life in the Irish myth of the Feast of Age. These pigs provided the Tuatha de Dana with inexhaustible supplies of food; they were sacrificed, then resurrected like the goats in the Norse myth. In the myths, meat and sacrifice existed side by side. (Cavendish 1994; Mercatante 1974; Winzen 1955)

See also Blood and Flesh; Chicory and Endive; Meat

GOOSE AND TURKEY

Feasting on geese has long been a tradition in the Old World, as is clear from ancient mythology. The prevalence of goose gods in numerous cultures attests to the ritual importance of geese and to the fact that these rituals date back to antiquity. Geese were common sacrifices to pagan gods, and ritual consumption of the bird followed the sacrifice. The goose feast that came to characterize holiday celebrations in later times arose as a modern-day derivative of these ancient rites and sacrifices.

People in Europe, Central Asia, North America, and North Africa customarily sacrificed geese, particularly at the turn of the seasons. Like other migratory fowl, geese appeared and disappeared at crucial times in the yearly cycle, so eating them customarily accompanied ceremonial events in the solar and agricultural year. People have linked geese to the changing seasons for so long that originally the goose served as a sacrifice to the spirit of vegetation, in thanks for the harvest. After the goose was ceremonially killed, participants in the sacrifice feasted on its flesh in a ritual that they believed would ensure the regeneration of the earth. The ancient Egyptians sacrificed geese to Isis and Osiris in autumn, and the priests of Isis and Osiris ate the gooseflesh. The Egyptians also sacrificed geese to Ra, the sun god. The Egyptians and people of other cultures recognized the goose as a solar symbol and identified it with sun gods like Ra, who emerged from an egg laid by a primordial goose in the waters of the Nile. Tales of the goose that laid the golden egg quite likely stemmed from these ancient myths with their solar symbolism.

The symbolic association of the goose with the sun led to the bird's use as a feast animal served at festivals connected with solar movement. Because the goose followed the sun when it flew south in the winter and north in the summer, the ancient Chinese considered the goose a representative of yang, the force of fire and solar power, and they consumed geese in rituals conducted at dusk and dawn. The Romanians consumed ducks at the spring equinox, because ducks too were migratory fowl whose predictable patterns and regular returns gave them seasonal significance. The Egyptians, Scandinavians, Celts, and Slavs all ate goose on seasonal feast days. Goose was served at the Celtic Samhain, or Halloween; the Germanic Yule, originally the first day of the new year; and Michaelmas, the ritual feast of the winter solstice. The Michaelmas feast is probably the most famous goose feast, apart from that at Christmas dinner. The goose served at Michaelmas and at Christmas links both holidays to pagan solar celebrations. Other holidays celebrated in the European lands involved feasting on geese as well. On St. Martin's Day, for instance, people in Bavaria dined on the goose and then divined by its breastbone whether the winter would be severe or mild, wet or dry.

Turkeys, native to the New World, were more plentiful than geese during the period of early settlement. American settlers served turkey at Thanksgiving, making it the seasonal feast bird. In much of the Western world today, turkeys have replaced geese also at the Christmas feast; but for all practical purposes, these two birds share the same symbolism. Just as people of the Old World connected geese to the sun, some of the North American tribes connected turkeys to the sun; and just as people in the Old World divined the weather with goose bones, people in the Americas assigned similar magic to "wishbones" from turkeys. (Armstrong 1959; Coe 1994; Toussaint-Samat 1992)

See also Chicken; Eggs

GOOSEBERRIES

Gooseberries grew wild in Europe long ago, and it appears that the Europeans didn't begin to cultivate them before the sixteenth century. If the Greeks and Romans knew of them, they left nothing in their literature to indicate it. Of course, they had so many grapes that gooseberries, in any case, may have seemed insignificant. The people who did not have grapes, however, used gooseberries to make wine as well as jams and jellies. The Europeans named these berries gooseberries because they traditionally ate them with goose.

As people learned the properties and uses of plants, they often surrounded those plants with beliefs and superstition. In some cases they seem to have borrowed or adapted myths about new or previously unknown plants from the lands in which those plants originated or were first put to use. For instance, the Euro-

peans used to say that babies were born under gooseberry bushes—a belief that might have originated farther east, in Iran. Scholars do find mention of gooseberries in legends from lands to the east of Europe; but currants—close relatives of gooseberries—also grow in the East, where they seem to have achieved a more prominent place in myth.★

According to an Iranian legend, the first humans came from a currant bush. Only one bush existed at first, but then it separated, and Ahura Mazda, the god of light, gave the two currant bushes a soul. The belief in a common soul that inhabited both plants and humans prevailed in Eastern religions. This belief gave birth to myths in which humans and plants changed forms. In the Iranian myth, two humans beings arose from the currant bush, Maschia and Maschiana, so the Iranians considered it sacred.

Similarly, Hindus held the Indian gooseberry bush sacred. In legend, the bush grew from the tears of two goddesses, Parvati and Lakshmi, who wanted so desperately to offer something new to Lord Shiva that they cried in frustration and the tree sprang up from their tears to provide an offering. The Sanskrit name for the Indian gooseberry is *dhatrica* or *dhatri,* which meant nursing mother. The fruit of the gooseberry gave nourishment, as did the mother goddesses. The Hindus associate it with both Shiva and Vishnu, and they worship the tree as a deity worthy of veneration and offerings in its own right. (Folkard 1892; Gupta 1991)

See also Blackberries; Blueberries; Cranberries; Elderberries; Mulberries; Raspberries; Strawberries

---

★What westerners today call kiwi fruit was once referred to as Chinese gooseberries. They aren't related to gooseberries, but people called them such because they believed they tasted similar. Chinese gooseberries, or kiwi fruit, are brown and fuzzy and much larger than other fruits designated as berries. They weren't imported to the United States until 1960, and came then via New Zealand, so westerners named them after the kiwi, a fuzzy New Zealand bird people thought they resembled.

GOURDS
See Pumpkins and Gourds

GRAIN

The discovery and cultivation of grain was of such crucial importance to human advancement that numerous ancient myths were devised to explain the growing cycle of grain. The Greeks told of the grain god Adonis, who died and returned to life each year. The Egyptians told of Osiris, who rose from the dead as the Nile River overflowed its banks and fertilized the land. Seasonally slain gods followed suit in many other myths of agricultural societies in both the Old World and the New, expressing the notion that grain died and then was resurrected. It sprouted like magic, like an immortal or a precious gift from the earth goddess, and for this reason commanded the reverence of all who consumed it.

One of the most convincing indications that the ancients worshiped grain was that they immortalized the earth goddess in the heavens. The zodiacal constellation Virgo represents this earth goddess, and the bright star Spica represents her ear of corn. Fifteen thousand years ago, Virgo marked the vernal equinox; the sun moved into Virgo just as spring arrived and the grain goddess returned from the underworld and renewed the earth. In Egyptian myth, the goddess Isis created the Milky Way when she scattered grain along her route. Scholars have connected agricultural goddesses with this prominent sky figure, including Isis of Egypt, Atargatis of Syria, Ishtar of Babylon, and perhaps the best-known fertility goddesses of all, the Greek Demeter and her daughter Persephone.

No discussion of the mythology of grain seems complete without a description of the Eleusinian Mysteries of the eastern Mediterranean, and the role of Demeter, the earth goddess. The Eleusinian Mysteries were the core of the most famous religion in antiquity, which included among its sacred rites a harvest festival and a celebration of the agricultural secret revealed in the myths and nature of Demeter. These myths are particularly significant in that they not only explained and reenacted the first grain harvest but also encapsulated an entire cosmology: This earth goddess destroyed the grain each winter, then resurrected it each spring. Those who worshiped Demeter and upheld the directives of her cult believed that she had the power to destroy and resurrect human souls. Because Demeter and her myth offered the promise of life after death, the cult of Demeter attracted eager initiates.

The best-known myth of Demeter and the one that led to the formation of Demeter's cult involved the abduction of her daughter Persephone by Hades, the god of the dead. Hades took Persephone underground to become his wife, but Demeter struck a bargain with the death god and convinced him to return Persephone to earth for part of each year. Persephone's story mirrors the growing cycle of grain: Like Hades's wife, grain is buried and remains underground each winter, and then rises from the ground to new life each spring. But the myth gets more complicated from there. It has been said that the cultivation of grain civilized humanity, and that every harvest marked the end of uncivilized prehistory and the beginning of history. Demeter was venerated for having taught people the art of grain cultivation, helping them to tame nature and to unravel nature's precious secret—the immortality of the earth. The cult of Demeter lasted hundreds of years; some observers have even discerned traces of its existence in the nineteenth century.

According to legend, Demeter discovered grain growing wild and taught people how to cultivate it. She used the sickle, the first harvesting tool, to do this—an instrument the ancient Greeks identified with the sky god Kronos, who castrated his father Ouranos and took over control of the world. The Titans were Ouranos's children; and because Demeter taught them to sow and reap, they appear to have represented human beings in their

The Rape of Persephone, one of the most celebrated myths of the ancient world. Persephone represented the spring, and after her abduction by Hades, the god of the underworld, the goddess remained underground for three months each year, then returned each spring, like the grain, to renew the earth. (Scala/Art Resource, NY)

primeval state. Demeter's instruction brought about the humans' advancement to an agrarian civilization. The annual harvest celebration, and the Eleusinian Games that accompanied it, reenacted the discovery of cereal food.

The Eleusinian Games are recognized not only for their commemoration of the first harvest but for their apparent connection to human progress. As part of the rituals, people threw stones to symbolize the sowing of grain. The grain was on the ground first, then it sprouted, as humans did when they learned to walk upright. The people who ate the grain at the harvest festivals propelled themselves forward by moving from a hunting and gathering culture to a farming one. By eating grains, primeval people become strong enough to lift the upper part of their bodies from the ground.

The Rites at Eleusis centered around Demeter and her stepson, Demophoon. Demeter fostered Demophoon (later identified with Triptolemus after Hades abducted Persephone), and Demophoon too represented the grain. Demeter grieved so much over the loss of her daughter that she burned the grain, represented by the burning of Demophoon. Demeter held the child in the fire and roasted him, much as one would roast grain. She did this in an attempt to make Demophoon immortal, to burn away his mortality as roasting grain preserved the grain but destroyed its ability to germinate. Demophoon's real mother intervened, however, and the child retained his mortality. He was not completely roasted, but retained a residue of procreative seed. Demeter lay Demophoon on the ground in an act symbolic of death. Demophoon had to die to produce new life. Some scholars believe that this disturbing myth paralleled the mythical origin of human life, the event the ancients reenacted each year at the annual harvest festival. People compensate for their mortality by producing offspring. They rise like grain from the ground. People who participated in the Eleusinian Games rose from the ground, and perhaps represented not only

Demophoon, who was reincarnated and multiplied, but the act that elevated human beings from their uncivilized, primeval state. The myth of Demophoon, the dying and rising god that represented the renewability of life in the grain, was paralleled by the Mesopotamian myth of Attis and by the Egyptian myth of Osiris and Isis (Egypt's Demeter). Early peoples of North America created the Corn Mother, and of South and Central America, the Maize God. These deities all represented grain, and all died and were resurrected. The prevalence of similar agricultural myths in all ancient societies reveals the fact that cultivation of grain transformed the world. (Frazer 1950; Toussaint-Samat 1992; Wasson et al. 1978; Wilkins et al. 1995)

See also Amaranth; Barley; Bread; Cake; Corn; Millet; Oats; Quinoa; Rice; Rye; Sorghum; Wheat

GRAPES

Since antiquity the grapevine has served as a symbol of the benevolent nature god. It was the gods' gift to human beings, full of the power to inspire and to lift the spirit to a higher realm. In ancient belief, the nature god revealed himself in the grapevine. The plant assumed such significance in life that people accepted it as symbol of peace and abundance, like wheat, barley, and fig trees.

Grapes have been cultivated in the Middle East since antiquity; indeed, the biblical "Promised Land" was often called the Land of Grapes. The fruit there was said to be enormous—both the size of the clusters and that of the individual grapes, which reportedly often grew as big as plums. All ancient peoples familiar with the grapevine seemed to assign it special significance. For many, grapes symbolized fertility. In Indian myth, they symbolized the yoni, the female genitalia, and therefore they also represent the goddess of the earth. The ancient Egyptians also considered grapes a fertility symbol and the grapevine a Tree of Life. One of their myths recounts how Isis, who in one capacity served as the goddess of magic and herbal lore, ate grapes and became pregnant with Horus. (Perhaps for this reason, the Egyptians called grapes "Horus's eyes.") Osiris, the brother/spouse of Isis, was said to have introduced the cultivation of grapes to his people. In myth, he was Egypt's first wine maker, and ancient papyri show his shrines decorated with grapes and vines.

Much of the symbolism of grapes has to do with their use in making wine. Because red wine resembles blood, grapes came to symbolize blood sacrifice. People thought them impregnated with soul substance, just as was commonly thought of soma and nectar and other beverages that represented the Water of Life in various early cultures. The Hebrews called grape juice "the blood of grapes"; later, for Christians, the blood of grapes came to symbolize the blood of Christ. Grapes and wine permeate Christian symbolism, with biblical references to vineyards, grapes, raisins, wine, and vinegar numbering in the hundreds. Christ likened himself to the vine, which later became an emblem of the Christian church and of the Kingdom of Heaven. He also likened God to a husbandman, and the people of the world to the vine's branches. From long ago, monks all over Europe grew grapes and made wine, and more than thirty saints have served as patrons of grape growers and wine makers, including St. Bacchus, St. Vincent, and St. Martin. Because wine represents the blood of Jesus, most of these saints were martyrs. It has been suggested that wine represents not only the blood of the vine and the blood of Jesus but also the tears of grape growers.

People of many cultures connected grapes and grapevines with some of their most celebrated gods and heroes. Christian and Jewish myths generally credited Noah with the

In Greece and Rome, the grape harvest marked the beginning of a celebration to honor Dionysus (Bacchus), the god of grapes and wine. (Scala/Art Resource, NY)

cultivation of the grapevine, and Egyptian myths gave Osiris this honor. In Persian myth, the grapevine sprang from the tail of the primordial bull slain by Mithras, and in Greek myth, it sprang from a stick buried by Orion's dog. But the most popular myth of cultivation features Dionysus, the jovial wine god, whom the people envisioned crowned with grape leaves and carrying a staff, or *thrysos,* wrapped in grapevines. According to legend, a snake taught Dionysus how to cultivate grapes and to make wine. Dionysus watched as a snake slithered around the grapevines and sucked the juice from the fruit, and he marveled at the red juice that spilled onto his chin. Seeing this, Dionysus picked the grapes, put them into a hollowed-out pit, and crushed them to extract the juice. Trampling grapes in a hollowed rock was the earliest method of wine making, and according to this legend, Dionysus invented it.

Once Dionysus succeeded in extracting the precious juice from his grapes, he poured the juice into a golden cup and offered it to the nymphs, the satyrs, and the Sileni, who then became his followers. According to Ovid, Ampelus was one of these followers. One day, when Ampelus was picking grapes from a vine that snaked up an elm tree, he fell from the tree and died. Dionysus placed him in the sky as a reward and turned him into the star Vindemiatrix in the constellation Virgo. The Latin *Vindemiatrix* (or *Protrygeter,* which means grape gatherer in Greek) is a relatively faint star, but in ancient times its rising at dawn in August marked the beginning of the grape harvest. The grape harvest has always been a time of celebration. When Vindemiatrix rose in the sky, the Greeks began a celebration honoring Dionysus. The nymphs and satyrs drank the nectar, and it dispelled their fears and cares and brought them unbridled joy. The euphoria the nymphs and satyrs felt when they consumed the juice of the grapes was temporary, yet it left a powerful impact. For a time, this wonder juice made them feel equal to the gods.

The worship of Dionysus, the vine god, in time developed into a powerful cult—so powerful, in fact, that Lycurgus, the king of Thrace, was said to have felt jealous and threatened. In one legend, Lycurgus destroyed the grapevines of Dionysus in a fury, only to discover that one of the grapevines was his own son. In another legend, Hera too flew into a jealous rage. Hera's husband, Zeus, had conceived Dionysus with Semele, the moon goddess, and this angered the queen of heaven so much that she turned Dionysus and his followers half mad. (Kerenyi 1976; Reed 1992; Schafer 1963; Toussaint-Samat 1992)

See also Wine

GUINEA PIGS

Most westerners today think of guinea pigs as pets, but people in parts of South America consume them on a regular basis, just as their ancestors did. To the ancient people of the Andes, guinea pigs were a primary source of protein, preferred over beef and alpaca. In fact, they were practically the only source of meat protein readily available for everyday use. Before the Spanish Conquest, the Inca and their predecessors had domesticated guinea pigs along with llamas, alpacas, dogs, and ducks, but guinea pigs were the primary source of food. They called these animals *cuyes,* and nearly every family raised them. The people used their domesticated cuyes not only for making common meals but for consumption during religious rituals.

The Inca and earlier Andean peoples were primarily agriculturists, but there is evidence that they domesticated guinea pigs as early as 5600 B.C. The people of the Andes originally raised guinea pigs exclusively for consumption on religious occasions. The cuyes took on a crucial ceremonial role in the religious celebrations of the Inca. People consumed the meat of these prized animals at various celebratory occasions throughout the year. Generally the celebrants consumed every part of the cuy except the hair, the bones, and the gall bladder. People in Peru, Ecuador, Bolivia, and Colombia continue to raise guinea pigs and to consume them on festive occasions. They feast on them during Corpus Christi, which includes a series of celebrations, and at *jaca tsariy,* which in some areas of Peru marks the beginning of celebrations honoring local patron saints, and which literally means "to collect cuyes."

The ritual use of cuy continues to play a large part in Andean culture. Diviners use cuyes to foretell the future; they believe these animals can alert people to impending death or illness by making certain sounds, and they believe the people can then prevent the death from occurring if they kill the cuy. Andean healers use these animals in folk medicine, and they highly value them for their role in diagnosing disease. The healers go through a variety of food-related rituals before diagnosing a patient. First they chew coca and drink chicha, their popular maize beer. Then they rub the patient's body with a live cuy, believing that either the cuy will squeak when it comes into contact with painful or disease-stricken parts of the patient's body or that the part on the cuy's body that correlates with the part of the patient's body will show some sign of disease. After the completion of this part of the ritual, the healer splits open the cuy's abdomen and uses the inner organs to diagnose the illness and determine a cure.

Ancient medicine often was based on superstition, myth, and ritual, and the ritual of the cuy provides a classic example. The consumption of cuy meat also had superstitious attachments. Because the Andean people typically believed the consumption of improper foods caused illness, they also believed the consumption of proper foods effected cures. They believed, for instance, that the meat of a black cuy could cure chest ailments such as pneumonia, bronchitis, and tuberculosis. (Bolton 1979; Morales 1995)

H

nuts sacred. The Germans put hazelnuts on windowsills to calm storms. They believed these nuts both embodied the lightning and averted it.

The ancients also used the wood from the hazel tree to make divining rods. Divining rods were Y-shaped and thought to have occult powers—the power to detect subterranean springs or treasure hidden underground, and even the power to summon demons. The art of divining with rods is called rhabdomancy. It was popular among the ancient Greeks and was practiced extensively in the Middle Ages. People assigned both the hazel tree and the nut itself divining powers. Perhaps because hazel rods were used to detect hidden treasures, hazelnuts were thought to attract wealth. Some people in Russia believed that keeping hazelnuts in the house would guarantee the acquisition of wealth.

HAOMA
See Soma

HAZELNUTS

Many beliefs about hazelnuts stem from ancient associations of nuts with fertility. Hazelnuts, or filberts, came from Europe and the Middle East, and in ancient times and in some European countries even today they are scattered at weddings to bestow fruitfulness on the newly married couple. Over the ages, people developed numerous superstitions about hazelnuts—many of them connected with fertility, others stemming from the hazel tree's ability to blossom twice in one year. In Germanic lore, for instance, hazelnuts are considered symbols of immortality.

Some early Europeans associated hazelnuts with romantic love, birth, and lightning, all of which relate to fertility. Early peoples used hazelnuts in divinations relating to love and marriage, and they carried hazel wands in wedding processions to ensure numerous offspring in the marriage. They believed in the power of the hazelnut to bestow fecundity in people, animals, and plants alike. Lightning, too, made the earth fertile with the power of the sky and the gods who inhabited it: Teutonic peoples considered hazelnuts the embodiment of lightning, and their sky god, Thor, held hazel-

Hazelnuts symbolized fertility, and some ancient people linked them to lightning and the fertilizing power of the storm. The Teutonic peoples considered hazelnuts the embodiment of their storm god, Thor. (Bettmann / Corbis)

113

The use of hazel in divination meant that the ancients considered the tree and its products magic. In Roman myth, Mercury carried a winged hazel rod, and whomever he touched with it gained the gift of eloquence. Sorcerers and wizards carried hazel rods, and in Greek myth, Circe used her rod to change men into swine. The early Celts considered the hazel tree the tree of wisdom; nine hazel trees grew over Connla's sacred pool, and the nuts dropped into the pool, where salmon, including the salmon of knowledge, consumed them.

In Swedish legend, the hazelnuts themselves made people invisible. People in much of the Old World also used the nuts for divination. Perhaps the most notable example of this use was on All Hallows' Eve (Halloween), when hazelnuts were placed on the fire to foretell the future of love relationships. The people who performed this ritual called the hazelnuts by the names of certain lovers, and if the nuts blazed up in the fire, they believed the passion the lovers experienced would grow and flourish. (Baring-Gold 1868; Folkard 1892; Lehner and Lehner 1960)

See also Almonds; Chestnuts; Peanuts; Pines and Pine Nuts; Walnuts

HERBS

Myths testify to the ancient uses of herbs for food, medicine, and magic. With an intimate connection to plants and attentiveness to nature's powers, ancient peoples assigned herbs powerful properties. In myths and legends, herbs could heal disease or inflict death, and both humans and legendary creatures used them to effect both good magic and evil.

The legendary and symbolic meaning attached to plants trickled down from generation to generation, and it was often said to have originated with the gods. Some ancient peoples believed that the herbs attained their curative powers because the gods created them. The Sumerians compiled the first guide to curative plants in 2200 B.C., a time when most medicines were made from plants and herbs. Many of these herbal medicines remain effective today; modern drugs are often synthetic refinements of curative herbs. In the fifth century B.C., Hippocrates wrote of the healing powers of herbs, listing about 400 herbs in common use at the time. In the first century A.D., Dioscorides compiled another herbal guide that listed 600 plants and their uses.

From antiquity, people have worshiped certain trees and plants for their healing and seemingly magic properties. They performed magic rituals in their cultivation and use to ensure their effectiveness. The early Christian church attempted to ban the cultivation of some herbs and the associated rituals, in order to suppress pagan religion. Nevertheless, Christian monks kept much herbal knowledge alive. In these early times, monks served as healers of both body and soul, and they knew that the earth held a complete storehouse of herbal remedies to cure ills of all sorts.

People in all areas of the world had knowledge of herbs, and they used them for perfumes and seasonings as well as for medicine. Witches were said to use them for making magic potions or poisons, which led to the connection of herbs and herb lore with witchcraft and demonology. Although some herbs were poisonous, many others had the ability to heal and soothe, and still others could intoxicate, transporting the mind to another realm. Those familiar with these abilities knew that herbs had great power. Spices too had power, and the mere scent of them, wafted up to heaven, nourished the gods. But while mythmakers connected spices to the gods and the celestial sphere, they connected herbs to the magic of the earth. Herbs could kill or drive someone mad on one hand, or promote longevity and avert evil on the other. The versatility of herbs testified to the power of the earth and to nature's miraculous provisions. (Cavendish 1994; Grieve 1967)

See also Chicory and Endive; Flowers; Ginseng; Mandrakes; Spices

Herb planting gained significance long ago because humans assigned herbs powerful, and even magical, properties. (The Pierpont Morgan Library/Art Resource, NY)

HONEY

The ancients considered honey a divine substance. Mythmakers linked it to nectar and ambrosia, the heavenly dew that miraculously flowed from the celestial regions, dripped from the world tree,★ and fortified the gods. In the Old Testament, the Promised Land flowed with milk and honey. Clearly, ancient people connected the golden elixir to holy places. They used it for libations and offerings, to cleanse and to purify; and because it connoted immortality, they used it in funeral rites, obviously considering it a worthy enough food to nourish the dead in the otherworld.

Early mythmakers believed that honey existed long before bees, because myths commonly tell of gods nourished by honey in the early stages of the universe's creation. In an ancient Orphic text, honey flowed from oak trees, and Kronos, the high god, became intoxicated from this honey and fell into the first sleep of the world. By the time Zeus entered the picture, however, so too did the bee Melissa. A Greek myth recounts how the goddess Rhea gave birth to Zeus in a cave on Mount Ida, and how she hid him there for a time to protect him from his father's wrath. Melissa fed Zeus in the cave, and she protected him as well. Bees often lived in caves, and their honey would have provided a source of sustenance for the infant Zeus. The Popul Vuh, the origin myth of the Quiche Maya, traces the origin of bees to a universal hive at the center of the earth. Ancient people from many parts of the world connected both bees and caves with the earth's generation, and dated honey to the creation of the world.

Civilizations all over the world considered honey sacred and magical, especially because it was created by a seemingly mystical process no one fully understood. The sanctity of honey perhaps stemmed from the myths of the Mordvinian Ugro Finns and their creation

story of the chief god, chkai, a bisexual king bee responsible for creating the human race. Because these people believed that humans were born from bees, they held bees sacred. They envisioned the earth as a beehive, ruled by the bee god chkai, who laid eggs from which all the other bees and creating goddesses were born.

The veneration of honey and of the bees that created it permeated ancient cultures in which honey was not only eaten but also made into an intoxicating drink—mead—that was consumed at public festivals and offered to the gods. Those who venerated honey believed that the gods themselves had inspired bees to create it; and by drinking mead brewed from honey, they hoped to gain godlike insight. The peoples of northern Europe consumed mead in great quantities. People in ancient India made a similar beverage, called *madhu,* from honey that they believed came from the flowers of the Mahua tree. In Indian myth, the Asvins, the twin horsemen of the sun god Surya, acquired honey from celestial bees and brought it down to earth in a three-wheeled cart called the *madhu-vahana*. This myth, like that of the Finno-Ugric Mordvins, identified honeybees as creators. The bees made the honey in heaven, the Asvins brought it to earth, and Krishna, the high god, drank the mead made from the honey, which like the honey itself had a divine quality.

The divine quality of honey led mythmakers to place this substance in the gods' possession. In the myth of Zeus and Melissa, mortals were not allowed to consume honey. When people entered Zeus's cave and attempted to steal his honey, the bees savagely attacked them. Zeus spared the honey thieves' lives by turning them into birds. Honey was forbidden to human beings not only because of its mystical quality but also because of its purity. The ancient Persians used honey to cleanse mortals of sin, which they believed possible because honey came from sinless bees who created the precious fluid without touching the flowers. This act, it appeared, led some

---

★ The world tree, a concept common to many European and Asian cosmologies, marked the center of the world and symbolized strength, life, and immortality.

people to consider bees virgins. In a famous Greek myth, Aristaeus, a shepherd, possessed bees, but the Dryads killed his bees after he pursued their sister Eurydice, the wife of Orpheus, inadvertently causing her death when she stepped on a poisonous snake. After that, Aristaeus was forbidden to come in contact with the virginal bees and the pure honey they produced.

Because of its purity and other virtues, the ancients used honey in marriage rituals. Honey could cleanse and purify as well as promote fertility and act as an aphrodisiac. The Slavs used honey in love potions. The Magyars of Hungary smeared honey on the genitals of young men and women to make them attractive to the opposite sex. At weddings in parts of India where in ancient times it was used to propitiate evil spirits, honey is still used to ensure fruitful unions.

Cultures around the world used honey for a variety of purposes—as a purifier, love charm, curative, preservative, and offering to the dead. The use of honey as an offering to the dead probably arose from the ancient belief that honey warded off demons, an extension of its evident curative powers. Ancient Babylonians used honey to exorcise evil spirits from the sick, and people in the Balkans offered honey to the demons of disease. The practice of offering honey to the dead is an ancient one. Vedic priests offered honey to Yama, the god of death; ancient peoples of Russia offered honey cakes to their dead; and Scandinavians sometimes poured honey mead on graves. Occurrences of such death rituals appeared in myth as well. In Homer's *Iliad,* the Greek warrior Patroclus received jars of honey at his funeral pyre, presumably to take with him to the otherworld; and in Homer's *Odyssey,* the enchantress Circe urged Odysseus to offer honey to the dead soothsayer Teriesias.

As honey was thought to sustain the dead in the afterlife, it was used as a preservative for food storage and in preparing dead bodies for burial. In Greek myth, the god Glaukos died when he fell into a pot of honey. His father,

Minos, asked the diviners how he might find the boy and restore him to life, and they answered that whoever could offer the best simile for Minos's cow of three colors would gain the ability to resurrect Glaukos. Polyidos, a wise seer of Corinth, compared the cow to the fruit of the bramble bush. He then restored Glaukos to life. In this myth, the honey pot served as a tomb where Glaukos's body was preserved until he was resurrected.

Honey was big business in ancient Egypt and Greece, where people found many uses for it. The Egyptians reserved honey for royalty and used it in funerary and temple offerings. The Greeks connected it to the Great Goddess rites and the myths surrounding Dionysus. According to Ovid, Dionysus, the vine god, invented honey. He did this when the satyrs he was traveling with made music with their instruments, and bees, unknown at the time, flew out of the woods and allowed Dionysus to lead them to a tree, where they confined themselves and made honey. The Egyptians gave honey an equally enchanting origin. In their myth, the sun god Ra cried, and tears dropped from his eyes. The tears turned into a bee, which immediately began making honey.

It is no surprise that honey, as the first sweetener, the first means of making intoxicating beverages, and in some myths, the first food, figures prominently in myths and rituals all over the world. In a creation myth of the Caduveo people of the Gran Chaco of central South America, a falcon saw honey forming in gourds, and told the creator god to take it out of the gourds and put it instead in the middle of trees so that humans had to work to retrieve it. Some Brazilian tribes ascribed to honey a great religious-ceremonial significance, and conducted a honey festival every September and October, at the end of the dry season. The people began gathering honey in March or April for this festival, storing the prized possession in gourds, and hanging them from the ceiling beams of their ceremonial huts. After an elaborate ceremony, they consumed the honey. These Brazilian tribes have numerous myths relating to the origin of the festival, which they created to ensure good hunting for the remainder of the year. (Darby et al. 1977; Deerr 1949; Dumont 1992; Kerenyi 1976; Levi-Strauss 1974; Toussaint-Samat 1992)

See also Candy; Manna; Maple Syrup; Mead; Milk; Nectar and Ambrosia; Sugar and Sugarcane

HORSE

Hippophagy refers to the eating of horses—a practice repugnant to many today but a common one in the past. Stone Age hunters ate wild horses, as did early pastoral peoples of Asia and pre-Christian peoples of northern Europe, including peoples of Scandinavia, Germany, Britain, Ireland, Italy, Greece, Russia, and Ukraine. People may have eaten horses as early as the fourth millennium B.C. Some archaeologists investigating the remains of horses at Dereivka, a Kurgan site in Ukraine, believe that these ancient Indo-Europeans hunted horses for their flesh, and perhaps domesticated them for this reason.

Magico-religious concepts have long surrounded the horse and its domestication. Common people ate horses and sacrificed them to their deities. These animals symbolized power, so their sacrifice and consumption was a sacrament, and whoever partook of the sacrament gained the power of the horse. Upon the birth of a child, the Patagonian Indians of South America performed a ritual to endow the child with equine qualities. They killed a horse, sliced open its belly, and removed its stomach. They then placed the infant in the horse's stomach cavity and ate the horse's flesh. Through this ritual, the child not only gained the horse's power but became a centaurlike creature, half horse and half human.

Horses are renowned for their tremendous strength; this might explain why they became linked symbolically in many cultures with natural powers such as sun and water. This as-

A symbolic map of the universe found on a shaman's drum, which was traditionally covered with the skin of a horse, in the Altai Mountains, Siberia. Pictured on the left is a horse beneath a tree prepared to be sacrificed (below) and (above) the same animal sacrificed, its skin attached to a ritual construction called Tayilga. (Museum of Anthropology and Ethnography)

sociation made horses fitting sacrifices to gods associated with the sun and the sea, such as the Greek gods Poseidon and Helios. Both sun and water were, likewise, agents of fertility, responsible for enriching the soil and growing the grain. So horses entered into the symbolism of farming peoples, who used a mare to represent their mother goddess. In India, as this mother goddess galloped, she spread the rain. Horse sacrifices in India had much to do with this belief about horses and their connection to the monsoon rains and the harvest. The horse was a particularly potent fertility symbol, considered by many the resident spirit of the cornfields, which protects the harvest and enables the grain to grow.

The people of ancient India and ancient Rome performed horse sacrifices due to their beliefs in the horse's strength in battle as well as its ability to make the fields fertile. Some ancient rituals connected the two concepts. The Roman horse sacrifice to the war god Mars was an annual event, performed on 15 October, following a chariot race. One of the horses that pulled the winning chariot was sacrificed as a representative of war but also as a representative of the corn spirit and a symbol of the harvest. Mars, in addition to being war god, protected the harvest from natural disaster, and October marked the end of the military season as well as the beginning of the season of cold and rain when the people concentrated on tending the fields. The Romans slaughtered the horse, in part, in thanks for the harvest. At the ritual, the horse's head was cut off and decorated with loaves of bread to symbolize the corn spirit. The blood of this horse was saved for a lavish festival later in the year.

A particularly macabre horse sacrifice accompanied the inauguration of the king of Ireland, and this too appeared to have a connection to the harvest. The people killed a mare, cut up the flesh, and boiled it. The future king then bathed in the bloody broth, drank it, and ate chunks of the horse's flesh while sitting in the water. Like the Patagonian ritual, this Irish ritual was sacramental and was performed to endow the future king with the qualities of the mare. Once the ritual was completed, the man gained official authority as king, and like the horse that he had consumed, was thought to have gained the ability to ensure good harvests.

Not long after the advent of Christianity, Pope Gregory III forbade hippophagy because of its association with the worship of pagan gods. In fact, most major religions attacked the consumption of horses at this time, and eventually people in much of Europe came to view the practice as repugnant. Yet in some areas, hippophagy persisted. Christian monks in Switzerland ate horses into the eleventh century, and the people of Denmark were still feasting on horse as late as the sixteenth century. Toward the end of the nineteenth century, the sale of horse meat was legalized in France, Germany, Austria, and Scandinavia. (Farb and Armelagos 1980; Harris 1985; Simoons 1994; Toussaint-Samat 1992)

See also Blood and Flesh; Meat

ICES AND ICE CREAM

In Greek myth, Prometheus civilized the world when he stole fire from the gods and gave it to human beings. Once in possession of fire, humans could mold metals, warm themselves during cold winters, and cook their food. Mastery over fire and heat clearly lifted people to a higher level, and cooking food distinguished them from animals. Heat and warmth became associated with technological progress. In ancient times, people feared the cold and thought eating cold foods was dangerous. In times past, people considered cold synonymous with evil and death. They feared the icy grip of death, and they knew that people turned cold when they died.

Early people cooked in order to make raw foods edible, not because they wanted to eat them hot; yet, for a long time, people feared cold and iced foods for their negative associations. Eventually, though, people began to long for cold drinks during hot summers and sought ice to chill them. They also learned that ice could preserve their food. Long before they knew how to make it, people found ways of storing and transporting ice for their own use.

For thousands of years people saved ice to satisfy their desire for cool drinks. The earliest icehouses existed in Mesopotamia, beside the Euphrates River, about 4,000 years ago. The rich used the ice in these pits to cool their wines. Alexander the Great dug pits and filled them with snow so that his army could have cool wine in the summer. Roman emperors had ice brought from the mountains, and the kings of Egypt had snow shipped to them from Lebanon. In the nineteenth century, Peruvians cut blocks of ice from glaciers in the Andes and lowered them down the mountains to make iced drinks and ice cream. Middle Easterners, especially in the Turkish Empire, frequently consumed iced fruit drinks, and the people of Greece sold snow in the markets of Athens from as early as the fifth century B.C. Today's sherbets and wine coolers likely originated with the wine-flavored ices consumed by early peoples, and today's snow cones likely originated with the ices made long ago from real snow mixed with honey and fruit.

It was said that people sometimes died from drinking cold water, and it is possible that they did because the snow from which they made the water was unsanitary. Yet from as early as 1100 B.C. people in China constructed underground icehouses and addressed a hymn to the goddess of cold; and ancient Chinese texts compare the pure heart of a Confucian gentleman with a jade vase full of snow. The mythology of snow and ice is marked by contradictory associations: It was deadly yet alluring, stultifying yet beautiful. Snow could freeze the earth but was also white and pure, like milk, so it came to symbolize the same cleanliness and purity people associated with milk. Northern Europeans loved milk and milk products. The early Germanic people who settled in Britain glorified milk, considering it a wholesome food and not merely a drink. Some of these positive associations with ice and milk have carried over to ice cream. (David 1994; Visser 1986)

See also Milk

INSECTS

The practice of eating insects proves that what people consider acceptable as food is purely a matter of culture. From antiquity, people have recognized the food value of insects. Greeks and Romans ate beetle larvae, and the Chinese ate crickets. The people of Ceylon have long eaten bees, and the people of India and Mexico ate ants, considering winged ants a particular delicacy. Insects provided a lot of protein in the early human diet, and they still do, particularly for peoples living in Africa and in the Middle East. It has been estimated that 80 percent of the world's inhabitants eat some kinds of insects.

Some people of the Tonga Islands in the South Pacific say that when their kings die, their spirits travel to Bulotu, or paradise, but that when people of the lower classes die, their spirits remain on earth and feed on insects. Westerners tend to equate insect eating with the lower classes; but although the practice is pervasive in certain traditional, tribal societies, it is by no means restricted to them. Many modern Africans include insects in their diets; stories circulate of tribal Africans stirring locusts into soups and plucking and eating termites straight off the wood. But not many people realize that people in much of the world ate insects at one time or another: The Japanese ate ants, the ancient Greeks liked cicadas, and the native tribes of California held a Feast of Grasshoppers when the insects swarmed in large numbers. Mohammed reputedly considered locusts a special treat; legend has it that his wives used to give him trays of locusts as presents. Many kinds of insects supply protein, and some people think their taste is similar to that of nuts. People of the ancient world considered grasshoppers and locusts particularly nutritious, and in fact these insects appear in the dietary laws of Leviticus as recommended food for the Israelites.

The Greek historian Diodorus Siculus described a class of locust eaters called Acridophagi who lived in Ethiopia and reportedly died before the age of forty as a result of eating locusts. They died when winged lice bred in their bodies and eventually consumed them. Instances of people eating locusts must have made a profound impression on the ancients, in one way or another. The people of Arabia have eaten locusts from remote antiquity; the people of Persia also ate them, as did the people of Israel, Syria, and other Middle Eastern areas. Locusts often saved the Arabs of the Sahara from famine, so they felt blessed when the locusts arrived. In Arab legend, a king locust ruled over the swarm and led the migrations.

The Chinese believed something similar, as did other locust eaters of antiquity who greatly anticipated the insect's arrival. Despite Diodorus's assessment, many people in Africa also considered the swarms of locusts that descended upon their villages a blessing. For example, in a legend of the Khoi, a great magic man or shaman who resides in the North releases the locusts from a deep pit and sends them southward to supply the people with food. The Khoi obviously considered locusts desirable food. African rainmakers even chanted incantations to bring the locusts to feed the people. According to the Bible, John the Baptist fed on locusts—though most scholars believe that the reference is actually to carob pods. The carob tree is native to the Mediterranean, and the fruit of the carob tree grows in large, flat pods called husks or locusts. According to the New Testament, carob pods primarily fed cattle, but people ate them in times of famine. John the Baptist may well have survived on either carob pods or insects during his forty days in the desert. (Cowan 1865; Harris 1985; Jensen 1963)

See also Carob

JUJUBES

Jujube trees grew in large areas of the Old World, and they grew prolifically in China, India, Egypt, and tropical Africa. The people of these areas relied on the fruits for their nutritive value, just as they did on figs and dates. The Chinese have used jujubes for food and medicine since ancient times. The Hindus of India considered their jujubes sacred to Vishnu, one of their trio of primary gods. People in Egypt used the jujubes that covered the Nile valley as funerary offerings; and it has been suggested that the Lotophagi in Homer's *Odyssey* ate not lotus but the fruit of the jujubes growing on the African coast.

Two different species of jujubes grew in the Old World, and the people who knew of jujube trees have long valued the nutritious fruits they produced. The Chinese considered their jujubes valuable enough to offer to the royals. Although the people of India considered their jujubes fruits of the poor, they not only dedicated them to Vishnu, but they sanctified them in the great religious epic the *Ramayana*. In the *Ramayana,* Rama, an incarnation of Vishnu, went in search of his wife Sita, who had been kidnapped by the demon Ravana. While searching for Sita, he encountered a poor Bhilni, a lower-caste devotee, who offered him some jujube fruits, tasting each fruit first to see if it was ripe enough. Rama accepted the fruit from the Bhilni, knowing that regardless of the way he offered it, he offered it with a pure heart. (Customarily in Hindu practice, upper-caste Hindus refuse to consume food prepared by the lower castes, much less food they put into their mouths, which would violate ritual purity. But because the Bhilni offered Rama the food with a pure heart, the god considered the fruit itself pure.) After Rama accepted the Bhilni's offering, the jujube fruit became sacred.

Jujubes surfaced in several places in both Hindu epics, the *Ramayana* and the *Mahabharata,* and because of its mythological significance, Hindus use the jujube frequently in religious ceremonies. They offer the fruit primarily to Shiva, but they consider it sacred to Vishnu as well. Hindus sometimes call Lord Vishnu "the lord of the jujube tree," and they call the tree itself Vadari or Badari, and Vishnu, as lord of the tree, Badrinath—also the name of a place of pilgrimage where reputedly a sacred jujube tree once grew. The sacred jujube is a recurrent motif in world myths. Some Indian myths say that the sacred Ganges rises from below a jujube tree on Mount Kailash. The Koran identifies the jujube as the Tree of Paradise, placing it on the highest point of the seventh heaven, at the right hand of God's throne. Some Chinese myths identify the jujube with paradise. They refer to this sacred tree as the Tree of Life, or the "Jujube of 1,000 [or 10,000] years." (*Funk & Wagnall's* 1972; Gupta 1991; Simoons 1994)

See also Lotus

K sacred beverage over a deity's image. Throughout history people associated inebriation with spiritual enlightenment, or at least they considered it a means of approaching the supernatural powers. For this reason, kava ceremonies assumed a sacred character, and people learned to associate the kava plant with the bodies of their gods. Origin myths of kava often attribute the plant to great gods, tribal chiefs, or spirits of the dead as well as to animals such as pigs and rats, which frequently gnawed on kava roots. Most commonly, kava is said to have grown from a dead body that had been buried underground. In Samoan myth, kava and sugarcane both grew from the grave of Ava, the son of the creator god Tagaloa.

A Samoan legend of the first kava ceremony involved Tagaloa, the creator god, and the first man, Pava. The two sat facing each other, and because the space between them was considered sacred, strict rules forbade the participants from moving through that space in any way. But in this legend, Pava's son violated this rule and stepped into the sacred space. Pava killed his son when he did this, even though he knew his act obliterated any hope of continuing the human race. Tagaloa remedied the situation. He lifted the kava cup and dripped the liquid onto the boy's body, and the boy was instantly resurrected. From then on kava served as a covenant between humans and God. Kava became linked to resurrection.

Numerous varieties of kava grow in the South Pacific islands, each one distinguishable by its color and by the size of its root sections. In Hawaii, commoners used only the most common variety, the chiefs used the rarer varieties, and the most highly prized variety of all was reserved strictly for the gods. In Hawaii, kava is sacred to the god Kane, and the drink is used most often in sacrifices to Kane and Kanaloa. In myth, these gods both cultivated the plant and drank the beverage. Kane and Kanaloa were creator deities, and as they traveled along the surface of the sea through

KAVA (AWA)

The word *kava* refers to both a plant of the pepper family and an inebriating beverage brewed from the roots of the plant. South Pacific islanders still consume the drink in sacred ceremonies that have continued to play an important role in their social and religious lives. The kava drink produces tranquilizing effects while allowing the mind to remain clear. It was originally made by women and children who chewed the roots into a pulp, then spit out the pulp, diluted it with water, and let it ferment. Because the fermented drink acted as both a narcotic and a sedative, it enjoyed popularity not only among healers but among great tribal chiefs wishing to bring peace to their villages. People of that time offered the roots and the drink to their gods, and many continue to do so today.

The kava ceremonies of the Pacific Islands have much in common with the tea ceremonies of China and Japan. Both types of ceremonies are sacred and elaborate, and both serve the purpose of uniting the community. Kava ceremonies are complex, as are tea ceremonies, and participants must adhere to strict rules. In some societies of long ago, only women prepared the kava and only men consumed it. In Samoa today, only a village virgin can prepare the kava and serve it to the chiefs. Many ceremonies involve offering kava to the gods, generally by pouring or sprinkling the

A kava ceremony in Samoa. (Jack Fields/Corbis)

the islands, they caused the first food plants to grow, kava among them. In preparing the sacred drink, it was necessary to mix the kava roots with water. So Kane and Kanaloa were also water finders. As they traveled around the country, they established springs and made sure that the water in the springs ran clear so that the chiefs could drink from them. Kane and Kanaloa appeared in human form, and they lived in an earthly paradise—a floating cloud land between heaven and earth. It was there that they drank kava and ate the fruit of a magic garden that never stopped producing.

Kane and Kanaloa drank kava because the islanders considered the drink worthy of gods. Drinking kava, in myth as well as ceremony, was both an honor and a privilege; Hawaiian legends commonly tell of gods struggling to gain the privilege of drinking this miraculous beverage. In one Hawaiian legend, just after heaven and earth were separated, the sky gods forbade Kanaloa and the earth spirits to drink

kava, and the latter revolted. The gods defeated the earth spirits, however, and banished them to the underworld, where Kanaloa, the leader of the revolt, became ruler of the dead. As ruler of the dead, Kanaloa was also known as Milu, an equivalent to the evil Maori goddess Miru. Miru lived in the underworld and kept stores of kava, which she used to stupefy men before she cooked them.

In myth and in practice, people consumed kava for both evil and benevolent purposes. Sorcerers used kava to ward off demons, and some peoples of Polynesia consumed it during times of dispute because both the drink and the ceremony reduced feelings of hostility and anxiety among the consumers. Some myths indicate that kava originally may have been used to suppress the appetite. One such myth explained the origin of this sacred plant: The King of Tonga visited an island of starving people, and because they had no food to offer him, a woman cooked her baby for him to eat. In gratitude, the king gave the baby a burial befitting a prince. Then—in keeping with precedent (other myths in which miracles occurred in order to right injustices)—the kava plant grew from the baby's grave, to alleviate the hunger plaguing the people. (Beckwith 1970; Cox and Banack 1991; Ratsch 1992)

See also Alcoholic Beverages; Ayahuasca; Balche; Beer; Chicha; Mead; Pulque; Sake; Soma; Wine

KIWI FRUIT
See Gooseberries

fade. Furthermore, some mythologists have identified the orange as the "golden apple" Zeus gave to Hera on their wedding day. This was one of the golden fruits that grew on a tree in the Garden of the Hesperides.

Over the centuries, there has been much confusion over the identity of these fruits. Some people have called them apples, and others, oranges, quinces, or citrons. Around the time of Christ, when the Greeks first became acquainted with citrons, they suggested that citrons must have been the famous fruit that grew on the tree in the Hesperides's garden. Images on coins dating from the second century A.D. depict Heracles with the fruit and the tree, which looks like a variety of citrus.

Citrus fruits have enjoyed a favorable reputation since ancient times. Lemon juice enlivens the flavor of other foods, and under the right conditions, the fruits grow the year around. People have long found the scent as well as the taste of lemons appealing, and have used lemon oil in perfumes, soaps, and medicines. Many African peoples originally used lemons for their curative properties. The Romans and Egyptians used citron as an antidote against poison, at a time when poisoning was a common form of murder. Lemons and citrons have served literally hundreds of purposes, from preparing a wide range of foods and aromatic oils, to relieving all sorts of physical ailments, to cleaning and polishing furniture and silver. The appeal of the fruit has lasted so long and extended so far that it's no surprise it found its way into myths. In Indian legend, when a courtesan named Cancalaksi was attacked by a leopard and killed, she was saved from eternal damnation by a service she had performed in life to honor Vishnu. Yama, the death god, insisted that she belonged with him because she had worked as a prostitute. But Vishnu rewarded her for her thoughtful act of rubbing a citron on the walls of his temple. This simple cleansing procedure so pleased the god that it won Cancalaksi entrance to heaven.

LAMB
See Goat, Lamb, and Ram

LEEKS
See Onions and Leeks

LEMONS AND CITRONS
Lemons grow all over the world, in areas separated by great distances. They grow in Japan, India, South Africa, and California, and they're cultivated extensively in the Middle East, in a region roughly coinciding with ancient Mesopotamia and including modern-day Syria, Palestine, and Egypt. Lemons are usually associated with the Mediterranean region, but they most likely originated in India. The citron (or *etrog*)—a smaller citrus fruit that resembles today's cultivated lemon and that might be its ancestor—played a significant role in myth and religion, particularly among the Jews, and in India and China among Hindus and Buddhists.

Citrus fruits have traditionally symbolized love. The Japanese and the Jews in Roman times used citrons to decorate their bridal chambers, and the Greeks and Romans considered both oranges and limes symbols of marriage. The orange, in particular, has mythological links to everlasting love, as do orange blossoms. Orange trees, and indeed all citrus trees, are evergreen, so like true love, they never

Today, citrus is a primary food crop around the world, and the citron is still one of India's most popular varieties of citrus and grows in many parts of the country. The most common mythological references to the citron are the recurrent motifs in Indian art: The Hindu elephant-headed god Ganesha is depicted holding a citron in his hand, and the god Kuvera typically holds one in his. Kuvera was a Vedic earth spirit, and later on, a god of earthly treasures. The Buddhists adopted Kuvera as one of their deities. Buddhist myths call the citron in Kuvera's hand "Buddha's hand," and in China they call it *fo-shou*. This variety of citron has five lobes. The Chinese revered it as one of their three sacred fruits—which they referred to as the Three Greatest Blessings—along with the peach and the pomegranate. The peach symbolized longevity; the pomegranate, fertility and eternal life; and the citron, happiness, wealth, and protection. Buddha's true hand symbolized protection as well. In legend, Buddha cursed citrons because of their bitterness; then, feeling remorseful, he transformed the shape of the fruit to resemble his hand. Though the "Buddha's hand" citron was inedible, it had a powerful scent, and the Chinese used the fruit as a temple offering to the household gods.

Hindus and Buddhists attached great significance to the citron, as did Jews, who made this fruit a vital part of their religious observance. The Jews called citrons *etrogs,* and they believed them to be the fruit of the "goodly tree" mentioned in the Old Testament. The Jews accepted the citron as the goodly fruit at the turn of the Christian era. They also adopted the citron as a symbol of Jewish national and religious identity. The people needed perfect fruits for ritual use, and they planted citrons everywhere to ensure an adequate supply for harvest festivals. Citrons, or etrogs, distinguished Jewish harvest festivals from similar festivals among other religious groups in the Middle East. Even today pious Jews include them in their autumn feast, the Feast of Booths (or Feast of Tabernacles).

This festival commemorates Israel's journey through the wilderness, and in the past, it involved prayers to God to ensure the fruitfulness of the land. During the feast, the Israelites carried branches of palms, willows, and citrons to symbolize God's precious gifts to the people. In addition to the identification of the citron as the goodly fruit of biblical times, some people also identified the citron as the forbidden fruit in the Garden of Eden. (Farb and Armelagos 1980; Goor and Nurock 1968; Simoons 1991; Tolkowsky 1938; Visser 1986)

See also Apples; Apricots; Limes and Linden Trees; Oranges; Quinces

LENTILS
See Peas and Lentils

LETTUCE
Certain folk beliefs about lettuce stemmed from the appearance of this food in early myths. Some peoples of the Middle East ate lettuce in times of mourning, echoing the vegetable's role in the death myth of Adonis. Many Egyptians ate lettuce to enhance their fertility, and they continue to believe it has the powers of an aphrodisiac. The Egyptians associated lettuce with the vegetation god Min and his white bull, who ate lettuce to gain potency. The connection of lettuce with fertility relates partially to its milky juice, which has been likened to semen. Furthermore, lettuce grew to resemble either the sex organs of the female or those of the male. The erect growth of the early Egyptian form of lettuce resembled a phallus, and people therefore linked it with reproduction.

The ancient Egyptians depicted Min with an erect phallus and a black body symbolizing the fertile soil. At the annual harvest festival, the pharaoh arranged for Min's statues to be removed from their shrines and for offerings of lettuce to be made to the god; then the god's statues were replaced in their sacred homes. People marched in procession at Min's festival, carrying heads of lettuce and representations of checkerboard gardens of lettuce, in celebration of fruitful harvests. The pharaoh is depicted as reaping grain at Min's festival, and even fathering an heir. The myth of Min clearly indicated that the Egyptians connected lettuce with fertility. But people in other cultures associated this food with death and sexual impotence. The lore surrounding lettuce is full of contradictory notions.

The ancient Greeks considered lettuce a plant of death and impotence because of the crucial role it played in the death of Adonis. In one version of the myth, Aphrodite, Adonis's lover, concealed Adonis in a lettuce bed (in a variant, Adonis hid himself there) to save him from a wild boar. In each rendition of the story, the vegetation god either took refuge or was hidden in a bed of lettuce, either wild or cultivated. But the boar gored him anyway, and he died among the lettuce heads. In the myth, death and impotence went hand in hand. Aphrodite fell in love with Adonis, and she didn't want him to be a hunter, for fear something would happen to him—and it did. The Greek epicurean Athenaeus asserted that the mythmakers hid Adonis in the lettuce to express the fact that eating lettuce causes impotence, often viewed as a form of death.

Still another version of the Adonis myth exists, one in which Aphrodite hid not Adonis, but Phaon, in the lettuce. Phaon was the ferryman of Lesbos, and he was such a kind man that he often ran his boat for free, refusing to take payment from those who could not afford it. Aphrodite discovered this when she disguised herself as an old woman and asked Phaon to take her across the water on his ferry. He allowed her to ride for free. She rewarded his kindness with a vase of alabastron—a perfume that made women fall in love with him. But it is unclear whether it was the alabastron or the lettuce itself that had this effect. As mentioned before, early forms of lettuce often resembled the male sex organ, and early people familiar with these forms may have believed that men who came into

contact with them would become irresistible to women. Legend has it that Sappho, the Greek lyric poetess, fell prey to Phaon's charms. But after Phaon became beautiful and attractive, he seduced many women, and Aphrodite hid him in the lettuce as well, to protect him from these women's husbands. This made Phaon impotent, just as it had Adonis.

The ancient Greeks may have identified lettuce with impotence for the same reason the Egyptians identified it with fertility: its shape. Ancient people often assigned properties to plants according to their appearance, and the lettuce the Greeks knew differed from that of the Egyptians. The Greek lettuce was short and round rather than phallic in shape, and they identified it with eunuchs—castrated men incapable of achieving erections. Furthermore, the Greeks identified the milky juice not with semen but with the soporific juice of the opium poppy, and possibly with breast milk. Breast milk, the Greeks said, inhibited fertility, because nursing mothers cannot conceive.

Although lettuce had contrasting properties in Greek and Egyptian myths, both Adonis and Min served as vegetation gods, and lettuce played a crucial role in both of their festivals. The Egyptians held their harvest festival to honor Min and to rejoice in the fruitful harvest. The Greeks held theirs to honor Adonis and to commemorate his death, an event they linked with the birth and death of corn. People commonly sowed greens at Greek harvest festivals, particularly lettuce. These plants grew quickly but also died quickly because they had no roots. The lettuce beds symbolized the transitory existence of the vegetation god, and were referred to as "Gardens of Adonis." (Detienne 1977; Ratsch 1992; Visser 1986)

LIMES AND LINDEN TREES

Two kinds of lime trees appear in myths: the linden tree, a native of eastern North America and Europe; and the true lime tree, a native of India. Most of the myths about lime trees refer to the linden, a flowering tree grown as an ornamental, which bears no fruit but secretes a sugary substance similar to honey and a sweet, aromatic fragrance when in bloom. Linden tea is popular in France, and honey from linden flowers is highly valued for use in medicines and liqueurs. Lindens are commonly referred to as lime trees and therefore are often confused with the trees that produce citrus fruits.

In the Germanic countries, myths abound about linden trees. In Scandinavian tales, elves, fairies, and other strange beings lived among the linden branches, and in Swedish tales domestic spirits resided there. In German and Tyrolian tales, dwarves and dragons inhabited lime trees. In the myth of the hero Sigurd, the dragon Fafnir lived ninety years in the ground, ninety years in the desert, and ninety years in a lime tree. Linden trees were popular in the Germanic countries long ago—so popular that almost every hamlet in Germany had one on the main square. Some of these trees had survived for hundreds or even a thousand years, and the townspeople used to gather under them to hear bards recite legends about them.

Many early Europeans revered linden trees and immortalized them in myth. The Cheremiss, a Finno-Ugric people who lived along the Volga River, for instance, revered the lime tree not for limes but for manna, a sugary substance exuded from the tree that people throughout Europe likened to celestial honey, the food that rained down from heaven and nourished the gods. The Cheremiss held sacred ceremonies in lime groves in which they prepared a honey mead that young maidens served to men as a ritual drink. This ritual reveals both the importance of the lime tree to northern Europeans and the connection they appear to have drawn between lime trees and women. In Estonia and Lithuania women made sacrifices to the lime tree, believing it had the power to grant them fruitfulness and happiness in domestic affairs. Estonian and Lithuanian men made similar sacrifices to oak trees.

Readers of ancient myths can hardly deny that ancient people recognized spirit within their trees, spirit analogous to human spirit, spirit that prompted mythmakers to tell tales of humans and trees living interchangeable lives. Ovid's legend of the lime tree emphasizes this spiritual connection, revealing another kind of bond between lime trees and women and oak trees and men. Ovid's myth centers on Baucis, a kind woman who lived happily with Philemon, an old shepherd, in a modest cottage in Phrygia. One day, the gods Jupiter and Mercury arrived at their cottage in disguise, and Baucis and Philemon kindly welcomed them in, whereas her wealthy neighbors rejected them. As a reward to the couple, Jupiter and Mercury destroyed the homes of the selfish neighbors in a flood, but they changed the cottage of Philemon and Baucis into a temple. Then they made the couple themselves priests of the temple. Philemon and Baucis had one wish: that they would die at the same time. So Jupiter granted their wish and changed both of them into trees: Philemon into the oak, and Baucis into the lime tree. The myth of this kind couple is only one of many ancient tales that reveal a belief in a common soul animating all living things, and that involve a kind and god-fearing couple saved from destruction by transformation into trees. Since the time of Philemon and Baucis the lime tree has served as a symbol of conjugal love. (*Funk and Wagnall's* 1972; Lehner and Lehner 1960; Porteous 1968; Tolkowsky 1938)

See also Lemons and Citrons; Manna

LOTUS

Several plants identified as the lotus have been used and cultivated for food since antiquity. They have played an important role in myth and ritual, and have served as symbols of the sacred nature of the universe. The ancients commonly ate aquatic plants, and the lotus plants of Asia and Egypt were types of water lilies. The Vedic Indians ate the stalks and roots of their lotus; the Egyptians made bread from the seeds of theirs; and people in other parts of North Africa ate the fleshy fruit of their lotus trees—yet another type of plant altogether. Each of these plants held mythological significance. People in many parts of the world revered the lotus as sacred and magical.

The people of Egypt no longer consider their lotus sacred, but many people of India, Africa, China, Japan, Persia, and parts of Russia continue to venerate the lotus. The lotus remains a strong religious symbol among Hindus and Buddhists; to these groups it symbolizes the vulva, divine birth, spiritual power and life, purity, beauty, and perfection. Buddhists and Hindus ornament their religious buildings with lotus flowers and tell myriad legends about the precious lotus flower. They consider the lotus an important fertility symbol, in part because its flower resembles the female genitalia, and in part because the plant rises from the water, and water has always symbolized the origins of life and fertility.

Water, to the people of India, represents the divine essence of the universe. The Hindu goddess of love, Lakshmi, was born of the lotus. The lotus and Lakshmi both arose from the depths of the primordial sea and were and continue to be associated with purity. Lakshmi's lotus was pure gold and had a thousand petals. The petals encased the sleeping Brahma, the creator deity, like a womb. Brahma was born from the lotus womb and the water, and then created the world.

In Hindu religious thought, the lotus that bore Brahma was Padma, a manifestation of Lakshmi, the wife of Vishnu. The lotus goddess Padma dwelled within the flower and was sometimes depicted by a single stalk of lotus, which was also a symbol of good fortune. Padma does not appear in the early Vedas but surfaces later, after people in India learned the art of agriculture. Both the lotus and its goddess represent abundance. Though the lotus goddess probably existed in some form early on, quite likely, Padma, as goddess of agriculture, arose when the people saw their land

Lotus and palmette reliefs. The lotus played an important role in myth and ritual, and served as a symbol of the sacred nature of the universe. (Erich Lessing/Art Resource, NY)

produce lush vegetation; they no longer had to rely on hunting and gathering to have food. Padma had two sons who personified mud and moisture, the primary ingredients of fertile soil.

The lotus of Greek myth was not the lotus lily of Hindu myth but a different sort of plant—one that had sweet, orange, fleshy fruit and that commonly grew in Libya and other parts of North Africa. Homer, in the *Odyssey,* spoke of the Lotophagi, or the lotus eaters, a group of people Odysseus encountered in his travels while living on the African coast. This lotus tree was reputed to be magic. In Greek myth, it was once the nymph Lotis, the daughter of Neptune, whom the gods transformed in order to help her escape the violent god Priapus. Dryope, another nymph, passed by Lotis in tree form and picked some of the fruit. She too instantly became a lotus tree. The Lotophagi Odysseus encountered ate from these trees continually. They did not change forms, but they fell prey to the magic. The Lotophagi made wine out of the fruit, and upon drinking the wine, entered into a state of euphoria. The fleshy-fruited tree that so entranced the Lotophagi was possibly a type of date palm.

The Egyptians ate a different fruit from a different lotus. The Egyptian lotus apparently grew everywhere in Egypt. Like the Asian lotus it was an aquatic plant, but it was often referred to as the sacred bean. The fruit of this plant was the size of a filbert, and the seeds were used to make bread. This Egyptian lotus, like the lotus of Asia, had deep mythological attachments. The Egyptians associated their lotus with the primordial sun; they revered it as the first flower of creation and believed that Atum, the sun, lay hidden within its petals. This connection made sense because the lotus closed its petals at night and opened them in the sunlight. Because it arose from the water, the lotus was also associated with Nun, the primordial ocean.

The rise of the lotus from the water symbolized the birth of the world out of primordial mud. The lotus, and the deities within it, rose from the darkness of the waters into the light. Atum entered the lotus flower when the sun set, and was reborn when the petals opened. This expressed, metaphorically, that the sun rose for the first time at Heliopolis in the beginning of the world and each morning after that. In another Egyptian sun legend, the lotus rose out of the Sea of Two Knives and opened its petals to reveal the scarab beetle, a common Egyptian sun symbol. This scarab beetle changed into a child who wept creative tears, tears from which sprang the human race. In the myths of Brahma, of Buddha, and of the scarab beetle, the magical, mystical lotus played a large role in the creation of the world. (Darby et al. 1977; Folkard 1892; Gupta 1991; Majupuria 1988)

See also Flowers; Jujubes

LUPINES

Many early peoples ate leguminous foods such as lupines and chickpeas during times of scarcity. The ancient Greeks consumed them, as did early American foragers. Various kinds of lupines grew throughout the Mediterranean and what is now the western United States. Legumes, in myth and symbol, had associations with death and the underworld, particularly in Europe. People commonly consumed legumes at funerals and offered them to the dead, believing that because beans sprouted quickly after their burial, they had some mystical tie to resurrection.

In addition to their identification as leguminous plants, lupines had another quality that attracted the ancients. There are two species of lupine, a sweet species and a bitter species. The bitter species contains an alkaloid capable of causing intoxication. Both species of lupine had medicinal value, but the bitter lupine had ritual value as well. The ancient Greeks believed it had magical powers and could help them contact the dead. In ancient Greece, on the banks of the river Acheron, sat the Oracle of the Dead, a secret shrine that attracted large numbers of pilgrims wishing to invoke the spirits. Before the invocation began, these pilgrims consumed large quantities of bitter lupines to facilitate the communication. (Baumann 1993; Ratsch 1992)

See also Beans; Peas and Lentils

MAGUAY
See Pulque

MAIZE
See Corn

MANDRAKES

Since antiquity, people have both feared and revered the mandrake, so legends have accumulated around this mysterious plant for centuries. The mandrake was alternately considered a sedative, an aphrodisiac, a producer of insanity, and a panacea. The mandrake was considered magical, and its magic so powerful that people often used it as a talisman. Women carried it as a charm against sterility; men carried it to arouse the passions of their lovers. Others carried it for its supposed value in divining secrets or bringing prosperity.

The mandrake is native to the Mediterranean region and has a sweet fruit that resembles plums or apples. Some groups of ancient people called it the "love apple" because they believed it granted fertility and acted as an aphrodisiac. The mandrake is not a food, per se, yet people did consume it, often by making drinks from its sap. The ancient Greeks identified the mandrake with Circe, the enchantress, who made a love potion from the potent plant that put male victims at her mercy.

Then she magically turned them into swine. The Greeks also identified the mandrake with Aphrodite, who they sometimes called Mandragoritis, or "she of the mandrake." Aphrodite was the goddess of love and pleasure, and the root of the mandrake was used to assist in love relationships and promote fertility.

The Egyptians likewise appear to have connected the mandrake with fertility. In Egyptian myth, Ra, the sun god, ordered Hathor, the fertility goddess, to consume a drink made from the mandrake. Many Egyptologists believe that the Egyptians used the mandrake to make their Elixir of Life—a fluid that they believed endowed them with good health and vigor.

Many people revered the mandrake, but others feared the strength of its magic. For this reason, much of the lore about mandrakes centered around its identification as the embodiment of evil. Though the mandrake was a vegetable, its root had a curiously human shape. In Christian legend, in fact, God created the mandrake as an experiment before he created human beings. People who invested the natural world with spirits believed that plants with poisonous sap had evil spirits. They typically likened the mandrake, with its long, forked root, to the Devil.

Because mandrakes typically have deep roots, extending (in people's imaginations) into the earth's dark recesses, legends connected the plant with ill will. Some legends said the plant thrived on the flesh of dead criminals buried underground, or that it sprang up in the first place from the blood and breath of those hanged on the gallows. This notion possibly arose because of the root's human shape, and because ancient people often attributed the origins of plants to the bodies of people slain or dismembered. Equally disturbing myths arose because the mandrake often glowed in the dark, a particularly eerie sight. The Arabians called the plant Devil's Candle, not knowing that glowworms living in the leaves caused the phenomena.

The root of the mandrake, with its curiously human shape, inspired legends telling of its powerful magic. (Dover Pictorial Series Archive)

In the most popular legends of the mandrake, the plant has the power to injure or kill any person who attempts to uproot it. The mandrake shrieks horrendous shrieks, these legends say, whenever anyone tries to pluck it. Then the ill-fated person dies. These legends so horrified people that they often made their dogs harvest mandrakes—generally, black dogs, which they associated with evil and death. Sometimes the dogs did die. The ancient Chinese told similar legends about ginseng and shang, the shape of which, like the roots of the mandrake, resembled a human being. In these legends, too, ginseng and shang shrieked when pulled from the ground, and both of them grew beneath the graves of the dead. The horrific shrieks attributed to the mandrake were sometimes believed to drive people insane. (Bennett 1991; Heiser 1969; Ricciuti 1978; Simoons 1998; Thompson 1975)

See also Ginseng; Herbs; Nightshades; Thornapples

MANGOES

The mango is native to a large area of the ancient world, from India to New Guinea. People in India and Nepal today often consider the mango the king of fruits; they worship it as a tree of destiny and believe it brings prosperity and wealth to the people. Hindus of India today—as did those of the ancient world—tell legends of mango trees and plant them with much ceremony and ritual. One of the best known of these rituals involves the marrying of mango trees to other trees. Hindus believe that the mango fruit can be consumed only after these ceremonies are performed for the trees, perhaps believing that the trees will produce a good crop only if they are "married."

Today, groves of mango trees stretch over large areas of India, as do tamarind, fig, and jasmine trees. Hindu tree marriages generally involve the mango tree as the bridegroom and either the tamarind, the fig, or the jasmine as the bride. Great pomp and circumstance follow the marriage, which can become quite costly because the owner of the grove generally invites many Brahmans to the feast. (Brahmans are people of the upper castes, originally of the first four castes, which according to legend were created from the mouth of Purusha to become spiritual teachers.) In another type of ceremony, men, or sometimes men and women both, are married to mango trees, or brides and grooms are married to each other in mango groves. In Hindu myth, Krishna married Rukmani, the incarnation of Lakshmi, in a mango grove. Lakshmi was the goddess of love and fertility, and as Rukmani, she bore Krishna ten sons and one daughter. Hindu mythology connects the growth of mangoes with reproduction, sex, and the production of sons. Legends tell how Kama, the Hindu god of love and lust, had a bow made of sugarcane and a favorite dart tipped with a mango flower that emitted the smell of the alluring fruit. Presumably, when Kama shot the arrow, the mango played a role in effecting his love spell. Similarly, in the *Ramayana,* Rama became aroused seeing a mango tree in bloom.

Given the mythological connection between mangoes, love, and sex, it appears likely that mango tree marriages developed as fertility rites. Sometimes these rites were performed at the marriage of a man and woman, and other times, several years later, if the woman had not yet produced offspring. In a typical instance, the husband plants a mango tree and the wife a fig. The woman attaches the stem of the female tree to the trunk of the male tree. Then she waters them. They do this by a pond or a pool of water, and they take great care to ensure the growth of these trees. People performing these ceremonies believe that the trees directly relate to the marriage, and that the vitality and reproductive power of the trees directly affects the woman's fertility. Some people in India today continue to believe that the mango tree grows new leaves at the birth of male offspring.

The marriage of trees, some say, reveals the commonality between people and plants. Throughout history, rituals around the world centered around plants for this very reason. Plants grew, reproduced, died, and were resurrected. They had energizing spirit, and they offered people the promise of life. Some current-day Hindus and Buddhists continue to consider the mango tree sacred. Hindus consider the mango tree a manifestation of Prajapati, the lord of all creation. Buddhists connect the mango with Buddha himself, who was once given a grove of mango trees in which to rest. In parts of India and Southeast Asia today, many people believe that benevolent spirits live in mango groves.

Mango trees produce lovely flowers and luscious, juicy fruits. They clearly would have been tempting foods to ancient Asians and the peoples of Oceania. For early peoples, the mango tree conjured up positive images, and for this reason they characterized the mango as a benevolent plant spirit, and often as a manifestation of a beloved deity. Hindus tell a myth that explains how the daughter of Surya the sun god became a mango spirit. Surya's daughter married a powerful king but had to change herself into a lotus flower to escape from a Rakshashi (a wicked enchantress). The king searched for his wife, and while doing so, came across the lotus flower growing in the forest and plucked it. The Rakshashi burned the lotus flower to ashes in anger, and from the ashes, the mango tree magically arose.

Over the next few years, the powerful king continued to search for his wife. Finally he came across the mango tree, and he fell in love with the mango fruit. The king plucked a ripe mango from the branches, and to his delight, his long-lost wife emerged from the fruit. (Barooah 1992; Cooper 1978; Eliade 1958; Frazer 1950; Gupta 1991)

MANIOC

Manioc, also known as cassava or yucca, is a rootlike plant that grows in the tropics. Its starchy rootstock is used in making flour, bread, tortillas, tapioca, laundry starch, and alcoholic beverages. Early people living in tropical areas told myths to explain the existence of manioc, which was an important staple food source, a primary source of starch that is stored inside the plant's tubers. Approximately 250 million people eat manioc today, primarily in South America and West Africa. The hardy plant flourishes in areas with dry soil and is resistant to drought. Long ago, people knew they could rely on manioc when all other crops fell prey to nature's destructiveness.

Manioc was likely cultivated first by the ancient Maya, and fortunately, it grew quickly and easily from stem cuttings. Early people also found it easy to cook; they simply placed the roots over a fire, peeled them, and ate them. The Maya weren't the only ones to eat manioc: The crop constituted a staple food for groups of people throughout South and Central America. In a myth of the Tacuna Indians of the central Andes, an ant introduced manioc to a woman who had no knowledge of fire, so she warmed the manioc by placing it in her armpits. People familiar with manioc knew that cooking it was essential, because raw manioc contained poison. Two varieties of the plant exist, one sweet and one bitter. Oddly enough, the bitter, rather than the sweet, was used as the staple food, and this was the variety that contained the poison—hydrocyanic acid. People learned that they had to remove the poison before they ate it, and they did this by grating, pressing, and heating the tubers. Then they used the acid to poison arrowheads and darts.

Origin myths of manioc likely arose both because the plant provided essential nourishment and because it was dangerous to eat. Many of these myths explained how the people learned to cultivate the plant or how people learned of the plant's existence. Manioc was widely cultivated in Africa: in the rain forests; in the grasslands of Uganda; in Niger and Sudan; and in Angola, south of the Congo River. In the Congo, east of Angola, Bushongo recount in legends how manioc came to their kingdom. A wise king of Bushongo named Samba Mikepe was said to have brought manioc to his people. He traveled westward and gained his wisdom long before he became king, and it was on this journey that he learned of manioc. Much later, during Samba Mikepe's reign, a large locust swarm descended on the Bushongo and destroyed all their crops, and Samba Mikepe knew just how to save his people from starvation. He cultivated manioc, knowing that locusts could not destroy the crop. The Bushongo had manioc in abundance. They used it first as a vegetable, and later for making bread. Soon other peoples in the Congo basin also began to cultivate the crop.

Manioc became such a important staple to so many Africans that, after a while, it seemed to them that manioc had always existed in their land, but in fact it didn't come to Africa until after Columbus's time. Samba Mikepe likely traveled to San Salvador in his westward travels; the people there must have taught him how to cultivate manioc, and he in turn introduced it to his people. In some South American legends, a child born to a young woman and the spirit of manioc taught the people how to cultivate the crop. In Christian legend, St. Thomas did the honors.

In a myth of the Mundurucu of Brazil, Karuebak, a woman known as the mother of manioc, revealed the secret of plant growth: Karuebak told her nephew to bury her in a ditch so that food crops would grow from her body. Her nephew obliged, and sure enough, manioc as well as maize, bananas, watermelon, and sugarcane grew on the spot. But the boy neglected to heed Karuebak's warning—that no one could walk over the area or the food would not grow. When indeed he did walk over the area, he stunted the plant growth. Worse than that, a sorcerer got angry about being excluded from the knowledge of growth and food, and cursed Karuebak to die under the ground. This curse caused problems for the people. Many of them began to eat raw manioc and died from the poison. The ones who cooked it turned into honeybees, but they produced a bitter honey thought to be poisonous. Cultivators of manioc learned how to extract the poison and utilize the foodstuff early on, but the fact that the poison appeared at all must have led them to consider the magic of manioc particularly powerful.

As early South Americans came to rely on manioc for food, they also began to make beer from it. Women and children chewed the manioc, and their saliva helped to ferment it. In a myth of the Machinguenga, a group living in Brazil and Ecuador, the moon gave humans cultivated plants and taught them how to chew. The moon married a human girl, and manioc and the other cultivated plants were the moon's daughters. The moon watches over his daughters, and in essence, guards manioc. He sees to it that the people care for this precious food crop properly—and knows if they don't, because then his manioc daughter weeps and complains bitterly to her father. She also complains if the people eat manioc by itself and do not season it properly. But if the people combine it with meat or fish, considered superior foods, she tells her father that the people are treating her well, as she does when they make her into beer. Being fermented and made into beer is what manioc daughter likes best of all. (Jones 1959; Levi-Strauss 1974)

MANNA

One of the most perplexing food mysteries originates from the Old Testament story in which God told Moses he would cause bread to rain down from heaven to feed the Israelites as they traveled through the desert on their way to the Promised Land. This bread from heaven, or manna, whatever it was, sustained the Israelites for forty years—from the time they left Egypt until the time they arrived in Canaan. According to the Old Testament, manna fell from heaven to save the Israelites from starvation; the Lord sent it, just as he had said he would. So people associated manna with other magical, sweet, sugary foods people typically connected with the deities, such as honey, soma, nectar, and ambrosia.

Biblical scholars have suggested various explanations for this manna. The Israelites and other people in antiquity knew only that it fell from the sky, but they had no idea where it originated. Mythological tradition, of course, indicates that manna originated in the celestial sphere and dropped to earth like heavenly dew. But scholars searched for answers in nature. Some identified manna as a kind of lichen that is carried by the winds. Certain lichens break loose from the ground after long periods of drought, and the winds carry them extremely long distances and then drop them. In biblical times, nomadic tribesmen found these lichens and made bread from them during times of famine. These lichens appeared so suddenly and so mysteriously that they truly did appear to drop from the sky—just like the manna God promised.

Other scholars have identified manna as quail dung. According to the Bible, as the Israelites traveled across the Sinai peninsula, they longed for cucumbers, the refreshing fruits they had known in Egypt. Then two things happened. Migratory quails descended upon them, and soon afterward, manna fell from heaven.

At this time in history, millions of migratory quails frequented the Sinai peninsula, and people likely consumed their flesh and their dung. But most scholars today believe that manna came from tamarisk trees, which grew abundantly in the area; when small insects punctured the branches to feed on them, the

According to the Old Testament, the miraculous manna, or "bread from heaven," sustained the Israelites on their journey to the Promised Land. (Giraudon/Art Resource, NY)

trees exuded a sugary sap, often called honeydew.★

Manna in nature does refer to sweet substances exuded from plants or trees, and it was commonly associated with hot, arid lands of the Old World. After the insects punctured the trees, the liquid they did not consume hardened and dropped to the ground. Long ago, Bedouins and other peoples living in the desert collected the substance and made it into breads and cakes, foods that offered seemingly miraculous relief from famine. The identification of manna with the juice of the tamarisk tree would support earlier, mythological explana-

★Another theory identified the biblical manna not as the fluid of the tamarisk tree but of the scale insects that fed on the trees. These insects drink the sap from twigs of tamarisk trees, and the sugar from the sap passes through the insects' bodies and falls like droplets of sweet honeydew onto the ground.

tions for miracle food: According to the Bible, manna fell from the sky. In Sumerian myth, the tamarisk tree grew in heaven and was sacred to Anu, the sky god. Furthermore, the Sumerians referred to Anu's sacred tree as *manu*, and ancient Sumerian texts connect *manu* with the tamarisk or the date palm, commonly regarded as the Tree of Life.

Yggdrasil, the Norse Tree of Life, apparently had a connection to manna as well, as did the mead tree of Greek myth and the cosmic linden tree of Finno-Ugric myths. Yggdrasil and other cosmic trees were not tamarisks, but they did exist in the celestial sphere and they did exude honeylike substances that dropped to earth and fueled the belief in supernatural sustenance. Manna provided sustenance for both body and spirit. It was not only material food but supernatural food—nourishment for the soul. It supported the notion that God could provide. The ancients apparently believed that manna would return at the end of the world; and interestingly, in Norse myth, manna did appear at the end of the world, at Ragnarok, an apocalyptic event commonly referred to as the Twilight of the Gods. According to myth, at the Twilight of the Gods, life ended and then began again. Human life was renewed by Lif and Lifthrasir, one man and one woman who remained inside Yggdrasil during the apocalypse and survived on the dew, or manna, the tree produced. (Donkin 1980; Dumont 1992; Harris 1793; Langdon 1964; Moldenke and Moldenke 1952; Simoons 1998)

See also Honey; Insects; Nectar and Ambrosia

MAPLE SYRUP

North American peoples have been tapping maple trees for sap for thousands of years. The practice began with the Ojibwa, Cree, Iroquois, Algonquin, and other tribes of the American North. These peoples used maple syrup as a sweetener and a food source long before the Europeans arrived in their land.

The Algonquins called the maple syrup *sinzibuckwud,* which meant "drawn from the wood," and many early peoples considered the flowing sap within the wood an affirmation of the spirits in nature. Native Americans believed that spirit inhabited and empowered the natural world and that the moisture flowing upward through the bark from the maples' root systems indicated movement and life within the trees.

Native Americans perceived the sap flows as an affirmation of nature's renewal as well as of nature's spirit. Because the sap started flowing just before the arrival of spring, the movement affirmed the rejuvenation of the earth after a long and seemingly dead winter. Early people learned to understand the rhythms of nature, and the people of the American North learned that only during a brief period of time could they tap their maple trees and extract fluid. They accomplished this by driving wooden sticks into the tree trunks and collecting the sap and water in bark containers. The process of maple tapping, to early people, represented a transfer of life force. The maple trees gave of their spirit and life fluid to feed human beings and to see them through the long, cold winters.

Maple trees are extraordinary in many respects. They live up to 400 years, and some of them reach 80 to 100 feet in height. There are 148 species of maple, but only two of them produce sap for maple sugar—the sugar maple and the black maple—both native to the American Northeast and parts of Canada. An average sugar maple can yield between ten and twenty gallons of sap a year, and it takes from forty to sixty gallons of sap to make one gallon of syrup. Fortunately, the northern forests are overrun with maple trees, and the climate is perfect for sap production. Maple trees often have been transported to Europe for transplanting, but there they don't produce enough sap to make syrup. Hence, it has long been believed that the production of maple syrup only occurs in America, where many people carry on the ancient practice

The Native Americans considered the maple sap they used to make syrup a gift from the gods. The maple trees gave of their spirit and life fluid to feed human beings and to see them through the long, cold winters. (Library of Congress)

of celebrating the season of sap gathering and sugar making.

The celebration of "sugaring," as people call the process today, has a long tradition in the American North. The Ojibwa appear to have ritualized the process centuries ago, when according to a tribal legend the spirit of the maple tree, called Ininatig or "man tree," spoke to the people and instructed them to cut his skin, extract his fluids, and use those fluids to save themselves from starvation. People suffered during the harsh northern winters; many starved, and many others had barely enough food to survive. But Ininatig saved them. He told one starving man to collect the clear, sweet sap, to boil it to make syrup, and then to stir it until it turned into sugar. He even told him how to make sugar candy.

Because Ininatig provided the Ojibwa people with the strength they needed to survive, the people continue to honor this generous tree spirit. Each spring, they celebrate the maple trees. Native Americans today, as in the past, recognize a reciprocity between human beings and nature. Because the people depend on plants and animals to survive, they show them respect; they have learned that if given proper respect, nature gives its gifts generously.

Today's maple festivals developed as celebrations of seasonal renewal and as offerings of thanksgiving to the spirits for the gift of maple syrup. Ininatig gave this gift to the Ojibwa, and Manabozho gave it to the Algonquin. Another Ojibwa tale attributes the maple's sap to Nokomis, the primordial earth mother, who is featured prominently in Ojibwa myth. In this particular story, Nokomis hid in a grove of maple trees to escape the wendigos, cannibalistic demons who personified the death grip of the winter. The wendigos chased Nokomis across the land, but when they saw her disappear in a forest of bright colors, they believed that fire had destroyed her, and they turned away and left the old grandmother alone. This "fire" was nothing more than the maple trees' autumn foliage. Because the trees saved the earth mother, they received their sweet, nourishing sap as a reward.

In another legend, a squaw discovered maple sugar when she was cooking moose meat and ran out of water. To finish cooking the moose, she tapped the maple tree for liquid, and used the sap. The meat was sticky, but smelled unusually delicious. Her husband took a bite, and to her delight, loved the taste. From then on, people continued to tap the maple trees for the sweet, wonderful substance. It became North America's first sweetener, and an essential source of food. Native Americans today continue to hold maple festivals and to recount the legends of the maple benefactors in order to pass on the proper respect for nature to new generations. (Casselman 1997; Elkhort 1991; Gay and Gay 1996; Levi-Strauss 1974, 1978)

See also Candy; Honey; Sugar and Sugarcane

MEAD

Mead is a generic name for intoxicating drinks make from honey, water, and other ingredients such as herbs and spices. It has been called the recreational drug of the ancients, humanity's first beer, and possibly humanity's oldest alcoholic beverage. The Africans, the Maya, the Indo-Europeans, and particularly the Germanic peoples drank mead in great quantities. Though eventually many of them drank mead at every feast and festival, they originally consumed it in rituals to make contact with the gods.

People of the Germanic tribes were famous for making mead, and mead is frequently mentioned in their myths. In one Norse myth, mead spouted from the udders of Odin's goat, Heidrun, and Heidrun fed on Yggdrasil, the world tree, a symbol of life and strength and a model for order in the world. In another popular myth, dwarves brewed the first mead, after stealing the necessary ingredients from the gods. The two races of Norse gods, the Aesir and the Vanir, warred constantly; but one day they called a truce, each side spitting into a cauldron to seal their agreement. From this primordial mix emerged Kvasir, a wise old man who knew all the answers of the universe. (The name Kvasir comes from the root *kvas,* which means "strong beer.") Two dwarves, envious of Kvasir's knowledge, desired to possess it for themselves. They killed Kvasir and drained his blood into three large vessels. Then they mixed his blood with honey and made the first mead. Whoever drank the mead became wise, like Kvasir. They could compose poetry and utter words of wisdom. The mythmakers labeled this the mead of poetry, or the gift of inspiration.

Dwarves were typically associated with wisdom in Norse mythology, even though they ultimately lost the precious mead. The dwarves killed a giant and his wife with whom they had quarreled, and then had to give the giant's son, Suttung, the mead of poetry in exchange for their lives. Odin and the other gods proceeded to win the mead from the giants. Odin was the high god, and he was quite resourceful. He managed to obtain the magic liquid from Suttung's daughter, Gunlod, who had trapped it deep inside a mountain cave. Odin disguised himself as a serpent, entered the cave, and seduced Gunlod, getting her to agree to give him three drinks. In three gulps, he emptied all three vessels. Odin then transformed himself into an eagle and flew back to Asgard, the home of the gods, and there he spat out the mead into three new vessels. Mead, and the gift of poetry and inspiration, belonged to the gods at last. Odin regularly fortified himself with mead and dispensed it to the others.

The mead of the Germanic myths appears to have an equivalent in the Indian soma, the elixir of immortality consumed by Indra and other Hindu gods. In Hindu myth, Indra—taking on the form of an eagle—rescued the precious soma from a mountain cave. Mead and soma served similar purposes. They were not simply intoxicating drinks but elixirs of life. They fortified the deities with wisdom, inspiration, and immortality, and elevated humans to a mental state appropriate for communing with their most venerated gods.

The mythmakers credited these beverages with supernatural powers: Blood and spittle formed the basis of the magic mead, and in myths around the world, blood and spittle served as magic, creative agents. Spittle also served as a fermenting agent, and Kvasir, the sage, personified the divine spittle. Having no knowledge of yeast, early people stumbled on other ways to produce the desired results. The ancient Peruvians, for instance, in brewing chicha, their maize beer, chewed some of the maize kernels first, mixing them in afterward with the rest. Human saliva breaks down the starch in the maize, and turns it into the maltose and glucose needed to produce alcohol.

If in the Norse version of the making of mead the gods' spittle did act as yeast, the spittle certainly formed a crucial part of the myth. The cauldron that held the mead was an equally important element. Northern peoples had large supplies of cauldrons and drinking horns, and Norse mythmakers continually placed emphasis on mythical cauldrons and on the unending supplies of mead they produced. Odin was said to keep his cauldron in a magnificent hall in Valhalla, the otherworld where kings and warriors went when they died. The Valkyries attended Odin and welcomed warriors into Valhalla, serving them mead and inviting them to feast in Odin's great hall. Aegir, the Norse sea god, also had a gigantic cauldron in which he brewed mead for all of the gods who feasted in his great hall underneath the waves in the depths of the North Sea. Both Odin's and Aegir's cauldrons of mead produced inexhaustible supplies, from which the Norse gods continually replenished their wisdom and inspiration. (Simoons 1998; Toussaint-Samat 1992; Turville-Petre 1964)

See also Alcoholic Beverages; Ayahuasca; Balche; Beer; Chicha; Honey; Kava; Pulque; Sake; Soma; Wine

MEAT

Throughout history, two contradictory notions have defined people's views on the consumption of meat. At one extreme was the view that killing and eating animals fostered ferocity and led to cannibalism; at the other extreme was the view that killing and eating animals was a sacred act, a ritual performed with the intention of offering the animal's flesh to the gods. The decision to eat or not to eat meat depended on the religious significance people attached to the animal's flesh and the killing act. People of some cultures consumed meat because they wished to honor the deities. People of other cultures avoided meat for this same reason. The Hindus and Buddhists prohibited the eating of meat because they adhered to the concept of ahimsa, or the sanctity of all living creatures. People of many cultures considered the consumption of meat inseparable from the practice of blood sacrifice; and for some, blood sacrifice constituted the most important part of religious belief.

The Masai, a pastoral people of East Africa, live exclusively on meat, milk, and blood from domestic livestock, primarily cattle. They don't kill specifically for food, because in Masai myth, Enkai, the Supreme Being, prohibited humans from killing livestock. But a woman once broke the rules and slaughtered an ox, and as punishment, Enkai killed the woman. Afterward, Enkai gave men permission to kill livestock under certain conditions. The Masai today venerate cattle and eat meat only in a ritual context. In the Masai creation myth, Enkai gave cattle to the people, lowering the animals from the sky on a string. The Masai believed that when Enkai gave people this precious gift, he sanctioned the use of pastoral foods, including meat and blood. In contrast to the belief that consuming meat and blood leads to savagery, the Masai believe that consuming these products defines humanity. By consuming only pastoral foods, the Masai say, they separate themselves from wild beasts, the beasts who hunt and kill and feed on people.

Masai warriors with a slaughtered ox. The Masai of East Africa believe that their creator god Enkai gave cattle to the people as a precious gift, and by doing so, sanctioned the use of meat and blood as food. (Roger De La Harpe; Gallo Images/Corbis)

Certainly meat consumption in the ancient world had as much to do with survival as it did with religion, but many early people connected survival and religion in their minds. In prehistoric times, people had few if any meat taboos. Taboos developed later, particularly in the Asian lands and among totemic people who believed that certain animals were their ancestors. It is difficult to determine the extent to which religious beliefs molded the dietary habits of prehistoric hunters; but certainly people revered the gods for the game animals they provided, long before the advent of agriculture. Among pious people, all food was god-given, whether it be fruits of the earth or flesh from the animals. To those who believed that the gods sent the animals to the hunting grounds as a gift, meat eating became a necessary act, a way of thanking the higher powers for providing sustenance.

Meat eating in the ancient world often involved sacrificing a part of the animal's flesh and blood to the gods before consuming the food. Those who considered blood sacrifice a pious act considered the killing itself sacred. They compared the act of taking life to the act of giving life, and therefore made it a ritual only designated people could perform, and often people were chosen to represent the deities themselves. In Greek myth, Prometheus, in an attempt to provide for human beings, sacrificed an ox, allotting the best share to the people on earth and leaving the gods only the smells rising from the burned fats and roasting meat. From then on, human beings were doomed to eat meat. It is interesting to note that in the Bible, Adam and Eve lived solely on plant food in the paradise of Eden. They lived in harmony with the animals. It was not until they ate the forbidden fruit from the Tree of Knowledge that they came to know evil; and it was not until after God flooded the world that he gave humans permission to eat meat. Meat eating defined the human condition, and as in the Prometheus myth, set humans in opposition to the gods. (Arhem 1989; Detienne and Vernant 1989; Farb and Arm-

elagos 1980; Simoons 1994; Toussaint-Samat 1992)

See also Bear; Beef; Blood and Flesh; Buffalo; Buffalo; Deer; Dog; Goat, Lamb, and Ram; Horse; Ox; Pork

MELONS
See Watermelons

MESQUITE

Mesquite beans were a primary food source for early peoples of the Sonoran desert, including the Yuman, the Mohave, the Cocopa, the Pima, and the Papago. The women in these tribes gathered the beans, spread them out on the roofs of their homes to dry, then used them to make a porridge that often saved them from starvation during the winter months. The people depended nearly entirely on desert plants for food, and mesquite seeds and pods met their nutritional needs. These products are high in protein, carbohydrates, and calcium, and fortunately for Mexican desert dwellers, they're easy to find. Mesquite produces exceptional yields of pods, even in Sonora, where rain falls only every few years. Hunters-gatherers in the area have therefore relied on the plant as a primary food source since ancient times.

The Native American gatherers ate more than fifty different kinds of grass seeds. They gathered these seeds and ground them into flour for bread, often combining them with either cornmeal or mesquite flour. Because the native peoples of Mexico have long considered mesquite beans an indispensable food source, they incorporated them long ago into their myths and legends. The Aztecs made them an essential part of their creation story. The Aztecs believed in a succession of world ages, each ruled by a different deity and each ending in a cataclysmic natural disaster. This creation myth explained the evolution of life, as well as the evolution of food. In the first age, giants inhabited the world, and they ate nothing but acorns. In the second age, people inhabited the world, and they ate nothing but mesquite. (Some versions say they ate pine nuts.) In the third and fourth ages, the people ate *cincocopi* and *acicintli,* both of them precursors to corn; and in the fifth and current age, they ate true corn. Although acorns, mesquite beans, cincocopi and acicintli sustained the world's inhabitants in various eras, the Aztec considered true corn the perfect food. (Montellano 1990)

See also Acorns; Corn; Pines and Pine Nuts

MILK

Milk is the essence of the mother goddess. The gods and kings of many lands received the nourishing liquid from her breast and entered into a state of everlasting bliss. Egyptian myths, in particular, are full of images of suckling deities, with the mother goddess appearing in numerous forms. As Isis she suckled Horus; as Nut she suckled souls of the dead; and as the cow goddess Hathor she suckled pharaohs and princes, including Osiris, after their deaths. Because the Egyptians believed that pharaohs became infants again after death, and because infants needed milk, the Egyptians believed these pharaohs needed milk in the otherworld as well. The mother goddess was there to provide it.

The mother goddess appeared most commonly as a woman, as a cow, or as a sacred tree. A Scottish-Gaelic legend tells of a goddess who personifies the milk-giving tree and who possesses the milk of wisdom. An African legend tells of Takane, the daughter of a great tribal chief, who feeds her young brother from a milk-giving tree in her garden. In a legend from South Africa, a tree provided milk for a poor family, possibly long before people learned to obtain milk from animals. Milk-yielding trees became a primary theme in world myth because various types of fruit (the fig and the coconut, for instance) produced milky juice. The Egyptian goddess Hathor embodied the sycamore fig, and the Aztec goddess Mayahuel embodied the maguey (agave). In myth, milk was holy food that flowed from the breasts of mother goddesses and from trees of life. These trees often had female attributes that validated their role as nurturer. As embodiments of trees, Hathor and Mayahuel both had many breasts. The nipple-like spines at the ends of the maguey leaves represented Mayahuel's breasts, and the figs represented Hathor's breasts. In both cases, the milk from the plant was the milk of the goddess.

The sycamore fig, in Egyptian myth, grew on an island in the Celestial Lake, at the source of the Celestial Nile (the Milky Way). The ancients commonly believed that the Milky Way—which they envisioned as a path of divine milk—was a heavenly river from which earthly rivers originated. The Greeks referred to the Milky Way as the milk of Hera, the wife of Zeus, who nursed their children to make them immortal. The Greeks clearly connected milk with the land of gods and goddesses and with the promise of eternal life. The milk in Greek myth did not flow from a tree, but it did exist in paradise. In Hindu myth, milk-yielding trees grew side by side with fruit-bearing trees, also a symbol of paradise, on the north side of Mount Meru and the south side of Mount Nila.

The mythic location of these trees in paradise meant that milk served the function of Elixir of Life. The source of the elixir was the mother goddess, who appeared in various forms—not only those of a woman, a cow, and a tree but also of a host of other animals that suckled gods and goddesses, kings and pharaohs. Vulture goddesses, for instance, suckled the pharaoh of Egypt; a goat suckled the Greek god Zeus; and a she-wolf suckled the Roman princes Romulus and Remus.

The cow goddess was one of the earliest objects of worship, and her milk was a sacred substance, clearly a gift from the gods. It's interesting to note, however, that not everyone elevates milk to such high status. In fact, many people view the product with disdain. Some Africans who keep dairy cattle don't consume

The sacred cow Hathor, a form of the mother goddess, suckling Amenhotep II. (Borromeo/Art Resource, NY)

their products because they liken milk to urine. Others refuse milk specifically to women and to people who they believe would be easily seduced by evil powers. Taboos on milk exist in much of East Africa and the Sudan as well as in East Asia, but in most cases they apply only to common usage—even these cultures recognize milk's superiority for ceremonial purposes. Some people in Africa who have an adequate supply of milk animals but don't milk them believe, in part, that only the favored classes or sorcerers have the right to consume milk. In an African myth from Burundi, Imana, the Supreme Being, removed a cow from her home in a celestial lake and sent it to the first princess on earth as a gift.

The cow gave birth, produced milk, and nourished the princess.

The notion of milk originating in a celestial lake or somewhere in the celestial sphere is a common one, and perhaps best illustrated by the Hindu creation myth describing the primordial ocean. This was a milk ocean, formed when the sacred cow, Surahbi, released a stream of milk and filled up the cosmic space. The milk of Surahbi was food for the gods, and the milk ocean clearly contained soma (or *amrita*), the nectar and ambrosia that made the gods immortal.

Bodies of divine milk appeared in Norse myth as well. In the beginning of time, when Audhumla, the ice cow, arose to feed Ymir, the primordial frost giant, four rivers of milk flowed from her teats and pervaded all four corners of the world. In Hindu myth, Surahbi's four children were the cow goddesses of the four quarters. Just as celestial milk from the Milky Way flowed into rivers on earth and provided nourishment for plants and people, celestial milk from these divine cows fell to earth and filled oceans, rivers, and streams. Rain, in other words, was milk from the celestial cow. In Egyptian myth, Nut, as cow goddess, released milk from her breasts and watered the earth with rain.

Like rain, milk was a life-giving substance, and as milk was considered sacred nourishment for gods, it was often considered a giver of immortality. The first settlers of Rome were shepherds, and they offered milk to their gods, just as the kings of Egypt and the cattle-raising peoples of ancient India did to theirs. In a legend from Thailand, Sujata, the daughter of a rich landowner, offered the richest and purest milk to Buddha. She gathered 1,000 cows into a meadow, milked them, then fed their milk to 500 of them. Then she milked the 500 and fed their milk to 250 of them. This went on and on, and the milk got richer and richer. The last 8 cows had extremely rich milk. Sujata mixed it with rice and fed it to Buddha, who was meditating under a fig tree. This milk sustained him until he achieved enlightenment.

The mythmakers of India also drew connections between milk and light. They likened Ushas, the dawn goddess, to a mother cow, and her rays of light to a stream of milk. In the Hindu myth of the Panis cows, both light and cow's milk are characterized as bright and radiant.

The cow emerged as a powerful symbol in the Vedic period, and today cow worship is an essential part of Hindu ritual. The cow gives of herself, particularly milk and milk products, for human use in sacred rituals. Gods such as Indra and Agni received milk oblations and thus they highly valued the cows that provided them. Some Hindus today believe that gods live inside cows—330 million gods, to

be exact. So the people protect cows; they do not destroy them. In myth, Surahbi was the mother of all cows, and in some myths she was born from the ocean of milk when the gods and demons churned it to obtain the Water of Life. In the myth of Krishna, however, Surahbi arose from the left part of Krishna's body. Krishna wanted milk, so he miraculously caused Surahbi's birth. Surahbi produced lots of milk for Krishna, and Krishna worshiped Surahbi; so people, in turn, worshiped all of her children. In another explanation of the sanctity of the cow, Brahma, the Hindu creator god, created cows on the same day he created Brahmans (India's highest caste), giving the cow a status far above that of other animals. In another myth, Indra put the milk into the cow, probably at the beginning of the universe. (Darby et al. 1977; Mackenzie 1970; Mahias 1988; Neumann 1955; Sharma 1980; Simoons 1998)

See also Beef; Butter; Dates; Figs; Honey; Meat; Nectar and Ambrosia; Water

MILLET

Though people in the United States and Europe today generally think of millet as fodder for horses, millet is an important staple grain for poor people in much of Asia, Russia, and western Africa, just as it was for Europeans through the Middle Ages. Like other staple grains, millet represented the earth's nourishment and the harvest. In southern Europe, people cultivated millet extensively as an alternative to oats and barley. It grew prolifically and produced astounding supplies. In China, millet had special significance because it required the earliest sowing and yielded the earliest harvest of all grain crops. The Chinese have worshiped the spirits of millet and of the soil since ancient times. Because they believed that this precious grain ensured their survival on earth, they used millet and millet wine ceremonially and in ritual sacrifices.

The myths and beliefs surrounding millet closely parallel the myths and beliefs about other staple grains. These tales recount the supernatural origin of the crops and attempt to explain how people on earth received these divine gifts. The Mossi of Volta, for instance, believe that a bird first produced millet during a great famine. A starving woman caught the bird and planned to cook it, but then discovered millet droppings in the bird's cage. Whoever gave the gift of grain received special reverence, for they supplied a precious and irreplaceable commodity. The Chinese said that Hou Chi gave people the gift of millet. They called him "Prince Millet" or "Lord Millet" and worshiped him as the god of cereals and the patron deity of agriculture.

In Chinese mythology, Hou Chi was god of the earth, a descendant of Huang Ti, god of medicine, and the firstborn son of Chiang Yuan, who gave birth to the first human beings at the beginning of the world. Hou Chi planted beans and rice, wheat and gourds, and then millet, which grew abundantly. T'ang, the founder of the Shang dynasty, placed Hou Chi in charge of millet; then when the Chou dynasty supplanted the Shang, Hou Chi gained recognition as the celestial ancestor of the Chou emperors. This meant that like the emperors, Hou Chi had a responsibility to ensure the survival of the harvest—particularly the millet, which the people considered vital because they believed its cyclic growth maintained the relationship between the earth and the sky world. As the celestial ancestor of the Chou emperors, Hou Chi lived among the stars and protected the agricultural cycle. The Chinese immortalized their grains by placing them among the constellations; they had celestial millet, a celestial granary and Imperial celestial granary, and a celestial sickle and pestle—they recognized all of them in configurations of stars that shone in their night sky at particular times of the year. The Chinese called their celestial millet T'ien-tsi, a configuration of four stars they believed presided over the grain harvest.

Like ancient people in many parts of the world, the Chinese were remarkably astute sky watchers, and they used the movements of the stars and the constellations to guide their actions. They understood that T'ien-tsi's first yearly appearance in the sky foretold the ripening of the millet. If the constellation shone clearly, the harvest would be abundant; but if the constellation was obscured or invisible, there would be famine.

People in lands other than China placed millet in their sky myths as well. The Dogon of Africa, for instance, believed that millet first existed in the sky and that their Great Blacksmith Ancestor stole it and brought it down to earth. The early Germanic peoples believed that millet landed on earth when a great storm dragon hid in the clouds and spat flames of blue lightning down from the sky; he sowed the millet on earth so that he himself could eat it. When the dragon spat red lightning, gold landed on earth. The early Germans appeared to draw a connection between gold and millet, for they married them in the myth of the storm dragon. Although in western Europe it was generally the poor who consumed millet, some Europeans believed that whoever ate the grain on New Year's Day would become rich.

People of early times often defined wealth by the quantity of foods they possessed; an abundant harvest and a reliable store of grain they considered symbols of prosperity. In a myth of the Togo people of Africa, a man named Kaddo had fields and fields of millet, so much that his granaries filled to overflowing, and because of this, people all over the land knew him as the wealthiest man in the village. Kaddo wallowed in his wealth. He loved his high stature. But unfortunately this made him a greedy man. Kaddo refused to share his millet with the villagers, even when they suffered from starvation. Kaddo called for all the villagers to help him solve his problem: what he should do with his abundance of millet, because clearly his granaries could no longer contain it. Though they suggested that he share his wealth with the hungry people, Kaddo decided instead to build a wall of grain around his house. He wanted to display his wealth and to keep it all to himself. Kaddo called for the women in the village to grind his millet into meal, then to add water and make bricks out of it, and finally, to stack the bricks and construct a great wall. This they did, and Kaddo proudly displayed his wealth, even in the face of starving people. But then the tides turned. A great famine plagued the land and Kaddo's field suffered. Soon he had no grain left, and for the first time, he too felt the desperation of hunger and need. Kaddo began to consume his wall, but the famine dragged on. Soon Kaddo had nothing left to eat at all. The story of Kaddo reveals the importance the African people placed on the millet they grew. Possessing it made them wealthy; but they had to share their wealth, for only then could such possession be considered fortuitous.

A German legend told of another man who had a garden of millet, and he too was considered wealthy. The wealthy man noticed that during the night someone had cut the grain and taken it away, so he had his sons stay awake in order to catch the thief. The oldest son took his turn the first night and fell asleep, and the second son took his turn the next night and fell asleep as well. The third son, however, surrounded himself with thorns, and as he started to drift off to sleep, the thorns pricked him and he woke up. This boy caught the thief—a horse—eating the millet. Later on, when the boys heard about a princess who was held captive in a castle on top of a glass mountain, the youngest son mounted the horse, climbed the mountain, and rescued her. As it turned out, the colt had once belonged to the princess herself, and had climbed and descended the glass mountain many times, as it took the princess down the mountain every night for a ride in the fields. The boy and the princess were married. The horse, like the millet, brought the boy good fortune. (Courlander 1975; Folkard 1892; Skinner n.d.; Staal 1984)

See also Amaranth; Barley; Bread; Cake; Grain; Oats; Quinoa; Rice; Rye; Wheat

MINT

Mint is an aromatic herb that people have used since ancient times both as a condiment and as a medicinal. It was highly valued by the ancient Hebrews, the Greeks, and the Romans, all of whom used mint much more frequently than people do today. Mint was alluring, but at the same time stultifying. The ancients considered it an aphrodisiac, yet also believed that it made women sterile and men impotent. Mint was believed to stimulate desire, but because the plant had no fruit, it was also believed to prevent that desire from being fruitful.

The ancient Romans revealed their perception of mint's dual nature in their myth of Mintha, the lover of Hades, the god of the underworld. Ovid's *Metamorphoses* tells of how Mintha attracted Hades's attention and the two entered into a relationship based on illicit sex. Hades's wife Persephone felt betrayed and abandoned by her husband, went into a jealous rage, and vowed revenge on Mintha. In one version of the myth, Persephone tore Mintha apart, reducing her to dust, and Hades changed her dust into the garden mint plant. In another version, Persephone's mother, Demeter, tore Mintha apart. She trampled her into the earth, but Persephone rose from the ground as mint, and much to Demeter's dismay, continued to seduce with her fresh, sweet smell.

Demeter and Persephone were earth goddesses, and the hostility between the two of them and Mintha is an important part of the myth. Because mint had no fruit, the conflict between Mintha and Demeter and Persephone pitted sterility against fertility; and because mint grew wild and uncontrolled in the fields of Eleusis, the conflict pitted the wild against the cultivated. Demeter represented the cultivated grain and thus the civilized state; the wild mint, on the other hand, represented the precivilized condition. When Demeter saw mint growing wild in her fields, she despised the plant as something untamed—a sign of the lust that had characterized Mintha's relationship with Hades. The opposition between the wild and the cultivated played a large role in the Eleusinian myth, as did the opposition between concubinage and the marital state. Demeter so hated the mint plant that she condemned it to sterility, changing it into a fruitless plant. But as a fragrant herb, mint never lost its allure. It became sacred to Hades, and it came to symbolize the illicit sex that characterized the death god's relationship with Mintha. (Detienne 1977; Folkard 1892)

See also Grain; Herbs

MORNING GLORY SEEDS
See Ololiuqui

MULBERRIES

Mulberries gained mythic recognition largely because of their red color, an attribute that traditionally symbolized blood. Some ancient cultures created taboos against red foods because of this connection, and others prized them because they grew from the blood of highly revered gods. In either case, the association between redness and blood provided a convenient basis for explaining the origins of mulberries.

One of the best-known legends of mulberries appeared in Ovid's *Metamorphoses,* in the tale of Pyramus and Thisbe. Ovid asserts that in all of ancient Babylon, Pyramus was the most handsome man, and Thisbe, the most beautiful woman. Although their parents had forbidden them to see each other, the two met secretly at the wall that separated their homes, and there they talked and kissed through a crack. But these meetings did not satisfy the lovers' desire to see each other. One day they decided to meet at the Tomb of Ninus, near a mulberry bush, whose fruits at that time were white in color. Thisbe got there first, but a lioness came and scared her away. Thisbe dropped her veil, and the lioness picked it up in her mouth and began to play with it. The lioness, however, had just finished devouring a lamb, and her mouth was still bloody from

the kill. When the lioness left the Tomb of Ninus, she left Thisbe's veil on the ground, stained with blood. Pyramus arrived at the meeting place soon after this, and when he saw the veil, he assumed that his beloved Thisbe had been killed. He plunged his sword into his heart in grief. Then Thisbe returned, saw her dead lover, and killed herself as well. The blood from Pyramus and Thisbe splattered out of their bodies and onto the white mulberries, which have been red ever since.

The mulberry tree in the myth of Pyramus and Thisbe was merely a prop, but in Chinese myths the tree played a more important role. Mulberries themselves were probably eaten in antiquity, but they had little nutritional value. The tree and the leaves, however, had great value in providing nourishment for silkworms. China thrived on the silk industry, and the industry thrived on the strength of the worms and their cocoons. So the Chinese had gods of silkworms in every stage of life, as well as gods of the mulberry trees that fed them. Ts'an Ts'ung, a god and the king of Shu, was said to have taught the people about mulberry trees and the technique of sericulture, or silk production. Hua Kuang Ta Ti was the lord of all silkworm deities, and his worshipers made offerings to him continually. Ts'an Hua Wu Shen were the five patron sages of the silkworm, the deities who guarded and protected these insects during their molting period. San Ku Fu Jen was the goddess of mulberry trees. The people invoked her to produce good leaves to feed the silkworms, and to watch over and protect all the mulberry trees that grew outside the city walls.

The Chinese have a legend about a good fairy who ensures that all of the mulberry trees in China produce abundant supplies of silk: It is said that the fairy was so pleased by a gift of mulberry preserves that she vowed to make the trees produce a hundred times as much silk as they previously had. An ancient Chinese myth also reveals the importance of the mulberry tree to sericulture, and thus to the vitality of China: When a young girl was picking mulberry leaves one day, she found a baby boy in the hollow of the mulberry tree. She gave the baby to her lord, who gave it to his cook to care for, and the boy, Yi Yin, grew up to be a wise member of the Shang court. The ancient Chinese venerated their mulberry groves, and some groups continue to do so today. Yi Yin was born of the sacred mulberry, and his myth validates the notion of sacred trees in general—trees of various species that many cultures believe gave birth to their important deities. Yu Yin, the mulberry mother of Yi Yin, was greatly revered for her contribution to China's silk industry. (Day 1969; Skinner n.d.)

> **See also** Blackberries; Blueberries; Cranberries; Elderberries; Gooseberries; Raspberries; Strawberries

MUSHROOMS

Mushrooms have always been objects of mystery. They sprout from the ground suddenly and grow so rapidly that they fire the imagination and stimulate myths and legends of all sorts. Ancient peoples believed that their gods ate mushrooms, and that when people first ate them, they understood the concept of divinity based on the mushrooms' hallucinogenic powers. Perhaps the very notion of the miraculous stemmed from experiencing such powers firsthand. Hallucinogenic mushrooms were revered in the ancient world. Varieties that were consumed for food were both considered a delicacy and viewed with suspicion. The Mexicans held all mushrooms sacred, and the Egyptians forbade commoners to consume them. The Egyptian pharaohs apparently wanted to keep the mystery of the mushroom to themselves.

Before people understood the growth conditions of fungi, they came up with fanciful explanations for the appearance of these strange fruits. From antiquity people connected mushrooms with fire. The ancient people of Corinth—the seat of a great fire cult—believed that they themselves were descended from mushrooms. Mushrooms often sprang up after storms, so the early Greeks and Romans typically attributed their growth to the lightning; these people believed that the bolt of the great god Zeus created the fungi. Early people in Mexico also appear to have linked mushrooms with what they perceived as sexual intercourse between a lightning bolt and the earth. The fly agaric mushroom, a poisonous species often used by shamans to induce trances, grew abundantly in North and Central America. Pagan legends associated mushrooms with lightning until the late eighteenth century, but Christian legends explained these poisonous mushrooms in a different way. In one Christian legend, Christ and Peter walked around the land begging for bread. When the peasants offered them bread, the brown crumbs that fell to the ground caused poisonous mushrooms to grow, and the white ones gave rise to edible varieties.

One of the best-known explanations for the origin of mushrooms identifies them as the product of fairy rings. The fungus spawns often form circles of dark green grass that for some reason people believed denoted the areas where fairies danced at night. In legend the mushrooms appeared wherever the fairies' feet touched the ground, and these magical beings had the ability to hold anyone captive who stepped inside the circles where they danced and romped. These strange mushroom formations fired the imaginations of people, who not only connected them with fairies but also with witches and devils. Some people referred to them as "devil's bread" or "devil's food," and others believed they grew from the spittle of witches or sorcerers.

Most likely the connection to demonic forces applied to the poisonous properties of the fly agaric mushroom. People typically connected poisonous mushrooms with the Devil's work. In a legend from Silesia, poisonous mushrooms grew when the Devil, who was in a bad mood, was walking through the woods and met up with an old woman. He cut her into pieces and scattered the pieces around on the ground. Mushrooms as wrinkled as an old woman sprang up wherever the pieces of her body fell. In a Germanic myth, Woten, the highest god, rode through the forest one night every winter with his dogs and followers behind him. Devils pursued Woten all the way, and his horse, Sleipnir, ran so fast that drops of bloody foam fell from his mouth. Wherever the foam fell, mushrooms sprouted the following spring. These were poisonous mushrooms, the fly agaric, which have red caps with white spots. An early belief that arose in Yorkshire, England, connected the growth of these mushrooms with stallions' semen.

Poisonous mushrooms caused the deaths of many rulers and important personages in the Old World. It has even been suggested that the Buddha, who many thought died after eating swine, or pork, actually died after eating swine mushrooms, their powers potent enough to carry him to heaven.* In Rome, Agrippa, who wanted the emperor's crown for her son, Nero, obtained a concoction from a woman who made poisons, put it into a mushroom, and gave it to her husband Claudius. Nero became emperor and thereafter referred to the mushrooms he ate as "the dish of the gods."

Taoists considered the *ling-chih* one of the most important plants of the gods. These were particularly rare mushrooms said to make people immortal. Chinese folklore has many legends of the search for the ling-chih, and Japanese folklore does as well. The Japanese called the ling-chih *reishi*. It grew on plum trees in Japan, and ancient Japanese texts hailed it as a food that arrests aging.

The fly agaric mushroom enjoyed widespread ceremonial use among the early Siberians. Until the Siberians learned of alcohol from the Russians, these mushrooms were

their only intoxicant. Alaskan and Siberian shamans used the fly agaric to help give them strength and to help them go into trances. They dried and ate them or mixed them with reindeer milk, water, or the juice of various plants. They also drank the urine of reindeer that had consumed the fly agaric, knowing that the hallucinogenic properties of the mushroom passed through the animal's body and were excreted in the urine.

Shamanic cultures of these northern lands believed that supernatural beings inhabited the mushrooms; the Koryak of Siberia believed that evil beings called *nimvits* inhabited them and that only the shamans could control these beings. The Chukchee believed that the mushrooms actually constituted another tribe. The Koryak called the fly agaric *wapaq,* and they said that Raven, their culture hero, taught the people how to use wapaq after the god Vahiyinin created it by spitting on the earth. In a Koryak legend, Raven caught a whale, and was unable to heave the whale's heavy body back into the water. So Vahiyinin made the magic mushrooms spring up to feed Raven and give him the strength he needed to lift the whale. The fly agaric's powers amazed Raven and the Koryak people. Not only did it give them strength but it also had the ability to induce hallucinations. Due to the mushroom's hallucinogenic properties, some have suggested that the fly agaric was the "plant" the Vedic Indians identified as soma. Soma produced a juice that when consumed also bestowed enormous physical strength, and most importantly, immortality.

Fly agaric might have made its consumers feel immortal in the same way that shamans who partook of the mushroom believed they could ascend to other worlds. The ancient Greeks may have consumed the mushroom during Dionysian festivals; it was said that the followers of Dionysus drank a magic potion and had visions. The name of the mushroom might well have come from the feeling of flying that it transmitted to those who partook of it. Symbols in ancient Mayan codices

---

*It was said that Siddhartha, the Buddha, abandoned vegetarianism and died at the age of eighty-four after feasting on pork. Some scholars assert that he died from eating "swine," not pork, and that this "swine" referred to the swine mushroom. Others said he died from eating bamboo shoots that had been trodden on by pigs.

resemble this type of mushroom, which indicates that the Maya also assigned mushrooms mythological significance. It appears that the Maya likely had mushroom cults in which worshipers consumed the sacred, hallucinogenic fungi during religious rituals. (Dobkin De Rios 1976; Graves 1957; Kleijn 1965; Morgan 1995; Ratsch 1992; Schultes and Hofmann 1979; Wasson 1972)

See also Cactus; Mead; Nightshades; Ololiuqui; Plums; Reindeer and Caribou; Soma

MUSTARD SEEDS

People in Asia and the Middle East have cultivated the mustard plant for thousands of years. In biblical times, the people of Palestine cultivated black mustard largely for its seeds, which they used to make oil for the ritual purpose of anointing. The ancient Hebrews and other Eastern peoples used large quantities of this oil, so they highly esteemed their mustard seeds. Not only did they use the oil for anointing but they used the seeds for healing ailments of all sorts.

The ancient Greeks assigned mustard seeds far-ranging healing properties and attributed the discovery of mustard seeds to Asclepius, their highly revered god of medicine. The Greeks also used mustard seeds (because of mustard's "fiery" nature) as an aphrodisiac, and mixed them with oil and honey to produce a form of birth control. Pythagoras recommended them as an antidote to poison, particularly the poison from scorpion bites. Early peoples of England and North America also used mustard seeds to counteract poison as well as to cure epilepsy, heart troubles, and toothaches; to cleanse the body; to clarify the blood; and to relieve the pain of gout and all sorts of other aches and pains. North American Indians used mustard medicinally too, and for many of these same ailments.

Mustard was widespread in early England and North America, and in the Middle East it was one of the most common garden herbs. Ancient Middle Eastern legends recount tales of gigantic mustard plants—larger than human beings, and hardy enough to accommodate nesting birds in their branches. In biblical times, mustard trees reportedly did grow up to fifteen feet tall, and birds did build their nests in them. The large plants attracted attention in ancient times, as did the small seeds. The mustard plant produced seeds smaller than any other seeds the people knew at the time; so the Hebrews, for instance, used the phrase *grain of mustard* to mean something infinitesimally small. People began to utilize the vast difference between the small seeds and the large plants in parables. A passage in the book of Matthew compares the Kingdom of Heaven to a grain of mustard seed, revealing that it started as the smallest of all seeds and grew to be the greatest of all herbs. It also compares the mustard seed to the modest amount of faith necessary to behold the miracles of the Lord.

The ancients quite obviously held mustard in high esteem. They invested it not only with healing powers but with powers of fertility and magic as well. In Hindu myths, mustard seeds enabled people to travel through the air, helped them locate treasures within the earth, and gave them the ability to effect transformations. In one Indian legend, a Brahman had a young wife who became a witch and betrayed her husband by giving her affections to their cowherd. Her husband discovered the two of them together and nearly killed them; but his evil wife saw him first, and changed him into a buffalo. The wife then sold her husband to a buffalo trader. By and by, the trader learned his newly acquired animal was a man in disguise. A good witch changed him back and gave him some magic mustard seeds, which he sprinkled on his wife, turning her into a mare.

Another Indian legend reveals the fertilizing powers of mustard seed: A farmer and his wife had tried for some time to have a child, but the woman did not conceive until she consumed some magic mustard. The farmer plowed a field over the site of an ancient temple where a nymph named Bakawali had lived, and mustard grew on the spot. Later, after his wife consumed the mustard seed, she miraculously gave birth to a baby girl. Even more miraculously, this baby girl appeared to be Bakawali herself, reincarnated in another form—transformed by the power of mustard. (Moldenke and Moldenke 1952; Penzer 1924–1928; Skinner n.d.; Walker 1979)

See also Herbs

must have consumed something that made them so. In Mesopotamian myth, however, the gods generally ate the same things the people ate. They ate fish and sheep and cereals and oils—foods that worshipers offered as sacrifices. The Mesopotamian myth of Adapa, however, mentions the Bread of Life and the Water of Life offered in heaven. So the Mesopotamians also appeared to identify immortal food. They may not have identified them as nectar and ambrosia, but in essence that's what they were. The Bread of Life fed the gods and the Water of Life quenched their thirst.

Early mythmakers seem to have used the words *nectar* and *ambrosia* interchangeably. In some myths, ambrosia was food and nectar was drink; in other myths, it was the other way around. Some writers described nectar as a drink made of honey and fruit, and ambrosia as a kind of porridge made from honey, fruit, olive oil, cheese, barley, and water. Others described ambrosia as an herb that grew on earth (some identified it as parsley or wild sage), an herb they believed prolonged human life just as the ambrosia of the gods preserved their immortality. But it was generally believed that

NECTAR AND AMBROSIA

Nectar and ambrosia, in the myths, were the foods of the gods, foods that preserved their immortality and that flowed miraculously in some mythical paradise. Oftentimes, world trees grew in paradise and produced these divine foods. The supernatural Tree of Buddha, the *haoma* tree (a sacred vine of the Zoroastrians), and the Tree of Life in many lands all produced immortal sustenance.

People in many early cultures believed that their deities ate special foods unknown to humans: The gods were immortal, and they

The Greek gods partaking in nectar and ambrosia on Mount Olympus. (Scala/Art Resource, NY)

mortals would suffer deadly consequences if they ate the gods' ambrosia or drank the gods' nectar, whatever those divine foods might be. Some said mortals who partook of these delights turned into fairies. Quite often the ancients connected ambrosia with honey. The classical Greeks commonly offered honey to their gods; Odysseus reportedly brought sacrifices of milk as well as of honey. The Greeks also baked honey cakes for the dead to feed Cerberus, the dog who guarded the entrance to the underworld.

People tend to connect nectar and ambrosia with Greek myth, and often envision Zeus, the high god, partaking of the godly food while seated on his throne on Mount Olympus. In Greek myth, Amalthea the she-goat nursed Zeus with her milk, and the bee Melissa nourished him with her honey. But the nectar and ambrosia of Zeus had their equivalents in many cultures. Often it was not milk and honey but fruit growing on the magical Tree of Life that bestowed immortality. In Hindu myth, Indra's heaven had five trees, under which the gods drank ambrosia, which the Hindus called *amrita,* or soma. Chief among these five trees was the ambrosia tree, also known as the *parijata* tree.

Trees grew on earth and in the sky world, and no distinction was made among them until ambrosia fell upon the earth. After that, the earthly trees seeded and multiplied, but they were not everlasting and immortal as were the trees in heaven. Earthly vegetation is only considered immortal because it dies, sprouts again, and reproduces, but the trees of heaven produce continually. The ambrosia tree of Buddhist belief was also called the Cloud Tree, the Tree of Wisdom, or the Tree of Buddha. It was a tree of gemstones that sprang up through the center of the universe when Buddha was born, and its flowers glimmered like jewels.

The ancients also identified various other plants as producers of immortal sustenance. In a Hindu myth (recounted in the *Ramayana*), the *gaduchi* was a medicinal plant that pro-

duced heavenly nectar, or amrita. Ravana, the demon king, wanted to marry Sita, Rama's wife. He wanted to do so partly because Rama's younger brother had cut off Ravana's sister's nose, and the demon king wanted revenge.

Ravana used his magic to create a golden deer, and because Sita longed for the deer, Rama and his brother left to chase it. While they were gone, Ravana abducted Sita and carried her off to his kingdom. Rama and his monkeys attacked the kingdom and killed Ravana. Rama fought evil, which made the high god Indra happy. He sprayed all the monkeys who had died in the battle with nectar, or amrita, the Elixir of Life. Some drops of the precious liquid fell on earth, and wherever they landed, gaduchi plants sprang up. Because these plants grew from the nectar of the gods, Hindus held them sacred and believed they could grant immortality.

The ancients clearly believed that nectar and ambrosia originated in heaven, often on the moon. The Hindu myth of churning the ocean connected amrita, the Hindu nectar or ambrosia, with dew from the moon. The primordial sea in this myth was a large ocean of milk, which the gods and demons had to churn in order to make the magic elixir rise from the depths. In the process of churning the ocean of milk, the gods and demons dropped potent herbs into the ocean, to flavor the ambrosia. Finally the substance arose, embodied in the moon god, Chandra, who later came to be identified as Soma. In the *Vishnu Purana,* the amrita or nectar appears to represent lunar light as well as dew. The moon received this nectar from the sun and distributed it among the gods, men, animals, and plants. When the moon waned, it was thought that thousands of deities were drinking the moon's nectar to renew their immortality. When it waxed full, people believed that the moon dew again would drip down onto the earth, to sustain people, animals, and plants. (Baumann 1993)

See also Honey; Manna; Milk; Soma

NIGHTSHADES

The mention of nightshades evokes legends of black magic and witchcraft. Witches have a reputation for poisoning people, and nightshades for supplying the means for doing so. Many members of this infamous plant family do indeed have toxic properties (e.g., belladonna), but others are familiar foods that people eat every day. Tomatoes, eggplants, and potatoes, for instance, all belong to the family of nightshades, and early people viewed them with skepticism and connected them with insanity.

Tomatoes and potatoes suffered from bad press when they first arrived in Europe. The Spaniards encountered them first in the New World, and it took a long time for people of the Old World to accept them as nourishing foods. The people of Europe knew that nightshades had a long history steeped in magic and superstition. The poisonous nightshades gave witches the ability to cast evil spells, they heard—to stupefy their victims, to put them into deep sleeps, and to drive them insane. The nightshades that had these abilities were inebriating plants such as henbane, mandrake, and belladonna or deadly nightshade.

The deadly nightshade is one of Europe's most poisonous wild plants. Its generic name, *atropa,* is derived from that of the Greek Fate Atropos, who was said to determine the time of a person's death by cutting the thread of their life. In Europe, particularly in the Middle Ages, witches were believed to feed deadly nightshade to people they wanted to harm or kill. People heard the legends about this plant and believed in its power to accomplish the unthinkable. They believed that deadly nightshade got the name *belladonna* because the plant had the ability to transform itself into a lovely but deadly enchantress. They also believed that witches rubbed their bodies with the plant in order to fly.

Witches in medieval Europe did use deadly nightshade as the primary ingredient in their magic brews, as had the shamans, sorcerers, and soothsayers of other lands and earlier times.

Nightshades, as the legendary ingredients in witches' brews, have long been associated with evil magic (Dover Pictorial Series Archive)

They used these plants in love potions, in divination, and in treating illnesses attributed to demons. The ancient Egyptians knew of these plants and their inebriating properties, as did the Sumerians and ancient Greeks. The Germanic peoples added henbane to their beer and mead to increase the potency of those beverages, and they called the deadly nightshade the Berry of the Valkyries, or *Walkerbeere,* and associated it with Woten, their god of ecstasy, and with the berserkers, frenzied warriors who consumed large quantities of mead and savagely destroyed their enemies. The Greek followers of Dionysus added belladonna, or deadly nightshade, to their wine, which likewise put them into a frenzied state. The Chinese added henbane to wine and fed it to patients, to enable them to contact the spirits. Henbane gained a reputation for enabling its consumer to contact spirits, particularly evil ones. In legend, when witches crushed henbane and burned it, the noxious fumes summoned demons from the underworld. (Heiser 1969; Ratsch 1992; Schultes and Hofmann 1979)

See also Alcoholic Beverages; Cactus; Eggplant; Mandrakes; Mushrooms; Ololiuqui; Potatoes; Thornapples; Tomatoes

OATS

Myths of oats have much in common with myths of wheat, barley, rye, corn, and other cereal grains. Grains generally were associated with the fertility of the earth and of the soil, and served as symbols of the earth's renewal. Oats originated in Central Asia, whence their cultivation is thought to have migrated into Arabia, Egypt, and northern Europe, together with the introduction of the horse.

Oats were a principal crop grown by people in the northern countries, but they appear to have gained a bad reputation in Norse mythology. Norse myths link Loki, the often malevolent trickster, with oats—"oats of the devil," they are called in the myths, or "Loki's oats." Loki is a complex figure—basically a trickster, but often an adversary to the gods as well. In one legend the earth mother put werewolves at the corners of the grainfields to scare off predators, but Loki sneaked past them and scattered his oat seeds. The myth fostered a connection between oats and naughtiness.

Harvest traditions in northern Europe fostered a connection between oats and evil. People in Germany and neighboring countries typically personified the last sheaf of oats as a horse, a cow, a wolf, or a goat. All of these animals represented not only the last sheaf but the spirit of the growing oats. Traditions involving the Oats Goat still exist in eastern Europe, particularly in Prussia, where people sometimes create a goat effigy from the last sheaf of oats harvested. Sometimes the goat effigies are fashioned of wood or straw. Children fear the Oats Goat, just as they fear the rye wolf and similar personifications of grain, because adults use such characters as scare tactics to keep children out of the fields. These fearsome animals cause sickness to harvesters and harm intruders, the adults tell their children, and when the wind blows, the adults explain it as the Oats Goat moving about through the fields. In Prussia and Bavaria, the people who embrace these superstitions sometimes release a real goat into the fields, and later, sacrifice and eat the animal at the harvest supper. (Kahn 1985; Lehner and Lehner 1973)

See also Barley; Bread; Cake; Corn; Millet; Rice; Rye; Sorghum; Wheat

OCTLI
See Pulque

OLIVES AND OLIVE OIL

Wild olive trees are indigenous to the eastern Mediterranean where they line the low coastal areas of Greece and the surrounding islands. They're evergreen trees, and they've been cultivated in the Mediterranean and the Middle East since Neolithic times. Olives occupy a prominent place in mythology and custom, and the olive tree's branches and oil were used in much of the ancient world to bestow kingship, consecrate holy objects, and anoint people of honor and bodies of the dead. The olive figures prominently in the myths and customs of Greece, in particular, where it served as a symbol of peace and of constancy; an emblem of achievement; and a sacred, immortal, and divine fruit.

The myths of both Greece and Rome connected olive trees with the high gods, and

Cameo depicting the contest between Poseidon and Athena over the naming of Athens. The gods decreed that the city should be named for whoever gave the people the best gift, and Athena won the contest by giving humans the olive tree. (Erich Lessing/Art Resource, NY)

being born under an olive tree signified divine ancestry. The Greek twins Apollo and Artemis were born under an olive tree, as were the Roman princes Romulus and Remus. (Myths also connect Apollo and Artemis to the date tree, and Romulus and Remus to the fig tree.) The gods taught the cultivation of olive trees. In Egyptian myth, Isis taught their cultivation and use, and in Roman myth, Hercules spread olives around the Mediterranean as he traveled about performing his twelve labors. It was Athena, however, whom the Greeks credited with creating the first olive tree, and she performed this task in the myth of the naming of Athens. Poseidon, the sea god, and Athena, the goddess of wisdom, argued over which of them the city should be named for. The gods decided it should be named after whomever gave human beings the best gift. Poseidon gave humans the horse. He struck the ground with his trident, and a horse sprang up on the spot. (In some versions of this myth he produced a saltwater spring in this manner.) Athena struck the ground with her spear, and an olive tree grew. The olive, the gods decided, symbolized peace, and the horse symbolized war. So Athena won the contest, and the new city was named Athens.

The Greeks continued to use the olive as a symbol of peace from the naming of Athens onward, and they considered it a sign of the vitality of Athens and its people. The victors of war received olive branches from the losers as a peace offering and an emblem of achievement, and the winners of the Olympian Games received crowns of olive leaves as their prize. The Olympian Games occurred once every four years, and during the games the people conducted ceremonies to honor Athena. They paraded up the Acropolis to a statue of the goddess carved out of olive wood.

Olive trees, because of the Athena myth, came to mean revitalization and constancy, in part because the olive tree lived an exceedingly long time. In Homer's *Odyssey*, Odysseus used the trunk of an olive tree to build his marriage bed. Because the trunk remained in the ground, it made his bed constant and immovable, like his bond with his wife Penelope. When Athena won the patronage of Athens, Poseidon, in anger, flooded the land, and then sent his son to cut down the olive tree. The boy chopped himself up but missed the tree, which remained intact. This tree embodied the constancy and stability of Athens. When the Persians burned the Acropolis, the charred stump of the olive tree remained, and from it a green branch grew. Parts of the new growth were moved outside the city and planted, and twelve new olive trees grew from them. These trees, the Moriae, also symbolized constancy and stability, as they too were immovable, like the tree trunk of Odysseus's marriage bed. The Moriae were protected by a curse—anyone who damaged the trees would fall victim to the gods' wrath. The Spartans raped the countryside and the olive groves, but fearing the curse, left the Moriae alone. From the fruit of these trees, the Greeks pressed the precious olive oil used to anoint the winners of the Olympian Games.

The Greeks anointed the winners of the Olympian Games with olive oil to honor Athena, the goddess of the olive tree. Anointment with olive oil was a sign of respect in many lands in ancient times, and olive oil reputedly relieved tension and fatigue. The olive harvest was an important event in ancient Greece. It occurred in winter, when sailors who could not sail during the cold months were available to help perform the task.

Because the olive had to suffer (to be pressed) in order to produce riches (oil), the Greeks made it a symbol of victory over adversity. They also made it a symbol of regeneration and included it in immortality myths. Olive trees appeared to be immortal. They were known to live for centuries, and even if they were cut down, their roots tended to send forth new shoots. (Goor and Nurock 1968; Lehner and Lehner 1960; Rosenblum 1996; Toussaint-Samat 1992; Visser 1986)

OLOLIUQUI

Many Native American tribes long ago gained familiarity with various hallucinogenic plants and used them frequently to commune with gods and ancestors, to divine the future, to gain self-knowledge, to diagnose disease, and to discern the location of criminals, missing persons, or lost objects. The Aztec, the Maya, and the Zapotec knew the morning glory as a magic plant that enabled them to commune with the gods. They also deified the plant in its own right, recognizing in it the power to transport them to the spirit realm and to help them tap into otherworldly powers. Some people believed that evil powers moved the plant and that a demon lived within the seeds. But nevertheless these pre-Columbian Americans consumed the magic morning glory seeds, or ololiuqui, and had visions. They believed that whoever lived inside the seeds communicated with them when they ate the seeds; the hallucinations they experienced convinced them that they could see and speak with the spirits.

The morning glory plant received deep reverence in ancient Mexico, and the seeds made ideal tools for Aztec priests to use in divination. The priests talked to the seeds, consulting them as the ancient Greeks did oracles; and Mayan healers ate the seeds, believing that they gained power from them to diagnose and cure the sick. Just a few morning glory seeds put these healers into a trance, which once achieved, enabled them to locate the spirits responsible for the disease and to banish them. Like peyote and other plant materials, morning glory seeds produced hallucinations similar to those induced by LSD. The ancients experienced a sense of heightened awareness or clairvoyance after ingesting them. Today, Zapotecs continue to use ololiuqui to achieve the clairvoyant state they believe necessary to heal the sick.

Ancient Americans made potions of the ground morning glory seeds to relieve pain. They used ololiuqui for pleasure but also in religious rituals, particularly during feasts to the high god Tezcatlipoca. Aztec priests and magicians called their sacred ololiuqui "green snake weed," perhaps in part because it climbed and snaked like a vine. The priests consumed the green snake weed in seclusion, respecting its power. Because they did respect its power, and indeed feared the strength of the spirit present in the plant, they also adhered to strict rituals in the collection and care of the seeds. They purified themselves with incense before collecting the seeds; they stored the seeds in small baskets that were passed down through generations of priests and diviners; and they deified the seeds, making offerings to them as though they were gods. (Miller and Taube 1993; Schultes 1982; Schultes and Hofmann 1979)

See also Cactus; Frogs and Toads; Mushrooms

ONIONS AND LEEKS

The onion was likely one of the first plants cultivated. Its layered structure and pungent odor so impressed the ancients that they developed beliefs about the onion that have survived to the present day. The offensive odor of the onion led many to fear its power. Its appearance and structure, however, fostered a different view: The onion was likened by some to a pearl—gold on the outside and white on the inside; and like a pearl, they thought, it symbolized oneness and unity. Furthermore, the onion was spherical in shape, consisting of a series of orbs, one inside the other. To the ancient Egyptians and the Druids, this structure suggested that the onion and the leek represented the universe, with each layer a different level of heaven or hell.

Because the onion and leek symbolized the universe, the ancient Egyptians considered the bulbs sacred. They swore oaths with their right hand on an onion, which to them symbolized eternity—a never-ending succession of worlds upon worlds. But the pungent odor of the onion led even those who revered it to associate it with demons. Some believed that it characterized the underworld or that its smell indicated the presence of evil forces on earth. Yet, others believed that onions and leeks, as well as their near relative garlic, had the power to ward off evil, to protect against the evil eye, and to cure ailments and diseases of all sorts.

The association of onions and leeks with dark forces so permeated ancient thought that many people considered them impure foods. Garlic, because of its strong odor, suffered from the same bad reputation. But contrasting views of onions persisted, at least among some people in ancient Egypt: The Egyptions inserted onions into the bandages and body cavities of mummies, and they carved pictures of them on the interior walls of the pyramids. Onions may have been a staple food among certain social classes; the laborers who built the pyramids are believed to have consumed them in large quantities, which might have fostered a reverence for the bulbs. Many Egyptian priests, however, avoided onions. Despite the onion's significance, there seems to have been a pervasive belief in its unholiness. Plutarch wrote that Egyptian priests avoided onions because they believed that the onion plant budded and thrived as the moon waned, and withered as the moon waxed. They therefore associated the plant with evil. In myth, the moon waned as the evil god Seth devoured the eye of Horus. Seth, the embodiment of chaos, extinguished the forces of goodness and light and threatened to annihilate the world.

Seth was a particularly evil deity in Egyptian myth. Not only did he devour the eye of Horus but he murdered his brother Osiris, dismembered his body, and threw it into the Nile. Seth epitomized evil in many ways, and the onion, because of the moon connection, suffered dearly for its association with him. Without the benefit of this myth, however, people in other lands connected the onion with death gods and with demons who had

the power to lure people into a state of unconsciousness or death. But ancient people often believed onions could revive them. In order to ward off the evil and to incur the onion's powers of revival, some people wore onions and garlic around their necks or inserted them into their clothing. For these same reasons, people often rubbed garlic juice in their eyes and ears or inserted garlic into their nasal passages. Some said it repelled the forces of death. It has been suggested that the people who inserted onions inside the body cavities of mummies may have done so to stimulate the dead to breathe.

If early people did believe onions could revive the dead, this certainly meant that the ancients recognized odor as a powerful force. Not only did the onion rouse the senses but in legend, it stimulated strength and bravery and aroused sexual appetite. Clearly, it had the energizing ability. In classical myth, the power of the onion made itself known when the Roman goddess Latona lost her appetite during pregnancy, and she got it back when she ate some onions. The onion was then consecrated to Latona as well as to her son Apollo because this miraculous food restored their health and vigor.

People who gave onions restorative properties or believed onions guarded against evil regarded them as symbols of protection. Assigning them protective powers likely stemmed from the belief that onions cured diseases. The Britons regarded leeks as symbols of protection, because in legend, they protected the British army from incurring battle wounds. Perhaps onions worked in this manner because their pungent smell drove away the enemy. In the sixth century A.D. the Saxons invaded Wales, and St. David, the patron saint of Wales, instructed the Britons to wear leeks on their caps. Because the leeks protected them as well as distinguished them from the enemy, the leek came to symbolize victory, and the Welsh made it their national emblem. (Simoons 1998)

See also Garlic; Spices

ORANGES

Oranges are native to Southeast Asia. The ancient Egyptians knew nothing of this fruit, and the Greeks made no mention of them either; but the Chinese cultivated them in antiquity, and the Japanese identified them as the fruit of life. In Japanese myth, the emperor sent a hero named Tajima-mori to the Eternal Land, possibly southern China, to bring back the magical fruit, so that the emperor might gain immortality. But Tajima-mori returned too late. The emperor had already died, and the magic of oranges could no longer help him. Though the Chinese identified the fruit of life as the peach, they considered oranges magical also, believing that the fruit brought good luck and joy and warded off evil spirits.

Oranges possibly gained respect in myth and legend because of their color. Ancient peoples seem to have believed that orange or red fruits had magical properties, connecting them with blood and life force. The golden color of oranges also led some mythmakers to link them with the sun. In Flemish legend, a young prince once went in search of a bride hidden within a magic orange in a land of sunshine and orange groves.

Because oranges were golden like the sun and decidedly magical, some scholars have identified them as the forbidden fruit in the Garden of Eden. Oranges also grew the year around, so ancient people regarded them as a fertility symbol. A fertility ceremony in the Yangtze region involves the marriage of orange trees, and a Japanese myth tells of the

Two bridesmaids at the wedding of Karis Mond to John Sumner at St. Paul's Church in Nightsbridge, England, wear elaborate headdresses of orange blossoms. (Hulton Deutsch Collection/Corbis)

marriage of Prince Jimmu to an orange tree. From far back in history, throughout much of Europe and North America, brides wore orange blossoms on their wedding day because they recognized the fruit as a fertility symbol. By representing the orange at this auspicious time, people believed that they could appeal to the spirit of the orange tree, and the spirit would in turn bless them with a fruitful marriage.

Although no mention of oranges per se appears in early Greek writings, some scholars believe that the Greeks did know of them, and that the use of the orange blossom as a bridal flower might have originated from a Greek myth in which Zeus gave Hera an orange on their wedding day. This fruit was termed "the golden apple," but the ancient Greeks tended to call every fruit an apple, and it is quite likely that this particular fruit was something else entirely. According to myth, the Golden Apples of the Hesperides grew from the seeds of this fruit. The Hesperides were three nymphs, Aegle, Arethusa, and Erythia, who together with a dragon named Ladon guarded the "golden apples" that grew in a magnificent garden owned by Atlas. It was only in this garden that the fruits could survive. Heracles, in one of his twelve labors, obtained some of these fruits by tricking Atlas and slaying the dragon. Outside the garden, however, the fruits spoiled; so Athena returned them to the Hesperides, their rightful owners.

If the Golden Apples of the Hesperides were indeed orange trees, then the Greeks apparently considered the orange an irresistible fruit. Atalanta was a beautiful maiden who wished to remain a virgin forever. She was also the swiftest mortal alive, and she stipulated that any man who wanted to marry her must beat her in a race. Hippomenes won the race by using the golden apples, or oranges, to delay her progress. He dropped three of them during the course of the race, one by one, and Atalanta stopped each time to retrieve the fruit, which she apparently could not resist.

In Malaysian legend, an elephant was the first to succumb to the orange's appeal. Long ago, when only animals existed on earth, an elephant found an orange tree and ate so much of its luscious, ripe fruit that he burst, and more orange trees grew from the contents of his stomach. By the time human beings appeared, they found the trees and discovered the irresistible fruits for themselves. From then on, elephants never ate oranges, but people did.

Oranges eventually traveled from the Far East to Europe, across the ocean to the Canary Islands, and then on to Latin America and the Caribbean islands. A Haitian tale of the orange tree tells of a young girl who lived with a stepmother so cruel and heartless that she denied the girl food. Weak from hunger, the girl stole three juicy oranges from her stepmother's table and ate them. When her stepmother discovered that the oranges were missing, she threatened to kill the girl, who ran away in fright. The girl grew tired of running and stopped to pray. After a while, she fell asleep. When she woke up, an orange seed fell down upon her, as if by magic. She planted the orange seed and it grew. It produced the juiciest oranges imaginable. She brought them home, and upon seeing the delectable fruit, her stepmother begged the girl to tell her where she had found them. The girl had learned a secret that would make her magic orange tree produce; she sang to the tree, and it bloomed. So she took her stepmother to the tree and she sang to it, and it grew high into the sky. Then she sang to it a second time, and it shrank down again. When the tree was low enough, the stepmother climbed up to pick the fruit. Then the girl sang again and the tree grew higher and higher, until the branches finally broke and the stepmother fell to her death. The girl had gained her freedom and her riches from the magic orange tree. From that day on, she had plenty of juicy oranges to sell at market, and she never had to go hungry again. (Tolkowsky 1938; Toussaint-Samat 1992)

See also Apples; Quinces

OX

The ox figures in one of the most famous myths of all time—the Greek myth of the culture hero Prometheus, who butchered an ox and served it up to humans and gods. This incident was recounted as the first blood sacrifice and the precedent for human consumption of animal flesh. Before Prometheus killed the ox, humans and gods had lived side by side in a Golden Age of harmony with one another and with the animals, sharing their food and feasting together at common banquets. After Prometheus killed the ox, this was no longer possible. Prometheus set gods and humans apart, giving the gods the incorruptible spices while tying humans to the flesh and blood characteristic of their mortal state.

The ox of the Prometheus myth was domesticated, not wild, and therefore an animal whose death and consumption constituted a true sacrifice. Hunters who pursued wild animals killed them as enemies, but those who slaughtered their domestic oxen truly gave something of themselves. The ox was a close companion of human beings; harnessed to the plow, it worked alongside them, helping them till the soil. In principle, the sacrifice of a domestic ox was comparable to that of cultivated grain.

The myth of the ox slaughter appears in Hesiod's *Theogony* and in *Works and Days*. Prometheus slaughtered and carved up the ox, giving humans the meat and all the edible parts, and gods the bones. Before laying the bones on the sacrificial fire, Prometheus disguised them by wrapping them in fat and sprinkling them with spices, hoping to trick the gods into believing that they were being offered meat. But in reality, Zeus tricked Prometheus. From then on, humans could satisfy their hunger only by consuming the flesh of sacrificed animals, already decaying and deprived of life. In *Works and Days,* Zeus also hid the grain deep within the earth. From then on, humans not only had to sacrifice their animals in order to eat but they also had to labor in the fields in order to obtain grain.

The Golden Age had ended. Humans were doomed to eat the grain from the fields they worked and to sacrifice the animals that helped work them.

The sacrificial ox played a primary role also in myths of India, Africa, and China. The Chinese considered this animal so vitally important that they identified it with a major constellation, which they called Niou. In ancient times, Niou reached the highest point in the sky at midnight on the day of the winter solstice. At this time of year, snow covered the ground in ancient China, and the people could no longer use their oxen for plowing the fields. It was then that the ox served its ceremonial purpose. When Niou reached the highest point in the sky at midnight, announcing the solstice, the people killed an ox and sacrificed it to the Sun, the Moon, and the Stars, the celestial gods who guarded the order of the universe. The ox fed the gods first, and then the people.

The ox seemed an appropriate sacrifice to the Chinese, because like the Greeks and other peoples, they assigned the ox particular value for the essential role it played in plowing their land. The Nuer of Sudan continue to rely on oxen to plow their land, and they also periodically sacrifice the animals to their deities, considering oxen the sacrifice of choice. Just as the Chinese sacrificed an oxen after they had completed their yearly work, the Nuer do something similar. During times of drought and illness, when these people believe they must propitiate their deities, they sometimes substitute another domestic animal, or a cucumber or other cultivated produce, for the ox. If they use a cucumber, they stab it as they would a sacrificial animal and carry out the same ritual. When Prometheus sacrificed the ox, he determined that sacrificial animals had to be domestic ones and plant foods had to be cultivated. So for ritual purposes, the cucumber becomes the ox, and the Nuer people believe it pleases the gods as well. (Detienne and Vernant 1989; Staal 1984; Vernant 1981a, 1981b)

See also Blood and Flesh; Meat; Wheat

PARSLEY AND CELERY

The celery of ancient times was a close relative to wild parsley, native to the eastern Mediterranean, and thus a logical plant to appear in Greek myths. The ancient Greeks called celery and parsley by the same Greek name. Although people in other areas of the ancient world consumed the plants, the Greeks used parsley and celery primarily for making wreaths, garlands, and crowns to wear on festive occasions. Parsley had a double meaning in Greek myths, symbolizing bravery and triumph on the one hand, and death on the other. The people of ancient Greece strewed parsley over graves and dead bodies but also used it to adorn the winners of the Olympian Games.

In Greece, the practice of making crowns out of parsley began in Nemea at the Panhellenic games, which in the classical period rotated among Nemea, Delphi, Isthmia, and Olympia. In a Greek myth, seven warriors known as the Seven Against Thebes stopped in Nemea on their way to battle. There they met a slave girl named Hypsipyle, who held the infant Opheltes, son of Lycurgus (the king of Nemea), in her arms. When the warriors asked Hypsipyle to lead them to water, she put the infant down on the ground by a spring for a moment, and the guardian serpent of the stream struck the infant and killed him. Parsley, or wild celery, grew from the ground by the stream, from the infant's blood.

P Amphiarius, one of the seven men, was a great seer as well as a courageous warrior, and he knew that the infant's death foretold disaster for their mission and death for their chiefs. He renamed the infant Archemorus, which meant "Beginner of Doom." Then Amphiarius and the other warriors gave Archemorus an elaborate funeral, and founded the Nemean Games in his honor. They used the parsley that grew by the spring to crown the winners of the games. In June 1996, the Nemean Games were reinstated in Greece, and participants again used wild parsley to crown the winners. The herb came to symbolize triumph and bravery, but it also suffered for the unfortunate event that led to its origin. Parsley never lost its association with death, or its reputation as an ill omen.

The crowning of athletes with wreaths of celery or parsley in ancient Greece symbolized triumph, but it appears that the practice may have originated in ancient rites involving human sacrifice. Some scholars have suggested that the wreaths were surrogates for the sacrificial victims, which at one time the victors of the games ultimately became. Parsley retained its funereal associations throughout the classical era in Greece and Rome, and these associations appear eventually to have spread through other parts of Europe. The Greeks associated parsley not only with Archemorus but also with Persephone, the queen of the underworld; they dedicated the herb to her and they frequently used it at funerals and burials. Furthermore, in the *Odyssey,* celery, or wild parsley, is said to have grown all over the island of the death goddess Calypso, which reinforced the herb's connection with death. The Greeks decorated tombs with wreaths of parsley and often spoke of someone on the verge of death as being in need of parsley, or similarly, in need of celery. The ancient Egyptians also appear to have connected celery with death. They used it to adorn mummies, and they too referred to the dying as being in need of celery.

A Fantastic Cave Landscape with Odysseus and Calypso, painting by Jan Brueghel. (Scala/Art Resource, NY)

The Greek myth of Archemorus presented a powerful argument for the classification of parsley and celery as death plants. But the physical characteristics of the plants might also have contributed to this classification. Celery resembled the poisonous hemlock, a plant that was used in the classical age to kill criminals. Furthermore, celery took a long time to germinate, which perhaps led to the British folk belief that parsley (or celery) goes to the underworld before it sprouts. In Great Britain, the superstitious connected parsley not only with death but also with witches and devils. Parsley, they said, visits the Devil; and the transplanting of parsley invites crop failure and death. People in Devonshire, England, believed that parsley beds had guardian spirits that wrought revenge on anyone who dared uproot the plants. (McDonald 1971; *Oxford Dictionary of Plant-Lore* 1995; Schultes and von Reis 1995)

PEACHES

Myths of China and Japan abound in stories about peaches. In these lands, the peach has long symbolized longevity and immortality. In Taoist myth, the peach tree served as the Tree of Life, twisting upward from earth to sky and supporting the universe on its outstretched branches. The Peach Tree of Life stretched 1,000 leagues across. It produced the most marvelous fruit once every 3,000 years, which bestowed immortality on anyone who ate them. Gods, emperors, and magicians all struggled to obtain these peaches by traveling to the garden P'an t'ao in the Khun-lun Mountains and climbing the magnificent tree, which was guarded by Hsi Wang Mu, the Queen Mother of the West.

The myth of Hsi Wang Mu and the notion of the peach as the fruit of life permeated Chinese culture. The peach tree is indigenous to China. People of India, in fact, had no folklore of the peach but simply referred to it as the "Chinese fruit." The Peach Tree of Life, however, reputedly grew in Tibet, on the highest peak in the Khun-lun Mountains. According to the myth, Chang Tao-ling, the first Taoist pope, sent a man named Chao Sheng and 300 disciples to this peak, and there they saw the peach tree near a pointed rock, its fruit-laden branches stretching out over a forbidding abyss. Chang Tao-ling challenged his disciples to pick the fruit, but only Chao Sheng attempted to do so. He climbed out onto the rock and up the tree and gathered 302 peaches in his cloak. Then he dropped them to Chang Tao-ling, who distributed them to the disciples. Chao Sheng, Chang Tao-ling, and the 300 disciples ate the peaches, became immortal, and ascended to heaven.

The mythical fruit tree of Hsi Wang Mu's garden was known as the Peach Tree of Life for good reason. Its peaches worked their magic on all of Chang Tao-ling's disciples, and on others as well. Wu Ti, the fourth emperor of the Han dynasty, wanted desperately to gain immortality, and he knew he had to find either the Water of Life or the magic fruit tree to do so. One day a bird flew into his palace garden, and he followed the bird to Hsi Wang Mu's mountain. The mythical queen came out of her garden to meet the emperor, accompanied by a dwarf servant who bore seven peaches of immortality on a tray. She gave Wu Ti one of the peaches, and he became immortal, just as he desired.

In Chinese myths, the queen's garden, next to the Lake of Gems, was where the Immortals held their banquet, a feast called Pan-tao Hui, or the Feast of Peaches. The Immortals gathered once every 3,000 years, when the fruit ripened, to celebrate the queen's birthday and to feast on meat and peaches. Hsi Wang Mu herself furnished the peaches, which were served by her daughters to their guests seated in pavilions next to the mythical lake. In Taoist myth, Hsi Wang Mu was the wife of the August Personage of Jade, the highest god in the pantheon, and she lived with him in a magnificent jade palace. Sometimes the gods allowed humans into the queen's garden and rewarded them with peaches for good deeds they had done in their earthly lives.

Hsi Wang Mu's peach tree was also the focus of a number of earthly ceremonies performed and attended by mortals. Because the tree was believed to have originated in paradise and to have connections to deities of all sorts, people considered the fruit magical. Not only did Shou-lou, the Chinese god of longevity, emerge from a peach but the tree itself provided a passage to heaven from earth. All of the tree's products were considered divine. At the entrance to heaven were gates presided over by two gods named Shen Shu, or Holy Shu, and Yu Lu, and there were other gates as well, through which goblins passed. This myth led to ceremonies that involved peach wood figurines of Holy Shu and Yu Lu, and the use of peach wood in exorcisms.

The use of peaches and peach wood in exorcisms appeared in Japanese culture as well. In Japanese myth, also, a peach tree intersected two worlds—in this case, the earth and the underworld. The ancient Japanese text *Kojiki* recounts how Izanami, the creator goddess, descended beneath the earth and sent eight thunder demons to chase her husband, Izanagi, out of the underworld. Izanagi managed to get hold of three peaches from the tree on the way out, which helped him fend off the demons. From then on, peaches were considered useful in exorcising demons.

Another Japanese myth of note centered around a demon slayer named Momataro, a name that means "little peachling." This myth emphasized the Japanese perception of the peach as a symbol of reproduction. In this story, a woman was washing her clothes at the riverbank one day when she saw a giant peach drifting along in the water. She managed to pull it to shore, even though it was the most gigantic peach imaginable. She took the peach home to her husband, and to their surprise, a baby boy emerged from the center of the fruit. The man and woman were delighted, as they had no children of their own, and they believed that the gods had given them this baby. The boy grew up, and decided to leave his parents in search of treasure on the Isle of Demons. Momataro succeeded in fighting the demons and returning home with the treasure. He gave the treasure to the couple who had raised him, in return for their having released him from his prison within the peach. (Mackenzie 1994; Simoons 1991; Toussaint-Samat 1992; Werner 1995)

See also Cherries; Cinnamon; Plums

PEANUTS

Peanuts are not nuts, actually, but legumes. They grow from a vine of the pea family and are native to South America, most likely to Bolivia and the Andes region. Archaeological evidence indicates that the ancient Maya and Inca cultivated peanuts. Depictions of peanuts have been discovered on Inca funerary vases, and remains of peanuts have been found at Inca burial sites, sometimes in a bag with other primary foodstuffs such as maize, beans, chili peppers, and coca.

Peanuts grow underground, and the ancients appear to have connected them with underworld powers, just as they did other leguminous foods. In ancient times, however, peanuts grew above ground and lacked the thin red skins present on some kinds of peanuts today. The Chinese had a legend to explain both of these changes: Long ago, a young boy in charge of watching over his family's peanut crop constantly struggled to protect his peanuts from crows who preyed on his fields. One day an old man appeared by the fields, tired and hungry and weak from traveling so far in the hot sun. The boy gave the man food and water, and in return for his kindness, the man gave the boy a magic jewel. This old man was actually a mountain spirit, it appeared, and this spirit instructed the boy to bury the jewel three feet underground with his bare hands. The boy dug until his hands bled, but he completed the task. When he

returned to the peanut field the next morning, to his amazement, all the peanuts had followed the jewel underground. This made the boy extremely happy. He didn't have to spend all day watching the fields anymore, for the crows could no longer destroy his crop. When harvesttime came, the boy had a plentiful harvest, enough to provide for the entire village.

The Chinese legend of the peanut stressed the importance of hard work, sacrifice, and kindness. The boy of the legend was actually Lo Pin-wang, one of the four savants of the T'ang dynasty. To the Chinese, the peanut symbolized Lo Pin-wang's goodness. The peanuts retreated underground and spared the kind boy from the hard work that kept him in the fields and away from his studies; and in honor of Lo Pin-wang, the peanuts that grew underground had thin red inner skins, believed to have formed from the blood of the boy's fingers when he planted the magic jewel. (Hu 1996; Lehner and Lehner 1973; Rosengarten 1984)

See also Almonds; Hazelnuts; Walnuts

PEARS

People in much of Europe viewed the pear as a symbol of fertility and womanhood. The fruit had a shape similar to that of a woman's body as well as that of the womb. In China, people also considered the fruit a symbol of virginal purity, because of the pear tree's delicate white blossoms, and of longevity, because pear trees often lived an exceedingly long time.

Some Europeans also recognized longevity and even immortality in their pears. A Gaelic legend referred to the apples of Avalon as pears, and these fruits grew in paradise and held the secret to everlasting life. People in Switzerland often planted a pear tree at the birth of a girl. They believed that some mystical connection existed between the two lives, and that the survival and welfare of the tree influenced the survival and welfare of the girl. A legend from Austria told of a certain pear tree in the countryside that people believed would bear fruit only as long as the German Empire flourished. True to legend, the pear tree died when the empire dissolved, remained lifeless for over sixty years, then miraculously bore fruit again after the establishment of the New Empire. There's something so awe inspiring about deciduous fruit-bearing trees that people placed them in miracle legends from the beginning of time. The trees' ability to bloom after their winter death and to bear ripe fruits testified to the miraculous fertilizing powers of nature. People in the Balkans and elsewhere in eastern Europe must also have recognized the pear tree as a fertility symbol, as their annual rituals involved the burning of wood from pear trees to ensure the growth of their crops.

The ancients derived symbol and meaning from nature in many ways. By equating physical traits such as size, shape, and color, for instance, they paired fruits and other objects of nature with the appropriate deities. The pear tree gained symbolic significance largely because of its shape. Not only does the pear tree form a pyramid but so too does the fruit itself; so both of them came to symbolize a woman's fertile womb and the goddesses who embodied the womb's powers. The ancient Egyptians dedicated the pear tree to Isis. The Romans and Greeks considered the pear tree a symbol of sexuality and a sacred manifestation of the love goddess Venus or Aphrodite, and of Hera, the goddess of heaven. The white blossoms of the pear tree made it sacred to the moon and to moon goddesses like Artemis, Athena, and Luna. Chinese myth posited a pear tree on the moon, in the celestial sphere, under the auspices of the moon goddess Heng O and her companion, a white rabbit. The lunar pear tree produced wonderfully juicy and fragrant fruits, and a Chinese legend recounts how a young boy acquired graftings from this celestial tree to improve the quality of his pear trees on earth. The young boy lived in a small fishing village by the sea, and he invested a great deal of time and labor in caring for his pear trees, which constantly struggled to grow in the salty soil and produced small, sour fruits.

The boy's luck changed one day when he encountered the lunar rabbit on earth and saved the animal from the clutches of a hungry owl. The rabbit, embodying all the magic the ancients connected to the moon and the celestial sphere, rewarded the boy for his kindness. He plucked out a few of his magic hairs and told the boy how he could use those hairs to ascend to the moon himself, remove some branches from the celestial pear tree, return to earth, and graft them onto his own pear trees. The notion of the celestial pear tree growing on the moon might have stemmed from the tree's longevity, its white blossoms, or their sweet fragrance. Ancient people typically associated a sweet aroma with godly realms. Heng O gave the boy her magic pear graftings willingly, and ever since then, the Chinese people have offered pears to their moon goddess at the Harvest Moon festival. (Bayley 1913; Hu 1996; Mercatante 1976; Reed 1992; Toussaint-Samat 1992)

See also Apples; Avocados

PEAS AND LENTILS

Since antiquity, legumes have served as a staple food for agricultural peoples, particularly the poor. Lentils were likely one of the first cultivated crops, and peas have been found at sites of the ancient lake dwellers of Switzerland as far back as the Stone Age. Lentils and peas grew wild in the Middle East and Central Asia long ago, and they fed the poor peoples of Egypt and throughout the Holy Land. When these crops moved westward, Europeans also came to rely on them. Legumes could be safely stored for many months, and they often saved the poor from starvation.

A biblical story in the book of Genesis tells of the twin brothers Jacob (a farmer) and Esau (a hunter). Esau begged Jacob for some lentil pottage, but Jacob refused him until Esau agreed to sell his inheritance—to give up his rights as firstborn child—in return for a bowl

Jacob and Esau, from the biblical story in the book of Genesis that told how Esau gave up his birthright for one bowl of lentil pottage. (The Jewish Museum, NY/Art Resource, NY)

of the pottage. Lentils provided essential food to people in biblical times. Esau was starving, and the pottage sustained him.

Long before Esau, the Neolithic peoples of the Middle East had harvested lentils, and the people of Egypt grew them extensively along the Nile River. The Egyptians used their lentils not only as food but as medicine and as money. They also used them as funerary offerings to the god Horus, a practice that most likely stemmed from Horus's legendary birth from Isis, the moon goddess, and from the ancient belief linking lentils, peas, and other legumes with the moon and with resurrection. The moon appeared to die and to resurrect itself each month, just as legumes died when they were buried underground, but then quickly germinated.

In folk beliefs throughout Europe, people tended to connect beans, peas, lentils, and other legumes with death and the underworld. People commonly offered legumes to the dead, placing them in coffins or serving them at memorial feasts in honor of the dead, a tradition that survives today. In western Europe, people commonly serve legumes at funerals as well as on All Souls' Day, a Catholic feast day commemorating all the souls who have departed this world and moved on to the otherworld. The Europeans call the legumes they serve on this day "soul food," and they generally serve it to the poor. The celebration of All Souls' Day apparently has its origins in an early Celtic festival in which the living served food to the dead, believing that the dead returned to earth on this day and must be fed. Believing that these wandering souls could be easily annoyed and that they had the ability to harm the living, feeding them seemed a reasonable way to keep them happy. Legumes, as symbols of death and the underworld, seemed a logical food to offer them.

Serving peas or lentils on All Souls' Day authenticated the link early people recognized between legumes and death. By extension, some people linked these foods to evil forces, which typically were associated with the world underneath the ground. The link people recognized between legumes and death also led to the avoidance of lentils and peas at times of the year when people of the past felt particularly concerned about evil influence. On Twelfth Night, for instance, superstitious Germans believed that ancestral spirits walked the earth; so the living abstained from eating peas and beans, for fear that harm would befall them.

On St. John's Eve, the time of the summer solstice, legumes entered into the picture for their supposed connections not only to evil influence but also to fire. Perhaps due in part to the climbing ability of certain legumes as well as the sulfurous odor that resulted from eating them, legumes in general became linked in the popular imagination with solar fire. In medieval legend, for instance, peas were associated with lightning (and perhaps with hail): At the summer solstice, dragons were believed to carry peas through the air and to hurl them down from the sky to fill up wells. So people lit fires on summer solstice to scare away the dragons. Other legends linked peas to fire as well: The Germanic dwarves known as Zwergs, who forged Mjollnir, the mighty hammer of Thor that hurled fiery thunderbolts, were said to love peas. In legend, these little people often took to pillaging the pea fields and stealing away with their treasures. (Folkard 1892; Simoons 1998; Toussaint-Samat 1992)

See also Beans; Lupines

PEPPERS

Black pepper, one of the earliest known spices, is produced from the berry of the pepper vine, a plant native to Burma, Assam, and India, where people have used it far longer than any other spice. More than 2 million acres of India are devoted to the production of spices today, and pepper is the primary crop. Sometimes called the "king of spices," pepper gained popularity as a foodstuff faster than any other spice.

Before the domestication of pepper, early peoples used other plants to season their food. In Europe they used myrtle berries, and in Asia, *fagara*. Fagara comes from trees and shrubs that produce aromatic, spicy fruits that when toasted and ground into a powder make what people today call Chinese or Szechuan pepper. The Chinese first used fagara as an additive to sacrificial wines and meats, and later as a common seasoning for everyday foods. Fagara served as a flavor enhancer long before pepper, but true pepper seemed far more exotic. The Chinese considered pepper healthful for the body and believed that it stimulated sexual desire. Pepper moved into Europe as early as the fifth or sixth century B.C., when people there began to use it to season their foods. It quickly gained acceptance as a medicinal substance, and later, in the thirteenth century, as a panacea. People attributed both medicinal and aphrodisiac properties to peppercorns.

Perhaps more common than black pepper in the southwestern United States and in Central and South America are red pepper, cayenne, and paprika; these products come from hot peppers called chilis, of which more than 1,600 varieties exist today. Chili peppers are actually fruits of a plant in the nightshade family, which originally grew throughout South America, the West Indies, the Caribbean, and Mexico. In these areas, people have been growing and eating chilis for more than 8,000 years. By the time the Spaniards arrived in these lands, chili peppers were a primary crop, second only to maize in importance. Some early peoples of these regions used pepper not only as a food but as an instrument of torture. The Caribs rubbed pepper into the wounds of boys before they became warriors, and the Maya rubbed pepper onto the genitals of girls who had violated the rule of sexual chastity. South American tribes also burned chili peppers to drive away Spanish invaders with the offensive smoke.

Because of the widespread use of pepper in the New World, myths and legends of pepper plants abound. The Inca called peppers *uchu,* and they so respected this food that they gave the same name to the first king of Peru, the legendary founder of the Inca race. In legend, Uchu was one of eight brothers and sisters who founded their race, all of them godlike beings who arose out of an opening in the rocks. All eight taught the Indians the art of agriculture and told them which plants were fit to eat. Pepper played such an important role in the Peruvian diet that it was considered a hardship to go without. Perhaps for this reason, boys who were going through rites of passage in order to become warriors were required to abstain from the eating of peppers.

Early peoples of the southwestern region of North America grew many varieties of chili peppers, and they too considered them important enough to create myths and legends around them. Many of these peppers were fiery hot, and the mythmakers attempted to explain this characteristic of the fruits as well as their origin and dispersal. In Zuñi Pueblo legend, the Twin War Gods set their sights on stealing the rain gods' thunder and lightning, and they sent a centipede up to the rain gods' altar to steal the thunderstone and the lightning shaft. When the Twin War Gods obtained these weapons, they began playing with them, and violent storms ravaged their home. Rain poured through the roof, flooded the house, and extinguished their fire. The Twin War Gods, in distress, had to climb to the roof of their house to escape, but there they played with the weapons again, and this time, so much water fell from the sky that it drowned their grandmother. A fiery pepper plant grew from her grave. The Zuñi Pueblo linked their fiery peppers to the fiery tongue of their grandmother as she scolded the Twin War Gods for

courting disaster. When the Twin War Gods plucked the pepper plant up from the ground, they sowed its seeds over the land, and thus the Zuñi explained the many peppers growing in their soil. (Foster and Cordell 1992; Heiser 1969; Simoons 1994)

See also Spices

PERSIMMONS

Ripe persimmons are wonderfully juicy and sweet. Different varieties ranging in color from yellow to red grow in North America, China, India, and Japan. One variety of persimmon indigenous to China, India, and Japan resembles a plum, and is commonly called the "date plum." These luscious fruits are also known as Jove's Apples. The bright color of persimmons, combined with their sweet flavor and aromatic scent, made them particularly alluring, and led some people of times past to identify these fruits as the golden apples in the Greek myth of the Garden of the Hesperides.

The Chinese, in particular, have a high regard for persimmons, and because of their bright color, consider them symbols of joy. Many varieties of the fruit grow in China. Scholars have found remains of these fruits in ancient tombs and mention of them in ancient writings, suggesting that the Chinese regarded persimmons as valuable fruit far back in history. The Chinese continue to use persimmons as offerings to the moon goddess Heng O at the annual harvest festival celebrated to thank the goddess for her influence over the year's crops. They choose foods to offer Heng O based on their perception of these foods as symbols of kindness, and they tell legends about the foods to reinforce their symbolism.

One Chinese legend about persimmons features two kind and generous beekeepers, a man and his son, who distributed much of the honey from their apiary to the poor. This act went against Hsueh Te, a corrupt officer in the Ch'in dynasty who wanted everything for himself. Hsueh Te sent his army to steal the honey from the beekeepers and put them in their place. Upon learning of Hsueh Te's plan, the two men hid their honey in a pot and buried it underneath a persimmon tree. But Hsueh Te and his army quickly discovered it. The youngest beekeeper smashed the pot in anger and let the honey drip into the ground to nourish the persimmons. Hsueh Te lost control after the boy did this, and he tied the boy to the persimmon tree and burned him to death. But the boy seemed to fortify the tree with his lifeblood and goodness. The tree grew large and produced an abundant supply of fruit. The persimmons became as bright red as the boy's blood, and as sweet tasting as the honey from his apiary. The people of China remember the young beekeeper when they eat persimmons, and they consider the fruit a symbol of his generosity. To this day, the Chinese not only present these fruits to their moon goddess but they also make dried fruits or cakes out of persimmons and give them as gifts. They also attribute healing and fertilizing powers to persimmons because of their many seeds. (Hu 1996; Simoons 1991)

See also Apples; Apricots; Lemons and Citrons; Oranges; Quinces; Tomatoes

PINEAPPLES

Pineapples have been widely cultivated in the American tropics for centuries. It appears that they originally grew wild in Brazil and Paraguay, and then the Tupi-Guarani tribes who inhabited these areas distributed them throughout South America as they acquired new territory. The Tupi-Guarani peoples called pineapples *nana,* but the Spaniards renamed them pineapples. Early Europeans commonly called any kind of fruit an apple; and the Spaniards thought the "pineapples" they found when they arrived in South America resembled the pinecones that grew on the large stone pines of southern Europe.

Pineapples and pinecones have nothing in common botanically, yet their resemblance led people to link them in myth and symbol. Both have been linked to fertility, for example. For a time, scholars thought that early peoples also linked the pineapple with the Babylonian creator god Marduk and the Phrygian mother goddess Cybele. However, more recent studies have led scholars to conclude that pineapples were unknown to people of the Old World. Although Old World depictions of pinecones—particularly the stone carvings found on walls at Nineveh in ancient Assyria—do somewhat resemble pineapples, Marduk and Cybele had more definite associations to pine trees, and scholars now believe that pineapples moved eastward only after the Spaniards discovered them in the New World.

When the people of the Old World did learn of pineapples, they recognized some of the same symbolism the people of South America and the Caribbean lands recognized. The pineapple symbolized friendship and hospitality to the Caribs. These people often hung pineapples outside their huts as a kind of welcome mat, inviting people to visit. But in Europe, other factors also came into play. Because pineapples were difficult to cultivate in European soil, the fruit quickly became an expensive product. Europeans began to associate pineapples with nobility because only the rich could afford them. Interestingly, the pinecones of the Holy Land also served as symbols of nobility. They grew into hardy, lofty trees, nearly sixty feet in height. In Europe, the pineapple remained a symbol of hospitality and friendship, just as the nobility stood for hospitality and friendship as well as wealth and privilege. The link people recognized between pineapples and hospitality led to the use of pineapples as an architectural motif. Images of pineapples adorned entrance halls and dining rooms and served much the same purpose as the pineapples hanging outside huts in the Caribbean.

A number of scholars who have identified pineapple motifs on ancient altars have suggested that the pre-Columbian Americans may have invested their pineapples with religious

The link people recognized between pineapples and hospitality led to the use of pineapples as an architectural motif. Images of pineapples adorned doorways and hallways as a welcome symbol. (Library of Congress)

significance; but apart from ceremonies honoring a Mexican god named Vitziliputzli, who is shown holding pineapples in his hand, it appears that the early Americans rarely used these fruits for ritual purposes. People in the New World certainly ate pineapples, and some used them for making sweet wine. People living on the coast of Panama, in some parts of Tierre Firme, and in the Orinoco Valley fermented pineapples to make wine, and some also used the decayed fruit to make poison for arrows and blowgun darts. People long ago fermented all kinds of fruits and plants to make wine, and they did this easily and with little knowledge of the plant they put to use. But it typically took a long familiarity with a plant before they learned to use it medicinally. The early people of Peru most likely cultivated pineapples as early as A.D. 100, and the Caribs and many other peoples of South America considered the pineapple an important medicinal plant, particularly for the restoration of appetite and for relief from stomach disorders. (Coe 1994; Collins 1951; Lehner and Lehner 1973; Verrill 1937)

See also Pines and Pine Nuts

PINES AND PINE NUTS

Because the pine tree is an evergreen and lives an exceedingly long time, it has been hailed by people of many lands as a tree of immortality. The Semitic peoples considered the pine a symbol of life. So did the Chinese, the Japanese, the Greeks and Romans, and many peoples of the New World. These beliefs stemmed from ancient times and led to the consumption of pine resin, pine nuts, and decoctions made of pine needles as elixirs of life. Its abundant seeds enhanced the pine's reputation as a symbol of fertility, long life, and resurrection.

The ancient Greeks devised several origin myths of the pine. In one myth, a nymph named Pitys loved the North Wind, Boreas, but flirted with the forest god Pan. Boreas got jealous and threw Pitys against the rocks, and

miraculously, Pitys instantly became a pine tree. The North Wind frequently blew so severely that it broke the pine's branches, and the Greeks explained the resin that appeared there as Pitys's tears. The Greeks also offered an explanation for how the pine tree became evergreen. According to myth, Cybele, the Great Mother, changed a shepherd into a pine, and Zeus made him an evergreen tree, thus allowing the shepherd to live forever. The shepherd was none other than Attis, a god whom the Romans elevated to cult status and who had equivalents in most every culture. In one version of the Attis myth, Cybele loved Attis so dearly that when he fell in love with a nymph, she drove her lover so insane with her jealousy that he castrated himself. He died from his wounds, and the pine tree grew from his blood. In another version of the myth, Cybele imprisoned Attis in the pine tree, but every spring he arose from it. His myth became a resurrection myth, a story the ancients told to explain the fertility of the earth and nature's capacity for renewal.

Attis was likely of Semitic origin; but when the cult of Attis spread to Greece and Rome, his worship became inseparable from the worship of Cybele and the pine. The Greeks worshiped Attis as god of the pine. The Romans instituted what most people today would consider a barbaric ritual, performed to initiate the priests of Cybele. First the people cut down a pine tree and paraded with it through the streets. They danced and drank wine mixed with pine nuts. They slashed themselves with knives and let their blood flow over the tree. The next day, a wild orgy followed in which people wantonly engaged in sex to symbolize impregnation of the earth. As part of the ritual, the initiates had to castrate themselves, as had Attis, before they could enter Cybele's priesthood. Such rituals validated the importance of the myth, reinforcing the pine's connection with resurrection. The ancient Egyptians also performed a ritual connecting the pine to resurrection. They imprisoned the image of Osiris each year in a hollow pine log. He too was resurrected. The pine, like Osiris and Attis, never died.

In the myths of China and Japan, the pine tree similarly represented a tree of life, and products made from the sacred pine were considered elixirs of immortality. Certain Chinese sages considered the juice of the pine an anti-aging potion, so Chinese people often drank tea made from the tree's sap. Sometimes they made drinks from the pine needles and cones or from a certain mushroom, hailed as the fungus of immortality, that habitually grows at the base of the trees. The Chinese still consume these pine products, believing that they contain "soul substance." They consume cypress seeds and products of other evergreen plants for the same reasons. In Chinese myth, the god of longevity often sat beneath a pine tree; and in legend, men and women often escaped death by eating pine resin.

It appeared to the Chinese that pine trees had miraculous life powers. They grew incredibly large, lived long lives, and withstood intense heat and intense cold. They stayed forever green, and they lost their sap, or lifeblood, when people cut them. In legend, pine trees had "soul substance" because they received their lifeblood from rain released by the dragon gods. Long ago, many people believed that particularly ancient pines turned into dragons. Some pine trees lived thousands of years, and those that lived 3,000 years appeared to have accumulations of resin underneath their bark, which created dragon-like shapes in the branches. Some people of ancient China saw these malformations and believed that they too indicated special power in the trees. It was no wonder that people consumed decoctions of pine in hopes of curing their ailments and prolonging their lives. People typically pounded and consumed the resin that formed the dragon shapes, believing that the potion they derived would enable them to live hundreds of years.

Just as stone pines grew in much of the Old World, the North American forests abounded in piñon pines. The people of the New World considered the products of their pines medicinal, but they also knew them as valuable sources of food. The nuts of the piñon pines, or piñon nuts, are highly nutritious, and they provided essential nourishment to the tribes of southwestern North America before they learned to cultivate corn, beans, and squash. They also became an important part of tribal myths and rituals. The Santa Clara Tewa of New Mexico identify one pine tree they believe to be the oldest tree on earth, and in myth, this tree produced the first food for human beings.

Many people of the Southwest valued pine nuts, pine pitch, and pine branches. Some tribes used piñon branches to make ritual wands, and some used the pitch for protection against evil powers. The Hopi smeared the pitch of piñon pines onto their foreheads to protect them against sorcerers, and the Navajo smeared the pitch on corpses before they buried them. (de Groot 1892–1910; Frazer 1950; Mirov and Hasbrouck 1976; Rosengarten 1984)

See also Pineapples

PLANTAINS
See Bananas and Plantains

PLUMS
Plums appear in several early myths of China and Japan. The Chinese considered the plum one of the "five renowned fruits of antiquity," along with the peach, the apricot, the jujube, and the chestnut. Plums tasted so juicy and so sweet that they conjured up images of paradise, a place defined by sweet aromas and tempting fruits. In Chinese myth both the plum and the peach symbolized longevity and immortality. In legend, Lao Tzu, the founder of Chinese Taoism, was born under a plum tree, and the people revered him not only as a philosopher but as an Imperial ancestor and an immortal god. In Japanese myth the plum stood alongside the peach and the pine as one

of the three trees of life, or sometimes, as the only Tree of Life. It grew on the island of Peng-lai, or Horaizan, and had a golden trunk and golden branches, silver roots, and luscious fruit.

Both the Japanese and the Chinese connected plums to immortality and fantastic places. The Chinese also connected it to their most famous fantasy creature, the dragon. In myth, the plum tree arose from the blood of a dragon's ears. The dragon's ears were cut off as punishment, and where the blood dropped to the ground, the plum tree grew. Perhaps the Chinese told this myth because of the bloodred fruit of the plum. Certainly they knew its color and texture well, and ancient people typically equated red juice with blood; they believed the juice of grapes represented the blood of sacrifice, for instance. Dark, fleshy plums have the reputation of being so juicy that they quench thirst solely on sight. In Chinese legend, an artist traveling across the desert painted a plum that looked so tasty and juicy that it made his mouth water. All he had to do was look at the picture he painted, and his thirst dissipated immediately.

The Chinese placed plums in their myths and legends because the fruit and the tree made quite an impression. The Japanese planted plum trees primarily for their blossoms, but the varieties that bore fruit were valued also for their medicinal properties. Plum trees gained their mythic significance largely because the trees bloomed early in the spring while snow still covered the ground, and the flowers remained on the seemingly lifeless branches for a long time. For these reasons both the Japanese and the Chinese connected plum trees with longevity and immortality—and not only plum trees but the fungus that grew beneath them. The fungus of immortality may well have been the *ling-chih,* a type of mushroom that grew on plum trees in Japan and that reputedly arrested aging. The Japanese called the ling-chih *reishi,* and by pairing it with the plum tree, they strengthened the mythological bond between the plum and longevity and immortality. In myth and leg-

end, pairing the plum tree with the nightingale and the butterfly also strengthened this bond. Both the nightingale and the flowering plum serve as harbingers of spring, in essence, as evidence of the earth's immortality as it reawakens from its winter death. The butterfly, which feeds on plum trees, and in myth, on the Plum Tree of Life, symbolizes immortality as well because it emerges from the chrysalis and reawakens from "death." (Reed 1992; Toussaint-Samat 1992)

See also Apricots; Chestnuts; Jujubes; Mushrooms; Peaches

POMEGRANATES

Myths and legends of the pomegranate reveal that the ancients both recognized and revered this fruit. The plant comes from Southeast Asia, and the fruit itself appears in myths of many lands, particularly of India, China, Mesopotamia, Greece, and Rome. The pomegranate had distinct characteristics that beckoned mythmakers to assign it significance. It attracted attention because of its crownlike blossom, its red color, and perhaps most importantly, its many seeds, which people all over the world linked to fertility and procreation.

Ancient mythmakers elevated pomegranates to high status, attributing symbolic significance to all of these traits. The red color and the seeds invited the greatest number of myths, but the Greeks had an explanation for the crownlike blossom as well. In Greek myth, Dionysus created the pomegranate when he changed a beautiful nymph into the tree that bore its fruit, and it was he who shaped the fruit's blossom into a crown. An oracle had prophesied that the nymph would wear a crown, which presumably meant that she would marry a god or a king. Dionysus did not marry the nymph but instead changed her into a pomegranate tree.

Mythmakers of many lands offered explanations for the origin of the pomegranate. The Mesopotamians called the fruit *rimmon,* and they likewise called their sun god Hadad-Rimmon.

In myth, Hadad-Rimmon died and was re-born as the pomegranate tree—the plant sprang from his blood. In Babylonian myth, it sprang from the blood of Tammuz, who was gored by a boar; and in another Greek legend, it sprang from the blood of Menoeceus, who sacrificed himself to the war god Ares in order to save Thebes. In yet another legend from Greece, a man lost his wife and fell in love with his daughter, Side, and this so distressed Side that she killed herself, believing she had no other means of escape. The gods turned the girl into a pomegranate tree and her father into a small falcon called a sparrow hawk. The Greeks used this myth to explain why sparrow hawks never land on pomegranate trees.

Myths of pomegranates springing from blood made sense to ancient peoples because they considered red foods symbols of blood and life force. As for the pomegranate, its red color and its many seeds made it a fertility symbol as well. In Mesopotamian myth, the god Attis was conceived when his virgin mother Nana put a ripe pomegranate to her bosom. (Other myths say it was an almond.) In ancient China, women offered pomegranates to the goddess of mercy when they prayed for sons. The link between seedy fruits and fertility still lingers in some areas of the world today. In Morocco, people use either pomegranates or figs to promote crop fertility. Believing they can assure a plentiful harvest by doing so, they squeeze the juice on the horns of oxen who plow the fields or they crush the fruit on the blades of the plows.

Customs in both the Middle East and the Mediterranean link the pomegranate to fertility, and to marriage as well. Arab brides smashed pomegranates in their tents to bestow blessings of fertility. Turkish brides counted the seeds to determine the number of children they would bear. The ancient Mesopotamians served pomegranates at wedding feasts; and the Chinese threw pomegranates on the bedchamber floors of the newlyweds, because they too considered the bursting of the fruit and the scattering of seeds a blessing

Persephone with the pomegranate Hades offered her in the underworld. (Tate Gallery, London/Art Resource, NY)

for a fruitful marriage. In Greek myth, the pomegranate tree and its fruit were sacred objects in the cult of Hera, the patroness of marriage and goddess of fertility and childbirth. The Greeks cultivated pomegranates near Hera's temples, and in one temple, the goddess is depicted holding a pomegranate in one hand.

In many of these traditions, pomegranates symbolized the marriage bond, and eating them sealed the union between husband and wife. In Greek myth, Hades, the god of the underworld, used the pomegranate in an attempt to seal his marriage to Persephone, daughter of Demeter, the earth goddess. Hades kidnapped Persephone one day when he ascended to earth, then took her back to his realm underneath the earth to be his bride. Demeter set out after Persephone, but Hades tempted Persephone with pomegranates so that she would have to stay with him forever. In myths and legends, eating the food of the otherworld was strictly forbidden; whoever consumed the food would remain in the otherworld. But Persephone ate only a few seeds of the pomegranate Hades offered her (some sources say only one seed). This was enough to keep her there only part of each year. Persephone had to remain in the underworld every winter, but she could return to the earth with Demeter every spring.

Persephone's myth shows that the ancient Greeks considered the pomegranate a symbol of the underworld and a representation of all seeds that germinate underground, emerge into the light, then return to death and darkness once again. The use of the pomegranate in this myth also reveals a number of beliefs about the red color of the fruit. Some cultures instigated a taboo on red-colored fruit, believing that it should be offered only to the dead. Hades may have offered the pomegranate to Persephone for other reasons. Some scholars say that Hades used the pomegranate to make his marriage to the earth goddess indissoluble, and that this revealed the use of pomegranates in ancient marriage rites. But in any case, Hades clearly used the fruit to tempt Persephone. In this same vein, Persians and Jews believed the biblical Eve used a pomegranate to tempt Adam.

Pomegranates were popular fruits in ancient Mesopotamia, and many scholars believe they were the original forbidden fruits. They grew in the famous hanging gardens of Babylon, and possibly on the Tree of Knowledge in the Garden of Eden. Many people certainly considered pomegranates sacred. They served as one of the three sacred fruits of Chinese Buddhists, along with the peach and the citron. To these people, the pomegranate not only symbolized fertility but eternal life as well. In Christian myth, the pomegranate symbolized the Virgin Mary, and the bursting seeds represented both fertility and the resurrection of Christ. (Folkard 1892; Goor and Nurock 1968; Simoons 1991, 1998; Skinner n.d.)

PORK

Pork plays a role in many myths and religions. The flesh of the pig, though highly regarded by some cultures, was widely abhorred by others. Beliefs about pigs ran the gamut from their association with evil to their association with resurrection and fertility. This makes it difficult to determine definitively why so many people avoided pork. Clearly, some appear to have dismissed pigs as unclean and therefore unfit for consumption, whereas others so revered them that eating their flesh constituted a violation of their sanctity.

People of many cultures revered the pig as a sacred animal, and some, as the embodiment of a god. In ancient Greece, people associated the pig with vegetation deities such as Adonis, Attis, and Demeter, and their respect for these deities likely led to their avoidance of pork. The ancient Egyptians connected the pig with Seth, a particularly evil deity, and it appears that for this reason some Egyptians refused to eat pork. In the guise of a pig or a boar, Seth attacked the eye of Horus, which represented the moon, a force of light and goodness. The attack itself represented a temporary triumph of evil over good. The connection between pigs and the moon occurred frequently in Egyptian myths, and pigs were commonly sacrificed to moon gods. Seth attacked Horus and his eye during the waning moon, a time when ancient people thought evil forces roamed the earth. Because pigs mated during the waning moon, they too were considered evil as well as obscene. Whereas in parts of China and Oceania the pig symbolized prosperity and abundance, in much of the rest of the world it symbolized gluttony and uncleanness.

The Egyptians as well as other peoples of the African continent considered pigs unclean and therefore unfit for consumption. The Hebrews, perhaps most notably, continue to embrace this belief today. People of early times possibly considered pigs unclean because they made the connection between pork and diseases, particularly diseases such as trichinosis, cholera, and leprosy. The Greek philosopher Plutarch mentioned that those who drank the milk of pigs got leprosy. In Greek myth, King Teuthras killed a boar who professed to be the nurse of Artemis, and Artemis, in revenge, afflicted King Teuthras with the dreaded disease. That pigs were the source of leprosy was a prominent belief in Europe into the nineteenth century, and in Asia, some people still believe it. The Chinese highly esteem the flesh of pigs, yet they continue to invoke the protection of the God of Swine against porcine diseases. The people of India too sometimes sacrifice pigs to propitiate disease demons.

Despite the prejudice against pigs and the fear ancient people had of evil forces, people as far back as Paleolithic times killed and ate wild pigs. By 7000–6000 B.C., the pig had been domesticated. Pigs are a primary food source for the people of the Pacific Islands today, and domestication of these animals involved rearing them in family homes and respecting them as important contributors to society. In the myths, people of early cultures sometimes made a distinction between wild and domesticated pigs, although both contributed to society by supplying pork.

A myth from New Hebrides explains the origin of both kinds of swine. Long ago a man climbed a tree and the bark rubbing against his testicles made them swell to enormous size. Finally they burst, and out came ten pigs, five from each testicle. The man must have known this was about to happen, because before his testicles burst, he told his friends to put stakes in the ground. When the pigs emerged, the men caught some of them and tied them to the stakes. The pigs tied to the stakes gave birth to domestic pigs. The ones that escaped and ran into the forests gave birth to wild pigs.

Perhaps nowhere else do pigs play so important a sociological role as they do in the Oceanian lands. In this part of the world, pigs represent status, wealth, and fertility; they are a favorite food of people as well as a favored sacrifice to the gods. Logically, this kind of thinking led to myths and legends attesting to the pig's significance. A myth from Papua, New Guinea, tells how the pig was created for sacrifice and food. Long ago there were no pigs, so people were forced to eat other people. In order to save her children from being eaten, a goddess gave birth to a pig, then turned herself into a mother sow, nursed her piglet, and was subsequently slaughtered. The pig child grew up and gave birth to many piglets, who then supplied the people with food. The goddess, and the pig, saved humans from slaughter.

Meat eaters around the world believe that primary food animals exist to feed the people. Just as the Ainu believe of the bear, the Inuit believe of the salmon, and many North American people believe of the deer and the buffalo, the native people of Oceania believe that the pig was created for sacrifice and that its primary function is to supply pork. All of these people hold their game animals in the highest esteem, knowing that they exist to benefit the people, guaranteeing life and affirming the ability of nature to provide. As is the case when vegetation sprouts abundantly from the earth, the abundance of pigs affirms the belief in a fertile world.

Scholars have suggested that people connected the pig with fertility as far back as Neolithic times. The pig grew fast and fat quickly, just as the grains of the earth sprouted and ripened. People in ancient Greece certainly recognized the connection between the pig and vegetation, for there pig slaughters

In Papua, New Guinea, pigs represent status and wealth. They stand for fertility and they constitute a favored food for the people as well as a favored sacrifice to the gods. (Wolfgang Kaehler/Corbis)

played an important role in the autumn planting festival, the Thesmophoria. At the Thesmophoria, women killed suckling pigs, then ate the pork as a solemn sacrament. They mixed the flesh with corn seed that they then sowed into the earth. The Thesmophoria was a fertility rite, connected with the worship of Demeter, the earth goddess; and the use of the pig in such a rite indicated that like the earth goddess, the pig symbolized the fertile earth.

The myth of Eubuleus the swineherd further reveals the connection between pigs, fecundity, and agriculture. Most people know the myth of Persephone and her abduction by Hades, the god of the underworld. Persephone was abducted from the fields of Eleusis, one of the primary sites of the Thesmophoria and of Demeter's cult. But not only Persephone disappeared from this site; Eubuleus's pigs did as well, when the ground simply opened up and swallowed them. The disappearance of both Persephone and the pigs preceded a resurrection. The followers of

Demeter stored the flesh of sacrificed pigs and sowed it in the soil with the seeds of grain. Vegetation sprouted from the earth, just as it had when Persephone returned from the underworld.

The links people recognized between pork, grain, agriculture, fertility, and resurrection were certainly not unique to the Greek world. Just as the ancient Greeks mixed pig flesh with corn seed before sowing, so the ancient Egyptians sowed their land by letting their pigs trample on the earth and press the seeds of grain down into it. In Welsh legend a gigantic sow named Henwyn traveled around the land and caused wheat and barley to sprout from the earth. The pig's fertilizing ability may have had something to do with the animal's ability to till the land as well as to press seeds into the soil. Pigs tilled the land by rooting up soil with their snouts. Kamapua'a, the pig god of Hawaiian myth, was famous for this; he rooted up soil everywhere, causing springs to appear and creating landforms wherever he went.

185

Kamapua'a's creative deeds, his long snout, and his ability to till the female earth clearly made him a symbol of reproductive power, perhaps even an agricultural deity. In an even more overt reference to the pig's fertilizing power, Kamapua'a could change himself into fish or plants when no pigs were available for sacrifice. (Darby et al. 1977; Frazer 1950; Rappoport 1968; Simoons 1994, 1998; Toussaint-Samat 1992)

See also Blood and Flesh; Meat.

POTATOES

The New World has more than 200 species of wild potato, most of which grow in an area stretching from Colorado to Argentina and Chile. Archaeologists found the earliest domesticated potato in a cave in central Peru, and they dated it to about 8000 B.C. But archaeologists know that this tuberous food was domesticated in the highlands of Peru much later, between 3700 and 3000 B.C. It was first cultivated by the pre-Incan races of the Andes, and by the Aztec and the Maya as well. Quechua is the native language of the Peruvians, and the Quechuan name for potato is *papa*. At the time of the Conquest, the people of the Andes had about 3,000 kinds of papas of various flavors and textures, and an assortment of myths associated with this prolific and popular food.

The early Peruvians saw a bond between potatoes and heads—a bond that people of the Baltic lands recognized as well, as evidenced in the curious custom they have of pulling each other's hair, symbolic of the potato roots, while eating the firstfruits of the potato harvest. The Peruvians engaged in a much stranger practice. These people were expert surgeons, and they possessed surgical skills that far exceeded those of the Europeans of this time period. Because the Peruvians frequently needed to deal with serious head injuries their warriors suffered from clubs and slings, they learned to perform a surgical technique called trepanning, a procedure that involved removing the fractured part of the

skull to relieve pressure on the brain. According to Incan myth, whenever a trepanning operation was performed, a new variety of potato appeared. Peru has the remains of more trepanned skills than found anywhere else in the world, as well as more varieties of potatoes.

Because potatoes constituted a staple food for the peoples of the New World, their myths logically reflected a connection to fertility. The Peruvians considered the potato a living thing, inhabited by a soul or spirit. The people who inhabited the area before the Inca came to rule worshiped the potato spirits and quite likely sacrificed children to them—they invested potatoes with that much power. People in Peru and Bolivia likened a pair of potatoes growing together to twins and considered them a good omen. Farmers hung these twins on posts at the heads of their fields as an example for the other plants to follow. The Indians of Peru also had other ways of influencing the production of crops, and numerous superstitions about when and how potatoes should be planted and harvested. For example, they buried stones shaped like potatoes in the ground, believing this had a direct effect on the abundance of the crop. Everyone in the family had to eat from the first crop, the people believed, or the potato spirits would take offense and spoil the harvest.

Potatoes did not move into Europe until the 1530s, when the Spaniards conquered Peru. When the potato finally did cross the ocean, the Swedes also buried stones to promote the fertility of the potato harvest, and the Baltic people also drew connections between potatoes and human heads. But although the Europeans may have adopted some New World beliefs regarding potatoes, in the early years and in general, European people hesitated to connect this unfamiliar food with fertility. They had difficulty accepting the new food, even in Ireland, a country known today for its cultivated potatoes. The growth of the potato seemed weird and unnatural, possibly even supernatural. The edible plants the Europeans knew had seeds, not tubers; and furthermore, the potato tubers looked misshapen, and they reproduced with no seeds each time they were replanted. Many of the upper classes particularly hesitated to eat potatoes, believing them a food suitable only for the poor.

The first potatoes imported from the New World did not produce fruitful crops in Europe. The summers were long there, and these potatoes were used to growing in the short days of the tropics. Though in Ireland the potato had more success because the climate remained mild until November, the Irish too remained skeptical of the food for a long time. The potato belonged to the nightshade family, the same family to which the mysterious (and some thought, poisonous) mandrake belonged. Some Europeans believed at first that potatoes were poisonous too, and that they caused leprosy and fever. Gradually, popular attitudes changed, and potatoes became a novelty food eaten by the upper classes. In the second half of the eighteenth century, European monarchs encouraged the production of potatoes to relieve widespread famine, and the poor soon learned to depend on them rather than on grains for sustenance. (Benham 1981; Coe 1994; Heiser 1969; Lehner and Lehner 1973; Toussaint-Samat 1992; Verrill 1937)

See also Eggplant; Nightshades; Tomatoes

PULQUE

The Aztecs of Mexico cultivated the maguey, or agave plant, primarily for its sap, which they fermented and brewed into an intoxicating beverage called pulque. Pulque, formerly called *octli,* had important nutritive value in a diet lacking in green vegetables, but it was primarily used in religious rituals and ceremonies. When the Aztecs drank this wine, they entered a state of exaltation similar to that experienced by participants in the orgiastic rituals of the Greek Dionysus and the Roman Bacchus.

Current-day Mexicans cultivate maguey plants alongside their fields of maize, beans, squash, and other primary crops. These people have cultivated the maguey since ancient times—for food, fiber, medicine, magical charms, and pulque, a precursor to the mescals and tequilas their ancestors used to brew after the Conquest. In pre-Conquest times, the Aztecs worshiped the maguey plant in many forms, primarily as Mayahuel, a lovely virgin goddess associated with maternity and fertility. Mayahuel personified the plant, so the Aztecs depicted her as having many breasts, because the leaves of the maguey plant resembled breasts in a crude way, with the dark spines at the ends of the leaves resembling nipples. Pulque was rich in vitamins, and the early people of central Mexico identified it with mother's milk.

Some Mexicans today consider pulque as holy as did their forebears in pre-Conquest times. The myth of Mayahuel lives on in the story of the Virgin of Guadalupe. Some current-day Mexicans refer to pulque as "the milk of our Mother," the Virgin of Guadalupe, who clearly replaced Mayahuel as the maguey goddess. In early myth, Mayahuel resided in the plant. She was abducted from heaven and taken to the Sonoran desert, where demons killed her and chopped up her body. Quetzalcoatl, the Aztec god and culture hero, then used her bones to make the maguey plant.

This mythical origin of the maguey plant appeared in *Histoyre du Mechique,* generally attributed, at least in part, to Fray Andres de Olmos, a renowned chronicler of Aztec language and culture. In the myth, Quetzalcoatl and the other gods decided that they needed something other than food to bring pleasure to people's lives, and they knew that Mayahuel, the maguey goddess, could provide it. Mayahuel lived with her grandmother, the fearsome star demon Tzitzimitl, in the sky, and Quetzalcoatl kidnapped her from her sky world while she slept. Quetzalcoatl accomplished this by transforming himself into his wind-god aspect, Ehecatl. Ehecatl made love to Mayahuel, then changed himself and his goddess into two branches of a forked tree, and the two remained on earth, entwined together. When Tzitzimitl discovered her granddaughter missing from the sky world, she became wild with rage and she sent the other *tzitzimime* to destroy her. In Aztec myth, the tzitzimime were darkness demons who battled the sun, dove headfirst from the sky like shooting stars, and threatened to annihilate the world. At Tzitzimitl's request, they dove straight down to the forked tree and split it in half. Then they devoured Mayahuel's branch. Quetzalcoatl transformed himself from tree branch into god, and buried Mayahuel's bones. From the goddess's grave the maguey plant grew, and from then on, the Aztecs had their miraculous beverage. They brewed pulque from the sap, partook of the drink, and overcame their sadness.

Mayahuel may have been the most important of the pulque gods and the source of the maguey plant itself, but the Aztec worshiped other pulque gods in connection with the lovely goddess. The Centzon Totochtin, or the Four Hundred Rabbits, were the children she nursed, and they formed her entourage, all of them male gods associated with drunkenness. Ometochtli, or Two Rabbit, served as their chief.

The Four Hundred Rabbits were orgiastic deities, and their worship was similar to the worship of the Greek wine god Dionysus. Some say that Patecatl, Mayahuel's consort, was one of the rabbits as well, and the most important of them. He came from the Gulf coast, where pulque was first processed, and became linked with the root of the maguey plant, which the Aztecs ground and steeped in the fermenting brew. Although initially Patecatl may have been linked with other plants that the Aztec added to the pulque to help it ferment, he was later worshiped as a god of medicine and credited with giving the pulque its magic power. (Brundage 1979; Marshall 1979; Miller and Taube 1993)

See also Alcoholic Beverages; Ayahuasca; Balche; Beer; Chicha; Kava; Mead; Milk; Sake; Soma; Wine

PUMPKINS AND GOURDS

The Inca of Peru, the Chinese, the Africans, the people of India and Southeast Asia, and nearly all the native peoples of North America cultivated pumpkins or gourds. Many people used them for food; they ate the seeds as cereal and they ate the young plants as fruits, sometimes seasoning them with herbs and preserving them. Whereas pumpkins were more commonly cultivated for food, gourds were most commonly used as vessels. The vegetables themselves contained a multitude of seeds—and seeds, as symbols of life's beginnings, held all sorts of possibilities.

The early people who cultivated pumpkins and gourds assigned them great symbolic significance. These fruits symbolized life and abundance, as the myths devised about them reveal. Because pumpkins and gourds contained so many seeds, they also contained magic—the great magic that the ancients associated with creation. In Indian myth, Sumati, the wife of King Sagara, had 60,000 sons at one time, which she accomplished by giving birth to a gourd. Her sons emerged from the gourd shell. Some versions of this myth name the fruit as a pumpkin, and others as a cucumber—both are botanical relatives of the gourd that have hard rinds and many seeds.★ In ancient India, both the gourd and the cucumber symbolized offspring.

The gourd seeds may have produced sons in the Sagara myth, but in other myths, the seeds of gourds or pumpkins produced the sun, the moon, the stars, and the entire human race. In Burmese mythology, a primordial spirit created the pumpkin, then other spirits added arms, legs, eyes, and other body parts, until finally they had created a human being. In Chinese myth, human beings arose from a pumpkin after the Deluge destroyed the world. Only a brother and sister survived, and they did so by escaping in a pumpkin or a gourd.

★Pumpkins were domesticated in the New World, so most likely the Sagara myth or other myths that attach pumpkins to India are post-Columbian. Some gourds, as well as the cucumber, were domesticated in India.

They married and had a child, a pumpkin child, and from the seeds of that pumpkin came all the races of the world.

In Indian myth, a magic pumpkin contained all the oceans of the world, and oceans have always symbolized life and abundance. This story tells of a sage named Iaia, who buried his only son in a huge pumpkin, and then carried the pumpkin to the foot of a nearby mountain he could visit, as one would a grave site. One day, Iaia opened the pumpkin, and to his surprise, found it full of water, whales, and gigantic fishes. The creatures jumped out, and some neighbor boys, hearing the commotion, hurried to the foot of the mountain and picked up the pumpkin to inspect it. The boys dropped the pumpkin and cracked it, and the water poured out and inundated the earth. In a variation of the story of Iaia, the water that flooded the earth flowed into the sea and turned the water bitter, like the bitter juice of the gourd. Before this event, the legend said, the seawater was fresh and sweet, and Iaia and his son used to fish in the water. But primarily Iaia's story deals with the gourd of creation, or the gourd as a symbol of nature's creative power. In another Indian myth, one of the gods of the Todas came from a gourd.

In Hawaiian myth, Papa, the earth goddess, gave birth to a gourd, and Wakea, her partner, formed the world from it. The cover became the sky; the pulp, the sun; the seeds, the stars; the white lining, the moon; the ripe white meat, the clouds; and the juice, the rain. Then the calabash itself became the land and the ocean. In a myth from Brazil, the sun and the moon threw fresh gourds into the ocean, and those gourds turned into human beings. In an Indochinese myth, the creator spirit dropped gourds from the sky world into the ocean, and two primordial beings ate them. This myth features the gourd of creation, but it also appears to parallel Tree of Knowledge myths. But unlike forbidden fruits, the gourds dropped from heaven appear to have been intended for consumption. When the two primordial

beings ate the gourds, they discovered sexual passion. Then they planted the seeds of their gourds and two other gourds grew—one that produced human beings and one that produced animals.

If gourds and pumpkins contained the oceans of the world and enough seeds to produce the human race, ancient mythmakers obviously considered them magic vessels. The pumpkin in Cinderella was magic, and in an Italian version of Cinderella, the pumpkin, or gourd, held Cinderella herself; a woman gave birth to this gourd and left it in the forest, then a king found it and eventually married the girl inside it. This Italian Cinderella story is called Zucchetina, a name that means "little gourd." Most probably it was this little gourd that led to tales of pumpkins that changed into coaches. African mythmakers told numerous tales of magic gourds—of gourds that could talk, of gourds that held magic forces, and of a gourd that a magic man sent out to search for food. Many African myths also feature gourds as symbols of wealth and prosperity. In Hawaiian myth, the gourd symbolized fertility as well. Hawaiian mythmakers used a food gourd to represent the fertilizing powers of their god Lono. Long ago, each Hawaiian home had a food gourd, and in it the people kept food, fish, and kava. They used their gourd for prayers. The gourd of Lono, the people believed, blessed the family with fertility and wealth.

People of the past respected gourds both as food and as vessels. As vessels, they often stored the Elixir of Life, such was the strength of their creative power. In Japanese myth, a genie kept a gourd full of the Elixir of Life. Taoist magicians kept gourds to imprison evil spirits. The Chinese so respected gourds that they placed them in the sky among the stars of Delphinius. The constellation Hou-koua ("good gourd") and the constellation Pai-koua ("rotten gourd" or "frozen gourd") appeared in the sky as reminders to watch the harvest closely and keep the gourds from freezing too deeply. In ancient China, people ate their gourds in September, when they were fresh; if they left the gourds in the fields much longer than that, they would freeze. The Chinese used to remove the gourd shells and soak the flesh in alcohol and rice water to make gourd wine. If the gourds froze too hard, they became useless, and a useful gourd harvest was important to the Chinese—for food and wine as well as for the vessels to hold them. The emperor even had his own gourd plantation called the "Fruit Garden of the Emperor," and from this garden he produced a supply of wine for his guests and cups with which to drink it.

The Chinese Taoists were among the many people who used gourds as vessels and who told myths about the gourd's magic abilities. In Taoist myth, the double or twin gourd was particularly magical: It incorporated both the yin and the yang (the dual principles of nature), and it symbolized Li T'ien-kuai, the second of the Eight Immortals. It also symbolized the link between heaven and earth. Li T'ien-kuai, who possessed such a gourd, had the ability to leave his earthly body and ascend to heaven. But once when Li T'ien-kuai performed this feat, his soul returned to earth and discovered his body missing, so he entered the body of a beggar who had recently starved to death. As a beggar, Li T'ien-kuai carried a gourd that contained magic medicines. He used them to revive the dead mother of his disciple Yang, and later, to make Yang himself immortal. (Beckwith 1970; Cooper 1978; Heiser 1979; Willis 1993)

See also Cucumbers; Squash; Watermelons

color and for their aromatic scent. The Greeks used them in marriage rituals, presenting them to the bride and groom to eat together before their wedding night. The Greeks began using quinces in marriage rituals in the sixth century B.C., when Solon, an Athenian statesman, issued a decree that a couple had to eat quinces before they had marital relations. This rule likely stemmed from the quince's sweet and pungent scent, reminiscent of love and sex, which led the ancient Greeks to regard quinces both as fertility symbols and as love tokens.

Quinces appeared as more than just tokens in the Roman myth of Cydippe, a young maiden who had attracted the attentions of a youth named Acontius. Cydippe was sacrificing to the goddess Diana one day when Acontius threw a quince into the temple with a message attached, reading, "I swear by the

QUINCES

Quinces are native to central and western Asia, and they were likely imported to Crete, where they eventually gained a reputation as love charms among the Greeks and Romans. Quinces were appealing, both for their golden

In Greek mythology, Hippomenes used the quinces in a race in order to entice Atalanta and win her affections. (Scala/Art Resource, NY)

191

divinity of Diana to become the wife of Acontius." Acontius knew that if the young girl read his message out loud in Diana's temple, the words would gain the potency of a solemn oath. Cydippe did read the words aloud, and indeed she did marry Acontius. Here the quince, which the Greeks called a golden apple, played a crucial role in facilitating love and marriage.

It is difficult to determine just how often quinces appeared in ancient myths. Because the Greeks did call quinces golden apples, mythological scholars easily confused them with other fruits of similar color, such as apricots, oranges, and true apples. Like other golden fruits, quinces variously have been identified as the forbidden fruit in the Garden of Eden; the apples of Milos, identified with Aphrodite; and the golden apples of the Hesperides, guarded by the dragon Ladon, which had the power to bestow immortality. Some scholars also identified quinces as the fruit that Hippomenes used to win the race against Atalanta. (Other scholars have identified these fruits as oranges or apples.) In the classical myths, Atalanta was a beautiful young princess who wished never to marry and to remain a virgin forever, but she had many suitors, and she decreed that she would marry whomever could beat her in a foot-race. Whoever entered the contest and did not win, however, would pay with his life. Several men did pay with their lives—Atalanta had them beheaded. But Hippomenes, using three "golden apples," or quinces, met her challenge and won. Hippomenes dropped the fruits one by one during the race, and Atalanta stopped each time to retrieve them. Hippomenes had obtained these golden fruits from Venus, the love goddess, who had given him the irresistible objects for protection—and they did protect him. They protected him from death by seducing Atalanta with their powers. In essence, they served as aphrodisiacs in this myth, delivering the maiden from infertility and allowing her to submit to Hippomenes's love. The Greeks and the Romans consecrated quinces to Venus. The goddess of love was believed to have a chariot filled with them, as well as with myrtle and roses; and in ancient art, she often appeared with a quince in her hand. (Baumann 1993; Folkard 1892; Hyams 1971)

See also Apples; Apricots; Oranges

QUINOA

Quinoa is a high-protein grain that was virtually unknown to people outside South America until recent years. The grain grew wild in the South American highlands thousands of years ago. People living in the area around Lake Titicaca began cultivating it around 5800 to 4500 B.C. For thousands of years, millions of people in the Andean region relied on quinoa to fulfill their nutritional needs, and they revered the grain as a god-given food. In Quechua myth, a sacred bird, the turtledove, or *kullku,* delivered quinoa to the people. He brought them three seeds: quinoa, *canuhua,* and *kiwicha.* Of the three, quinoa became the primary staple crop.

When the Inca came to rule in the Peruvian Andes, they too relied on quinoa as a nutritional staple and held it sacred. They called it "mother grain," and they made it the focus of sacred rituals performed in worship of their sun god. In legend, the sun sent Manco Capac and his wife Mama Ocllo, the first Incan couple, to the world. They emerged from Lake Titicaca and followed the sun's instructions for building their empire. Much to do with building the empire involved the cultivation of crops. The sun gave Manco Capac a golden planting stick and told him to find a place where he could sink the golden planting stick into the earth with one thrust. He should build the empire there, the sun said. Then he taught Manco Capac the cycle of seasons and how to plant. Manco Capac found the place the sun had told him about, named it Cuzco, and built the sun a great temple. Then he began to build the empire. The Inca knew that to build an empire, they not only had to conquer the inhabitants of the land but also to unite them, and to provide enough food to keep the people from starving. So they developed an astute knowledge of their indigenous plants and developed advanced methods of cultivation. Quinoa became the Inca's most important crop. They boiled it, ground it into flour, cooked the leaves, and fermented the grain to make beer, or *chicha*. They also worshiped the quinoa seeds as their empire's source of origin and survival.

The Inca worshiped quinoa as they did the sun who gave them the grain and the divine king who sowed the seeds. But when Francisco Pizarro and other Spaniards arrived, they abolished all forms of pagan worship and destroyed the quinoa crops the people had worked so hard to develop. Hernán Cortés destroyed the amaranth crops of the Aztecs for the same reason. The Spaniards obliterated the Incan empire in a single year by attacking everything the people held sacred. They replaced quinoa with barley. Barley fed the people but had no religious associations. It also had far less nutritive value, and many people died of malnutrition. Some of the Inca continued to grow quinoa in secret in remote areas, just as the Aztec did with amaranth. But potatoes and maize became the primary staple crops. Gone was the time when quinoa had ruled, and the Incan emperor, revered as god-king, had broken the soil with his golden spade and planted the first quinoa seeds of the year, offering them to the sun. (Foster and Cordell 1992; Rogers 1987; Wood 1989)

See also Amaranth; Chicha; Grain

R that looked much like a carrot. The Chinese called this elongated form lo-phu, and the Japanese called it daikon. The Japanese name connected this radish in myth with Daikoku, a famous culture hero and Buddhist guardian deity responsible for good harvests.

Agricultural peoples of Japan today often keep a shrine to Daikoku in their kitchens. The harvest god is a combination of the guardian deity and culture hero the Buddhists at first worshiped as separate spirits. He guarantees prosperity and good fortune in rural communities. Not only do the Japanese have altars to Daikoku in their kitchens but they perform rituals involving the marriage of Daikoku to a radish. They place the radish on an altar to Daikoku as his bride, as they believe that the symbolic marriage guarantees fertility of the soil, because both Daikoku and the radish represent abundant harvests. The Japanese perform this ritual and similar rituals around the time of the winter solstice, a crucial time in the yearly cycle, to placate the gods who have the ability to return spring and growth to the earth.

The significance the Japanese placed on Daikoku for his ability to renew the harvest made his bride, the radish, an important food in harvest festivals, an auspicious offering to the deities, and a sacred food for human beings. The Chinese myth of Mu-lien outlined dire consequences for a woman who plucked a radish carelessly from the ground. The woman, Mu-lien's mother, had been banished to hell and condemned to eternal starvation for refusing to respect all forms of life. Mu-lien had worked hard to rescue her, but when she emerged from the underworld, she immediately consumed the radish that had sprouted up from the ground and offered the promise of renewal. (Some myths identify this vegetable as a carrot.)

Radishes obviously tempted the woman as would forbidden fruit, and the red color of the radish added to its allure. But people who

RADISHES

Few people today consider radishes popular foods, yet they surface in folktales and legends for several reasons. In antiquity, people valued radishes primarily for their seed, which the ancients made into oil; people likely used radish oil long ago in embalming the dead, particularly as an enema to clean out the intestines. Others took notice of these vegetables because of their red color, which had both sacrificial and sexual connotations. Radishes had other distinctive qualities as well: a particularly acrid taste, and long ago, a propensity to grow to enormous size. A Jewish legend told of a radish so big that a fox hollowed it out and made his home inside it. The Greeks and Romans told stories of radishes weighing up to 100 pounds.

Because radishes grow and ripen best in cold weather, they symbolize renewal and the promise of coming spring. Early people ate radishes when they feared death, believing that the promise of renewed spring offered a promise of renewed life as well. Jews traditionally served radishes at Passover because they connected them with renewal. The Japanese and Chinese connected them also with prosperity. The kinds of radish that grew in the East differed from those that grew in the West. The western varieties moved eastward in ancient times, but the people in the Eastern lands developed their own form, an elongated radish

In Japanese Buddhist myth, Daikoku, a guardian deity of good harvests, represented the radish. (The Newark Museum/Art Resource, NY)

pick root crops often suffer dire consequences for the theft. In the legend of Mu-lien, the greedy woman was returned to hell for her offense.

In the popular fairy tale of Rapunzel, Rapunzel suffered for her theft as well. Radishes grow in the ground, and supernatural forces seem to control them. In German legend, an evil mountain genie called Rubezahl represented the radish. He imprisoned a princess in a castle, and because she begged for companionship, he gave her some radishes, which he touched with his magic wand and changed into girls. Though the radishes stayed human only so long as they kept their leaves, the clever young princess came up with a plan. She distracted Rubezahl by asking him to count the radishes he gave her, and while he was thus occupied, she stole his wand. Know-ing the wand had the power to change rad-ishes into other forms, she turned one of them into a horse and rode away to freedom. (Christie 1985; Dorson 1963; Folkard 1892; Skinner n.d.; Westfahl et al. 1996)

See also Carrots; Turnips

RASPBERRIES

Hunter-gatherers familiar with raspberries valued them highly as a sweet, nourishing food during times of scarcity. Raspberries played a ritual role in harvest ceremonies, and a magic role in fairy tales and legends. Berries of all sorts have enjoyed a connection with magic, and raspberries were no exception. For one thing, they seemed to make perfect food for fairies and other little people. In a Finnish tale, the diminutive Raspberry King inhabits the raspberry bushes, and has lived inside them for thousands of years.

The Finnish tale of the Raspberry King embodied the notion of power and magic in food plants. The Raspberry King ruled over the berry bushes; but in order to keep him humble, the Sky God decreed that the king emerge from the bushes for one day every 100 years in the form of a caterpillar. One day, two sisters were collecting the king's raspberries to make jam, and they spied the little caterpillar and spared his life. The king gave them juicy raspberries as a reward. It seems fitting that someone with supernatural powers controlled the distribution of the fruits, because the appearance of nuts and berries seemed miraculous in early times. Before people learned the art of agriculture, nuts dropped from the trees like supernatural gifts, and raspberries and other fruits seemed to appear on the vines like magic.

The ancients perceived magic in all kinds of foods, and fruits in particular attracted the mythmakers because of their bright colors and aromatic scents. Raspberries, because of their shape and color, share the same symbolism with some other fresh fruits. Raspberries look like miniature hearts, as do strawberries and pears, so the Greeks and Romans connected them with love and put them under the dominion of Eros and Venus. The raspberry's pungent aroma and red color conjured up images of godly delights; the Greek myths, for instance, placed them on Mount Olympus.

The brambles of raspberry bushes also enter into their symbolism. Some peoples of the Philippines hang raspberry vines on their doors to keep the spirits of the dead from entering their homes. They do this after someone in their home has died, believing that if the spirit tries to reenter the home, it will get tangled in the brambles. Some peoples of India and Nepal use raspberry bushes for similar purposes. In a funerary ritual in Nepal, for instance, people jump over raspberry twigs after the death ceremony. They too believe that the raspberry brambles repel the spirits, and that if they perform this ritual, the ghosts of the dead won't go near the raspberry bushes or try to come into the house. (Bayley 1913; Leach 1961)

See also Blackberries; Blueberries; Cranberries; Elderberries; Gooseberries; Mulberries; Strawberries

REINDEER AND CARIBOU

In precontact times, the indigenous peoples of Alaska and Siberia relied on reindeer and caribou meat to survive. Reindeer husbandry is the traditional occupation of many people living in the northern latitudes still today, of people in Alaska and Siberia, and of the Lapps in Norway, Sweden, and Finland. The reindeer herdsmen of these areas relied on their close relationship with the animals to guarantee the success of the hunt. They developed an intimate relationship with the herds and learned to understand their breeding, foraging, and migration habits.

The relationship that developed between the hunter and hunted was not unique to reindeer societies but permeated hunting societies throughout America and in many other areas of the world. Like these other hunters, the reindeer herdsmen perceived animals as soul spirits and influential natural powers, and they knew the importance of communicating with them. Typically, shamans played a large role in facilitating this communication because they knew how to travel to the spirit world and tap into its mystic powers. Legend tells of a certain shaman who learned where the caribou migrated by going into a trance and traveling with a guardian spirit to a house in the forest. There he saw the gigantic King Caribou standing over the door and guarding the house while the herds walked underneath him to safety.

The legend of the guardian caribou exemplifies the belief in a Master of Animals who protects the game from hunters who fail to respect nature. People in traditional

Reindeer hunters developed an intimate relationship with their herds, and perceived animals as soul spirits and influential nature powers. (Library of Congress)

hunting societies often place strict taboos on killing more than one can eat, and they employ the use of legendary game masters to whom hunters must appeal in order to receive prey. These kinds of beliefs defined other myths of the northern lands, leading to many similar tales of shamans traveling to the realm of guardian spirits and winning their permission to obtain food. Sedna, the Inuit sea spirit, served the same purpose as the King Caribou. Both guarded the game animals and protected the sanctity of nature, and both granted only a certain number of animals to hunters.

Sedna, the King Caribou, and similar nature spirits validated not only the belief in animal spirits but in the necessity of propitiating these spirits before taking food from them. Sedna and the King Caribou protected the game but at the same time helped the hunters. These legends underscored the hunters' dependence on the animal masters for survival, and their need to respect the animals

in order to guarantee continuation of the species. People of the Americas particularly embraced the concept of sanctity in nature, and of the sanctity of the nature spirits, be they plant or animal. They recognized plants and animals as living spirits much like themselves, moved and motivated by the same life force. In this line of thought, food sources had souls, so to eat was to take part of the life force of the plant or animal. Life force gave food its sanctity. Perhaps one reason the herdsman of the north had such profound respect for the reindeer and their guardian masters was that they understood famine all too well. They knew nature could deny or provide, and they respected the spirits so that the spirits would give freely of themselves.

The reindeer herdsmen may have relied on their herds to provide food for everyday consumption, but their respect for the animal spirits moved them to use the reindeer meat in ritual ceremonies as well. The Lapps had a custom of killing and consuming a reindeer as part of a memorial feast to honor a dead relative, for instance. They used the reindeer to carry the dead to their graves, then they killed and ate those very reindeer in honor of the dead people they carried. Then they buried the reindeer bones in a chest in the earth. Sometimes, if the dead person was a wealthy man, ritual slaughters and reindeer feasts continued for several years after the person's death. The Lapps believed these sacrifices guarded the living against poverty. Similar rites and beliefs existed among the Samoyeds, who practiced all kinds of horrendous rituals to bring about the death of the reindeer. The reindeer had belonged to the deceased and served him in life, and thus had to die with him and serve him in the spirit world as well.

The herds of reindeer and caribou that lived in the northern lands served their herdsmen well. These animals existed to benefit the people—to feed them and clothe them and even to reveal to them the secret powers of nature. An interesting practice surfaces in the study of the reindeer herdsmen and the foods they consumed from their animals. Not only did the herdsmen eat the reindeer meat but they also drank the animal's urine. Siberian shamans learned from the reindeer to use the hallucinogenic fly agaric mushroom to go into trances and commune with the nature spirits. They discovered that reindeer ate the mushrooms as well as drank one another's urine afterward. They also went to great lengths to drink the urine of human beings. By doing this, these reindeer taught the people the mushroom's secrets. The people too began drinking the urine of both reindeer and humans, and Siberian shamans in particular drank urine to elevate their minds and to enter the spirit world. In past times, Siberian shamans dressed like reindeer, with fur and antlers, possibly to honor the animals for their contribution to survival and for teaching people how to tap into nature's powers. (Dobkin De Rios 1976; Leeds and Vayda 1965)

See also Bear; Buffalo; Deer; Mushrooms; Salmon; Whale

RICE

For ages, rice has served as a symbol of life, fertility, and abundance. That's why people throw it at weddings—to bestow blessings of fertility on the newly married couple. Rice's connection with fertility stems from its abundant growth in many parts of the world, and from the common reliance on this grain as a staple food. For this reason, many peoples have long considered rice sacred. This miracle grain sustained their lives, so they created gods and goddesses to embody it, and they set up shrines to worship these deities as benevolent providers.

One of the best-known rice deities is Inari, a Japanese god who has over 40,000 shrines in villages all over Japan. Inari appeared around 800 B.C., and is still worshiped today, sometimes as a goddess, and other times as a god: an old man with a beard, either carrying bundles of rice or sitting on top of them. Inari lives in the mountains, but he comes down the slopes each spring when the Japanese people begin cultivating their fields. He protects the fields all season long, so they hold a festival to honor him. Inari brings food and prosperity, wealth, and even friendship. Then he returns to the mountains in autumn. Inari has power because rice itself has power—the power to give strength, to sustain life, and even to drive away evil.

Inari goes by many names because rice deities protect every rice field in Japan. Almost all of the country's agricultural rituals involve the production of rice, and the Japanese perform rituals at various stages in the growth of their rice plants. They welcome the rice deity before cultivation begins, and they bid him farewell at the end of the harvest. The people of Japan consider rice the most sacred thing on earth, so Japanese farmers make it their sacred duty to produce good crops.

Rice farming has for centuries been accompanied by rituals in all rice-growing regions of Japan. The most popular Japanese folk festival is called Hatsuuma, and it's held on 12 February of each year. During this festival, the

Japanese gather at shrines to Inari to pray for a good crop. Other ceremonies and rituals take place at various times of the year: for instance, during the typhoon season, when the Japanese make offerings to appease the wind god; and in early spring, when they make offerings to the field god. Sometimes the people offer these gods *kagami-mochi,* or layered rice cake. During harvesttime, they offer them ripe grain. At the end of the harvest, the Japanese hold a harvest festival, and the people make offerings to their village gods to thank them for help during the growing season.

Rice farming played such a significant role in Asian life that mythmakers credited its introduction to supernatural intervention. Japanese mythmakers said that Amaterasu, their sun goddess, introduced rice farming to the people. She sowed rice first in the fields of heaven, then gave the ears to her descendant, the Imperial grandson Niningi-no Mikoto, to plant in Japan. In one myth, she sent Uke-Mochi, the food goddess, to produce rice from her mouth. Chinese mythmakers said that their mythical emperor Shen-Nung taught the Chinese to cultivate rice. Other myths offered different explanations. One Chinese myth credits the dog with the introduction of rice. Some myths from both China and Japan credit a mouse or a rat. In Japanese myth, it was a priest who first saw the rice, but a mouse who led him to it. Once, while meditating, this priest couldn't help but be distracted by a mouse scurrying around with something in his mouth. The priest managed to tie a thread to the mouse's leg, and was then able to follow him. The mouse led him to a place he had never seen before, a watery land where rice grew in abundance. The priest then sent for his people, and they began to cultivate the precious food.

Rice is the most extensively cultivated grain crop in the world, so similar legends arose also in other cultures. The Arabs said that the first rice grains came from the sweat of Mohammed. In a myth from Madagascar, the daughter of the Supreme Deity brought rice from heaven. In Indonesian myth, a snakelike god named Anta had a daughter named Samyam Sri, who was murdered by the gods to protect her from molestation by a man who was married to her wet nurse. (Because the woman had nursed Samyam Sri, this was considered incest.) Plants grew from her murdered body, rice from her eyes and chest. In an African myth from Malagasy, a woman took her child to the riverside one day and the child found a grasshopper. The child asked the mother to catch the grasshopper for him, and she did, but the grasshopper ran away. The child grieved so much that he died. The mother prayed to God for her dead child, and God told the woman to bury her son in a marsh. This the woman did, and soon the first rice plant grew, and eventually, bestowed the gift of grain.

In an Indo-Chinese myth, rice existed always, but it was not until the goddess Kuan Yin squeezed milk from her breasts into the rice plants that they became filled with grain. Rice cultivators developed different varieties of rice, some of them with reddish grain, and the myth of Kuan Yin illustrated how ancient mythmakers incorporated the use of color in the tales that they told. The goddess Kuan Yin squeezed milk out of her breasts and produced white rice; then she squeezed again, until blood flowed out of her nipples. The blood and milk, mixed together, produced red rice.

The femininity of rice deities confirmed the role of rice as a giver of life. Perhaps their gender also had something to do with the fact that rice is white, like mother's milk, and a delicate crop; it has to be treated gently, especially at budding time. In Japanese myth, rice and other primary crops grew from the body of the goddess Ogetsu-hime, killed by the storm god Susanowo. The ancients typically equated the soul of rice with the soul of women, and they typically recognized the rice mother as a giver of life—a giver of human life. The Indonesian rice goddess Dewi Sri is goddess of the earth and mother of the Javanese people. She's equated with the In-

Japanese women harvesting rice, the lifeblood of their society. (Library of Congress)

dian Lakshmi, the goddess of agriculture, prosperity, and love, and one of the most beloved deities in the Hindu pantheon. Lakshmi, like rice, gives wealth, and in one aspect, she embodies the rice. Dewi Sri is an ancient deity, described as a pregnant goddess when the rice stalks grow in the paddies. The Javanese and many other people personified their rice, and thus gave their rice goddess capabilities analogous to those of humans. They also endowed her with a spirit or a soul. In Japanese myth,

Izanagi, the mother goddess, lived in the sky world but returned at harvesttime every year to visit her descendants and infuse life power into the soul of the rice plants.

The concept of soul in grain is an ancient one. Rice cultivators, and indeed all grain cultivators, invested their crops with spirit. This was certainly true in the ancient world, and it remains so today among some groups. People adhere to the belief in rice spirits because they recognize the interconnectedness between rice and people. So they treat the grain delicately, and they take care to preserve its soul. Some people believe that the rice loses its soul when the grain is reaped, so at this time, they grieve the death of the spirit. They also take special care to prevent the soul from escaping during the process. In the Pacific Islands, women make dolls out of rice before the harvest, believing that the soul of the grain is transferred to the doll. In Sumatra, people pound the rice rather than grind it in a mill because they believe the mill bruises the rice so badly that the soul in the rice flees. Rice tastes better, they say, with the soul inside it.

Rice growers around the world realize the intricate tie between their people and their primary crop. Rice is their lifeblood, their fertility symbol, their benevolent goddess of prosperity, wealth, and abundance. Rice gives them strength and life; their myths clearly reveal this belief. In Buddhist myth, rice gained sanctity when it revived Siddhartha from near death. The Bodhisattva was starving, and moved by his weakness, a village girl named Sujata milked 100 cows and fed the milk to 50 of them. Then she milked the 50 cows and fed the milk to 25 of them; then 25 cows, and gave the milk to 10 of them. Then she milked the 10 and gave 1 cow the milk. This milk Sujata used to cook rice, adding sugar to make a rice pudding. Siddhartha went on to achieve enlightenment and become a Buddha. Because this rice pudding saved the Buddha's life, rice itself became sacred. (Dorson 1963; Gupta 1991; Lehner and Lehner 1973; Rabbitt 1940; Toussaint-Samat 1992; Visser 1986)

See also Barley; Bread; Cake; Corn; Grain; Millet; Oats; Rye; Sake; Sorghum; Wheat

RYE

Rye was a reliable staple grain in the Old World. It thrived in cold climates, making it an ideal crop and food source for peasants in the northern countries. Long ago, the harvest was accompanied by elaborate rituals. Peasants immortalized their grain crops by personifying them and assigning them leading roles in harvest ceremonies. Variants of Old Woman were among the most common personifications of grain, including Old Barley Woman or Old Corn Woman, Rice Mother, and Calleach (old woman or hag). All of these "women" personified the harvest in general, and the last sheaf of grain specifically. People across the globe personified the last sheaf of grain, and some farmers today continue to regard it as an emblem of abundance. But long ago and in some traditions, people feared that evil spirits took up residence in the last sheaf: Regarding rye, the Rye Woman or Rye Witch inhabited the last sheaf. She was a frightening field spirit who chased, and often killed, children who entered her fields.

An equally frightening personification of rye was the Rye Wolf (in Germany, Roggenwolf), an evil animal that was said to inhabit rye fields and terrorize children. In German folklore, this evil being was passing through the field whenever the rye waved in the wind. Roggenwolf moved about the fields, retreating farther and farther into them as harvesters carried away the grain, until finally he took up residence in the last sheaf. In some traditions, the word *wolf* applied either to the reaper who reaped the last sheaf or to the wagon that carried it away. Rye harvesters typically made the last sheaf into the shape of a wolf, and in some traditions, the reaper of the last sheaf had to act like a wolf—howling and pretending to bite the other harvesters. In other traditions, whoever harvested the last sheaf was said to "kill the rye wolf." In some areas of Germany, folk belief dictated that children be told of Roggenwolf's presence and forewarned that he would devour them or carry them away if they dared tread on his grain.

The belief in Roggenwolf is easy to understand, given the common notion in northern Europe that devils haunted rye fields. The peasants greatly feared devils, so they often left the last sheaf of rye for them, in hopes that these demons would argue over it while the people carried the rest of the rye, unnoticed, out of the fields. The belief in rye demons quite likely stemmed from the fact that rye is susceptible to ergot, a fungus that turns the grain black. Ergot contains lysergic acid, a poisonous alkaloid that doesn't destroy the rye but often kills the people who eat it. Lysergic acid is also found in morning glory seeds, which the Aztecs of Mexico used as a hallucinogenic drug. Ergotism, caused by the consumption of infected rye bread, caused hallucinations similar to those caused by the ritual consumption of morning glory seeds. People who suffered those hallucinations but did not understand them had every reason to attribute them to supernatural influence.

Ergotism reached epidemic proportions in Europe in the Middle Ages. Entire villages were stricken with madness, and the people, not knowing the cause, attributed it to demonic forces. They called the plague St. Anthony's fire, because they believed that only prayers to St. Anthony, the patron saint of the poor, offered any hope of relief from this sickness, which at the time had no known cure. It wasn't until 1670 that scientists discovered the cause of the plague and identified ergot as a parasitic mold that grew on grain, particularly on rye. The ergot caused purple-brown spikes on the ears of grain.

Before this time, people referred to these purple-brown spikes as rye-wolves, offspring of the demonic Rye Mother who inhabited the fields. Ergot of rye most often afflicted children, and it infested the grain especially in the warm summer months, when children tended to play in the fields. In Limoges in A.D. 943, many children died in rye fields, and people attributed their deaths to the Rye Witch. Some children claimed they saw this

Rye Witch, and they described her as an ugly old woman with bony arms and black breasts and a mass of tangled hair. The Rye Witch, the children said, smeared a black, evil substance on the rye, and lured the children into the fields, coaxing them to eat her food. If they refused to eat, she smothered them. This legend possibly arose because someone actually believed they saw such a witch. The hallucinogenic properties in the rye may have caused the children who ate infected bread to see horrific sights.

The physical effects people suffered from consuming ergotized rye strengthened the belief in rye demons. Those children who consumed enough of the infected rye bread suffered convulsions and died. There were two types of ergotism: convulsive ergotism, which caused mental disturbances, and gangrenous ergotism, which caused the extremities of infected people to turn black and rot away. For pagan peoples whose folk beliefs emphasized the presence of demons, it was easy to misconstrue the blackness of the gangrenous limbs as proof that an evil spirit of some sort, be it witch or wolf, did indeed inhabit their fields. It has even been suggested that ergot of rye was responsible for the "witchcraft" practiced at Salem in later years. The effects of convulsive ergotism paralleled how people believed a person possessed by demons would act. Some of the accused "witches" of Salem lived on farms and may have been exposed to rye poisoning, which would have caused them to manifest delusional or psychotic behavior. (Caporael 1976; Dodge 1979; Frazer 1950; Ricciuti 1978; Schultes and Hofmann 1979; Wasson et al. 1978)

See also Barley; Bread; Cake; Corn; Grain; Millet; Oats; Rice; Sorghum; Wheat

S of poison brewed by the witch Medea. Medea, they said, used this crocus to make her enemies choke to death. The superior saffron crocus, in contrast, arose from the union of the king and queen of heaven, Zeus and Hera. The two deities, who had been arguing over who should win the Trojan War, ended their quarrel in a bout of lovemaking on Mount Ida. On the very spot where they had made love, saffron later sprouted and grew.

People past and present have prized saffron largely because of its color, ranging from deep gold to a reddish hue. Both red and gold achieved a high status in color symbolism. Gold symbolized divinity and royalty, and red symbolized passion and vigor on one hand, and blood and death on the other. The Greeks called saffron the "blood of Heracles," a tribute to its divine powers, and they mixed it with wine. They also called it the blood of Crocus. In a variant myth about the origins of saffron, Hermes, the messenger god, created the plant after he mortally wounded his friend Crocus by accident. Where Crocus's blood fell to the ground, saffron sprang up.

The prevalence of saffron in Greek myth attests to the significance the early Greeks attributed to the plant, both for its color and its aromatic scent. The Greeks continually clothed their gods and heroes in saffron, just as the peoples of the East did their Buddha. In the *Iliad,* for instance, Homer described Eos or Aurora, the goddess of dawn, as "saffron robed." The Egyptians, like the Greeks, assigned special powers to saffron, including the power to heal, largely because of its color. Pliny described it as a panacea, and people of his time wore it as an amulet to protect themselves from disease. According to the Doctrine of Signatures, like cures like, so people who adhered to this doctrine used saffron to cure jaundice, based on their belief that yellow cured yellow and could thus remove the yellow color from their skin. The Tamils, a Dravidian people of south India, use saffron to lighten the color of their skin. (The early Aryans associated the

SAFFRON

Saffron—produced from the pollen of the saffron crocus—has been widely used throughout the Old World for its color, flavor, and fragrance. It is native to the eastern Mediterranean region, and it has been cultivated in Mesopotamia, Persia, and northwest India since antiquity. The earliest reference to saffron cultivation dates from 2300 B.C. Saffron was abundant in ancient days, and ancient people used it as a flavoring, a dye, a perfume, and a potent sexual stimulant. Both its flavor and its fragrance contributed to the belief that it was an aphrodisiac. (It was mentioned in *The Arabian Nights* as an aphrodisiac, and people generally appear to have associated it with courtesans.) The ancients believed not only that saffron stimulated desire but also that it drove away evil and melancholy, cured certain diseases, and had magic properties.

The use of saffron as a condiment likely originated in Persia and India and was introduced later to Europe. Because saffron grows ideally in the Mediterranean region, Spain is the leading producer today. Saffron is difficult to grow and therefore remains the most expensive spice in the world. Attempts to cultivate the saffron crocus have led to inferior varieties that were far less flavorful. Some varieties of the crocus are poisonous: The Greeks described the inferior meadow saffron, or spring crocus, as having sprouted from drops dark-skinned Dravidians with dark forces, and these perceptions lingered into the present day.) Pregnant Tamil women sometimes drink saffron potions to lighten their babies' skin. They also avoid eating fruits with dark skins for fear of their producing a darkening effect.

Saffron plays a primary role in the religions of India and other lands, where the people traditionally have considered its golden color sacred. They associate gold with royalty and divinity as well as with love, sex, and fertility both of human beings and of the earth. Because these people consider gold an erotic color, they use it in marriage ceremonies; and because they associate it with divinity, they make it into a paste and apply it to images of their gods and goddesses. The Chinese have been known to rub saffron on themselves, to make their bodies resemble the golden body of the Buddha. Gold has traditionally symbolized enlightenment and wisdom, and thus Buddha is often depicted as golden in color. For this reason, Buddhist priests may have used saffron to color their robes long before turmeric replaced it. Because turmeric is also golden yellow in color, it too achieved religious/ritual use among some peoples; in addition, it is far less expensive than saffron. Saffron remains the most expensive and most highly prized spice in the world today. (Basker and Negbi 1983; *Funk and Wagnall's* 1972; Simoons 1991; Toussaint-Samat 1992)

See also Cinnamon; Ginger; Spices; Turmeric

SAKE

Japanese myths abound with references to sake as medicinal and magical, an elixir of life and longevity. Since antiquity, Japanese Shintoists have incorporated the drinking of rice wine in their rituals. The production of sake dates back to 200 B.C., when people used the beverage only in religious ceremonies; somewhat later it came to be used also in ordinary life. But the consumption of sake continues to constitute an important part of shrine rituals throughout Japan.

Customarily in these rituals, worshipers offer the wine to the spirits first; then the people drink the beverage. Sake, they believe, contains spirit. The ancient Japanese literary works *Kojiki* and *Nihongi* say that sake is as good as if it were made by gods. It's the gods' favorite drink, the Japanese believe; and by consuming it in sacred rituals, people establish a spiritual communion with the divine.

Propitiations of sake ensure good crops and good health, wealth, luck, and happiness. In legend, sake was nothing short of magic, and the gods bestowed this magical gift on people worthy of its powers. One legend tells of Kosagi, a poor woodcutter and a model of filial piety, who used to buy sake for his father, to bring happiness and pleasure to his life. When times got hard for Kosagi, however, he could no longer afford to buy sake, and he took his father water instead. The gods took pity on Kosagi, and because they recognized his piety and goodness, they supplied the sake for him. Whenever he went to fill his gourd at the waterfall, the water turned into the precious elixir, so Kosagi and his father had a constant supply.

The magic of sake also was revealed in an ancient Chinese legend that made its way to Japan. The legend tells of what Chinese literature refers to as the "rice-wine dream." In one version of the legend, a man named Rosei received the gods' gift of sake. Rosei and an Immortal were waiting for dinner at an inn, and when the Immortal supplied the sake, Rosei had a fabulous dream of prosperity and good fortune. The legend revealed the miraculous powers of the rice wine not only to bring luck and happiness but also to stimulate the imagination.

The significance of sake lies in its source—rice—the life source of Japanese society. Japanese farmers invest their rice with spirit and breath. They say the roots of the rice plants contain breath, and they perceive their sacred crop as an entity alive and breathing in the fields. Rice gained sanctity because it had life-giving, divine properties; it nourished both body and soul, early people believed. Sake gained significance from its divine origin. In Japanese myth, rice existed first in heaven, and Amaterasu, the sun goddess, gave the precious grain to the world.

Sake continues to play an important role in the worship of Amaterasu. It appears that her brother Susanowo fermented the first sake, though this sake may have been made from millet or barley rather than rice. After his banishment from heaven, Susanowo came across a man grieving over the loss of his daughters. An eight-headed serpent had been devouring them, one by one, and the time had come, the man knew, for the dragon to kill the last of his precious children. So Susanowo instructed the man how to brew sake, and told him to fill eight vats with the drink and to set them out for the dragon to find. The dragon found the sake, consumed it all, and passed out from intoxication. Susanowo then slew the dragon and saved the maiden from destruction.

Susanowo's brewing of sake is described in both *Kojiki* and *Nihongi* and predates other references to sake in the literature. Sake and rice appear to date from time immemorial, but it also appears that the Ainu and other early inhabitants of Japan made millet wine before they made rice wine. The god Niningi-no Mikoto may have been the first to make sake from rice: A shrine near Kyoto, built 12,000 years ago, was dedicated to him along with his wife and son and Oyamatsumi-no-kami, the grandfather of his son and the son of Izanagi and Izanami, the creator deities. The Japanese today venerate Oyamatsumi-no-kami as the patron saint of sake distillers.

The Japanese recognize numerous sake gods, including Sukuna-bikona, a dwarf who is said to have sailed across the sea to Japan in a gourd and taught the Japanese the art of brewing the sacred drink. In some traditions, Sukuna-bikona created all medicinal herbs as well as discovered the spiritual potential within rice. Certainly the Japanese considered rice wine medicinal. People all over the country recognized the connection between sake and the deities, and between sake and the Japanese emperors as well.

Japanese emperors reputedly had divine ancestry and thus the natural ability to maintain intimate relationships with the spiritual world. Just as ancient peoples around the world used stimulants and alcoholic beverages to commune with the spirits, Japanese emperors consumed sake to invite the spirits, or kami, into their lives and their bodies. Each new emperor traditionally announced his rule during the Daijosai festival, and asked the kami for their help in ruling. Because the spirits inhabited the sake, they easily entered the emperors' bodies when the latter consumed the drink. New emperors offered sake to the kami and then drank the sake with these spirits to seal the bond between them.

Similar thinking permeates Japanese marriage ceremonies, in which the bridal couple drink sake together to seal their bond. This custom relates both to the sanctity of sake and to the entrance of the spirits into the marital union through this divine drink. Christians drink wine as part of Holy Communion for similar reasons. Wine symbolizes the lifeblood of Christ, and consuming it seals the spiritual union with God. (Casal 1940; Mackenzie 1994; Nelson 1996; Piggott 1997; Rabbitt 1940)

See also Alcoholic Beverages; Ayahuasca; Balche; Beer; Chicha; Kava; Mead; Pulque; Rice; Soma; Wine

SALMON

Salmon were such an important food source for so many early peoples in northern lands that it's no surprise that salmon myths and rituals permeate their cultures. Salmon live most of their lives in cold climates but migrate yearly from saltwater to freshwater, and back, in accordance with seasonal changes and spawning patterns. Early peoples who fished the northern waters took care not only to track the migration habits of the salmon but also to propitiate the spirits of nature who sent the fish swimming upstream for the benefit of

Salmon fishermen in the Arctic waters. The Inuit relied on salmon for food, and considered them powerful nature spirits who gave life to the people. (Library of Congress)

people. The people of the Pacific Northwest believed that the salmon spirits willingly offered themselves as a sacrifice and that the people had a duty to honor and thank them. Many of these tribes honored the salmon as a symbol of life because the salmon assured their survival, so they carried out special rituals to show proper respect to the nature spirits and the spirits of the fish.

Native peoples of the northwest coast of America had a special reverence for the natural world and the spirits they believed inhabited it. These people depended on the salmon for food, but they knew that it was only by the goodness of the nature spirits that they received any food at all. For this reason, northern fishermen felt it necessary to propitiate the spirits so the spirits would treat them kindly. But the people also feared nature's wrath. When the people of one tribe tortured the salmon by slicing them open, putting burning pitch in their backs, and watching them emit sparks of light as they splashed through the waters, the spirits took revenge

and caused a volcanic eruption. The spirits of nature, the people believed, did not hesitate to exhibit their destructive power when the people neglected to respect the natural world or caught more salmon than they needed.

Of all the nature spirits that inhabited the Arctic, the most powerful was Sedna, the Spirit of the Sea. Sedna was said to have populated the sea with salmon and other game animals, and Inuit shamans frequently visited her in the spirit world, to plead with her to send the salmon into the rivers and provide for the people. The Karok of California thought that the bark of the alder tree provided salmon, possibly because the bark looks like a salmon when it gets wet.

The food myths of hunting and fishing cultures typically reveal a belief that the game animals exist for the benefit of the people. Powerful nature spirits control them, but the animals have powerful spirits themselves. To the people of the Pacific Northwest, the salmon had tremendous power, as its benevolence guaranteed life. Usually, by the grace of these spirits, the people were able to catch a large supply. Then they smoked it and dried it to guarantee that the food would last several months.

People of the northwest coast performed First Salmon rites to propitiate the salmon spirits and thank them for the new supply of food. They performed these rites as a gesture of respect, in hopes of guaranteeing that the salmon spirits would continue to provide food, returning to earth in the bodies of other salmon, who would once again offer themselves willingly in sacrifice. In one such ritual, a salmon chief would formally greet the salmon when it first arrived in the waters, honor it with speeches and flattery, and then assure the fish that it would be paid the proper respect after it was killed. Part of this respect involved returning the bones to the river where the fish lived. This ensured that the salmon spirit could be reborn in its home beneath the sea. The assurance of resurrection meant that killing the salmon freed its soul. The freed soul then informed the other salmon of its kindly treatment, and thus ensured a continued supply of food in the future.

Food myths of the northern lands clearly indicate that Arctic peoples endowed salmon with magic powers. The Salmon of Knowledge in Celtic myth had particularly strong powers. This salmon lived in the waters of a sacred well, a well that itself had magic power within it. Magic wells and sacred waters characterized Celtic myths, and oftentimes the fish that swam in the water absorbed their sanctity. This particular sacred well existed long before the river Boyne replaced it—and no one, not even the gods, was permitted to approach the well or to have access to its waters.

The concept of sacred waters was an ancient one, and the Celts in particular believed that well water held the key to wisdom and universal truth. Although the Celts believed that people who drank or bathed in these waters and the fish who swam there absorbed the water's magic, apparently the Salmon of Knowledge got his wisdom by eating hazel-nuts. A magic hazelnut tree grew over the well, and its Nuts of Knowledge continually fell into the water, where the salmon devoured them. The Salmon of Knowledge swam in the well a long time. A Druid named Finnegas the Bard had tried unsuccessfully to catch the salmon for seven years, knowing that whoever ate him would become eternally wise. It was not until the Celtic hero Finn went to study with Finnegas that the bard succeeded in catching the salmon. But Finn, not Finnegas, was the lucky recipient of the wisdom. Though Finnegas caught the salmon, it had been prophesied that Finn should receive the gift; so Finn himself cooked and ate the flesh, and was said to have gained eternal wisdom, as well as the gift of prophecy, from it. (Rolleston 1990; Toussaint-Samat 1992)

See also Fish; Hazelnuts; Water

SALT

People throughout history have invested salt with more symbolic significance than any other food. People of all cultures recognized it as divine, primordial, and powerful—as essential a substance as iron or blood. Salt is pure, white, incorruptible, and impossible to break down into constituent elements. It has been said that all matter contains salt, so early peoples perceived it as the essence of life and of the human soul. In addition, because salt has the property of durability—the ability to penetrate and to preserve other substances—people assigned it magical properties. They made it a sacred religious object and an emblem of immortality.

In Chinese myth, a peasant discovered salt while working in the fields one day. He saw a phoenix resting on a mound of earth by the sea; and knowing that where the legendary bird perched, treasure was buried, the peasant inspected the mound of earth after the bird flew away, and retrieved a cupful of earth that he thought might have exceptional value. He reported his find to the emperor, but the emperor considered the peasant's gift a waste of time, and had the man executed. Then he placed the clump of earth on a shelf and forgot about it. Later on, during the wet season, this forgotten clump of dirt fell off the shelf and landed in some food the emperor's cook was preparing for supper. It enhanced the flavor of the food, and the emperor loved the taste. He sent people to the place where the peasant had retrieved it, and the Chinese soon learned how to process the rock to produce the highly coveted crystals.

Salt, the only consumable rock, has been and remains indispensable to human beings. It enhances the flavor of food and has been used to preserve it; but more importantly, it's an essential mineral in the human body. In the Bible, Jesus called his followers the salt of the earth. Though there were few of these followers, they were irreplaceable to Jesus; and like salt, the message they carried was powerful enough to penetrate the entire earth. The followers of Jesus persevered and endured, as did "the salt of the earth." Salt embodied durability and permanence and thus gained acceptance as a true immortal.

The durability of salt greatly influenced the myths and legends that surrounded it. Salt became a symbol of durability because it prevented decay. Early people's observations of this phenomenon led them to believe that salt warded off evil. Because salt did symbolize durability and permanence, it served as an emblem of eternity and immortality. For this reason, people of the Middle Ages believed the Devil hated salt, and they consistently used it in magical rites and rituals to avert evil influence. Superstitious people threw salt over their left shoulder, where the Devil was believed to lurk, effectively chasing him away.

Salt may not have truly abolished evil, but it certainly prevented decay. People used it extensively as a medicine, and they believed that it both prevented and cured diseases. Salt also had the ability to penetrate water and dissolve into it, and thereby impart its healing and purifying properties to the water. From far back in antiquity, people believed that salt-

water, in particular, possessed curative powers. In legend, healing goddesses dwelled in the sea and in other bodies of water, and people either drank or bathed in those waters to heal ailments of all sorts. Perhaps the connection between water and salt explains the religious significance of holy water and the use of salt in Roman Catholic baptismal ceremonies. Salt also was used in religious rites of other sorts, such as those performed to prevent newborn babies from becoming changelings.

The connection between water and salt stems from the mythological origins of salt as the child of the sun and the sea. Salt inherited qualities from both parents. It is clean and pure like water, and dry, white, and sparkling like fire from the sun. In Finnish myth, Ukko, the sky god, sent a heavenly spark from the celestial sphere down to the waves, where the spark became salt. So as the child of the sun and the sea, salt had the purest of all parents. Because both water and fire symbolized purity, salt became the essence of cleanliness and purity. For this reason, salt was used in exorcism rites in most religions. The ancient Romans also purified their sacrificial victims with salt to make them acceptable to the gods.

Because salt came from the sea, people connected it not only with the purity of the waters but also with the fertility of the waters. They likened it to the ultimate fertilizing fluid—semen—symbolized in the sea foam that gave rise to the Greek Aphrodite and the Hindu Lakshmi. Because Aphrodite and Lakshmi arose from the sea foam, they served as goddesses of sex and fertility. Because salt also arose from the sea (in one of its forms), it too served as a fertility symbol.

Beliefs about salt paralleled ancient beliefs about semen, and the consumption of salt frequently was connected to sexual intercourse and impregnation. People believed that salt led to fecundity, so they used it in love potions. The ancient Romans considered salt cellars favorite wedding presents and treasured heirlooms. The people of Germany and Scotland used salt in marriage rites, particularly to enhance the fertility of the couple and to guard against any evil influence that might interfere with that fertility. The sea has consistently served as the ultimate fertility symbol—the primordial, creative power—and the abundance of sea creatures was commonly attributed to the salt in the sea. Salt became a symbol of procreation.

Perhaps because Aphrodite sprang from the salt sea, the ancient Greeks used salt in the worship of their love goddess. Because of salt's high symbolic significance and the general perception that it was sacred, people of many other lands also used salt in sacrificial offerings. Homer said that salt pleased the gods. The Greeks, Romans, Jews, and Egyptians all used it in offerings. Egyptian priests prohibited the use of sea salt, however, because they associated it (like all things arising from or connected with the sea) with the monster Typhon. Instead, the Egyptians mined their salt in the quarries of Amon; the priests of Amon then ceremonially offered the mineral to the Egyptian king. Egyptians considered this salt purer than that from the sea, and the purity imputed to the salt largely contributed to perceptions of its intrinsic power.

The lasting and incorruptible quality of salt led to the popular belief that spilled salt is a bad omen. When the ancient Romans led sacrificial victims to their deaths, they placed salt upon their heads, and these victims knew better than to shake it off. In Hebrew religious rituals, the Jews salted their meat offerings because they considered the offering a covenant with the Lord; and when Leonardo Da Vinci painted The Last Supper, he created an overturned salt cellar at the side of Judas to indicate the apostle's betrayal. The ancients used salt to seal covenants, especially religious covenants, as well as pacts and pledges. Salt never spoils, so it symbolizes loyalty and the assurance that the bond of friendship will never be destroyed. In addition to offering salt to the gods, the ancient Greeks and people in some European countries offered it to guests as a symbol of life, hospitality, friendship, and good-

will. (Abbott 1932; DeLys 1997; Elkhort 1991; Jones 1964; Toussaint-Samat 1992; Visser 1986)

See also Tamarind

SESAME

Sesame plays a large role in myth and ritual, particularly among the Hindus of India. Most likely, sesame originated in India, though some scholars believe it originated in Africa. Sesame seeds are eaten as food and pressed to make oil, which is used both in cooking and for anointing. Both the seeds and the oil have ritual significance. Hindus make cakes of the seeds and offer them to spirits of the dead. They anoint themselves with oil to bring good luck and to keep away evil. Since antiquity, Hindus have linked sesame with death. For this reason they have traditionally used sesame seeds both in ceremonies for the dead and in ceremonies conducted to counteract the influence of demonic forces.

India today is the world's largest producer of sesame, and people in India continue to link sesame with death. The ancient mythological connections are numerous and widespread. In Hindu myth, Yama, the god of the dead, created sesame, so the people offer both the seeds and the oil to him, as well as to other gods of the underworld. Hindus also offer the Pitris, the souls of their dead ancestors, sesame seeds along with rice, barley, fruits, and even animal foods, which are believed to keep the Pitris gratified for long periods of time. Yama rules over the Pitris, so these spirits have a capacity for evil. Hindus also use sesame seeds in funeral rites for the newly deceased—those about to enter the realm of the dead and encounter underworld forces—believing that sesame will offer them protection from evil. For the same reason, Hindus give sesame cakes to friends attending funerals.

Hindus who offer sesame to the living believe that this sacred grain helps remove the contagion of death. That's why they give it to those attending funerals, and similarly, to those who come into contact with dying persons.

Some people believe that the spirit of a dead person can cling to the living, and that by rubbing the living with sesame oil they can effectively drive the spirit away. They believe that offering sesame cakes to those already dead may help the deceased acquire a new body, as the deceased long for continued life. It has been suggested that sesame seeds work in this manner because seeds in general symbolize life. Sesame seeds, in particular, appear to be effective charms not only for staving off death but also for removing sins and for giving the dead the strength they need for their long journey to the otherworld. In Oriental belief, an offering of sesame mixed with rice ensures that the dead person will be admitted to heaven.

In keeping with the use of sesame to remove evil influences, an interesting ritual takes place in parts of India today on the day of the winter solstice. In this ritual, the sesame acts as both a purifier and as a good-luck charm. The people hold a festival on this day to celebrate the end of the period, between July and January, when the gods are believed to sleep and demons to be in control of the land. Sometimes on this day, the men use sesame to clean their mouths, and sometimes newly married women wear necklaces made of sesame seeds to bring good fortune. The use of sesame in this manner does not conflict with the grain's connection to death but rather supports it. Using sesame for purity and good fortune affirms the belief in its ability to appease the death gods and to reverse the effects of evil. Black sesame works particularly well for this purpose. In some places in India, people offer black sesame to Sani, an evil deity who personifies the planet Saturn. Unhulled sesame comes in a range of colors, from white to black, and black sesame has particular power because of the association of black with dark forces. People offer Sani black sesame to propitiate him and to remove his evil influence.

Offerings of sesame not only propitiate evil deities, however. In Hindu belief, the power of sesame makes it an appropriate offering also to Ganesha and to Lakshmi, both deities of good fortune. Lakshmi, in addition to being the goddess of good fortune, plays an important role in effecting love and fertility. Sesame seeds are reputed to excite the passions and are believed to have made effective love charms and aphrodisiacs. The Arabs used them as a cure for impotence. They also make appropriate offerings to deities with the power to bestow life and fertility. Hindus offer sesame seeds not only to Lakshmi but also to Gauri, a wife of Shiva associated with the fertility of the corn and the harvest. The Greeks offered sesame cakes to Demeter. The ancient Greeks considered these sesame cakes sexual symbols. The people made them to honor Demeter, the earth goddess, and offered them to her at the Thesmophoria, an ancient harvest festival with accompanying rites and rituals that served the purpose of honoring and rewarding the fertilizing power of the goddess of the land.

Sesame was one of the nine sacred grains in ancient India, and people often used sesame not only to promote fertility but also to treat various physical ailments. There is no doubt that people past and present assigned sesame magical properties. Perhaps the most telling measure of sesame's reputed magic the world over is the effect the phrase "Open, Sesame!" had for Ali Baba in *The Arabian Nights* and in various European folktales. The utterance of these words not only opened doors but also secret passages in trees and mountain caves. The power of these words stemmed from the ancient belief that certain plants contained magic and that sesame was one such plant. This reflected the avid desire of ancient people to find power in nature and to utilize that power to control events in the world around them. (Gupta 1991; Simoons 1998)

See also Cake

SOMA

Soma was a leafless plant of East India that has remained unidentified to this day. R. Gordon Wasson, in his book *Soma: Divine Mushroom of*

Immortality, presented a convincing argument for the identification of soma as the fly agaric mushroom; other scholars have suggested various other candidates. The plant, whatever it was, was utilized to produce an intoxicating drink that the ancients likely consumed in a mixture with buffalo milk, butter, barley, and water. The ancient Hindus consumed this drink in rituals to honor their gods; and in myth, the most powerful Hindu gods consumed the magic elixir themselves. The high god Indra drank great quantities of soma, which gave him power, unparalleled strength, and immortality.

The soma that Indra consumed existed in the celestial sphere, and the plant that yielded the juice from which fermented soma was made grew on earth as its terrestrial counterpart. The people on earth invested both the juice and the plant with divine powers. In ancient Indian epics, the original soma plant grew first in Indra's heaven, after which an eagle named Syena brought it down to earth, to a mountain in the Himalayas called Mjuvat, where it continued to grow. The earthly soma plant gained such sanctity that the Hindus revered it as a god in its own right.

Soma was both the lord of plants and the personification of the juice. As a god, he could heal diseases and bestow riches. As a liquid, soma arose during the creation of the world, as the gods churned the ocean of milk. This celestial soma, this magic elixir, had the divine powers people all over the world believed existed in some form or another, somewhere in paradise. Both gods and demons coveted soma because they knew it contained the power not only to strengthen them but to make them immortal. So in Hindu myth, when the magic elixir rose from the milky waters, wars broke out between the gods and the demons to gain possession of it. Though some of the demons did manage to drink soma, ultimately the gods won it back.

Soma not only fortified the gods but represented the Water of Life and the vital fluid in all beings. People in ancient India identified the Water of Life with the moon, which they considered the storehouse of life's waters. Soma, like the moon, was nature's source of fertility and growth. The moon contained the soma, and the moon, as everyone knew, was immortal. The gods consumed soma, and thus the immortal properties of the lunar water. The moon got smaller and smaller, but then revived again to its full size. The liquid, and the god, symbolized the fertilizing power of the waters as represented by the watery nature of the immortal moon.

The Indians of the ancient world made a ritual of pressing the soma juice. They also made rituals of drinking it, and of offering it to their gods. Over time, the use of soma as an intoxicant died out; but in Vedic, or ancient times, when Indra ruled supreme, group inebriation from soma was an important part of religious life. When the participants in these rituals consumed the soma, they believed they could summon the gods into their presence. The inebriation they experienced brought them to an altered state of consciousness and helped them gain insight into the spiritual world. The ancient Zoroastrian text, the *Avesta,* refers to a similar juice, called *haoma,* that also came from a plant that grew in the mountains and was also consumed in rituals with a mixture of milk. The juice was golden in color, like soma, and was considered the most important offering to the gods.

Today, Zoroastrians in Iran still consume a substance representative of the ancient haoma, using either pomegranate juice and ephedra or rue and milk. The ancient mead of the Germanic tribes also served functions similar to those of soma and haoma. The mead contained honey, water, and certain herbs, such as henbane and rosemary. It too was consumed as a part of elaborate cultic rituals in which the participants experienced group inebriation. (Gupta 1991; Ratsch 1992; Wasson 1972)

See also Alcoholic Beverages; Ayahuasca; Balche; Beer; Chicha; Kava; Mead; Mushrooms; Nectar and Ambrosia

SORGHUM

Sorghum is a grain of the semiarid tropics, and has been consumed by the people of southern Arabia and West Africa since prehistory. The people of these areas cultivated sorghum extensively, and they put every part of the plant to use. They used the leaves and stems for animal fodder and the roots for fuel, and they pounded the grain into flour to make cakes, breads, and porridges. The people in sub-Saharan Africa relied on sorghum as a staple grain, but the people of ancient Egypt considered it less than desirable. The Egyptians invented leavened bread about 1680 B.C., but only the destitute ate bread made from sorghum. The wealthy ate bread made of wheat, and the common people ate bread made of barley.

The Egyptians practiced agriculture from at least 2000 B.C., and it appears that people in Yemen began even earlier to cultivate crops. In fact, they may have been one of the first groups to practice agriculture. Sorghum was one of the first cultivated crops in this region. Sorghum produces a lot of grain, so it proved to be a good crop for people in Yemen, whose arid lands commonly supported little other vegetation.

Sorghum cultivation originated in the hot, arid lands, somewhere in sub-Saharan Africa around 4000 B.C. Africans living south of the Sahara at this time viewed the crop much differently than did Egyptians; they certainly didn't associate sorghum with the poor, but considered a man with lots of sorghum very wealthy. Some of the people who lived in the area between Chad and Ethiopia connected sorghum with nobility, and the Yoruba-Dahomey of Nigeria learned to use it medicinally. The Yoruba-Dahomey god Osanyin presided over medicinal crops and symbolized the curative nature of the vegetable kingdom. He had an astute knowledge of plant lore and he knew the healing power of sorghum and other crops the people cultivated.

In a legend of the Bassari (from Togo), sorghum came to the people as a gift from the creator god Unumbotte. After Unumbotte made humans, he gave them seeds and told them to plant them. The first tree that sprouted after the people planted Unumbotte's seeds bore red fruit, and the animals hesitated to eat it. They saw Unumbotte eat it, but the animals weren't sure that they should, believing that it may have been some sort of forbidden fruit intended only for the gods. But just as in other forbidden fruit stories, a snake came around and told the humans to eat the fruit from the tree, and they did. This made Unumbotte realize their hunger and give them sorghum, yams, and millet to sustain them. (Arnott 1975; Smartt and Simmonds 1995; Visser 1986)

See also Barley; Corn; Grain; Millet; Oats; Rice; Rye; Wheat

SOYBEANS

In recent decades the popularity of soybeans has risen dramatically. From its limited production as an Asian food crop, the soybean has graduated to become the most widely cultivated legume in the world. Soybeans have been a standard in the Chinese diet for centuries—mostly in the form of tofu, soy sauce, bean curd, oil, and raw bean sprouts. The legume was a major food crop in China by the fourth and third centuries B.C., and within several hundred years, soybean cultivation had spread throughout Asia. It would take thousands of years before the legume came into popular use in the West.

Myths about soybeans sprang up long ago among the Chinese and Japanese. In a legend from Peking, two bandits named Yu Xi-ong and Gong Gang-shi survived on soybeans when they were lost in the desert, long before the rest of the world learned of the legume's existence. In a variation of this legend, the bandits captured some merchants, and the merchants fled to a hilltop, where they discovered the soybean plant. The plant had been placed there by Hou Tsi, an ancient agricultural god.

In Japanese legend, the creator gods Izanagi and Izanami descended from heaven and created Japan and all the gods and goddesses of the Japanese pantheon. But the god of the sea didn't like being wet all the time, so he came up from the water and killed the food goddess. From her corpse grew the soybean plant, along with beans, rice, millet, and barley. These soon became Japan's primary crops, and the Japanese held them all sacred. The Chinese referred to soybeans, rice, millet, barley, and wheat as the five sacred grains. Aside from supplying vital nutrients, soybeans had the added ability to repel most insects who ate silkworms, and silkworms and sericulture were vital to the Chinese economy.

Ancient Chinese philosophy rested on a fundamental belief in the interdependence of opposites, a belief that nature was a delicate balance of yin and yang. The Chinese classified drinking as yang and eating as yin; and within the spectrum of foods, they classified certain ones, such as grains, as yin, and others, such as meat, as yang. This classification rested on connections the Chinese made between meat and the element of fire and between grain and the element of earth. Fire was yang and earth was yin, and meat required fire in the cooking process, whereas grains and certain fruits and vegetables arose from the cold earth. The ancient hunters and gatherers of China consumed yang foods such as deer, rabbits, elephants, and rhinoceri. Then agriculture came to China, and they consumed yin foods in the form of the five sacred grains.

The Chinese attributed the origin of agriculture to a mythical emperor named Shen Nung. The people called Shen Nung the Divine Husbandman or the Divine Cultivator, and they believed that he taught the Chinese people what parts of the land to cultivate and what kinds of food to plant. Shen Nung gave all food plants to the people as a gift. The soybean proved to be particularly valuable, producing more usable protein per acre than any other crop. (Rosengarten 1984; Toussaint-Samat 1992)

See also Grain

SPICES

Like nectar and ambrosia, spices belonged to the gods. The gods subsisted on them, and their essence helped define the gods' nature. Ancient Greek myths connected the Olympian gods with aromatic fragrances. Pythagorean legends spoke of strange beings with no mouths, who lived on the moon and fed on smells alone. Because the myths identified gods and other supernatural entities with fragrance and perfumes, people tended to believe that the smell of spices wafted to earth from paradise like godly breath.

The ancients used spices both for culinary and for religious purposes. The nonfood spices such as frankincense and myrrh they used to make perfumes and ointments, or presented to the gods as sacrificial offerings. The first recorded evidence of aromatic plants extends back to the Sumerian clay tablets of 2200 B.C. and to the Egyptian papyri of 2800 B.C. (Reportedly, a 5,000-year-old herbal, compiled by the legendary Chinese emperor Shen Nung, also existed at one time.) The Egyptians reserved their aromatics for the pharaohs, princes, and priests. They made aromatics under supervision of the priests, and they used them in rituals and as embalming substances for high-ranking officials. Given these ritual uses, they were processed under the supervision of the priests. As to the dietary use of spices, the ancients used them to purify foods that they offered to their gods. The Bible stresses the importance of aromatics in sacrificial food offerings; the aromatic smoke of roast meat pleased the gods, whether Jehovah or Zeus and the Olympians.

In Greek myth, Prometheus established the practice of scenting food offerings with spices when he performed the first blood sacrifice. Prometheus killed an ox and carved it, and in doing so set the standard for sacrificial offerings in the future. He divided the ox into two portions: the meat and entrails, which he gave to human beings, and the bones, which he sprinkled with aromatics and then burned in sacrifice to the gods.

Consumed in the flames, the pleasing scent of the spices wafted straight up to heaven. The scent was believed to purify decaying flesh. The gods deserved spices as sacrifices, it was said, while humans had to rely on flesh and blood. Unlike flesh and blood, spices were incorruptible; and once touched by fire, they belonged solely to the gods. At first, the ancients reserved aromatic spices only for use as purifiers and only to scent the food offerings of sacred rituals. Gradually, spices developed into an accessory to food, and over time, they became an essential part of the ordinary diet.

Early people were captivated by aromatic scents, and they learned to use spices not simply as flavors and perfumes but as preserving agents. The preservation methods of the distant past were less than adequate, even in the Middle Ages, so the scent of spices greatly improved the foods' palatability. This may have been one reason people of the Middle Ages enjoyed spicy foods; clearly they had powerful allure. People of this era imagined that spices came from the Land of Spices, a legendary, distant world. Some people even imagined that all of the aromatic spices grew in this land on the same tree. Some of the spices were transported down the Nile, and the recipients of these products imagined that the Nile had its origin in heaven and that the spices came straight from there. Ginger, nutmeg, cinnamon, and cloves came from the Orient, that mysterious land in the East that people of the Middle Ages connected with Arabia. Because most spices grew in hot, dry climates where the sun's fire expended the most heat, the link between Arabia and the Land of Spices was firmly established.

The legendary phoenix, which burned up in its own flames and arose anew from the ashes, like the sun, is one particularly notable mythological reference linking spices with fire. The phoenix built its nest and funeral pyre out of spices, evoking the image of aromatic offerings wafting up to heaven. Pythagoras, the ancient philosopher and religious leader, linked spices with Arabia and with celestial fire—both of the sun and of the fiery Sirius, the brightest star in the night sky.

In ancient Greece, the rising of Sirius marked the hottest time of the year, a time when the sun's fire came closest to the earth. In Greek myth, the sun descended to earth, touched down in the Land of Spices, and made love to Leucothoe, the daughter of Orchamus, the king of the Persians and the ruler of the Land of Spices. The sun's behavior enraged Orchamus, and he buried the girl deep within the earth where the sun's rays could not penetrate her. But the sun covered Leucothoe with nectar, and she emerged from the ground as frankincense. Her sweet aroma penetrated the earth and rose to the sky. Once again Leucothoe was united with the sun. From then on, the Greeks said, spices connected earth with the celestial sphere. The aromas wafted upward to the sun and the sky gods, reestablishing a communication link with heaven. (Detienne 1977; Dodge 1979; Norman 1972; Schivelbusch 1992; Toussaint-Samat 1992; Verrill 1940)

See also Cinnamon; Ginger; Herbs; Meat; Ox; Saffron; Turmeric

SQUASH

People in antiquity made little distinction between cucumbers, gourds, squashes, melons, and pumpkins: All were fruits of a vine, and all had hard rinds and an abundance of seeds, although they varied in size and color.★ Some Asiatic varieties of bygone times actually reached a weight of 240 pounds. The sheer growth potential of the individual fruits, as well as the enormous number of their seeds, led to popular reverence for them as well as to their frequent mention in myth. For example, the squash varieties people today distinguish from pumpkins and gourds appear widely in myths of the Americas. Squash con-

★ Squashes and pumpkins were domesticated in the New World, so they did not appear in Old World myths until post-Columbian times.

stituted a primary food plant for Native Americans long ago, and along with corn and beans and sometimes tobacco, gained widespread reverence as a sacred plant.

A large subfield in world mythology is devoted to the origins of food plants. In the Americas, many different creation myths explained the origin of squash. In myths of the Southwest, the Great Spirit brought squash when she came to earth in the form of a woman. She fell asleep, and when she awoke, she walked over the land, and squash, beans, corn, and tobacco sprouted up from her footsteps. In Hopi myth, Muyinwa, the earth and fertility god who controlled all plant growth, sent squash and melons from his home beneath the earth. In a Cahuilla myth from California, squash arose from the stomach of Mukat, the creator. When Mukat was killed, the primary food plants arose from his body, including squash, watermelons, tobacco, corn, wheat, and beans.

Squash not only served as a principal food crop for early Native Americans but also had medicinal uses among some tribes. In a Pawnee myth, Red Spider Woman, who lived in the center of the earth and embodied the squash root, taught the people how to use squash for healing. In one version of her myth, the buffalo trampled Red Spider Woman into the ground, and squash grew from her body. In another version, it grew from the bones of a dead giant. Long before the birth of human beings, Tirawahat, the Great Spirit, flooded the earth to destroy the fearsome and powerful giants who inhabited it. Later, after the birth of humans, Black Meteor Star visited the earth and told a man where to find a root that grew in the grave of one of the giants destroyed in the flood. The man located the root, ceremoniously removed it from the ground, and divided it up among the tribal healers. Red Spider Woman appeared to the man that night and told him of its medicinal powers. (Coe 1994; Gill and Sullivan 1992)

See also Beans; Corn; Cucumbers; Pumpkins and Gourds; Watermelons

STRAWBERRIES

Ripe, beautiful strawberries are a delectable treat, and particularly appealing because they're one of the first fruits of the season: They ripen quickly in the spring, thrive during the warm months, but then quickly perish when exposed to drought or frost. Obtaining strawberries out of season was quite desirable for legendary people bent on finding magic in the realm of mortals. Folklore and ancient legend frequently feature a search for berries in winter—often strawberries. Finding them posed quite a challenge, and those who initiated the search knew that whoever received this assignment faced a seemingly impossible task.

It was just such an impossible task that inspired legendary stepmothers to send their children into the woods. Cruel stepmothers, or other cruel relatives most commonly assigned such tasks, believed that the children would surely die in the woods because they couldn't possibly return with the berries. In Teutonic myth, a young girl sent on a quest for strawberries did succeed in acquiring some, with help from a few little men living in the forest. Hungry and cold from her journey, she stumbled upon their house, and they invited her in to get warm. When she shared her crust of bread with them, the men rewarded her for her kindness by producing the fruit. They asked her to sweep the back doorstep, and when she did, she discovered the precious strawberries glistening beneath the snow.

The search for berries in winter was a popular theme in both European and North American legends, particularly in the legends of the Pacific Northwest and the Central Plains. Sometimes the source of the berries magically yielded an inexhaustible supply. In myths and legends, strawberries were highly coveted objects, perhaps as precious as gold. A legend that emerged among the mountain people of Saxony, Bavaria, and Bohemia tells of how a peasant child traveling to the area went into the forest to gather strawberries and saw a woman covered with golden moss. When the woman asked the child for some of the strawberries, the child gave them to her, and she ate them and went on her way. When the child got home, she witnessed a miracle—the precious strawberries she had gathered from the forest had turned to gold.

A legend of the Cherokee of North America offers an explanation for the origin of strawberries that similarly emphasizes their appeal: First Man and First Woman married, but after a while First Woman became angry with her husband and left home. She headed toward the Sun Land in the East. First Man grieved for his wife—he missed her so deeply—and finally he begged the Great Spirit to help him win her back. Some versions of the legend identify the helping spirit as the sun. The sun, or the Great Spirit, devised a plan to slow the woman down so that her husband could catch up with her. The sun caused huckleberries to appear along the woman's path, but she didn't see them and kept right on going. Then he did the same with blackberries and several other types of fruits, but she didn't see them either. Finally he put strawberries in her path—fresh, red, sweet-smelling strawberries that the woman could not resist. She bent down and picked them, ate them, and then turned around to pick some more from behind her. As she did this, she looked to the west and saw her husband coming toward her. She gathered a handful of the berries and ran to her husband, and the two ate them together.

Strawberries achieved significance in North American legends because many early Americans survived on nuts and berries during times of scarcity. Not only did they eat the berries raw but they also learned to preserve them for use during the long winters. In the Cherokee legend, after First Man and First Woman reunited and returned home with the strawberries, First Woman preserved the fruits she had picked by placing them in a jar of wild honey she had on her shelf.

Early peoples certainly loved the taste of strawberries, fresh or preserved, but they also used them for medicinal purposes. Hunters in central Europe used to eat the berries to sharpen their powers of perception. Others used them to cure nervous disorders, control heart palpitations, and purify the blood. In the lore of the Seneca, strawberries have had special significance since ancient times. Not only are they the first fruits of the year but they are believed to grow along the path to the sky world. For this reason, the Seneca associate them with spring, rebirth, and life in the heavens.

Norse mythmakers also incorporated strawberries in their myths of rebirth and life in heaven. Frigga, the Norse fertility goddess, hid the souls of dead children inside strawberries to transport them to Valhalla, the paradise where souls of warriors go after they've died in battle. Strawberries were sacred to Frigga, and later on, to the Virgin Mary, who assumed Frigga's role and attributes after Europe was Christianized. In Christian legend, the Virgin Mary demanded all the strawberries in the fields, and anyone who dared to eat her berries was cast out of heaven. This belief stemmed from Frigga's smuggling children into heaven inside strawberries. With children being disguised as strawberries, the people on earth had no right to eat them—for they might well be eating children. (Arnott 1975; *Funk and Wagnall's* 1972; MacFarlan 1968; Olcott 1919; Toussaint-Samat 1992)

    See also Blackberries; Blueberries; Cranberries; Elderberries; Gooseberries; Mulberries; Raspberries

SUGAR AND SUGARCANE

Most people crave sweets. In antiquity, people found sweetness in fruits and vegetables and in honey; and they learned to tap into nature's sugar supplies by practicing apiculture and by cultivating plants to produce even sweeter varieties. But sugarcane is something different all together. Because it was sweeter than even the sweetest fruit, early people considered it a divine luxury. People tended to connect the sweetness of taste with the sweetness of life in general. Many people believed that sugar averted evil. Consuming it, they thought, guaranteed happiness and welcomed good fortune and prosperity into their lives.

Sugarcane is native to the South Pacific islands, and a number of myths emerged there, among various island peoples, attesting to sugar's importance. These stories commonly trace human descent from sugarcane, as in a legend from the Solomon Islands in which the first man and the first woman sprouted from two knots of sugarcane and then begot the human race. In a legend from New Britain, two fishermen named To-Kabwana and To-Karvuvu (*to* is the Polynesian word for sugarcane) fished up sugarcane in their net. At first, the men threw the cane back into the sea, but it kept showing up in their net, so finally, they buried it. As it grew out of the ground, the first woman burst out of the sugarcane. She cooked food for the men, and then retreated back into the cane at night. One day the men captured the woman and one of them made her his wife. From this pair, all human beings were born.

As sugarcane traveled through East Asia and India to China, the people of these lands devised myths to explain the origin of the plant. In Indian legend, a hermit named Vishvamitra created sugarcane as food in a temporary paradise located between heaven and earth. A young prince named Trishanku had asked Vishvamitra to send him to heaven while he was still alive, and Vishvamitra granted his wish. But Indra cast the prince out of heaven. So Vishvamitra created a paradise for the prince, midway between heaven and earth, and he created the sugarcane, along with many other magnificent plants, as a gift for the prince. Indra, in anger, ordered all the plants destroyed, but he reconciled with the prince before the sugarcane disappeared. It was then sent down to earth as a gift to mortals.

In India as well as in other lands, people considered sugarcane a divine crop. It seemed to grow miraculously, and it possessed a sweetness fit for gods and royalty. In another Indian legend, sugarcane grew miraculously in the bedchamber of a king named Subandu. The Brahmans told Subandu that a prince would rise from this sugarcane, and a prince called Ikshvaku did arise. Many generations later, the Buddha descended from him.

Sugar held high significance among Buddhists, who named it as the first food Buddha accepted after achieving enlightenment. Hindus also elevated it to high rank, naming the juice of the sugarcane as one of the fluids that filled the four oceans, along with saltwater, melted butter, and wine. The Chinese drank the juice of the sugarcane long before they learned to made the hardened product.

In Chinese legend, a Buddhist monk named Tsen, who lived on the Plan-shan Mountain, introduced the making of dry sugar. One day, Tsen's donkey descended the mountain and destroyed a cane plantation belonging to a man named Noang-chi. Tsen taught the art of sugar making to Noang-chi to make up for the damage, and the people of China quickly recognized dry sugar as a product of great value.

In Hindu myth, Kamadeva, the Indian cupid, had a bow made of sugarcane, with strings made of bees and honey, which he used to effect his love spell and all the sweetness that came with it. The sweetness of sugar made it symbolic of many good things, among them love, wealth, luck, and happiness. In one Chinese legend, sugarcane symbolized triumph over evil. A ruler of long ago loved sweets, so he cultivated sugarcane on a large parcel of land. One day a rival tribe invaded his land and the ruler had to flee, with the invading army in hot pursuit. The army invaded the fields of sugarcane, but because it was dark outside, they couldn't see very well. Thinking the sugarcane stalks were large enemy swords, they retreated. Thanks to the sugarcane, the Chinese ruler regained his land.

The belief that sugarcane averted evil was widespread, and in China today, some people still believe that sugarcane brings wealth and harmony into the home. In certain provinces of south China, people place stalks of sugarcane on the sides of their doors not only to guard the door against evil spirits but also to welcome the God of Wealth into the household. The Chinese use sugarcane as a decoration during marriage ceremonies and during New Year celebrations, to ensure happiness and prosperity in the days to come. On New Year's Eve, Chinese families often cut sugarcane into sections and eat it together after their evening meal. They also use it to light the New Year's fire. They place the pulp in the fire pot, and the next morning they brush away the ashes to find glowing red coals. From these coals the family starts a new fire, believing that the sweetness of the sugarcane will bring good fortune and pleasure throughout the New Year.

The custom of starting new fires with sugarcane is rooted in an old Chinese legend. A man named Wei Ssu was getting up in years and decided he needed to appoint another member of his family to run his household affairs. He challenged his three daughters-in-law to build a fire for the New Year, giving each of them two stalks of sugarcane with which to build it. The first daughter simply used the stalks as logs, but they quickly burned out, leaving nothing but ashes. The second daughter shredded the stalks and used them as kindling, but her fire also died. The third daughter proved the most resourceful. She and her husband retreated to their bedroom and spent the evening chewing the sugarcane and having a wonderful time, laughing and enjoying each other's company. Then they spat the pulp into a fire pan and started a fire. A sweet aroma permeated the room, and the couple recognized it as a sign of good luck for the coming year. The fire burned all night and into the morning, when the clever woman then used the fire to make breakfast. Gossip of the young woman's resourcefulness spread around the town, and people followed her lead. Ever since that day, the people of China have chewed sugarcane and then kindled fires from the pulp, considering themselves blessed with sweetness, good fortune, and a harmonious life.

(Deerr 1949; Hu 1991; Lehner and Lehner 1973; Toussaint-Samat 1992)

See also Candy; Honey; Maple Syrup

SUNFLOWER SEEDS

People have long recognized the food value of flowers, and sunflowers have edible seeds, roots, and buds. In Europe, people cooked sunflower buds and sometimes ate them raw in salads. They ate the seeds too, and used oil pressed from the seeds in cooking. The Thompson Indians of British Columbia eat the sunflower root today; but because they believe the sunflower plant, like all plants, has a spirit, they propitiate that spirit before they can safely eat from the sunflower's body. Long ago, people in the Americas found sunflower seeds particularly nourishing. They relied on them during times of famine, and often ate them during religious ceremonies connected with the sun and the rain.

The sunflower looks like the sun; it's bright in color and it has petals that resemble rays. The Greeks identified the flower with their sun god Helios. It turned toward the sun, and thus was labeled a heliotrope. According to Greek myth, the sunflower originated with the sea nymph Clytie, Helios's lover until he deserted her and she died of grief. After her death, Clytie changed into a sunflower, whose face always turned toward Helios, following him on his daily journeys through the sky.

The Greeks weren't the only people to identify the sunflower with a solar deity. The people of India used the flower to represent their sun god Surya, and the people of ancient Persia used it to represent their sun god Mithras. Some scholars believe that among the Inca of Peru the sunflower symbolized Inti, their sun god and the founder of the Incan race. During rituals performed to honor Inti, chosen virgins called Maidens of the Sun wore large golden disks on their breasts that symbolized the high deity and that some scholars believe might have been stylized sunflowers. Some also believe that the partakers in these

The Greeks identified sunflowers with their sun god Helios. In myth, the sea nymph Clytie fell in love with Helios and was changed into the sunflower, who always turned toward her lover and followed him on his daily sky journeys. (Erich Lessing/Art Resource, NY)

rituals also ate sunflower seeds during the ceremony and perhaps considered them sacred foods.

Whether or not the Inca held sunflower seeds sacred, other people of the Americas certainly did. The tribes of the Central Plains venerated them, as did the tribes of the Southwest, which relied on the sunflower as the only domesticated food plant, before corn, beans, and squash arrived from Mexico. Sunflowers grew rapidly in the Southwest with little care, and the seeds provided essential nourishment. The people ate them raw or roasted, or ground them into meal to make breads and cakes. They even placed them on graves to feed the dead. People in India placed sunflowers on the graves of their dead too, believing them adequate nourishment to sustain the dead on their journey to the otherworld. The Southwest Indians say the seeds sustain their dead during the long trip to the Happy Hunting Grounds. (Lehner and Lehner 1960; Majupuria 1988; Niethammer 1974; Rosengarten 1984)

See also Flowers

SWEET POTATOES
See Yams

TAMARIND

Tamarind trees are native to tropical Africa, and people throughout the East cultivate them for their edible fruits. The fruits, though sour, produce seeds that the people of India and other eastern lands use to season their foods. They also use the pulp for beverages, sauces, and curries. Hindus pay strict attention to the plants of their world, and they frequently use them in religious rituals. But though the Hindus attach mythological significance to the tamarind, they fear that using the sour fruit in auspicious rites might sour the rites themselves. Many people of India fear the tamarind as an unlucky tree. Not only does the fruit taste sour but the tree puts off an odd smell. Some believe that evil spirits live inside the tree and that is why nothing can grow beneath it. Some even call it Yamadutaka, the messenger of the death god, Yama.

Not all people in India avoid the tamarind, however. Many consider it a sacred tree because Krishna and his herd of cows were said to frequent a tamarind in the forest. Tamarind trees appear in the myths of Rama as well. In the *Ramayana,* Rama, his wife Sita, and his brother Lakshmana fell asleep under a tamarind tree, which according to myth had large leaves at that time in history and provided good shelter. Although the wandering trio had vowed that during their exile they would live without comfort and shelter from the ele-ments, they had sought shade during the afternoon under the tamarind. That night, although a terrible storm raged, the tamarind tree sheltered the trio so well that they felt not one drop of rain. Rama woke up, and ordered Lakshmana to shoot down the tree's leaves with his bow and arrow, in order to keep the trio from dishonoring their vow. Lakshmana shot at the leaves and split them all in two, leaving the group exposed to the storm's power. Because of Lakshmana's arrow, Hindus believe, tamarind leaves today are small and divided, but the leaves are still useful. People consume them in vegetable dishes and use them medicinally.

The myth of how the god Ganesha got an elephant head explains the use of tamarind as a seasoning: Lord Shiva saw his daughter Usha and his son Ganesha playing one day, and he got angry because they were ignoring him. Shiva got so angry about this that he cut off Ganesha's head. Parvati, Shiva's wife, insisted that Shiva restore her son to life, so Shiva replaced the boy's head with the head of an elephant.

Meanwhile Usha, Ganesha's sister, watched all this, frightened, and hid in a barrel of salt. Parvati found Usha in the salt barrel and she became angry and blamed her for not watching Ganesha carefully and allowing the entire incident to occur. So Parvati cursed Usha to be born on earth. Usha begged for forgiveness, as she did not want to be born on earth, fearing no one would remember her. So Parvati relented somewhat. She sent Usha to earth, but preserved her memory with the use of tamarind. Because Usha hid in the salt barrel, Parvati decreed that during the month of Chet, people would season food with tamarind juice rather than salt. Because of this myth, Hindus traditionally have associated tamarind with Usha, and they remember her fondly, as the cooling juice offers some relief during the warm month of Chet. (Barooah 1992; Gupta 1991)

See also Chicory and Endive

223

TARO

Taro is a staple crop of the western Pacific Islands—as basic to the people of this area as rice is to Asians or bread is to Europeans. The staple foods of any country have strong ties to the concept of fertility and reproduction, and in the Pacific Islands, males produce taro, just as women produce children. The symbolic association of these two processes means that those who cultivate taro certainly consider it a precious and irreplaceable crop. The plant's importance led to a large number of myths, many of which offer explanations for its existence.

In some myths, taro came from heaven. In Samoan myth, Losi brought taro from heaven to earth, and serves as its protective deity. Another myth traces the origin of taro to the birth of a deformed child: The child died and was buried, and the taro plant grew from his grave. In one popular origin myth of taro, the plant grew from an embryo of Papa and Wakea, the creators of the universe. Some said that taro came from Hawaiki, a mythical island that was home also to numerous other food crops, and they credited various supernaturals with having dispersed the plant from there. Origin myths vary among Pacific Islanders, but everyone who grew taro appears to have recognized it as a miracle food and to have assigned it a supernatural origin.

The people of China likewise seem to have regarded taro as miracle food. When invading Japanese pirates terrorized Chinese soldiers and sent them to the woods in retreat, taro roots saved their lives and led them to victory. Food supplies had dwindled desperately during the war, and the weakened Chinese soldiers found the strange tubers growing abundantly all over the woods. They quickly began to use the starchy roots to satisfy their hunger. Refortified by the tasty and nutritious food, the soldiers reentered the battle and defeated the Japanese invaders. It seemed that the gods had placed taro in the woods to help the Chinese in their time of need.

In the Pacific Islands, all taro gardeners believe that the plant grows by magic. They employ magic, in fact, in each stage of cultivation from the planting to the harvesting. Men have the magic to plant the taro, whereas women have the magic to weed the garden and to care for the growing tubers. Taro magic involves casting spells—protective spells guarding the plants against disease and destructive weather, and fertility spells ensuring a successful crop. Superstitious gardeners attribute failure of the crop either to incompetence on the part of the spell caster or to evil magic performed by an enemy.

Taro gardeners perform magic in gardening to influence the spirits that are believed to reside within taro plants and to have ultimate control over the crop's survival. These spirits also are thought to have the power to bestow good health on the cultivators, provided the latter take care to adhere to customs and regulations in caring for their gardens. Taro spirits control the growth of the corms or tubers, and gardeners perform spells to persuade these spirits to enhance the growth or to send more taro into the garden. In Tikopia, Melanesia, the god Taromata guards and protects the taro, and the people dedicate the first seedlings to him. People of different regions recognize different taro spirits, but all of these spirits respond to magic. People believe in the existence of these spirits because they can hear their sounds: Taro spirits reportedly have the ability to walk around, and people sleeping near the garden can hear them moving about during the night. But walking around at night makes the taro spirits vulnerable to abduction, so people perform spells to guard against this too. No other plant in the Pacific requires continual magic, but with taro, continual magic is essential. Without it, people are convinced, their precious crop will not grow at all.

Because taro gardening takes high priority among the peoples of the western Pacific, most of the gardeners know a multitude of spells to perform throughout the growing period, and these spells have been passed down for generations. Most gardeners have more than one taro garden, and some have as many as ten or twelve, but the gardens often contain subsidiary crops such as sugarcane, cucumbers, yams, and bananas, none of which demand such constant care. Knowledge of taro gardening is essential knowledge, and cultivation of the crop is a sacred act. In some societies, gardeners consider every instrument used in the cultivation sacred as well. (Beckwith 1970; Fieldhouse 1995; Firth 1939; Hu 1996)

See also Yams

TEA

For Asians today as for their ancestors in the ancient world, tea drinking is a daily ritual. The tea plant is native to southern China, and an infusion made from its leaves was originally drunk for medicinal value. But as time went on, tea gained usefulness far beyond medicine. Buddhist priests considered tea drinking a holy sacrament. Taoists believed that tea was one of the ingredients in the Elixir of Life. Tea drinking in the East was and remains an important activity, practiced by nearly everyone and accompanied by much ceremony and ritual.

Eastern tea ceremonies arose because people considered tea drinking an enhancement of meditation and a means to achieving spiritual enlightenment. Because Buddhists in Japan regarded tea drinking as a religious act, they developed elaborate tea ceremonies called *chanoyu,* designed to symbolize the spiritual path to enlightenment. They employed tea masters who presided over the ceremonies. Rikyu was the most famous among these ancient tea masters. Lu Yu (also called Luwuh) was the first Chinese tea master and an authority on tea drinking. He wrote the *Tea Classic* (Ch'a Ching), the first comprehensive work on tea, which asserts that the tea-drinking ceremony is essential for the maintenance of harmony in everyday life. In ancient China certain people became deified after their deaths. Lu Yu, for his astute knowledge of tea and his abilities to discern water quality, was one such per-

A tea party in Yoshiwara. (Art Resource, NY)

son. Lu Yu reputedly could detect subtle differences in water purity. Pure water was a primary concern in brewing tea. The water had to be just right to make good tea, and people often went to great lengths to acquire the purest water. In legend, Lu Yu was sent by a certain dignitary down the Yangtze River to taste the water—and he declared it unfit. After Lu Yu's death, Chinese tea merchants believed he watched over them and protected them.

In the *Tea Classic,* Lu Yu asserted that Shen Nung, a mythical Chinese emperor said to have ruled around 2737 B.C., discovered tea. The name Shen Nung means "Divine Husbandman." This emperor was believed to have taught the people husbandry and to have discovered the medicinal value of various plants. It made sense that Shen Nung may have discovered tea too. According to legend, Shen Nung had experimented with hundreds of herbs, and once when he was burning a

The Japanese Chanoyu, or tea ceremony. Buddhists in Japan regarded tea drinking as a religious act, and developed elaborate tea ceremonies designed to symbolize the spiritual path to enlightenment. (Library of Congress)

camellia bush (which is botanically similar to a tea plant), he noticed an enticing aroma. This was the beginning of tea.

However, another mythical explanation of the first tea plant has emerged throughout much of Asia, in many variants. In one version of the myth, a hermit was angry because he tended to fall asleep, and he had no control over when this happened. The hermit had enough of this; and one day, when his eyelids closed, he tore them out and threw them down on the ground in a rage. A god witnessed this and made a tea plant grow from his eyelids. Blessed with the gift of tea, the hermit no longer fell asleep unwillingly.

Tea leaves look something like eyelids with lashes, and the consumption of tea hinders sleep. This perhaps explains the prominence of the eyelid myth. In one Chinese version, it was Bodhidharma, a Buddhist monk, who tore out his eyelids, angry that he had fallen asleep while teaching the doctrines of Gautama. Buddha transformed the eyelids into a tea plant. A Buddhist myth from Japan told of Daruma, an Indian sage, who was thought to be the son of a Hindu king. Daruma tended to get distracted from his meditations and often fell asleep against his will. Daruma cut off his eyelids, remorseful that he had failed to be the devoted sage he desired to be. His eyelids were transformed into the tea plant, and Buddhist priests from then on used tea to keep them awake during long meditations. (Blofeld 1985; Davis 1992; Lu 1974; Toussaint-Samat 1992)

See also Coffee; Herbs

THORNAPPLES

The thornapple has a rich history in myth and magic. People have consumed thornapple seeds for centuries in inebriating drinks and reputedly magic potions. Like other highly toxic members of the nightshade family, thornapple gained legendary fame for its use in medicine and magico-religious rites. People around the world respected thornapple for its power and considered it a plant of the gods and spirits.

Thornapple has been credited with supernatural powers of all sorts, including the ability to incite passion, grant fertility, and heal diseases. The Shagana-Tsonga of the North Transvaal in South Africa give it to girls entering puberty during their initiation ceremonies, believing that it enables them to communicate with the ancestor deities who can grant them fertility. People in India smoked their species of datura mixed with hemp to activate its aphrodisiac properties.

In most societies, however, people familiar with thornapple and other types of datura assign these plants particularly evil powers. The Native Americans called thornapple the devil's apple, and people in Europe thought it a plant of witches and demons. Some people in Peru thought thornapple enabled them to commune with the dead and others said it simply reduced people to foolishness. In legend, some Peruvian soldiers ate thornapple before going to the battlefield, and for days they did nothing at all but act like idiots—grinning, blowing feathers into the air, and laughing hysterically.

Despite their dangerously toxic properties, plants of the datura species enjoyed widespread use as inebriants added to beverages of all sorts. The people of India added thornapple seeds to wine. The ancient tribes of the Andes crushed the seeds and mixed them with *chicha,* a beer brewed from maize. In ancient Greece, devotees of Dionysus likely mixed it in their wine to incite the frenzy that characterized their worship. People in Morocco mixed the seeds with coffee and still do today, and people in Mexico mix them with tea and add them to mescal, a liquor made from agave. People in parts of Africa use datura to make *pombe,* a beer they use in ritual contexts, having discovered long ago that the thornapple increases the pombe's intoxicating effects.

People familiar with the power of thornapple quickly recognized its value in ritual and ceremony. People of Mexico, California, and southwestern North America consider this valuable plant a sacred hallucinogen much like peyote, and they developed shamanistic cults around its ritual use. The Navajo believe that thornapple has a powerful life force or spirit. They use all parts of the plant, but leave enough in the ground to ensure its survival. The Zuñi consider thornapple the most sacred plant on earth. In Zuñi legend, a boy and girl who lived inside the earth came out one day to see what was happening. They learned too much, according to the divine twin sons of the sun father, so these twins sent the boy and girl back into the earth forever. Flowers sprang up where they entered the earth— datura flowers, or thornapple. The Zuñi employ the ritual use of thornapple perhaps more than any other North American group. They say that the plant belongs to the rain priests and that only they can collect its roots. The rain priests use thornapple magically to contact the rain spirits and convince them to release the rains. (Ratsch 1992; Schultes and Hofmann 1979)

See also Alcoholic Beverages; Cactus; Mandrakes; Nightshades

TOBACCO

People today don't think of tobacco as food, but tobacco has been consumed in one form or another since antiquity. Before it was smoked and sniffed, it was chewed. Long ago, people who chewed tobacco did so to slake their hunger and thirst, in much the same way as they used other plants they considered gifts from the gods. The oldest known version of chewing tobacco was produced by early people of the New World, who made a dough out of ground shell lime and crushed tobacco leaves, shaped the dough into pellets, and then dried them. Native Americans considered the tobacco plant a magical and sacred herb. Those who traveled long distances relied on their chewing tobacco to alleviate hunger.

Tobacco is one of the oldest and most important plants cultivated in the Americas, and numerous myths recount its divine origin. In Iroquois legend, it grew from the singed hair of a powerful spirit. In Crow legend, it grew from the semen of a boy who was masturbating and spilled his seed on the ground. The boy then taught his people how to cultivate the plant. In Fox legend, the Great Spirit sent a man to search for this sacred plant, cultivate it, and distribute it. The man found the plant and carried out the Great Spirit's instructions. From then on, the Fox people used the sacred tobacco as an offering to Wisaka, their creator god and culture hero, and to the spirits of thunder. Tobacco pleased the gods, many groups in the Americas believed, and they offered tobacco to their deities. These people considered tobacco highly valuable. The Aztecs

deified tobacco as Ciuacoatl, the warrior snake goddess whose body became the tobacco plant. In a myth that originated far across the ocean, in tribal India, the gods made the plant grow from the ashes of the homely daughter of a king, who killed herself because no one loved her. When she materialized as the tobacco plant, she was at last well loved by men.

People throughout the Americas venerated the tobacco plant, many of them considering it a cure for all ills. They used it to treat fevers, asthma, eye problems, skin problems, bites and stings, nervous disorders, fatigue, poisonous bites, bruises, ulcers, plague, rheumatism, and other ailments. Many used tobacco also to ward off demons and the evil eye. Tobacco received a place in so many mythologies not only because the mythmakers considered it medicinal but also because they credited it with magic powers. People of Central America thought it protected against thunder and lightning and against the grip of the death

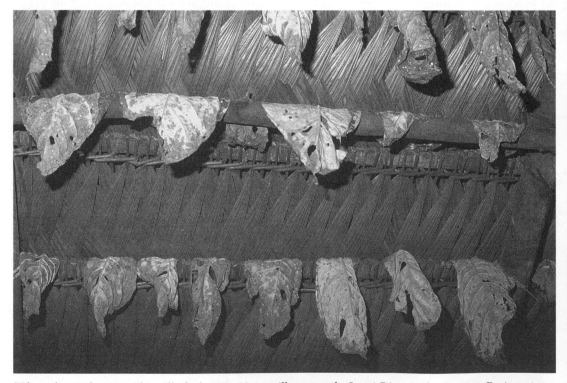

Tobacco leaves drying on the wall of a hut in a Yagua village near the Javari River in the Amazon Basin region of Peru. (Alison Wright/Corbis)

gods, who they believed had an aversion to tobacco.

The perception of tobacco as a sacred and magical plant led to its widespread use in religious rituals. Many people used tobacco both as a stimulant and an intoxicant. South American shamans frequently drank concoctions of tobacco mixed with other reputedly magic herbs in order to induce trances. The shamans boiled the tobacco leaves in water, or chewed them and spit them into a container and then steeped them in water. They consumed this potion orally, or in some cases, administered it nasally. The peoples of Middle America also used tobacco as an additive to more potent magical drinks, such as *chicha,* a maize beer consumed by Peruvian Indians and thought to be of considerable nutritive value. In this instance, tobacco served as a food substitute. According to anthropologist Claude Levi-Strauss, South American Indians counted tobacco as a food. In a myth of the Mundurucu, a man tells a boy that tobacco was intended as food for human beings. The chewing of tobacco, a common practice in pre-Columbian times in the Andes, alleviated hunger. Later, the coca leaf replaced the tobacco leaf as a food substitute.

Substituting tobacco for food occurred not only among people in the Americas but among people in other parts of the world as well. In a legend from tribal India, a poor family had nothing to offer their guests to eat so they killed themselves because hospitality was so important in their culture. The gods were so moved by this act that they decided to create the tobacco plant, the betel nut, and the areca nut. All three of these "foods" were plentiful in ancient India, and poor people needed no longer fear having nothing to offer. These particular foods therefore played a significant cultural role.

In another legend from India, Mahadeva, an aspect of Shiva, kept asking his wife Parvati for food. He asked over and over again through the years, until Parvati could stand it no longer. She went into the forest, picked up a leaf, and prayed to the god of vegetation to help her. Indeed he did help her, as the leaf she found was none other than the tobacco leaf. She filled a pipe with it and put it near the food. The next time her husband asked for food, she gave him the tobacco to smoke, and he promptly forgot about food. Parvati then started growing the tobacco on her own, and tobacco became known to the world. (Lehner and Lehner 1960; Levi-Strauss 1970; Schleiffer 1973; Thompson 1970)

See also Ayahuasca; Betel Nuts; Chicha; Coca; Coffee; Cola Nuts

TOMATOES

Tomatoes originated in Mexico and South America, where the plants most likely grew as weeds in maize fields. By the time of the Spanish Conquest, the peoples of the area had learned to cultivate tomatoes and had developed many different varieties. The Inca, the Maya, and the Aztecs all cultivated tomatoes. The Aztecs called them *tomatl*—a word that meant "round" and "plump," but it appears that the Aztecs also used this word for many other kinds of fruit. The tomatoes known today originated south of Mexico, in an area stretching from Ecuador to Chile.

When the Spaniards first brought tomatoes to Europe, in the sixteenth century, the people there were suspicious and afraid of them. They grew them out of curiosity and used them as ornamentals and medicinals, but it took another few hundred years for Europeans to accept these strange fruits as food. Perhaps this attitude had something to do with the taste of the tomatoes first cultivated in the Old World; they were warm-weather plants after all, and they may not have adapted well to the new climate and growing conditions. More likely, however, the skepticism with which people viewed tomatoes stemmed from their apparent link to poison. The tomato was a nightshade, and many nightshades (e.g., mandrakes and thornapples) were poisonous. So people may have thought tomatoes were poisonous too. Tomatoes looked like fruit but they didn't taste like fruit, nor did they resemble any vegetable the people knew.

The people of the New World grew many different kinds of tomatoes. When their yellow tomatoes were introduced to Europe, people called them golden apples, linking them to the golden apples of the Hesperides in Greek myth—the fruits that bestowed eternal life and granted fertility. Perhaps for this reason, tomatoes gained a reputation in the Old World as an aphrodisiac.

The French called them love apples, or *pommes d'amour*. But the aphrodisiac powers imputed to tomatoes also fueled Europeans' suspicions. Love potions, they knew, often included poisonous plants. Magicians in Thessaly reputedly used poisons in their love potions, and in myth, so did the wicked enchantress Circe—she used mandrakes, close relatives of tomatoes. One legend, however, traces the name *pomme d'amour* to its place of cultivation. The legend recounts how a Moor who first encountered the tomato in Spain took some seeds back to Morocco to plant. From then on, the tomato was appropriately dubbed Moors' apple, or *pomo dei mori,* which was mistranslated into French as pomme d'amour, a phrase that sounds similar but is vastly different in meaning.

This legend of the tomato's Moorish connections makes sense, because long ago, people in the Old World called all fruits apples, often differentiating them only by their place of origin. Citrus fruits were called Persian apples, for instance, and apricots were called Armenian apples. But if tomatoes were Moors' apples, so too were eggplants. The Arabs loved them as well. However, the matter is further complicated by the fact that the early Europeans also tended to name fruits for their outstanding characteristics. In this respect, the term "love apple" quite possibly did refer to the tomato's reputed aphrodisiac properties, just as "mad apple" referred to the eggplant, and specifically to the belief that eating eggplants made people insane.

Tomatoes and eggplants both suffered because of their identification as nightshades. Though the nightshade family has both edible and nonedible members, in ancient times people associated this entire family of plants with poisons and witchcraft. People typically used mandrakes, henbane, and other nightshades to kill their enemies. The tomato was a close relative of the eggplant—in fact, at first it was thought to be a kind of eggplant—and Europeans feared its effects long before they learned to appreciate its virtues.

The Hindus banned both tomatoes and eggplants from their diet, not because they were nightshades but because they were red in color. Hindus rejected meat, and by extension, some sects banned red foods that appeared to have a connection to blood. In contrast, tomatoes became wildly popular among Americans during the 1800s. Several doctors made outlandish claims about the tomato's virtues, and people began to say that the fruits could effect miraculous cures. (Coe 1994; Foster and Cordell 1992; Heiser 1969; Lehner and Lehner 1973; Smith 1994; Verrill 1937)

See also Eggplant; Mandrakes; Nightshades; Potatoes

TURKEY
See Goose and Turkey

TURMERIC

Turmeric has been used throughout the ages both as a condiment and as a dye. The people of India have long used turmeric to flavor their curries, and because the turmeric plant has yellow flowers and orange stalks, the addition of this condiment gives the curries their characteristic golden color. Because the plant grows quickly and because it does produce golden yellow flowers, turmeric has been assigned magical properties. Many people of Asia and the Pacific Islands consider yellow a sacred color, the color of gods and royals. Furthermore, the turmeric plant is aromatic, and aromatic spices of all sorts have long been considered effective in repelling demons.

The significance of turmeric in myth and magic rests largely on the symbolism of its color. In fact, the presence of the yellow rhizome is likely the reason people first domesticated the plant, as yellow had ceremonial significance far back in antiquity. Though people in Europe and America most often use turmeric as a condiment, people in Asia and Oceania use it just as often as a dye. In Mangareva, three gods are believed to protect the dye, and strict taboos and rituals accompany its preparation. The Polynesians consider red a sacred color, and they have a way of producing red by mixing the turmeric with coconut cream. Both yellow and red are thought to please the gods.

Turmeric as a dye plays an important role also in religious rituals, particularly in marriage rituals in India and other Asian lands. People use turmeric to anoint brides and bridegrooms; they rub turmeric oil on their bodies to turn their skin the auspicious gold color. They also color their wedding clothes with the oil or with turmeric water, and the bride and bridegroom smear it ceremonially on the walls of their home. In Hindu thought, turmeric has purifying properties, and its use in marriage rituals protects the couple from evil. It also fosters happiness, strengthens the bond between husband and wife, and facilitates the birth of children. Certain groups in India conduct turmeric water marriage ceremonies, which are considered as binding as any legal marriage. These people believe that the turmeric paste or water, when rubbed on the bride and groom, cements them together in an eternal and sacred bond.

Because turmeric enjoys wide regard as both a purifying and a protective agent, its ritual use extends beyond marriage to rites of birth and death. All of these rituals typically involve the dyeing of ceremonial robes and anointing of participants with turmeric water or oil. In India and Southeast Asia, birth rites may involve rubbing the mother with turmeric paste during childbirth, or rubbing both mother and child with the paste shortly after the birth. In Sumatra, midwives often chew turmeric and then spit it out onto the newborn infant. In southern India, Polynesia, and Micronesia, death rites may involve rubbing turmeric on corpses or pouring it over graves. Turmeric is supposed to please the ancestral spirits as well as repel the underworld forces. The use of turmeric in birth and death rites stemmed from the belief that the plant itself as well as its yellow color averted the influence of demons.

Popular attributions of magical properties to turmeric led people in Southeast Asia and the Pacific to use the plant in agricultural rituals. These people believed that by pouring the turmeric water over the soil, they could assure the fertility of the fields. In agricultural rituals as well as in birth, death, and marriage rituals, the color yellow largely accounts for the plant's value. Yellow pleases the spirits.

For this reason too, shamans in some of the Pacific Islands use turmeric as an amulet to protect people from sorcerers and ghosts, and they chew the roots of the plant and spit them out over a person possessed by demons. The protective powers of turmeric also made it a desirable medicinal plant. People in India and Indonesia believe that it heals wounds; in Bengal they use it to cure stomachaches and eye diseases; and in Sumatra they use it in treating all kinds of ailments, including jaundice, broken bones, and gonorrhea.

As scholars struggled to explain widespread and prevalent popular beliefs in the protective powers of turmeric, they discovered an interesting mythological connection between the plant and the soil: In parts of India, Hindu mythmakers appear to have assigned turmeric to the auspices of the earth goddess Gauri. This might be due in part to a coincidence in the color of the soil and that of the plant; in much of tropical Asia, the soil is yellow or red. In belief systems worldwide, the soil has long been assigned protective properties.

The connection between the earth and turmeric appears also to explain the use of the plant in marriage rituals. Hindus use turmeric powder in their worship of the earth goddess Gauri, who also presides over marriages, especially in rites associated with her spring marriage to the sun god. They regard the mythological marriage of Gauri to the sun god as a prototype of earthly marriage. Appropriately, *Gauri* means "golden yellow"; and as a personification of the earth and of ripened grain, this yellow goddess bestows fertility. Therefore, she is typically venerated at weddings, in which turmeric powder, yellow like the soil, sun, and grain, is rubbed on the bride and groom to impart the earth's protective and fertilizing properties. (Simoons 1998; Sopher 1964)

See also Cinnamon; Ginger; Saffron; Spices

TURNIPS

Turnips have provided people with reliable food since prehistoric times, particularly those living in northern Europe, between the Caucasus Mountains and the Baltic Sea. Root plants in general appeared frequently in the legends and lore of northern countries, not only because they served as staple foods but also because they grew underground and appeared to have some mystical connection to the earth powers. Peasant peoples living in cold climates saw the earth freeze every year, and they often had little but turnips and other root plants to eat during the winter. But people farther south valued turnips as well. The ancient Romans considered them the most valuable of all vegetables, and the British in the Middle Ages placed them on coats of arms to represent people who generously gave to the poor.

The Baltic Finns put their precious turnips under the tutelage of Agras or Agroi, the turnip god, who was also the patron of twins. The birth of twins has traditionally indicated supernatural influence, and twin turnips—two turnips growing together—was clearly a super-natural gift, and possibly a manifestation of Agras himself. When people of these lands found such a configuration growing in their gardens, they performed rituals and recited ardent prayers at their root cellars. They made it a point to marvel at the heaviness of the twin turnips, and they thanked Agras for his generous gift and prayed to the god for a good turnip year.

The Baltic Finns prayed to Agras because they knew the importance of their turnip crop. They stored the roots in turnip cellars, and in good years, they often had enough food to last through the winter. Turnips crop up frequently in Russian and Baltic folklore. In one Russian legend, magic children living deep in the woods so longed for turnips that they stole them from an elderly couple who had planted them on their roof. In return for the turnips, they left the couple a magic tablecloth that gave them all the food they wanted and a magic goat that gave them all the gold they wanted.

To humble Russian peasants, turnips may have seemed as good as gold, but to greedy fortune hunters they were a poor substitute. To fortune hunters in China, ginseng was the only root as good as gold, but unfortunately, turnips looked curiously like ginseng. According to legend, powerful spirits resided in ginseng roots—spirits that hated to be caught by ginseng hunters seeking to turn a profit from their extraction. So the ginseng spirits used their resemblance to turnips to throw the greedy hunters off. The fortune hunters knew that if they could uproot the precious plants, they would fetch outlandish prices on the market. But just when the hunters had discovered the location of the roots, the spirits of ginseng fled, leaving turnips in their place.

A Manchurian legend involving turnips and ginseng reveals the resemblance between these two roots while at the same time explaining why turnips grew on the Great Plain of Hopei. An evil and greedy man took what he thought were ginseng roots to the emperor, but the spirits of the roots played him a trick, and the emperor received nothing but turnips. When the greedy hunter first encountered the ginseng spirits, they had agreed to go with him as a gift to the emperor. But they asked to clean themselves off first. The man provided the spirits with a glass of water, and the spirits jumped into that water, turned it yellow, and flew away. They told the man to pour the water on the Plain of Hopei if he wished to grow even more potent ginseng. The man did as he was told, and the roots that grew there were the very ones he presented to the emperor. The emperor gorged himself on the roots, and afterward suffered a serious bout of diarrhea and vomiting. Believing that the ginseng hunter had tricked him deliberately, the emperor ordered the man beheaded. Once again, the ginseng spirits had succeeded in fleeing their captor. Not only did they rid themselves of that particular hunter permanently but they left turnips on the Plain of Hopei so that future hunters no longer had any clue as to where to find the ginseng.

Root legends often emphasize the dire consequences of pulling the plants out of the ground. An interesting twist to these tales appears in an Algonquin legend of a gigantic turnip that filled the hole to the sky country. Feather Woman fell in love with Morning Star one night when she and her sister were sleeping outside and she noticed the lovely bright light illuminating the sky. Morning Star also noticed Feather Woman, it appeared, because he came down to earth for the young woman, and he took her up to the sky world to be his wife before she could even say good-bye to her parents. She lived with Morning Star, the son of the sun and moon, in a shining lodge in the sky.

In this myth, a sacred turnip sealed the entrance to the sky world. One day, Moon gave Feather Woman a root digger and sent her off to dig up roots. He warned her not to dig up the large turnip, however, for if she did, it would bring her unhappiness. Predictably, this made Feather Woman quite curious about the turnip; yet for a long time she resisted touch-

ing it. One day, however, she couldn't resist any longer. She enlisted the help of two cranes, and together they uprooted the turnip—and left a gaping hole in the sky. It appears that the turnip in this legend was the key to happiness; for after Feather Woman could see down to earth, she longed for her family, and Morning Star had to return her to her earthly lodge. But Feather Woman was never happy again. Back on earth, she longed desperately for her husband, but he refused to take her back. Having committed a sin by uprooting the sacred turnip, she was forbidden to return to the sky country. (Holmberg 1964; Kimmins 1977; Spence 1989)

See also Carrots; Ginseng; Radishes

TURTLE

Ancient peoples of the New World and the Old consumed both the flesh and the eggs of turtles. The Chinese have eaten these foods since antiquity and consider them great delicacies. The ancient Maya ate both land turtles and sea turtles; and among the people of the Caribbean islands, salted tortoise was a popular dish. The people of the Cayman Islands particularly enjoyed turtle meat, and made omelets and fricassees from the eggs.

Early people attached great significance to turtles, as is clear from the role they played in myth and symbol. The turtle earned a reputation as a strong animal—in myth, strong enough to support the world. Hindus in India, for instance, envisioned Lord Vishnu as a tortoise, supporting the world while the gods and demons churned the ocean of milk to obtain the Elixir of Life. The ancient Maya envisioned a giant sea turtle floating in the ocean and supporting the world on his back. Turtles played a prominent role in the religious rituals of the Maya. The Maya ate them and they sacrificed them to the gods. Like many ancient people, they subscribed to the notion that people absorb the animals' essence when they consume its flesh. They believed that eating turtles gave them strength and endurance.

Among the Chamacoco of Gran Chaco, only the women eat turtles; the men believe that if they consume turtles they'll acquire the animal's sluggishness.

Turtles seemed to have supernatural powers to ancient peoples. These animals seemed impervious to disease, lived long lives, and could go without food for long periods of time. The Chinese considered the flesh of turtles strengthening, and they consumed it to guarantee good health and longevity. They considered green sea turtle a particular delicacy, and they roasted it, boiled it, and used it in soups and stews. They often presented these dishes as gifts to the royal court. Some Chinese connected turtles not only with health and longevity but with immortality. Some believed the medicinal value of turtle flesh was powerful enough to counteract evil.

In Chinese myth, the turtle guards the north quadrant of the world and serves as an emblem of earth, one of the four primal elements of nature. The phoenix represents fire, the dragon represents water, and the unicorn represents air. Of these four animals, only the turtle exists outside the mythological realm, so only the turtle can serve as food—food that offers the promise of both strength and prosperity. (Chang 1978; Simoons 1991)

See also Blood and Flesh; Meat

VANILLA

Vanilla comes from a tropical orchid indigenous to the jungles of Central and South America. It was unknown to the Old World until the beginning of the sixteenth century, when the Spaniards brought it back from Mexico. There are more than 35,000 species of orchid, and the vanilla orchid is the only one that produces edible fruit. It was the Aztecs who learned to convert the seedpods of this orchid into one of the world's most delightful flavorings.

The indigenous tribes of Mexico were harvesting vanilla pods as early as 6000 B.C. and using them primarily to flavor their chocolate drinks, called *xocoatl*. They also ground up vanilla flowers and wore them around their necks in amulets as medicinal charms. They used vanilla as a perfume, a medicine, a mental stimulant, an insect repellant, and an aphrodisiac.

It is remarkable that these early peoples knew how to extract flavor from orchids, because in their wild state the vanilla beans, or pods, look like string beans filled with millions of tiny seeds, and they don't smell or taste like vanilla at all. The production of the flavoring is a complicated process. A tribe of Aztecs called the Totonacs used a method known as "sweating" to cure the beans—spreading the pods on blankets in the sun, covering them at night so that the pods stayed warm and moist, and reexposing them to the sun the next day. After about twenty days of such curing, the pods became dark and wrinkled, and due to an enzymatic reaction, exuded a sweet aroma. The curers then dried the pods for several months.

The ancient people of Mexico cultivated orchids and processed vanilla for Montezuma. Hernán Cortés first tasted vanilla in Montezuma's court; but the Aztecs kept their curing knowledge a secret, and the intricacies of the process mystified the Europeans into the eighteenth century. When vanilla first arrived in the Old World, people used it as the Mesoamericans did, primarily to flavor their chocolate drinks. It was only about a hundred years ago that people began to manufacture vanilla extract.

The Aztecs called the vanilla bean *tlilxochitl,* a word that meant "black flower," although it was the cured seedpods that were black and not the flower. The Aztecs made the vanilla bean an important part of their religion, as they did the orchid from which they harvested the pods, the *xanath*. This orchid got its name from a mythological goddess who came to earth at the beginning of the world and fell in love with a Totonac warrior. Because Xanath was the daughter of a great fertility goddess, she was forbidden to marry a mortal, even though she loved him dearly. But Xanath changed herself into the vanilla vine and remained on earth forever. By creating the goddess Xanath, the Totonacs revealed their belief that the gods themselves gave the people vanilla. According to myth, the heavenly vanilla vine continued to bloom and produce fruit on earth to supply not only Xanath's warrior but all of the Totonacs with eternal happiness. Having received this heavenly gift, the people made it their duty to care for the vines, to guard them against theft, and to learn how to increase their pod productivity, which they did by performing what was called a "marriage of vanilla." When the Europeans transported the vanilla orchids across the ocean, however, they had a difficult time getting the flowers to bear fruit. The orchids that produce the vanilla are not self-pollinating, and in the wild they depend on insects to pollinate them. In the tropics, two particular species of bees and hummingbirds pollinate the pods, and scientists had to discover this before Europeans could profit from the vanilla orchid and the delightful flavor it produced. (Bruman 1948; Coe 1994; Foster and Cordell 1992; Robertiello 1987; Toussaint-Samat 1992; Verrill 1937)

See also Chocolate

WALNUTS

Walnuts have traditionally been regarded as symbols of fecundity and abundance. The Greeks and Romans, in particular, served them at weddings to bless the bride and groom with a fruitful marriage, and they injected them into their myths as symbols of love. In myths and legends, nuts of all sorts symbolized fertility, as well as regeneration and immortality. But although many people considered walnuts themselves auspicious objects, they considered the walnut tree an ill omen.

Ancient legends tell of walnut trees haunted by devils, demons, and evil spirits of all sorts. This belief continued from ancient times into the Middle Ages, when mythmakers connected this tree to witches and to the Devil himself. Some peoples considered the walnut a funereal tree and believed that the shadow of the walnut tree brought death. The ancient Greeks connected walnuts with Persephone, who was captured by Hades, and with other deities connected with death and the underworld. The Romans believed demons danced around the trees and that evil spirits lived in the branches. One particular walnut tree was believed to harbor the evil soul of Nero. The Romans also believed that witches held meetings under walnut trees; certainly pagan rituals were performed there. After the advent of Christianity, St. Barbatus cut down a walnut tree supposed to be inhabited by the Devil.

His home destroyed, legend has it that the Devil slithered away in serpent form, no doubt to take up residence somewhere else.

Sometimes the evil spirits who inhabited walnut trees did affect the nuts and the people who ate them. The spirits made the nuts useful charms for warding off lightning, fevers, and epileptic seizures. They symbolized fertility, and in Lithuanian myth, even regeneration. In the Lithuanian legend of the Deluge, walnuts saved the good people from drowning. As Perkuns, the storm god, ate walnuts, the flood waters rose, and the shells fell into the water. The good people climbed into the shells and used them as boats. Like the survivors of mythological floods in other lands, these people repopulated the world. Nuts had hard shells, and in myths and legends, they could achieve enormous size. Not only were they able to hold the flood survivors in the Lithuanian myth but St. Agatha of Christian myth, who escaped her persecutors by sailing the Mediterranean in a walnut shell. Some say she repeats this voyage every year.

The association of walnuts with gods and saints endeared this food to the people. In India, Lakshmi, the fertility goddess, loved walnuts, and her worshipers offered them to her. In Greek myth, the great god Zeus loved them, so the Greeks offered them to him, and they took care to cultivate them throughout the land. The association between walnuts and the great sky god survived in Roman times. People called walnuts "the nuts of Jupiter," because they believed that in the Golden Age, humans lived on acorns, but the gods lived on walnuts. Both Jupiter and his wife Juno played an important role in promoting love and fertility, so walnuts were employed for these purposes. For the same reasons, the Greeks served walnuts at weddings, and Roman bridegrooms scattered them around their bedchambers after their wedding feasts. Children hurriedly picked them up, and then offered these "nuts of Jupiter" to the sky god himself.

These Greek and Roman wedding rituals reveal the connection that people of the classical world recognized between walnuts and love, and the myth of Carya and Bacchus further reveals the connection. It also explains the origin of the walnut tree. King Dion of Laconia had three daughters, the youngest of whom was Carya. As a favor to Dion, Apollo, the sun god, had bestowed on all three of the king's children the gift of prophecy. But Apollo warned these young women that if they ever misused the gift, he'd take it away. In due time, Dionysus, the god of wine and revelry, fell in love with Carya. Her jealous sisters tried desperately to keep the lovers apart. Dionysus, in anger, turned the two sisters into rocks. When Carya died, he immortalized her and her love for him by turning her into a walnut tree. From then on it was said, the Greeks used the nuts to arouse love's powers. (Skinner n.d.)

See also Almonds; Chestnuts; Hazelnuts

WATER

Water has traditionally symbolized restoration, purification, invigoration, and wisdom. Mythmakers believed that water was a natural curative that healed disease. They thought it was a natural restorative, so they said it brought back lost youth. Nutritionists today recommend drinking eight glasses of water per day to cleanse the body and maintain good health. True, water cleanses, but in myths and legends, it did much more than that. Because it flowed from sacred springs in paradise, it conferred immortality on whoever drank it, and it had the power to banish demons.

Taoists said that the water in paradise flowed from a legendary stream in the Khun-lun Mountains and that the stream sprang from a jade rock. The Taoists called water the essence of jade. Because they linked it with paradise, they also linked it with heavenly dew, the Elixir of Life in the moon, prepared by a legendary hare who resided there. In Taoist belief, rainwater and dew both have medicinal and magical powers, provided that whoever drinks the dew receives a pure sample straight from heaven. If it comes into contact with anything from earth, however, it loses its power and its magic. The idea of the purifying power of water stemmed from the observation that water had cooling properties—properties, the ancients believed, that could counteract the "heat" of particularly evil powers and render them innocuous. For this reason many myths tell of water's ability to fend off evil spirits.

Legends typically feature a search by some mythological hero for the dew from heaven—the legendary Water of Life or Fountain of Youth that not only purifies but grants eternal youthfulness. Such a notion arose from the belief in water's restorative powers. In legends, drinking this water cured the sick, restored eyesight to the blind, and bestowed the gift of fertility on barren women. Often, it also resurrected the dead. Philosopher Huai-nan Tzu reputedly discovered the Elixir of Life in 122 B.C., when he drank this water and ascended to heaven. As he drifted upward, he dropped the vessel that contained this water, and his dogs and chickens lapped it up and ascended to heaven with him. Frequently in folktales and legends, heroes searched for this miracle water. They believed it flowed from a magic well or fountain that existed somewhere in Africa, Asia, or the otherworld.

The most ancient example of such a quest is recounted in a myth from Mesopotamia in which the goddess Ishtar descended to the underworld to search for her dead lover Tammuz and resurrect him with the Water of Life. Ishtar, having passed into the underworld, had to be sprinkled with the Water of Life before she could return to the world above. In other tales, the drinking of this water had the same effect as its sprinkling did in Ishtar's myth. Water's power to resurrect the dead stemmed from the notion that all life comes from water and that water therefore has the ability to preserve life. Myths of the Fountain of Youth, the well of life, and drinks such as the Indian soma, which the gods consume to renew their youth, all stem from this idea.

West Africans retrieving water from a well. People all over the world recognized power and spirit in water, and often considered well water sacred. (Library of Congress)

Mythmakers also said that the drinking of water brought wisdom. In Norse myth, the high god Odin sacrificed one of his eyes in return for permission to drink just one draught from a sacred spring, the Spring of Mimir, which flowed underneath the roots of Yggdrasil, the world tree. He pledged his eye to Mimir, the giant who guarded the spring, drank of the spring's waters, and gained eternal wisdom. The hero Finn of Irish legend gained his wisdom from water as well. He didn't drink the water but rather ate the Salmon of Knowledge, which had obtained its wisdom from having absorbed the waters of a magic well. Gods and heroes of many lands drank from sacred rivers such as the Ganges and the Nile, or from sacred sources of the Ganges and the Nile, which were believed to originate in the celestial sphere. The gods who resided in the celestial sphere established the link between water and wisdom. Islamic myths speak of "the heaven-sent waters of reality" and the "fountain of grace." They say that the drinking of water reveals spiritual truth, and they define the Water of Life as the knowledge of God and his powers.

Despite the miraculous properties mythmakers attributed to water, people of many cultures preferred other beverages. Many people avoided water, in fact. Hippocrates correlated water with disease, and numerous other reports exist of the impurity of water supplies throughout history. Because water was susceptible to contamination, in some countries—Egypt, for instance—people preferred to drink beer. Official reports on the problems of early settlers in America attributed sickness to a lack of beer and the subsequent reliance on water. Natives of the New Hebrides islands in the Pacific Ocean likewise avoided water; and because some native peoples of South America considered themselves water's enemies, the Spaniards made them drink water as punishment.

Such contradictory notions about water reflect the knowledge that water had power—both the power to create and the power to destroy. In Egypt, people linked water with Osiris, the god of the Nile, and considered an offering of water a symbol of resurrection. The Zoroastrians connected water with light and with both solar and lunar power, and therefore considered it sinful to drink water in the dark. Drinking in general symbolized the absorption of divine power and life; people believed this of water, of wine, and of blood, and they drew connections between all of these liquids and considered them sacred. Among the Tring Dayaks of Borneo, people mourning a death could not drink ordinary water but only rainwater that had collected on the leaves of vines, which they considered "soul water." Among Buddhists, drinking water had to be cool and clear, and it had to emit the fragrance of lotus flowers, which was considered purifying. Some Buddhists even grew lotus flowers in tanks to purify their water. Hindus also place great emphasis on the purity of water. The devout take great care in preparing foods made with water, and observe strict rules in consuming these foods. For instance, a Brahman will not touch food prepared by a non-Brahman if the food was prepared with water. If a guest who is not a Brahman comes to a Brahman's house, the host may eat only sweetmeats and fruit left by the guest, for sweetmeats are prepared with milk. In Hindu thinking, water has great powers, but those powers must be protected from anything impure. (Andrews 1998; Cooper 1978; Crawley 1931; Eliade 1958; Soyer 1977)

See also Salmon

WATERMELONS

Watermelons have much in common with pumpkins, gourds, squashes, and cucumbers. All of these foods have hard shells and an abundance of seeds, which made them handy containers as well as symbols of fertility. Mythmakers generally did not distinguish pumpkins from watermelons and other similar foods, so legends often confuse them. Cinderella traveled in a pumpkin in one version of her tale, a gourd in another, and she could just as easily have traveled in a watermelon. According to legends, watermelons, like pumpkins and gourds, reached enormous sizes in the ancient world; hollowed out, they could easily have accommodated a young woman.

Watermelons are native to central Africa and have been cultivated along the Palestinian coast and along the Nile River in Egypt since prehistory. Egyptian watermelons did grow quite large—reportedly, up to thirty pounds—and a single melon would have provided several pounds' worth of cooling juice. In these hot, arid lands, poor people used watermelon juice to refresh themselves, and mixed it with sugar to reduce fevers. Watermelons and cucumbers were favorite foods of the Israelites in Egypt, and the Bible recounts how these people longed for them as they traveled through the desert. In Arab legend, watermelons grew in paradise. Not all gourdlike fruits gained such esteem, however. The colocynth is from the same family as the watermelon, as is the elaterium, and both are toxic to humans. In the Bible, in the book of Kings, it appears that a man named Elisha made a pottage from the colocynth. When he discovered his mistake, he cursed all gourdlike fruits, including watermelons, that they would turn into stones.

Watermelons are grown extensively in China; they are called *kua,* a word also used for cucumbers, squash, pumpkins, and gourds. In legend, Kua Hsien, the Melon Fairy, rules over all of these fruits. The Chinese value melons for their cooling fruit and juice but also for their seeds, watermelon seeds being particularly popular. Chinese legend recounts the story of a poor family of melon growers in Hopeh. This family inadvertently offended a member of the upper class and was forced to retreat into the mountains of Kuan-tung, where they had no luck at all in growing melons. They planted their seeds on the mountainsides, but the fruits that grew remained small and terribly sour. An P'ing, the son of the melon grower, took to playing his flute under the full moon, and suddenly one day, he saw two maidens dressed in green sitting at the edge of the melon patch. He watched them and listened intently as they talked of melon seeds that would grow well in the mountains. When the two maidens discovered An P'ing listening to them, they disappeared, but one of them left a green silk purse on the hill where she sat. To An P'ing's amazement, it contained melon seeds. An P'ing fell in love with the maiden, who returned and gave him the seeds as a gift. The two were married, after which they planted the melon seeds together and grew miraculously large and delicious melons. An P'ing and his wife harvested large crops of these melons and sold them at a great profit. Villagers who were jealous of their good fortune suspected that the two of them were Immortals and that the fruits they produced came straight from heaven. Some of these villagers followed An P'ing up the mountain one day; and one evil, scheming man discovered An P'ing's melon garden and declared that the land where the melons grew did not belong to An P'ing at all but to his rich employer. The evil man took An P'ing's melons and kidnapped his lovely wife. An P'ing, of course, was not truly an Immortal, but his wife was; and when the men came to seize her, she changed them into a pile of green rocks. An P'ing regained the magic melon seeds, and taught the people of the area how to cultivate them. They soon became a primary food crop in China.

Watermelons moved to the New World with the arrival of the Spaniards, and the native peoples of the New World quickly adopted them as food plants. They are mentioned in ritual songs of the Santa Clara, and the Pueblo reportedly considered them valued gifts on ceremonial occasions. The indigenous peoples of both North and South America adopted watermelons with enthusiasm, creating origin myths of watermelons paralleling myths of their other primary food plants. In a Cahuilla myth from California, the melons grew from the eyes of Mukat, the creator.

In Toba myth, they arose from vomit. Several groups of South American Indians called watermelons evil, and believed that watermelons only became edible when the Indians themselves planted them. The Mundurucu called watermelons the Devil's plants; they said that humans domesticated watermelons and made them safe, but the wild ones came directly from the Devil. In one Mundurucu myth, the melons arose from the grave of Karuebak, an old woman cursed by an angry sorcerer. Karuebak died underground, and her body produced food plants, some of which caused problems for the people. These watermelons from Karuebak's grave were the original wild watermelons, the ones the people feared as evil. So the Mundurucu said that whoever ate these watermelons died, but whoever kept the seeds and planted them elsewhere created harmless, edible varieties and supplied food for the people. (Grosser 1888; Hu 1996; Levi-Strauss 1974)

See also Cucumbers; Pumpkins and Gourds; Squash

WHALE

Most everyone knows the fate of Jonah in the biblical story of Jonah and the whale, as well as the fate of Gepetto, Pinocchio's father, in the popular fairy tale. Most whale myths people recognize involve whales devouring humans rather than humans devouring whales; yet people who relied on the sea for food often relied on the whales to provide it. Biblical stories appear to indicate that God intended humans to consume whales. In the book of Job, the Bible speaks of Leviathan, a primeval sea monster; and Hebrew myths speak of two Leviathans, a male and a female, both of them destined for the table. In the myths, God killed the female Leviathan and preserved her body to serve to the righteous, and he left the male

Victims of the whale hunt. In killing whales for food, the Inuit employed all kinds of "magic" including the use of shamans to tap the nature spirits' powers and ensure the success of the hunt. (Library of Congress)

Leviathan in the sea to die in battle with another water monster and become food as well.

The search for Leviathan inspired myths based on the hunt for and conquest of whales and other large sea animals. People in the northern lands, particularly along the northwest coast of America and in Alaska and Siberia, relied on whales for food. Their sea remained frozen all winter, but in the spring the whales migrated and hunting season began. The hunting and harpooning of whales in the northern waters formed the basis of prominent whale cults, with a host of myths and rituals. In the myths, whale hunts began long before the land was formed; the land *was* the whale in fact, and some demiurge like Raven harpooned it.

Raven appears as creator deity in many Arctic myths. One myth involving primal harpooning told how Raven sailed over the sea looking for land, then spotted a whale and flew into its mouth. Inside the whale, Raven found an igloo with a lamp inside it and a woman tending the lamp. In some versions of the story, Raven violated the woman and she died inside the igloo. The lamp she tended went out and the whale died as well. The Inuit created stories such as this one to convey their

belief that in the beginning of time, not only did whales become land but humans and animals, and in this case, women and whales, had interchangeable souls. In this myth, the woman represented the whale's soul and the lamp represented the whale's heart. So by violating the woman, Raven harpooned the whale. Raven survived for a time inside the dead whale by feeding on the animal's flesh; then he managed to escape to a nearby boat, transform himself into a human being, and inform the boat's crew that he had killed the whale. Woman became whale, demiurge became whaler, and whale became land and food for human beings.

The native North American whaler is something of a shaman, transcending the boundaries of human strength to conquer the whale's soul. The Inuit believe that shamanism is essential in securing the availability of whales for food. In Inuit myth, Sedna the Sea Spirit controls all the sea animals, and she decrees feast or famine by determining when to send the whales and game animals to the people. Shamans, however, must communicate with Sedna; they must descend to her underwater home and persuade her to release her animals. The myth of Sedna appears in many sources and with varying details. In one variant, Sedna was once a beautiful maiden who was carried off by a raven to be his bride. To rescue her from the raven, Sedna's father had to travel to a distant island, escape with his daughter in a kayak, and battle tremendous storms that the raven created to sink their kayak.

Eventually, Sedna's father gave in to the raven's powers and surrendered his daughter to the sea. He pushed her off the boat, but she clung to the side. Grief-stricken but determined to carry through with the sacrifice, Sedna's father chopped off his daughter's fingers, one joint at a time. Sedna sank to the bottom of the sea, and her severed fingers became the sea animals; the largest ones became whales. Sedna is believed to have a tremendous amount of power. She watches over the sea animals and serves as the guardian of nature. When people commit crimes against nature—when they take too much food, for instance—Sedna withholds the animals and people begin to die of starvation. The shamans then attempt to appease her. In one version of her myth, when people commit crimes

against nature, the crimes settle in her hair like lice, and because Sedna has no fingers, she can't remove them. So the shamans have to comb her hair and make her happy. If they succeed, she releases the animals. If they don't, the famine persists.

The whale hunt was a dangerous and difficult endeavor, and the Inuit employed all kinds of "magic" to ensure its success. They used shamans, they sprinkled ashes on the ice to avert evil influence, and they adhered to strict rituals involving the representation of woman as the whale's soul. In most societies, while the men hunted the whales, the women stayed confined to their homes; yet the women too played a crucial role in the hunt. In one ritual, an Inuit woman led her husband to the water, lay down on the ice, and remained there while the man pushed off from the ice, turned the boat around, and touched the woman's parka with his weapon. During the time the woman lay on the ice, the Inuit believed she had become the whale's body. When her husband touched her parka, he claimed her, just as Raven did when he violated the woman in the igloo. In both cases, the woman became the whale's soul.

After the man had touched the woman's parka and thus laid claim to the whale, the woman assumed a passive role in the endeavor. She had to retreat to her home and remain passive so that the whale itself would remain passive. In Inuit belief, the woman mystically transmitted to the whale the passivity the animal should feel toward his hunter. If she succeeded and if Sedna gave her blessing, her husband harpooned a whale. The rituals involved in the whale cult often involved dancing and feasting inside the whale's rib cage after the man returned with his catch. But the Inuit showed utmost respect for the whale's soul. They mourned the animal's spirit before they feasted. Then they returned some of the flesh to the sea to be reborn. The souls of whales, like the souls of other animals the Inuit hunted, returned to the hunting grounds in another spirit form when properly appeased. This belief in

Haida shaman's rattle carved with the design of a killer whale. (Werner Forman Archive; Museum of Man, Ottawa/Art Resource, NY)

spirit inspired the belief in the interchange-ability of woman and whale; encouraged the use of shamans to influence the outcome of the hunt; and led to the creation of Sedna the Sea Spirit, who had to surrender the whales to feed the people. (Lowenstein 1994)

See also Buffalo; Deer; Meat; Reindeer and Caribou; Salmon.

WHEAT

Wheat is most likely the oldest known cereal grain. It is the grain that has served as a symbol of ancient harvest deities from the Hittite civilization to the civilizations of ancient Egypt and classical Greece and Rome. People learned to cultivate wheat throughout the European continent, and it soon became their staff of life, as important to the Europeans as rice was to the people of Asia and corn was to the people of the Americas. Because wheat was the staff of life, people considered it a divine gift, and they made it the focus of ritual from early times. Like corn, the word *wheat* was used in bygone times to refer to cereal grains in general, including barley and oats.

Wheat and barley are among the most ancient of Middle Eastern food crops, having been domesticated around 8000 B.C. By the classical era, wheat had assumed primary importance. Barley was less expensive and more plentiful than wheat, so it came to symbolize poverty and worthlessness; wheat, in contrast, came to symbolize goodness and richness, particularly of the soil. The people perceived wheat as a benevolent grain from a benevolent god, who according to the Old Testament chose to bestow the gift of the wheat harvest as a reward to the righteous and chose to destroy the wheat harvest as a punishment to evildoers. In the New Testament, Jesus used wheat in his agricultural parables to illustrate the notion of resurrection. He said that a grain of wheat is just a grain of wheat—it dies—but if it is put into the ground, more grains of wheat arise from it. Jesus too died so that many could live. The symbolism of wheat reveals

the ultimate truth: the birth of light from darkness and of life from death.

Long before Jesus, however, people understood the notion of death and rebirth when they witnessed the cycles of nature: the changing of the seasons, and the birth, growth, and death of plant and animal life. Early people organized their lives around the seasonal calendar. They celebrated the gift of grain by conducting elaborate agricultural rituals during critical times in the seasonal cycle. In Greek myth, the goddess Demeter gave wheat to the people, and the people who worshiped her understood the revelation of the harvest. When Demeter and her daughter descended to the underworld, the grain died, and when they returned, the grain arose anew from the ground. Initiates to Demeter's cult embraced her myths and conducted the rituals to ensure the productivity of the harvest—to please and appease the grain deities who had the ability to cause feast or famine. Other cultures around the world conducted similar harvest rituals. But Demeter, and other grain goddesses like her, nurtured not only the body but the soul. For the initiates in Demeter's cult, the Eleusinian Mysteries, worshiping the grain goddess guaranteed their own life after death.

People around the world considered wheat the temporary embodiment of the goddess—of Demeter or of whomever represented the grain. Ancient people often believed they witnessed the goddess passing by when they saw the wheat waving in the breeze. It was a common belief in the ancient world that wheat, or grain in general, had spirit; and people worshiped the gods and goddesses who embodied that spirit. They worshiped the wheat itself, and often the last sheaf in particular, which they believed harbored the wheat spirit. Some people perceived this wheat spirit as an old woman, others as an infant or a maiden. Some said that whoever cut the last sheaf of wheat absorbed the dying spirit and must then be sacrificed to ensure a good harvest the following year. Early people worshiped wheat and the gods who discovered wheat and taught them how to cultivate it. They worshiped gods who had control over the sowing and reaping, as well as those who guarded the harvest and protected it from specific diseases. Often they performed sacrifices to appease these deities. The Romans, for instance, sacrificed sheep to the god Robigus, the deity who had the power to protect the harvest from rust, one of wheat's worst enemies.

Many beliefs surrounding wheat applied to grain crops in general; wheat, along with barley, served as the basis for agricultural myths of many civilizations. The deities the people credited with the discovery and cultivation of wheat were culture heroes; they helped human beings advance by teaching them how to live off the land and control the production of food. The ancient Egyptians credited both Isis and Osiris with teaching them the cultivation of both wheat and barley. These gods helped their people move up the evolutionary ladder from hunters and foragers to agriculturists: Isis, by discovering the wheat growing wild, and Osiris, by developing cultivated varieties and making grain a staple food. Though the records of Egyptian civilization indicate that these people were agriculturists, many scholars believe that before Osiris's reign as king, the Egyptians were cannibals. So by introducing the cultivation of wheat and barley, Osiris saved his people from savagery.

Osiris was a dying and rising god, a vegetation deity responsible for the fertilization of the soil, and thus a logical deity to personify the wheat crop and star in the agricultural myths his people embraced. But Osiris's sister/wife Isis played an equally important role. She was the Greek Demeter or the Roman Ceres, the fertility goddess and earth mother responsible for the harvest. In Egyptian myth, Osiris died and was resurrected by Isis, who retrieved his body, broken to bits by his evil brother Seth, and pieced it back together.

In Babylonian myth, the vegetation god Tammuz also died and was resurrected. The goddess Ishtar descended to the underworld and brought him back to life, and just then,

the wheat arose from the ground. As the cult of Tammuz moved westward, Tammuz became known as Adonis, and the people who worshiped Adonis planted the so-called Gardens of Adonis to honor him in his vegetal form. They prepared baskets filled with soil and sown with wheat and barley and other quickly sprouting crops. The "Gardens of Adonis" have been interpreted as manifestations of the grain god's powers, and as charms promoting the growth of vegetation, as the rapid growth of wheat in these gardens was believed to make the wheat in the fields grow rapidly too.

The myth of Adonis became so popular that Adonis himself was labeled the dying and rising god. Aphrodite, the goddess of love, found Adonis so beautiful that she saved him from destruction by sealing him in a casket and sending him to Persephone to protect him in the underworld. Persephone too fell in love with Adonis, however; and when Aphrodite went to retrieve the god, Persephone refused to give him back. So Zeus had to issue a decree that Adonis remain with Persephone in the underworld for half of the year and with Aphrodite on earth for the other half.

Dying and rising gods like Adonis represented vegetation in general and wheat in particular, and the goddesses responsible for resurrecting them conferred the boon of the harvest on humankind. Not only did these goddesses discover wheat growing wild but they brought it back from death; they taught humans how to cultivate it. Therefore, wheat not only represents the victory of life over death but the knowledge of agriculture in general—the crucial civilizing force that moved human beings up the evolutionary ladder. (Frazer 1950; Toussaint-Samat 1992)

See also Barley; Bread; Cake; Corn; Grain; Millet; Oats; Rice; Rye; Sorghum

WINE

The grapevine is native to the Middle East, where people have cultivated it since the dawn of agriculture. Wine pressed from grapes is one of the oldest beverages consumed by humans, and a substance that people of many lands associated with the blood of gods. Early people believed that the fermentation of grape juice was a mystical process, and therefore produced a mystical product. In essence, they believed that wine was created for the purpose of establishing communication between humans and gods.

The practice of wine making predates recorded history, and most likely originated when people who had stored their grapes a long time discovered that the fermented fruit and its juices had intoxicating effects. The ancients made wine not only from grapes but also from many other fruits, including dates, figs, quinces, mulberries, and pears. The early peoples of various lands knew many different intoxicating substances. Some consumed hallucinogenic mushrooms, and others, plants such as the coca and the poppy; and their shamans used these substances to travel to other worlds. The consumption of wine, like the consumption of any intoxicant, became a religious rite. The drinking of wine in many cultures eventually replaced blood sacrifices, as is evidenced by the Christian Eucharist.

In Christian belief today, partaking in the Eucharist means partaking of the divinity of Christ. In the ancient world and among many people, consuming the blood of someone chosen to represent their god meant partaking in their divinity as well. To the ancients, the intoxicating effects of wine seemed to validate the belief that wine became divine blood. In the myths of some early peoples, wine arose from the body of a divine, primordial being. In Iranian myth, wine arose from the blood of the primordial bull, slain by the god Mithra, in an act that symbolized creation. Each year, the people of ancient Iran crushed grapes to reenact this sacrificial slaughter. Those who consumed the wine produced from these grapes believed they would thereby possess the bull's energy and vital force.

The ritual function of wine and other alcoholic beverages reveals its importance in early societies. In Japanese society, people drank sake, or rice wine, in rituals conducted to honor the kami, the divine spirits. In Scandinavia, the Vikings drank wine during sacrificial feasts honoring Odin for his power and the fertility gods Njord and Frey for their influence over the crops. The Greeks drank wine in rituals connected with Dionysus, the god of the vine and of ecstasy. In early Greek thought, wine was a gift from Dionysus and bestowed the capacity for spiritual vision. The Greeks characterized Dionysus as wild and orgiastic. In Roman myth, Bacchus performed the same functions as Dionysus in Greek myth. Bacchus too was clearly mad, yet endearing; wicked, yet jovial. The dual nature of the wine god appears to have been a reflection of the dual nature of the grape: the ability to alter the state of consciousness, perhaps to a dangerous, destructive degree, and the ability to exhilarate, to heighten the spirit, and to open the way to enlightenment.

In the cult of Dionysus, all who consumed the miraculous elixir partook in the madness of the wine god. But the cult of Dionysus had a much loftier purpose than that. Dionysus not only represented the vine but also agriculture in general. He died a violent death but was resurrected, like the fruits of the earth that came and went with the seasons. In myth, drunken fertility spirits called satyrs accompanied Dionysus, consistent with his role as an agricultural deity. The Egyptian Osiris was another equivalent to Dionysus. Osiris introduced grapes to his people as well as grains. The Egyptians most likely drank wine in honor of Osiris and made offerings of wine to him, just as they made offerings of wine to the dead, presumably because they believed wine should be enjoyed in heaven as it was on earth.

People today often take nature's gifts for granted. They drink wine to heighten their spirits, but they no longer consider intoxication sacred and miraculous. As revealed in the myths of Dionysus, people of the ancient world knew wine as a mood enhancer but also as a

Bacchus, the Roman god of wine and revelry. (Scala/Art Resource, NY)

means to spiritual enlightenment. They recognized a miracle in the fermentation process, and they witnessed a transformation, both in the grape and in the mind of the person who consumed the grape wine. So they created a god to embody the magic. To early people, wine seemed like a living being who progressed from one stage to another, and changed in the process, gaining divine properties. The imbiber of wine, and in Greek culture the devotee of Dionysus, assimilated the soul of the wine god. The euphoria caused by wine seemed like madness but was considered divine possession. Drinking wine appeared to make humans temporarily equal to the gods. Wine, in essence, was a metaphor for divinity.

The duality of Dionysus revealed the belief in wine and drunkenness as both good and evil. In Iranian legend, the fermented grape juice was at first considered poison. Prince Jemshed loved grape juice, and he stored it in goatskin bags in his palace in the desert. Once, when he went to get a drink, he discovered that the juice had changed somehow, and he thought it tasted horrible. He labeled the bags poison so that no one else would drink from them. Not too long after that, however, one of Prince Jemshed's wives decided to kill herself by drinking this "poison." She drank and drank but simply got happier and happier. This woman had wanted to kill herself because her husband no longer favored her over the other wives in his harem. But after her "transformation," she gained back the favored position. The wife of Prince Jemshed drank wine every night, and it changed her from a sad woman to a happy one. Her husband learned her secret when he discovered the empty bags. Recognizing the significance of the elixir he formerly considered poison, Prince Jemshed became the first wine maker. (Darby et al. 1977; Kerenyi 1976; Lehner and Lehner 1973; Otto 1965; Toussaint-Samat 1992)

See also Alcoholic Beverages; Ayahuasca; Balche; Beer; Blood and Flesh; Chicha; Grapes; Kava; Mead; Pulque; Sake; Soma

YAMS

Yams and sweet potatoes have been staple foods in Oceania since ancient times. They were one of the foods the Polynesians relied on during their sea travels; the yams kept them alive, whereas many other foods perished during long voyages. Because of the important role the yam played as a life-sustaining crop, Oceanian peoples felt the need to explain its existence. Many of them believed that the yam originated in the sky world and was brought to earth by a miracle.

In myths of the Pacific Islands, humans often had to steal yams and other foods from the gods. Sometimes the gods withdrew foodstuffs that already existed on earth. In a legend from Samoa, flying gods stole yams belonging to a high chief, and the chief sent his son to the spirit realm to retrieve them. In Maori myth, the star Whanui—who was the brother of Rongo-maui, the god of agriculture, fruits, and cultivated plants—served as keeper of the yam in heaven. Rongo-maui went up to heaven and stole the food from his brother, hiding it in his loincloth and using it to impregnate his wife. His wife then delivered to the people the first yam by giving birth to this sacred food plant in the water. In Oceania, women are the primary cultivators of yams, and perhaps for this reason women gave birth to them in myth. However, other myths emphasize the yam's connection with the soil. The people of Kiwai have a myth in which a man copulates with the earth and impregnates a female spirit dwelling underneath the earth, who then gives birth to yams. Still other myths attribute to yams a different origin. A myth from New Guinea identifies dogs as the first yam eaters. The people were starving, but the dogs were healthy. So one day a man followed a dog and found him eating heaps of yams from the bottom of a pond. The man picked the yams, and people began eating them. Another New Guinea myth places the first yams in a less desirable habitat. In this tale, a woman saw a man defecate in a creek, and later they found yams in that very spot. The woman took them home and planted them, and they became the world's first food plants.

Myths of the Pacific Islands often deal with famine because the people who lived there frequently experienced it—and yams often relieved it. In an African myth, the Ashanti people were experiencing a famine, and they knew nothing of yams until they met a man one day who possessed them. Some of the Ashanti villagers realized that they needed to obtain this valuable foodstuff, so they searched far and wide until finally they located some. The villagers were told that in order to obtain them, they would have to surrender one of their own people in exchange. For a long time no one in the village would give in to this request, and hunger continued to plague the people. In the end, an Ashanti woman saved her people from starvation by surrendering her only son. This myth not only explained how the Ashanti acquired yams and how the yams relieved famine but also the Ashanti rules of inheritance. Because of the woman's sacrifice, boys inherit property and wealth from their maternal uncles; when men die, they leave their possessions to their sisters' sons.

The myths and rituals explaining the acquisition of yams played a crucial role in the religious lives of early people. In some regions, people continue to perform these rituals, which involve reenacting the acquisition of yams from the sky world. In other regions, participants in these ceremonies use magic charms to achieve the desired results. The New Caledonians bury stones shaped like yams in their fields, believing that the stones will increase the yield. Many people believe in the power of a Yam Spirit. During a yam ceremony in Australia, the Yam Spirit moves from Altjerringa, the domain of ancestral spirits, to a mountain cave, and then to a totem stick decorated with vegetable down and planted in the ground during the ceremony. If the performers gain the favor of the Great Spirit, the yam's taproot descends into the ground and sends out shoots throughout the soil that eventually will provide yams to the people.

The Yam Spirit was a powerful force present in much of Oceania and in Nigeria as well. Yam planting in Nigeria, as in the Oceanian lands, was accompanied by elaborate rituals. In Nigeria, the Yam Spirit, called Ifejioku by some, has a special cult, and the people of the yam cult must adhere to certain rules before and after the planting. In one instance, an Ibo priest plants his yams first, so he harvests first as well. Then he gives his firstfruits to the Yam Spirit. The largest yam in the harvest is called the *juji,* and the Yam Spirit himself is thought to live within it. The priest keeps this yam for an entire year, until the next year's harvest, then kills a fowl and sprinkles the fowl's blood on the juji. He then leaves it as an offering at the shrine of the Yam god, along with some cola nuts. The Ibo consider it an offense to harvest yams and eat them before they perform this ritual.

The yam ceremonies performed in these cultures are similar to agricultural rites surrounding numerous other crops throughout the world. The gods, and in many belief systems, the ancestors, provide the food, so the people make ritual appeals to these entities to guarantee provision. An Orokolo myth identifies the moon god as the provider of yams, but many other myths identify goddesses. The goddess dies, descends into the ground, and then is resurrected as a food plant. In Oceanian lands this food plant is often the yam, and the gods who ensure a good harvest receive appropriate respect and reverence. (Courlander 1975; Knappert 1995c; Talbot 1967)

See also Breadfruit; Taro

YOGURT

Yogurt, like cheese, was discovered long ago, when wandering herdsmen carrying milk in sheepskin bags noticed that the milk had curdled. People likely discovered both cheese and yogurt in the beginning of the Neolithic era, when they first began to practice milking. Nomadic herdsmen milked their animals, then carried the milk in pouches made out of sheep's stomachs, the lining of which contains an enzyme called rennin, which curdles milk. The Middle Eastern climate was ideal for curdling milk; left in the heat, milk curdled in just a few hours. Depending on the degree of heat and the type of bacteria in the environment, the curds would be fine and develop into yogurt, or coarse and develop into cheese. Yogurt was most likely discovered by accident. As a product of milk, it was assigned similar properties.

Milk and milk products have always been considered nothing short of magical. In fact, it has been suggested that the *milk* in the biblical phrase *milk and honey* referred to yogurt. As soon as the wandering herdsmen discovered the curdled milk, they tasted it and found it to their liking. It was not long before they perceived health benefits that they attributed to the curdled milk.

In biblical legend, an angel told Abraham that eating yogurt was the secret of long life. Abraham ate it, and reputedly lived to the age of 175. Peasants in the Balkans live a long time, particularly in Bulgaria, and furthermore, many of them retain their ability to conceive late in life. Both of these abilities have been attributed to the fact that these people eat large quantities of yogurt, and that yogurt apparently has healing properties. In the 1500s, yogurt was believed to have healed the French monarch King Francois I from a severe depression. For a long time doctors visited the bedside of the ailing king, but no one could do a thing to help him, and he sank deeper and deeper into depression. Then Francois learned of a Jewish doctor who used fermented sheep's milk to make a magnificent brew. Everyone hailed the properties of the doctor's brew, so King Francois sent for the doctor. The doctor walked through southern Europe on foot with his flock of sheep, and upon arrival, gave yogurt to the king. King Francois drank the yogurt for several weeks and was cured. The French people thereafter referred to yogurt as the "milk of eternal life."

Milk has been hailed as the ultimate food, and milk products alone have been assigned the ability to sustain life, as is evidenced by African myths of the milk bird. The milk bird appears frequently in African myth, and in one variation of the story, this bird is an ancestor who guards an ancestral burial field by ensuring that no one cultivates or disturbs it. A man and a woman hoe this field by day, but at night, the bird sings and the weeds grow back again. But even though the couple is deprived of crops, the bird sees to it that these people do not starve. The man catches the bird, and the bird yields *amasi,* a kind of yogurt, to feed the man and his family. In the story, this yogurt, like milk, sustained life. The bird sang to the man and revealed its identity as the man's mother, the one who feeds and nurtures him in times of famine. (Elkhort 1991; Knappert 1995a; Lysaght 1994; Mahias 1988; Toussaint-Samat 1992)

See also Butter; Cheese; Milk

APPENDIX I:
FOOD MYTHS BY CULTURE

AFRICA
Alligator and Crocodile
Bananas and Plantains
Baobab
Beef
Butter
Cheese
Chicken
Coconuts
Coffee
Cola Nuts
Eggs
Figs
Fish
Insects
Jujubes
Lotus
Manioc
Meat
Milk
Millet
Ox
Pumpkins and Gourds
Rice
Sorghum
Thornapples
Yams
Yogurt

BALTIC AND SLAVIC LANDS
Acorns
Barley
Bears
Beer
Bread
Cake
Cherries
Eggs
Garlic
Hazelnuts
Honey
Horse
Limes and Linden Trees
Lotus
Manna
Millet
Mushrooms
Potatoes
Radishes
Raspberries
Reindeer and Caribou
Turnips
Walnuts
Yogurt

CHINA
Alligators and Crocodiles
Amaranth
Apricots

Bamboo (Shoots)
Bananas and Plantains
Barley
Birds' Nests
Cake
Candy
Carrots
Cherries
Chestnuts
Chicken
Cinnamon
Cucumbers
Dates
Dogs
Eggs
Flowers
Ginger
Ginseng
Goose and Turkey
Ices and Ice Cream
Insects
Jujubes
Lemons and Citrons
Lotus
Mandrakes
Millet
Mulberries
Mushrooms
Oranges
Ox
Peaches
Pears

CHINA, *continued*
Peppers
Persimmons
Pines and Pine Nuts
Plums
Pomegranates
Pork
Pumpkins and Gourds
Radishes
Rice
Saffron
Sake
Salt
Soybeans
Sugar and Sugarcane
Taro
Tea
Turnips
Turtle
Watermelons

EGYPT
Alligator and Crocodile
Asparagus
Barley
Beans
Beef
Beer
Bread
Cabbage
Cake
Candy
Chicken
Chicory and Endive
Corn
Cucumbers
Dates
Eggs
Figs
Fish
Goat, Lamb, and Ram
Goose and Turkey
Grain
Grapes
Honey
Ices and Ice Cream

Jujubes
Lemons and Citrons
Lettuce
Lotus
Mandrakes
Milk
Mushrooms
Olives and Olive Oil
Onions and Leeks
Parsley and Celery
Pears
Peas and Lentils
Pines and Pine Nuts
Pork
Salt
Spices
Water
Watermelons
Wine

GREECE AND ROME
Acorns
Almonds
Amaranth
Apples
Asparagus
Barley
Basil
Beans
Blackberries
Blood and Flesh
Blueberries
Bread
Cabbage
Cake
Candy
Cheese
Chestnuts
Cinnamon
Dates
Dog
Figs
Fish
Flowers
Garlic

Ginger
Goat, Lamb, and Ram
Grain
Grapes
Hazelnuts
Honey
Horse
Insects
Jujubes
Lemons and Citrons
Lettuce
Limes and Linden Trees
Lotus
Lupines
Mandrakes
Meat
Milk
Mint
Mulberries
Mushrooms
Nectar and Ambrosia
Olives and Olive Oil
Oranges
Ox
Parsley and Celery
Pines and Pine Nuts
Pomegranates
Pork
Quinces
Rye
Saffron
Salt
Sesame
Spices
Walnuts
Wheat
Wine

INDIA
Alcoholic Beverages
Bamboo (Shoots)
Bananas and Plantains
Barley
Basil
Beans
Beef

Betel Nuts
Bilva Fruit
Buffalo
Butter
Cake
Coconuts
Cucumbers
Dates
Dog
Eggplant
Eggs
Figs
Fish
Garlic
Ginger
Gooseberries
Grain
Grapes
Honey
Horse
Jujubes
Lemons and Citrons
Lotus
Mangoes
Meat
Milk
Mustard Seeds
Nectar and Ambrosia
Onions and Leeks
Peppers
Pomegranates
Pumpkins and Gourds
Raspberries
Rice
Saffron
Salt
Sesame
Soma
Sugar and Sugarcane
Sunflower Seeds
Tamarind
Tea
Thornapples
Tobacco
Turmeric
Turtle
Walnuts

JAPAN

Bamboo (Shoots)
Bear
Cherries
Cucumbers
Flowers
Lotus
Mushrooms
Oranges
Peaches
Pines and Pine Nuts
Plums
Pumpkins and Gourds
Radishes
Rice
Sake
Soybeans
Taro
Tea

THE NEAR AND MIDDLE EAST

Almonds
Apricots
Artichokes
Barley
Beef
Beer
Carob
Cheese
Chicken
Chicory and Endive
Coffee
Cucumbers
Dates
Dog
Eggplant
Figs
Fish
Garlic
Ginger
Goat, Lamb, and Ram
Gooseberries
Grain
Grapes
Herbs

Honey
Ices and Ice Cream
Insects
Jujubes
Lemons and Citrons
Lettuce
Manna
Meat
Mulberries
Mustard Seeds
Nectar and Ambrosia
Peas and Lentils
Pineapples
Pomegranates
Water
Wheat
Yogurt

NORTH AMERICA

Acorns
Alligator and Crocodile
Beans
Bear
Beer
Buffalo
Cactus
Candy
Chestnuts
Corn
Cranberries
Deer
Dog
Elderberries
Fish
Goose and Turkey
Gooseberries
Grain
Insects
Maple Syrup
Mesquite
Milk
Mushrooms
Mustard Seeds
Peppers
Pineapples
Pines and Pine Nuts

N. AMERICA, *continued*
Reindeer and Caribou
Salmon
Squash
Strawberries
Sunflower Seeds
Thornapples
Tobacco
Turnips

OCEANIA

Bananas and Plantains
Betel Nuts
Blood and Flesh
Blueberries
Breadfruit
Chicken
Coconuts
Dog
Eggs
Figs
Fish
Ginger
Insects
Kava (Awa)
Pork
Pumpkins and Gourds
Rice
Saffron
Sugar and Sugarcane
Taro
Turmeric
Yams

OLD EUROPE (CELTIC LANDS AND SCANDINAVIA)

Acorns
Apples
Artichokes
Beans
Beef
Beer
Blackberries

Blood and Flesh
Blueberries
Butter
Cabbage
Cake
Cheese
Cherries
Chestnuts
Chicory and Endive
Coffee
Cranberries
Cucumbers
Deer
Dog
Eggs
Elderberries
Flowers
Goat, Lamb, and Ram
Goose and Turkey
Gooseberries
Hazelnuts
Horse
Limes and Linden Trees
Manna
Mead
Meat
Milk
Millet
Mushrooms
Nightshades
Parsley and Celery
Pears
Peas and Lentils
Peppers
Pineapples
Pork
Potatoes
Rye
Salmon
Salt
Sesame
Strawberries
Thornapples
Tomatoes
Turnips

SOUTH AND CENTRAL AMERICA

Amaranth
Avocados
Ayahuasca
Balche
Beer
Blood and Flesh
Bread
Cactus
Carob
Chicha
Chocolate
Coca
Corn
Flowers
Frogs and Toads
Guinea Pigs
Honey
Horse
Manioc
Mesquite
Milk
Mushrooms
Ololiuqui
Peanuts
Peppers
Pineapples
Potatoes
Pulque
Quinoa
Sunflower Seeds
Thornapples
Tobacco
Tomatoes
Turtle
Vanilla
Watermelons

CHRISTIAN FOOD MYTHS

Amaranth
Blackberries
Blood and Flesh
Bread
Butter
Carob
Cherries
Dates
Eggs
Elderberries
Figs
Fish
Ginger
Goat, Lamb, and Ram
Goose and Turkey
Grapes
Herbs
Honey
Horse
Insects
Mandrakes
Mangoes
Manioc
Mushrooms
Pomegranates
Rye
Salt
Strawberries
Walnuts
Wine

APPENDIX II:
FOOD FUNCTIONS

APHRODISIACS AND LOVE CHARMS

People have always valued foods presumed to have aphrodisiac powers because sexual potency seemed intimately connected with fertility, longevity, and the regeneration of life. Almost every fruit and vegetable, at one time or another, has been hailed by someone as a sexual stimulant, particularly those foods with pungent odors, fiery flavors, soft, fleshy textures, or shapes resembling genitalia. The human desire to attract love has led to the consumption of foods of all sorts, many of which have been identified in myth as symbols or attributes of love goddesses such as Venus or Aphrodite. Many of these foods have properties connecting them to fertility as well as to love and sex, and many of the goddesses who are identified with these foods have the power to grant fertility as well as effect love spells.

See the following entries:

Apples	Flowers
Apricots	Ginger
Asparagus	Ginseng
Basil	Hazelnuts
Beans	Herbs
Betel Nuts	Honey
Birds' Nests	Lemons and Citrons
Chicory and Endive	Lettuce
Coffee	Limes and
Fish	Linden Trees
Mandrakes	Raspberries
Mangoes	Saffron
Mint	Salt
Nightshades	Sesame
Oranges	Spices
Peppers	Thornapples
Persimmons	Tomatoes
Quinces	Walnuts

ELIXIRS OF LIFE AND IMMORTALITY

People of the past believed deeply in the existence of supernatural forces, and they relied on those forces to grant them fertility and long healthy lives. The ancients suffered frightful mortality rates, and they experienced the innately human dread of death and pain. This fostered a deep desire for health, longevity, and the renewal of youth. It led to quests, both mythological and real, for a magical elixir that would cure disease, grant long life, and perhaps even bestow immortality. In myths around the world, plants and plant derivatives of all sorts are hailed as elixirs of life, fountains and wells offer stores of life-giving water, and trees bear everlasting supplies of magic fruit. Such beliefs were reinforced by the popular perception that gods obtained their immortality by partaking of one or another mysterious, magical substance.

See the following entries:

Apples
Bamboo (Shoots)
Beer
Butter
Cherries
Cinnamon
Dates
Eggs
Figs
Ginseng
Grapes
Hazelnuts
Herbs
Honey
Jujubes
Manna
Mead
Milk
Mushrooms
Nectar and Ambrosia
Peaches
Pears
Persimmons
Pines and Pine Nuts
Plums
Pomegranates
Quinces
Salt
Soma
Turtle
Walnuts
Yogurt

Baobab
Barley
Basil
Beans
Betel Nuts
Bilva Fruit
Blueberries
Bread
Breadfruit
Butter
Cherries
Chestnuts
Chicken
Coca
Coconuts
Corn
Cranberries
Cucumbers
Dates
Eggs
Figs
Fish
Grain
Grapes
Hazelnuts
Horse
Lettuce
Lotus
Mandrakes
Mangoes
Maple Syrup
Oranges
Persimmons
Pomegranates
Pork
Potatoes
Pumpkins and
    Gourds
Quinces
Radishes
Rice
Salt
Taro
Thornapples
Turmeric
Turnips
Walnuts
Wine

FERTILITY SYMBOLS AND SYMBOLS OF RENEWAL

Fertility has been a primary concern of all societies at all times in history. Because human life depended on the fertility of the fields and of women, people equated a lack of fertility with death and considered barrenness a disaster to be avoided at all costs. People today rarely understand the deadly threats that the ancients faced continually, and they rarely understand the perception of a world full of spirits with a need to be appeased. People of the past constantly tried to promote fertility by locating the sources of power in the world, by propitiating the right spirits in the right ways, and by consuming foods deemed to have fertilizing power. Foods hailed as fertility symbols had properties such as an abundance of seeds or the ability to produce prolifically. Consuming these foods and offering them to the gods gained special significance during crucial times in the seasonal cycle such as harvesttime, when people were especially aware of the necessity for renewal.

See the following entries:

Acorns
Almonds
Apples
Asparagus
Bamboo (Shoots)
Bananas and Plantains

FOODS ASSOCIATED WITH THE UNDERWORLD

Alligator and
    Crocodile
Barley
Blackberries
Carrots
Dog
Eggplant
Elderberries
Flowers
Grain
Kava (Awa)
Mint
Nightshades
Peanuts
Turnips
Walnuts
Water

FOODS FOR THE DEAD

A common practice throughout history, in most parts of the world, was the provision of food for the dead. The necessity of such a practice stemmed from the notion of the soul as an entity separate from the body, which leaves the body upon death, and which has a mind and needs of its own. People offered food to the dead as a way of honoring them or of providing for them as they continued to exist in another realm. Some peoples believed that after death the soul embarked on a journey to the other realm, and needed proper sustenance in order to get there safely. Foods commonly offered to the dead included those that people invested with spiritual significance or that were deemed appropriate in order to demonstrate respect. In past times particularly, people often feared that if they neglected to honor and provide for the dead, the dead would come back to haunt the living or would take revenge on them in some dreadful way.

See the following entries:

Amaranth	Honey
Asparagus	Jujubes
Beans	Lupines
Bear	Onions and Leeks
Betel Nuts	Parsley and Celery
Cake	Peas and Lentils
Chicha	Pomegranates
Eggs	Sesame
Figs	Sunflower Seeds
Garlic	Tamarind
Ginseng	Wine

FORBIDDEN FRUITS

Various fruits have been identified as the original forbidden fruit, the one the biblical Eve plucked from the Tree of Knowledge in the Garden of Eden. Most commonly said to be an apple or a fig, the forbidden fruit could be any fruit the people of the area held sacred, be it a pomegranate, an apricot, an orange, a quince, or even a coconut. Forbidden fruits grew on the Tree of Knowledge, which grew alongside the Tree of Life in a mythical paradise. Both trees bore fruit, and human beings had to choose between them. The Tree of Life signified immortality, and the Tree of Knowledge signified mortality, and they existed not only in the Garden of Eden, but in mythical gardens everywhere. When humans chose to eat the forbidden fruit from the Tree of Knowledge, they deprived themselves of eternal life and thus separated themselves from the gods.

See the following entries:

Apples	Oranges
Apricots	Peaches
Bananas and	Plums
Plantains	Pomegranates
Bilva Fruit	Pumpkins and Gourds
Cherries	Quinces
Figs	Radishes
Grapes	Turnips
Lemons and Citrons	

INTOXICANTS AND HALLUCINOGENS

While people today rarely distinguish between the sacred and the profane, people of the past often had a clear understanding of both. They embraced the sanctity of nature and felt awe-inspired by the unknown; they recognized the mystical quality of life, so they looked for magic everywhere. People in touch with the sacred recognized life spirit in the plants and animals of their world, and they found plants and animals with spirits so strong that consuming them revealed the realm of the gods. For this reason people who consumed these hallucinogens deified them and worshiped them as gods; shamans used them, as did healers and magic men of other sorts, and indeed anyone who wished to transcend the boundaries of the mortal world. Human beings engage in religious drug use to elevate their minds, commune with spirits, and visualize heaven. Plants and animals with intoxicating or hallucinogenic powers reaffirm the existence of sanctity on earth.

See the following entries:

Alcoholic Beverages	Carob
Ayahuasca	Chicha
Balche	Chocolate
Barley	Coca
Beer	Coffee
Cactus	Cola Nuts

Flowers
Frogs and Toads
Grapes
Herbs
Honey
Kava (Awa)
Lupines
Manioc
Mead
Mushrooms
Nightshades

Ololiuqui
Pulque
Reindeer and
    Caribou
Rye
Sake
Soma
Thornapples
Tobacco
Wine

Cactus
Cheese
Chestnuts
Coca
Coffee
Dog
Garlic
Ginger
Ginseng
Guinea Pigs
Herbs
Honey
Kava (Awa)
Lemons and Citrons
Limes and Linden
    Trees
Mandrakes
Milk

Onions and Leeks
Peppers
Pines and Pine Nuts
Saffron
Salt
Sesame
Soma
Strawberries
Tamarind
Taro
Tea
Thornapples
Tobacco
Tomatoes
Turmeric
Turtle
Yogurt

MEDICINALS

Today many people know to eat cranberries to cure bladder infections or prunes for their laxative effect, but people long ago had far more extensive herbal apothecaries. Healers derived their cures from plants and animals that were believed to contain magical properties. Witch doctors, herbalists, shamans, and healers of all kinds based their search for magic plants largely on the plant's shape, color, and other identifying characteristics. They believed, for instance, that plants growing in water absorbed the water's healing and purifying powers, and that plants that grew and bloomed year-round imparted immortality to human beings. The Doctrine of Signatures, a concept employed by herbalists of the Renaissance, held that like cured like, and that people could use plants to cure human ailments based on anatomical similarities. This meant that yellow plants cured jaundice, a disease that turns the skin yellow, for instance, and that plants shaped like hearts cured ailments of the heart. Most foods have been assigned healing properties by someone, at one time or another in history. The following foods have commonly been used for medicinal purposes in many different cultures.

See the following entries:

Alligator and
    Crocodile
Apples
Ayahuasca
Balche

Bamboo (Shoots)
Baobab
Bilva Fruit
Birds' Nests
Cabbage

OFFERINGS AND SACRIFICES

Because food is a basic need of the living, people of many different cultures have considered food offerings the best way to show devotion and reverence to their deities. People of the past most often attempted to propitiate the higher powers by surrendering the foods they valued most dearly—not the wild foods that the gods gave freely but rather the meat of domesticated animals and the plant foods cultivated by human hands. When people sacrifice their domesticated animals or their cultivated plants, they truly surrender to the gods, and they demonstrate their willingness to deny themselves in order to worship them. Sacrifice involves spiritual nourishment, but it involves physical nourishment as well. The gods who receive food offerings consume only the essence of the food, not the food itself, so after the gods consume their share, the priests and the common people partake of the material substance. Almost all foods at one time or another and in one culture or another were used as offerings or sacrifices to some supernatural being. The following foods represent some of the most common sacrifices.

See the following entries:

Amaranth
Balche
Basil
Beans
Bear
Beef
Beer
Betel Nuts
Bilva Fruit
Blood and Flesh
Buffalo
Butter
Candy
Chicha
Chicken
Chocolate
Cinnamon
Coca
Coconuts
Corn
Dates
Dog
Eggs

Fish
Goat, Lamb, and Ram
Goose and Turkey
Grain
Honey
Horse
Kava (Awa)
Lemons and Citrons
Lettuce
Meat
Milk
Millet
Ox
Pork
Rice
Salmon
Salt
Sesame
Spices
Sugar and Sugarcane
Turmeric
Wine
Yams

POISONS

Ancient magic relied on the use of plants and animals, and plants and animals with poisonous properties were always easy to obtain. Practitioners of black magic and witchcraft needed poisons to stupefy their victims, and they developed ways to tap into the earth's evil powers and extract powerful substances to stir into magic potions and to rub on poison arrows and darts. Poisoning has always had a close connection with witchcraft, and mythological witches such as Hecate and Circe had an intimate knowledge of plants such as deadly nightshade, mandrakes, thornapple, and henbane. But there's a fine line between killing and curing. Both require an extensive knowledge of plants and animals and how to combine them to make reputedly magic potions.

See the following entries:

Balche
Eggplant

Elderberries
Frogs and Toads

Herbs
Mandrakes
Manioc
Mushrooms
Nightshades
Pineapples

Potatoes
Rye
Saffron
Thornapples
Tomatoes
Wine

PURIFICANTS AND SYMBOLS OF PURITY

The notion of religious purity must be understood along with the notion of religious pollution. In some traditions, purity leads people to healing, renewal, and eternal life in heaven, whereas pollution ties them to the world of death and decay and dooms them to the powers of the underworld. Though the concepts of pollution and purity exist in nearly all the world's religions, the necessity for ritual purification takes primary significance in religions such as Hinduism and Buddhism where worshipers take care to consume only pure foods. Foods deemed pure are culture specific, but in general, they achieve purity based on their presumed sanctity and the religious symbolism people attach to them. Ingesting such foods often constitute religious sacraments, and these types of purification rituals take on primary significance during critical rites of passage such as birth, death, and marriage—the times when people are most vulnerable to evil influence.

See the following entries:

Balche
Basil
Beef
Betel Nuts
Birds' Nests
Blackberries
Butter
Cherries
Dog
Goat, Lamb, and
    Ram
Honey
Ices and Ice Cream

Lemons and Citrons
Limes and
    Linden Trees
Lotus
Milk
Pears
Salt
Sesame
Spices
Turmeric
Water
Yogurt

TABOOS

Food taboos are bans or restrictions on the consumption of certain substances based on religious beliefs and concerns. In antiquity, they constituted an early form of moral code, and each society developed bans based on factors unique to its culture. In past times, people who adhered to food taboos maintained a belief in a world inhabited by spirits. They believed that if they broke certain rules, they would incur the wrath of the spirits and incite them to inflict disasters on the community, such as crop failure, famine, sickness, or death. Taboos often developed around plant foods thought to be connected with death and the underworld powers, with blood and flesh, or with totems or ancestors. Food taboos have existed since Neanderthal man walked the earth, and modern variants of ancient taboos continue to this day in every society. Today people may not call their food restrictions taboos; yet cultural mores of some societies have led to widely accepted bans on the consumption of foods such as dogs, cats, or insects.

See the following entries:

Beans	Horse
Beef	Meat
Blood and Flesh	Milk
Buffalo	Mulberries
Chicken	Onions and Leeks
Dog	Pomegranates
Eggplant	Pork
Eggs	Reindeer and
Fish	Caribou
Garlic	Turtle

TOTEMS

Totemism assumes the existence of a supernatural relationship between human beings and nonhuman forces, most often those embodied in plants or animals. People who embrace totemism believe they descended from a specific plant or animal (their particular totem), and they generally consider the eating of a totem akin to the eating of an ancestor. Such consumption would be a form of cannibalism—a nearly universal taboo. In most traditional totemic cultures, the respect people feel for their totems prevents them from killing and consuming them; yet in some societies and some places, totemism appears to have encouraged the ritualistic feasting on the particular totemic plant or animal. People in these societies believe that their bond to the totem is strengthened by the ritual, physical absorption of its virtues and life force. The existence of totemic societies attests to the widespread belief that a common soul or life force unites all living things. For this reason myths and legends frequently mention transformations among plants, animals, and human beings.

See the following entries:

Alligator and	Cucumbers
Crocodile	Deer
Bananas and	Dog
Plantains	Eggs
Baobab	Fish
Bear	Meat

BIBLIOGRAPHY

Abbott, John. *The Keys of Power: A Study of Indian Ritual and Belief*. London: Methuen, 1932.

Achaya, K. T. *Indian Food: A Historical Companion*. Delhi: Oxford University Press, 1994.

Albert-Puleo, Michael. "Mythobotany, Pharmacology, and Chemistry of Thujone-Containing Plants and Derivatives." *Economic Botany* 32, 1978, pp. 65–74.

Alexander, Hartley Burr. *Latin America*. Vol. 11, Mythology of All Races. Boston: Marshall Jones, 1964a.

———. *North America*. Vol. 10, Mythology of All Races. Boston: Marshall Jones, 1964b.

Anderson, A. W. *Plants of the Bible*. London: Crosby Lockwood & Son, 1956.

Anderson, E. N. *The Food of China*. New Haven, CT: Yale University Press, 1988.

Andrews, Alfred C. "The Bean and Indo-European Totemism." *American Anthropologist* 51, 1949, pp. 274–292.

Andrews, Tamra. *Legends of the Earth, Sea and Sky: An Encyclopedia of Nature Myths*. Santa Barbara, CA: ABC-CLIO, 1998.

Anesaki, Masahanu. *Japanese Mythology*. Vol. 8, Mythology of All Races. Boston: Marshall Jones, 1964.

Apicius. *Cookery and Dining in Imperial Rome*. Trans. Joseph Dommers Vehling. New York: Dover Publications, 1977.

Arhem, Kaj. "Maasai Food Symbolism: The Cultural Connotations of Milk, Meat, and Blood in the Pastoral Maasai Diet." *Anthropos* 84, 1989, pp. 1–23.

Arinze, Francis A. *Sacrifice in Ibo Religion*. Ibadan, Nigeria: Ibadan University Press, 1970.

Armstrong, Edward A. *The Folklore of Birds: An Enquiry into the Origin and Distribution of Some Magico-Religious Traditions*. Boston: Houghton Mifflin, 1959.

Arnott, M., ed. *Gastronomy: The Anthropology of Food and Food Habits*. The Hague: Mouton Publishing, 1975.

Athenaeus. *The Deipnosophists: A Chaotic Miscellany of Food in the Classical World*. 7 vols. Reprint. Cambridge, MA: Harvard University Press, 1951.

Austin, Alfredo Lopez. *The Rabbit on the Face of the Moon: Mythology in the Mesoamerican Tradition*. Salt Lake City: University of Utah Press, 1996.

Balik, Michael J., and Paul Alan Cox. *Plants, People and Culture: The Science of Ethnobotany*. New York: Scientific American Library, 1996.

Baring-Gold, Sabine. *Curious Myths of the Middle Ages*. London: Rivingtons, 1868.

Barooah, Pramila Pandit. *The Tale of Trees*. New Delhi: Ministry of Information and Broadcasting Government, 1992.

Basedow, Herbert. *The Australian Aboriginal*. Adelaide: F. W. Preece and Sons, 1925.

Basker, D., and M. Negbi. "Uses of Saffron." *Economic Botany* 37(2), 1983, pp. 228–236.

Batchelor, John. *Ainu Life and Lore: Echoes of a Departing Race*. Tokyo: Kyobunkkan, n.d.

Bates, Marston. "Insects in the Diet." *American Scholar* 29, 1959, pp. 43–52.

Baumann, Hellmut. *The Greek Plant World in Myth, Art and Literature*. Trans. William T. Stearn and Eldwyth Ruth Stearn. Portland, OR: Timber, 1993.

Bayley, Harold. *The Lost Language of Symbolism*. 2 vols. Philadelphia: J. B. Lippincott, 1913.

Beckwith, Martha. *Hawaiian Mythology*. Honolulu: University of Hawaii Press, 1970.

Benham, Harvey. *Man's Struggle for Food*. New York: University Press of America, 1981.

Bennett, Jennifer. *Lilies of the Hearth: The Historical Relationship between Women and Plants*. Camden East, Ontario: Camden House, 1991.

Bernhardt, Peter. *Natural Affairs: A Botanist Looks at the Attachments between Plants and People.* New York: Villard Books, 1993.

Bickerdyke, John. *The Curiosities of Ale and Beer.* Reprint. London: Spring Books, 1965.

Birrell, Anne. *Chinese Mythology: An Introduction.* Baltimore: Johns Hopkins University Press, 1993.

Blofeld, John. *The Chinese Art of Tea.* London: George Allen and Unwin, 1985.

Bolton, Ralph. "Guinea Pigs, Protein, and Ritual." *Ethnology* 18, 1979, pp. 229–252.

Brothwell, Don, and Patricia Brothwell. *Food in Antiquity: A Survey of the Diet of Early Peoples.* New York: Frederick A. Praeger, 1969.

Bruchac, Joseph. *Native Plant Stories.* Golden, CO: Fulcrum, 1995.

Bruman, H. J. "The Culture History of Mexican Vanilla." *Hispanic American Historical Review* 28, 1948, pp. 360–376.

Brundage, Burr Cartwright. *The Fifth Sun: Aztec Gods, Aztec World.* Austin: University of Texas Press, 1979.

Burkert, Walter. *Lore and Science in Ancient Pythagoreanism.* Trans. Edwin L. Minar, Jr. Cambridge, MA: Harvard University Press, 1972.

Caldecott, Moyra. *Myths of the Sacred Tree.* Rochester, NY: Destiny Books, 1993.

Campbell, Joseph. *Historical Atlas of World Mythology.* 2 vols. San Francisco: Harper and Row, 1988.

————. *The Masks of God.* 4 vols. Harmondsworth, England: Penguin, 1977.

Camporesi, Piero. *Juice of Life: The Symbolic and Magic Significance of Blood.* New York: Continuum, 1995.

————. *The Magic Harvest: Food, Folklore and Society.* Cambridge, MA: Polity, 1993.

Caporael, Linda R. "Ergotism: The Satan Loosed in Salem?" *Science* 192, 1976, pp. 21–26.

Carrasco, David. "Cosmic Jaws: We Eat the Gods and the Gods Eat Us." *Journal of the American Academy of Religion* 63(3), Fall 1995, pp. 429 (35 pp).

Casal, U. A. "Some Notes on the Sakazuki and on the Role of Sake Drinking in Japan." *Transactions of the Asiatic Society of Japan,* second series, vol. 19, 1940, pp. 1–186.

Caso, Alfonso. *The Aztecs: People of the Sun.* Norman: University of Oklahoma Press, 1958.

Casselman, Bill. "Leafing through Maple Lore." *Canadian Geographic* 117(5), Sept.-Oct. 1997, p. 25.

Cavendish, Richard, ed. *Man, Myth and Magic: An Illustrated Encyclopedia of the Supernatural.* 21 vols. New York: Marshall Cavendish, 1994.

Chang, K. C., ed. *Food in Chinese Culture: Anthropological and Historical Perspectives.* New Haven, CT: Yale University Press, 1978.

Charsley, Simon R. *Wedding Cakes and Cultural History.* New York: Routledge, 1992.

Christie, Anthony. *Chinese Mythology.* New York: Hamlyn, 1985.

Cobo, Father Bernabe. *Inca Religion and Customs.* Trans. and ed. Roland Hamilton. Austin: University of Texas Press, 1990.

Coe, Sophie D. *America's First Cuisines.* Austin: University of Texas Press, 1994.

Coe, Sophie D., and Michael Coe. *The True History of Chocolate.* New York: Thames and Hudson, 1996.

Cole, John N. *Amaranth: From the Past to the Future.* Emmaus, PA: Rodale, 1979.

Collins, J. L. "The Antiquity of the Pineapple in America." *Southwestern Journal of Anthropology,* vol. 7, 1951, pp. 145–155.

Condit, Ira J. *The Fig.* Waltham, MA: Chronica Botanica, 1947.

Conway. "Mystic Trees and Flowers." *Blackwood's Magazine,* 1870.

Cook, Roger. *The Tree of Life: Image of the Cosmos.* New York: Avon, 1974.

Cooper, J. C. *An Illustrated Encyclopedia of Traditional Symbols.* London: Thames and Hudson, 1978.

Courlander, Harold. *A Treasury of African Folklore: The Oral Literature, Traditions, Myths, Legends, Epics, Tales, Recollections, Wisdom, Sayings and Humor of Africa.* New York: Crown, 1975.

Cowan, Frank. *Curious Facts in the History of Insects.* Philadelphia: J. B. Lippincott, 1865.

Cox, Paul Alan, and Sandra Anne Banack, eds. *Islands, Plants and Polynesians: An Introduction to Polynesian Ethnobotany.* Portland, OR: Dioscorides, 1991.

Crawley, A. E. "Food." Pp. 59–63 in *Encyclopedia of Religion and Ethics,* ed. James Hastings. Edinburgh: T. and T. Clark, 1925.

Crawley, Ernest. *Dress, Drinks and Drums.* London: Methuen, 1931.

Crooke, W. "Food for the Dead." Pp. 65–68 in *Encyclopedia of Religion and Ethics,* ed. James Hastings. Edinburgh: T. and T. Clark, 1925.

Crooke, William. "Egg-plant–Potatoes–Onions: Unlucky." *Panjab Notes and Queries* 3(27), Dec. 1885, p. 41.

Crossley-Holland, Kevin. *The Norse Myths.* New York: Pantheon Books, 1980.

Dalby, Andrew. *Siren Feasts: A History of Food and Gastronomy in Greece.* New York: Routledge, 1996.

Dalziel, J. M. *The Useful Plants of West Tropical Africa.* London: Crown Agents for the Colonies, 1948.

Daniels, Cora Linn Morrison, ed. *Encyclopedia of Superstitions, Folklore, and the Occult Sciences of the World: A Comprehensive Library of Human Belief and Practice in the Mysteries of Life.* Detroit: Gale Research, 1971.

Darby, William, Paul Ghalioungui, and Louis Grivetti. *Food: The Gift of Osiris.* 2 vols. New York: Academic Press, 1977.

David, Elizabeth. *Harvest of the Cold Months: The Social History of Ice and Ices.* London: Michael Joseph, 1994.

Davidson, H. R. Ellis. *Myths and Symbols in Pagan Europe.* Manchester, England: Manchester University Press, 1988.

———. *Gods and Myths of Northern Europe.* New York: Penguin, 1973.

Davidson, James. *Courtesans and Fishcakes: The Consuming Passions of Classical Athens.* New York: HarperCollins, 1997.

Davis, F. Hadland. *Myths and Legends of Japan.* New York: Dover, 1992.

Day, Clarence. *Chinese Peasant Cults: Being a Study of Chinese Paper Gods.* Taipei: Ch'eng Wen, 1969.

de Groot, Jan Jakob Maria. *The Religious System of China, Its Ancient Forms, Evolution, History and Present Aspects, Manners, Customs and Social Institutions Connected Therewith.* 6 vols. Leiden, The Netherlands: E. J. Brill, 1892–1910.

de Groot, Roy Andries. "On the Trail of Bird's Nest Soup: Caves, Climbs and High Stakes." *Smithsonian* 14(6), Sept. 1983, pp. 66–77.

Deerr, Noel. *The History of Sugar.* 2 vols. London: Chapman and Hall, 1949.

DeLys, Claudia. *A Treasury of Superstitions.* New York: Gramercy, 1997.

Detienne, M. *The Gardens of Adonis: Spices in Greek Mythology.* Trans. Janet Lloyd. Hassocks, Sussex: Harvester, 1977.

Detienne, M., and Jean-Pierre Vernant. *The Cuisine of Sacrifice among the Greeks.* Transl. Paula Wissing. Chicago: University of Chicago Press, 1989.

Dickson, P. *The Great American Ice Cream Book.* New York: Atheneum, 1972.

Dixon, Roland Burrage. *Oceanic Mythology.* Vol. 9, Mythology of All Races. Boston: Marshall Jones, 1964.

Dobkin De Rios, Marlene. *The Wilderness of Mind: Sacred Plants in Cross-Cultural Perspective.* Beverly Hills, CA: Sage, 1976.

———. "The Influence of Psychotropic Flora and Fauna on Maya Religion." *Current Anthropology* 15(2), 1974, pp. 142–164.

Dodge, Bertha S. *It Started in Eden: How the Plant-Hunters and the Plants They Found Changed the Course of History.* New York: McGraw-Hill, 1979.

Donkin, R. A. *Manna: A Historical Geography.* Vol. 17, Biogeographica. The Hague and Boston: W. Junk, 1980.

Dorson, Richard M., ed. *Studies in Japanese Folklore.* Bloomington: Indiana University Press, 1963.

Driberg, Tom. "Food and Drink." Pp. 926–933 in *Man, Myth and Magic,* ed. Richard Cavendish, vol. 7. New York: Marshall Cavendish Corp., 1994.

Dumont, Darl J. "The Ash Tree in Indo-European Culture." *Mankind Quarterly* 32, 1992, pp. 323–336.

Duran, Fray Diego. *Book of the Gods and Rites* and *The Ancient Calendar.* Norman: University of Oklahoma Press, 1971.

Eberhard, Wolfram. *Folktales of China.* Chicago: University of Chicago Press, 1965.

Edmonds, Margot, and Ella E. Clark. *Voices of the Winds.* New York: Facts on File, 1989.

Egerton, March. *Since Eve Ate Apples: Quotations of Feasting, Fasting and Food from the Beginning.* Portland, OR: Tsunami, 1994.

Eliade, Mircea, ed. *Encyclopedia of Religion.* 16 vols. New York: Macmillan, 1987.

———. *A History of Religious Ideas.* Vol. 1: *From the Stone Age to the Eleusinian Mysteries.* Chicago: University of Chicago Press, 1978.

———. *Patterns in Comparative Religion.* New York: Sheed and Ward, 1958.

Elkhort, Martin. *The Secret Life of Food: A Fest of Food and Drink in History, Folklore, etc.* New York: St. Martin's, 1991.

Farb, Peter, and George Armelagos. *Consuming Passions: The Anthropology of Eating.* Boston: Houghton Mifflin, 1980.

Feeley-Harnik, Gillian. *The Lord's Table: The Meaning of Food in Early Judaism and Christianity.* Washington, DC: Smithsonian Institution Press. 1994.

Ferguson, John Calvin. *Chinese Mythology.* Vol. 8, Mythology of All Races. Boston: Marshall Jones, 1964.

Fieldhouse, Paul. *Food and Nutrition: Customs and Culture.* London: Chapman and Hall, 1995.

Firth, Raymond. *Primitive Polynesian Economy.* London: Routledge & Sons, 1939.

Folkard, Richard. *Plant-lore Legends and Lyrics: Myths, Traditions, Superstitions and Folk-lore of the Plant Kingdom.* London: Sampson Low, Marston, 1892.

"Folklore of British Plants." *Dublin University Magazine,* Sept.r 1873, p. 318.

Fontana, David. *The Secret Language of Symbols.* San Francisco: Chronicle, 1994.

Foster, Michael Kirk. "From the Earth to Beyond the Sky: An Ethnographic Approach to Four Longhouses Iroquois Speech Events." Ph.D. dissertation, University of Pennsylvania, 1974.

Foster, Nelson, and Linda S. Cordell. *Chiles to Chocolate: Food the Americas Gave the World.* Tucson: University of Arizona Press, 1992.

Fox, William Sherwood, ed. *Mythology of All Races.* 13 vols. New York: Cooper Square, 1964.

Frazer, James George, Sir. *The Golden Bough: A Study in Magic and Religion.* New York: Macmillan, 1950.

———. *Totemism and Exogamy: A Treatise on Certain Early Forms of Superstition and Society.* 4 vols. London: Macmillan, 1910.

Fredman, Ruth Gruber. *The Passover Seder: Afrikomon in Exile*. Philadelphia: University of Pennsylvania Press, 1981.

Freeman, Mara. "The Celtic Tree of Life." *Parabola* 24, Spring 1999, p. 59.

Fuller, John C. *The Day of Saint Anthony's Fire*. New York: Macmillan, 1968.

Fuller, Linda K. *Chocolate Fads, Folklore, and Fantasies: 1,000+ Chunks of Chocolate Information*. New York: Hawthorn, 1994.

Fuller, Robert C. *Religion and Wine: A Cultural History of Wine Drinking in the United States*. Knoxville: University of Tennessee Press, 1996.

Funk and Wagnall's Standard Dictionary of Folklore, Mythology and Legend. Ed. Maria Leach. New York: Harper and Row, 1972.

Fussell, Betty Harper. *The Story of Corn*. New York: Alfred A. Knopf, 1992.

Gamble, Eliza Burt. *The God Idea of the Ancients*. New York: G. P. Putnam's Sons, 1897.

Garnsey, Peter. *Food and Society in Classical Antiquity*. New York: Cambridge University Press, 1999.

Gay, Kathlyn, and Martin K. Gay. *Encyclopedia of North American Eating and Drinking Traditions, Customs and Rituals*. Santa Barbara, CA: ABC-CLIO, 1996.

Gentry, Howard Scott. *Agaves of Continental North America*. Tucson: University of Arizona Press, 1982.

Gill, Sam D., and Irene G. Sullivan. *Dictionary of Native American Mythology*. Denver: ABC-CLIO, 1992.

Gimbutas, Marija. *The Goddesses and Gods of Old Europe, 6500–3500 B.C.: Myths and Cult Images*. Berkeley: University of California Press, 1982.

Glants, Musya, and Joyce Toomre, eds. *Food in Russian History and Culture*. Bloomington: Indiana University Press, 1997.

Glasgow, Vaughn L. *A Social History of the American Alligator: The Earth Trembles with His Thunder*. New York: St. Martin's, 1991.

Goldsmith, Elisabeth. *Ancient Pagan Symbols*. New York: G. P. Putnam's Sons, 1929.

Gonda, J. *The Functions and Significance of Gold in the Veda*. New York: E. J. Brill, 1991.

———. *Rice and Barley Offerings in the Veda*. New York: E. J. Brill, 1987.

———. *The Ritual Functions and Significance of Grasses on the Religion of the Veda*. New York: North-Holland, 1985.

Goor, Asaph. "The Place of the Olive in the Holy Land and Its History through the Ages." *Economic Botany* 20, 1966, pp. 223–243.

Goor, Asaph, and Max Nurock. *The Fruits of the Holy Land*. Jerusalem, New York: Israel Universities Press, 1968.

Gott, Philip P. *All about Candy and Chocolate*. Chicago: National Confectioners Association of the United States, 1958.

Gottesman, Jane. "An Ancient Field of Dreams (Greece's Nemean Games.)" *Sports Illustrated* 85(6), Aug. 1996, p. 6B.

Graves, Robert. *The Greek Myths*. Reprint. Mt. Kisco, NY: Penguin, 1988.

———. "Mushrooms, Food of the Gods." *Atlantic Monthly* 200(2), August 1957, pp. 73–77.

Green, Miranda *Celtic Myths*. Austin: University of Texas Press, 1993.

———. *Animals in Celtic Life and Myth*. New York: Routledge, 1992a.

———. *Dictionary of Celtic Myth and Legend*. London: Thames and Hudson, 1992b.

Greimas, Algirdas H. *Of Gods and Men: Studies in Lithuanian Mythology*. Indianapolis: Indiana University Press, 1992.

Grieve, M. A *Modern Herbal*. 2 vols. London: Hafner, 1967.

Grosser, William H. *Scripture Natural History*. N.p., Religious Tract Society, 1888.

Gupta, Shakti M. *Plant Myths and Traditions in India*. New Delhi: Munshiram Manoharlal, 1991.

Hamblin, Nancy L. *Animal Use by the Cozumel Maya*. Tucson: University of Arizona Press, 1984.

Harlan, Jack R. *Crops and Man*. Madison, WI: American Society of Agronomy, 1975.

Harris, Marvin. *The Sacred Cow and the Abominable Pig: Riddles of Food and Culture*. New York: Simon and Schuster, 1985.

———. *Cannibals and Kings: The Origins of Culture*. New York: Random House, 1977.

Harris, Thaddeus. *Natural History of the Bible: Or a Description of All the Beasts, Birds, Fishes, Insects, Reptiles, Trees, Plants, Metals, Precious Stones, etc. Mentioned in the Holy Scriptures*. Boston: I. Thomas and E. T. Andrews, 1793.

Hartmann, H. T., and P. G. Bougas. "Olive Production in Greece." *Economic Botany* 24, 1970, pp. 443–459.

Harva, U. "Finno-Ugric Mythology." In *Mythology of All Races*, ed. William Sherwood Fox. New York: Cooper Square, 1964.

Hastings, James, ed. *Encyclopedia of Religion and Ethics*. Edinburgh: T. and T. Clark, 1925.

Heffern, Richard. *The Complete Book of Ginseng*. Millbrae, CA: Celestial Arts, 1974.

Heiser, Charles B., Jr. *Of Plants and People*. Norman: University of Oklahoma Press, 1985.

———. *Seed to Civilization: The Story of Man's Food*. San Francisco: W. H. Freeman, 1981.

———. *The Gourd Book*. Norman: University of Oklahoma Press, 1979.

———. *Nightshades: The Paradoxical Plants.* San Francisco: W. H. Freeman, 1969.

Hewitt, J. F. *Primitive Traditional History.* 2 vols. London: James Parker and Co., 1907.

Hoffpauir, Robert. "The Water Buffalo: India's Other Bovine." *Anthropos* 77, 1982, pp. 215–238.

Holmberg, Uno. *Siberian Mythology.* Vol. 4, Mythology of All Races. Boston: Marshall Jones, 1964.

Hopkins, E. Washburn. *Epic Mythology.* Delhi: Indological Book House, 1968.

Howey, M. Oldfield. *The Horse in Magic and Myth.* London: W. Rider, 1923.

Hu, William C. *The Chinese Mid-Autumn Festival: Foods and Folklore.* Ann Arbor, MI: Ars Ceramica, 1996.

———. *Chinese New Year: Fact and Folklore.* Ann Arbor, MI: Ars Ceramica, 1991.

Hume, Harold. *Citrus Fruits and Their Culture.* New York: Orange Judd, 1907.

Hyams, Edward. *Plants in the Service of Man.* New York: J. B. Lippincott, 1971.

Isaac, Erich. "The Influence of Religion on the Spread of Citrus." *Science* 129, 1959, pp. 179–186.

Jacob, H. E. *The Tree of Life.* Leiden, The Netherlands: E. J. Brill, 1966.

———. *Six Thousand Years of Bread: Its Holy and Unholy History.* New York: Doubleday, 1944.

Jensen, Adolf E. *Myth and Cult among Primitive People.* Trans. M. T. Choldin and W. Weissleter. Chicago: University of Chicago Press, 1963.

Jobes, Gertrude. *Dictionary of Mythology, Folklore and Symbols.* 2 vols. New York: Scarecrow, 1962.

Jones, Alison. *Larousse Dictionary of World Folklore.* New York: Larousse, 1995.

Jones, E. "The Symbolic Significance of Salt in Folklore and Superstition." In *Essays in Applied Psycho-Analysis,* vol. II. New York: International Universities Press, 1964.

Jones, William O. *Manioc in Africa.* Stanford, CA: Stanford University Press, 1959.

Juengst, Sara C. *Breaking Bread: The Spiritual Significance of Food.* Louisville, KY: Westminster/ John Knox, 1992.

Kahn, E. J., Jr. *The Staffs of Life.* Boston: Little, Brown, 1985.

Kavaler, Lucy. *Mushrooms, Molds and Miracles: The Strange Realm of Fungi.* New York: John Day, 1965.

Keith, A. Berriedale. *Indian Mythology.* Vol. 6, Mythology of All Races. Boston: Marshall Jones, 1964.

Kerenyi, Carl. *Dionysos: Archetypal Images of Indestructible Life.* Princeton, NJ: Princeton University Press, 1976.

Kernan, Michael. "Around the Mall and Beyond." [Column.] (Smithsonian Associates Program on Spices) *Smithsonian* 27(12), Mar. 1997, p. 22.

Khare, R. S. *Culture and Reality: Essays on the Hindu System of Managing Foods.* Simla: Indian Institute of Advanced Study, 1976.

Khare, R. S., ed. *The Eternal Food: Gastronomic Ideas and Experiences of Hindus and Buddhists.* Albany: State University of New York Press, 1992.

Kimmins, Andrew, ed. *Tales of Ginseng.* New York: Morrow, 1977.

Kleijn, H. *Mushrooms and Other Fungi: Their Form and Colour.* New York: Doubleday, 1965.

Knappert, Jan. *African Mythology: An Encyclopedia of Myth and Legend.* London: Diamond Books, 1995a.

———. *Indian Mythology: An Encyclopedia of Myth and Legend.* London: Diamond Books, 1995b.

———. *Pacific Mythology: An Encyclopedia of Myth and Legend.* London: Diamond Books, 1995c.

Kull, A. Stoddard. *Secrets of Flowers: The Message and Meaning of Every Flower.* Brattleboro, VT: Stephen Greene, 1976.

Langdon, Stephen H. *Semitic Mythology.* Vol. 5, Mythology of All Races. Boston: Marshall Jones, 1964.

Leach, Maria. *God Had a Dog: Folklore of the Dog.* New Brunswick, NH: Rutgers University Press, 1961.

Leeds, Anthony, and Andrew Vayda. *Man, Culture and Animals.* Washington, D.C.: American Association for the Advancement of Science (Publication No. 78), 1965.

Lehner, Ernst, and Johanna Lehner. *Folklore and Odysseys of Food and Medicinal Plants.* New York: Farrar, Straus and Giroux, 1973.

———. *Folklore and Symbolism of Flowers, Plants and Trees.* New York: Tudor, 1960.

Levi-Strauss, Claude. *The Naked Man.* London: J. Cape, 1981.

———. *The Origin of Table Manners.* New York: Harper and Row, 1978.

———. *From Honey to Ashes.* New York: Harper and Row, 1974.

———. *The Raw and the Cooked.* New York: Harper and Row, 1970.

London, Bill. "Transplant in the Rockies." *Americas* (English edition) 39, May-June 1987, p. 38(4).

Lowenstein, Tom. *Ancient Land, Sacred Whale: The Inuit Hunt and Its Rituals.* New York: Farrar, Straus and Giroux, 1994.

Lowy, Bernard. "Amanita muscaria and the Thunderbolt Legend in Guatemala and Mexico." *Mycologia* 66(1), 1974, pp. 188–191.

———. "Mushroom Symbolism in Maya Codices." *Mycologia* 64, 1972, pp. 816–821.

Lu, Yu. *The Classic of Tea.* Trans. Francis Ross Carpenter. Boston: Little, Brown, 1974.

Lysaght, Patricia, ed. *Milk and Milk Products from Medieval to Modern Times.* Ninth International Conference on Ethnological Food Research. Edinburgh: Canongate Academic, 1994.

MacCullough, John A. *Eddic Mythology.* Vol. 2, Mythology of All Races. Boston: Marshall Jones, 1964.

MacDonald, Margaret R., ed. *The Folklore of World Holidays.* Detroit: Gale Research, 1991.

MacFarlan, Allan, ed.. *Fireside Book of North American Indian Folktales.* Harrisburg, PA: Stackpole Books, 1974.

———. *American Indian Legends.* Los Angeles: Ward Ritchie, 1968.

MacKay, Alistair. *Farming and Gardening in the Bible.* Emmaus, PA: Rodale, 1950.

Mackenzie, Donald A. *Myths of China and Japan.* Reprint. New York : Random House, 1994.

———. *The Migration of Symbols and Their Relations to Beliefs and Customs.* Reprint. New York: AMS Press, 1970.

Mahias, Marie-Claude. "Milk and Its Transmutations in Indian Society." *Food and Foodways* 2, 1988, pp. 265–288.

Majupuria, Trilok Chandra. *Religious and Useful Plants of Nepal and India.* Lashkar, Gwalior, India: M. Gupta, 1988.

Majupuria, Trilok Chandra, and Indra Majupuria. *Sacred and Useful Plants and Trees of Nepal.* Kathmandu, Nepal: Sahayogi Prakashan Tripureswar, 1978.

Manguson, John. "Sugaring Time: A Reflection on Nature and Sacrament." *Christian Century* 114(10), March 19, 1997, pp. 292–295.

Marshall, Mac, ed. *Beliefs, Behaviors and Alcoholic Beverages: A Cross-Cultural Survey.* Ann Arbor: University of Michigan Press, 1979.

Mason, J. Alden. *The Ancient Civilizations of Peru.* Harmondsworth, England: Penguin, 1957.

McDonald, Lucile. *Garden Sass: The Story of Vegetables.* New York: Thomas Nelson, 1971.

McKenna, Terence. *Food of the Gods: The Search for the Original Tree of Knowledge.* New York: Bantam Books, 1992.

Mercatante, Anthony. *The Magic Garden: The Myth and Folklore of Flowers, Plants, Trees and Herbs.* New York: Harper and Row, 1976.

———. *Zoo of the Gods: Animals in Myth, Legend and Fable.* New York: Harper and Row, 1974.

Miller, Mary, and Karl Taube. *Gods and Symbols of Ancient Mexico and the Maya.* London: Thames and Hudson, 1993.

Mirov, Nicholas T., and Jean Hasbrouck. *The Story of Pines.* Bloomington: Indiana University Press, 1976.

Moldenke, H. N., and A. L. Moldenke. *Plants of the Bible.* Waltham, MA: Chronica Botanica, 1952.

Montanari, Massimo. *Culture of Food.* Oxford: Blackwell, 1994.

Montellano, Bernard R. Ortiz. *Aztec Medicine, Health and Nutrition.* London: Rutgers University Press, 1990.

Morales, Edmundo. *The Guinea Pig: Healing, Food, and Ritual in the Andes.* Tucson: University of Arizona Press, 1995.

Morgan, Adrian. *Toads and Toadstools: The Natural History, Folklore, and Cultural Oddities of a Strange Association.* Berkeley, CA: Celestial Arts, 1995.

Mortimer, W. Golden. *History of Coca, the "Divine Plant" of the Incas.* Reprint. San Francisco: And/Or, 1974.

Muller, Max. *Egyptian Mythology.* Vol. 12, Mythology of All Races. Boston: Marshall Jones, 1964.

Nelson, John K. *A Year in the Life of a Shinto Shrine.* Seattle: University of Washington Press, 1996.

Neumann, Erich. *The Great Mother: An Analysis of the Archetype.* New York: Pantheon, 1955.

New Larousse Encyclopedia of Mythology. New York: Prometheus, 1968.

Newall, Venetia. *An Egg at Easter: A Folklore Study.* Bloomington: Indiana University Press, 1971.

Niethammer, Carolyn. *American Indian Food and Lore.* New York: Macmillan, 1974.

Norman, Barbara. *Tales of the Table: A History of Western Cuisine.* Englewood Cliffs, NJ: Prentice-Hall, 1972.

Okakura, Kakuzo. *The Book of Tea.* Tokyo: Kairyudo, 1939.

Olcott, Frances Jenks. *Wonder Garden: Nature Myths and Tales from All the World Over.* Boston: Houghton Mifflin, 1919.

Orbell, Margaret. *Illustrated Encyclopedia of Maori Myth and Legend.* Sydney: University of New South Wales Press, 1996.

Osborne, Harold. *South American Mythology.* London: Hamlyn, 1983.

Otto, Walter F. *Dionysus: Myth and Cult.* Bloomington: Indiana University Press, 1965.

Owen, John. "The Medico-Social and Cultural Significance of the (Baobab) in African Communities." *African Notes* (Ibadan) 6, 1970, pp. 24–36.

Oxford Dictionary of Plant-Lore. Comp. Roy Vickory. New York: Oxford University Press, 1995.

Pandey, Brahma Prakash. *Sacred Plants of India.* New Delhi: Shree, 1989.

Parrinder, Geoffrey. *African Mythology.* New York: Peter Bedrick, 1982.

Pavlik, Steve. "The Role of Bears and Bear Ceremonialism in Navajo Orthodox Traditional

Lifeway. *The Social Science Journal.* 34(4), October 1997, p. 475(10).

Penzer, N. M., ed. *The Ocean of Story, Being C. H. Tawney's Translation of Somadeva's Katha Sarit Sagara.* 10 vols. London [privately published], 1924–1928.

Perry, W. J. *The Primordial Ocean: An Introductory Contribution to Social Psychology.* London: Methuen, 1935.

Phallic Tree Worship. Varanasi, India: Bharat-Bharati, 1971.

Philpot, J. H., Mrs. *The Sacred Tree.* London: Macmillan, 1897.

Piggott, Juliet. *Japanese Mythology.* Reprint. New York: Peter Bedrick, 1997.

Pliny the Elder. *Natural History: A Selection.* Trans. John F. Healy. New York: Penguin, 1991.

Poignant, Roslyn. *Oceanic Mythology.* London: Hamlyn, 1967.

Porteous, Alexander. *Forest Folklore, Mythology and Romance.* Reprint. Detroit: Singing Tree, 1968.

Prakash, Om. *Food and Drinks in Ancient India.* Delhi: Munshiram Manoharlal, 1961.

Rabbitt, James A. "Rice in the Cultural Life of the Japanese People." *Transactions of the Asiatic Society of Japan,* second series, vol. 19, 1940, pp. 187–253.

Rappoport, Roy A. *Pigs for the Ancestors: Ritual in the Ecology of a New Guinea People.* New Haven, CT: Yale University Press, 1968.

Ratsch, Christian. *Dictionary of Sacred and Magical Plants.* Santa Barbara, CA: ABC-CLIO, 1992.

Ravel, Jean-Francois. *Culture and Cuisine: A Journey through the History of Food.* New York: Doubleday, 1982.

Reed, Mary. *Fruits and Nuts in Symbolism and Celebration.* San Jose, CA: Resource Publications, 1992.

Ricciuti, Edward R. *The Devil's Garden: Facts and Folklore of Perilous Plants.* New York: Walker and Co., 1978.

Robbins, Peggy. "Yard Dog of the South: The Alligator in Wetlands Legend." *World and I,* July 14, 1999, p. 234.

Robertiello, Jack. "Vanilla." *Americas* (English edition) 44(1), 1987, p. 58.

Robertson, Noel. *Festivals and Legends: The Formation of Greek Cities in the Light of Public Ritual.* Toronto: University of Toronto Press, 1992.

Rogers, Peggy Ellen. "A Supergrain for the Future: Revival in the Andes." *Americas* (English edition) 39, May-June 1987, p. 36(3).

Rolleston, T. W. *Celtic Mythology.* London: Bracken Books, 1990.

Rolph, George M. *Something about Sugar: Its History, Growth, Manufacture and Distribution.* San Francisco: John J. Newbegin, 1917.

Rosenblum, Mort. *Olives: The Life and Lore of a Noble Fruit.* New York: North Point, 1996.

Rosengarten, Frederic. *The Book of Edible Nuts.* New York: Walker, 1984.

Rubel, Paula G., and Abraham Rosman. *Your Own Pigs You May Not Eat: A Comparative Study of New Guinea Societies.* Chicago: University of Chicago Press, 1978.

Ruck, Carl. "The Wild and the Cultivated in Greek Religion." In *On Nature,* ed. Leroy S. Rouner. Notre Dame, IN: University of Notre Dame Press, 1984.

Sauer, Carl O. *Agricultural Origins and Dispersals.* New York: American Geographical Society, 1952.

Sauer, Jonathan D. *Historical Geography of Crop Plants: A Select Roster.* Boca Raton, FL: CRC Press, 1994.

Schafer, Edward H. *The Golden Peaches of Samarkand: A Study of T'ang Exotics.* Berkeley: University of California Press, 1963.

Schivelbusch, Wolfgang. *Tastes of Paradise: A Social History of Spices, Stimulants and Intoxicants.* New York: Pantheon, 1992.

Schleiffer, Hedwig. *Sacred Narcotic Plants of the New World Indians: An Anthology of Texts from the 16th Century to Date.* New York: Hafner, 1973.

Schultes, Richard Evans. "The Beta Carotene Hallucinogens of South America." *Journal of Psychoactive Drugs* 14(3), 1982, pp. 205–220.

Schultes, Richard Evans, and Albert Hofmann. *Plants of the Gods: Origins of Hallucinogenic Use.* New York: McGraw-Hill, 1979.

Schultes, Richard Evans, and Siri von Reis. *Ethnobotany: Evolution of a Discipline.* Portland, OR: Dioscorides, 1995.

Sen Gupta, Sankar. *Sacred Trees across Cultures and Nations.* Calcutta: Indian Publications, 1980.

———. *Tree Symbol Worship in India.* Calcutta: Indian Publications, 1965.

Sharma, B. V. V. S. R. *The Study of the Cow in Sanskrit Literature.* Delhi: GDK Publications, 1980.

Simoons, Frederick J. *Plants of Life, Plants of Death.* Madison: University of Wisconsin Press, 1998.

———. *Eat Not This Flesh: Food Avoidances from Prehistory to the Present.* 2d ed. Madison: University of Wisconsin Press, 1994.

———. *Food in China: A Cultural and Historical Inquiry.* Boca Raton, FL: CRC Press, 1991.

———. "Fish as Forbidden Food: The Case of India." *Ecology of Food and Nutrition* 3, 1974a, pp. 185–201.

———. "The Purificatory Role of the Five Products of the Cow in Hinduism." *Ecology of Food and Nutrition* 3, 1974b, pp. 21–34.

———. "Rejection of Fish as Human Food in Africa: A Problem in History and Ecology." *Ecology of Food and Nutrition* 3, 1974c, pp. 89–105.

———. *A Ceremonial Ox of India: The Mithan in Nature, Culture and History.* Madison: University of Wisconsin Press, 1968.

Skinner, Charles M. *Myths and Legends of Flowers, Trees, Fruits and Plants.* Philadelphia: J. B. Lippincott, n.d.

Slive, Daniel J. *A Harvest Gathered: Food in the New World.* Providence, RI: J. C. Brown Library, 1989.

Smartt, J., and M. W. Simmonds, eds. *Evolution of Crop Plants.* 2d ed. London: Longman, 1995.

Smith, Andrew F. *The Tomato in America: Early History, Culture and Cookery.* Columbia: University of South Carolina Press, 1994.

Sopher, David E. "Indigenous Uses of Turmeric (Curcuma domestica) in Asia and Oceania." *Anthropos* 59, 1964, pp. 93–127.

Soyer, Alexis. *The Pantropheon: Or a History of Food and Its Preparation in Ancient Times.* New York: Paddington, 1977.

Spence, Lewis. *Myths and Legends of the North American Indians.* New York: Dover, 1989.

Spruce, Richard. *Notes of a Botanist on the Amazon and Rio Negro.* Ed. A. R. Wallace. London: Macmillan, 1980.

Srinivasan, Doris. *Concept of Cow in the Rig Veda.* Delhi: Motilal Banarsidass, 1979.

Staal, Julius D. W. *The New Patterns in the Sky: Myths and Legends of the Stars.* Blacksburg, VA: McDonald & Woodward, 1988.

———. *Stars of Jade: Astronomy and Star Lore of the Very Ancient Imperial China.* Decatur, GA: Writ, 1984.

Talbot, P. Amaury. *Some Nigerian Fertility Cults.* London: Oxford University Press, 1967.

Tannahill, Reay. *Flesh and Blood: A History of the Cannibal Complex.* New York: Stein and Day, 1975.

———. *Food in History.* New York: Stein and Day, 1973.

Taube, Karl. *Aztec and Mayan Myths.* Austin: University of Texas Press, 1993.

Thiselton-Dyer, T. F. *The Folklore of Plants.* Reprint. Detroit: Singing Tree, 1968.

Thompson, C. J. S. *The Mystic Mandrake.* Reprint. Detroit: Gale Research, 1975.

Thompson, Eric S. *Maya History and Religion.* Norman: University of Oklahoma Press, 1970.

Tolkowsky, S. *Hesperides: A History of the Culture and Use of Citrus Fruits.* London: John Bale, Sons & Curnow, 1938.

Toussaint-Samat, Maguelonne. *History of Food.* Trans. Anthea Bell. Cambridge, MA: Basil Blackwell, 1992.

Turville-Petre, Gabriel. *Myth and Religion of the North: The Religion of Ancient Scandinavia.* New York: Holt, Rinehart and Winston, 1964.

Tyler, Hamilton A. *Pueblo Animals and Myths.* Norman: University of Oklahoma Press, 1975.

Tylor, Edward, Sir. *Researches into the Early History of Mankind.* Chicago: University of Chicago Press, 1964.

———. *Primitive Culture.* New York: Harper, 1958.

Tyrrell, William Blake, and Frieda S. Brown. *Athenian Myths and Institutions: Words in Action.* New York: Oxford University Press, 1991.

Ukers, William H.. "All About Tea." *The Tea and Coffee Trade Journal,* 1935.

———. "All About Coffee." *The Tea and Coffee Trade Journal,* 1922.

Utenkova, Yelena. "Hold the Maple Syrup: These Are Bliny." *Russian Life* 39(3), Mar, 1996, p. 32.

Vaillant, George C. *The Aztecs of Mexico.* New York: Doubleday, 1962.

Van Laan, Nancy. *The Magic Bean Tree: A Legend from Argentina.* New York: Houghton Mifflin, 1998.

Vernant, Jean-Pierre. "The Myth of Prometheus in Hesiod." In *Myth, Religion and Society: Structuralist Essays by M. Detienne, L. Gernet, J.-P. Vernant and P. Vidal-Naquet,* ed. R. L. Gordon. New York: Cambridge University Press, 1981a.

———. "Sacrificial and Alimentary Codes in Hesiod's Myth of Prometheus." In *Myth, Religion and Society,* 1981b.

Verrill, A. Hyatt. *Perfumes and Spices: Including an Account of Soaps and Cosmetics.* Boston: L. C. Page, 1940.

———. *Foods America Gave the World.* Boston: L. C. Page, 1937.

Villiers, Elizabeth. *The Good Luck Book.* Reprint. London: Studio Editions, 1994.

Visser, Margaret. *Much Depends on Dinner: The Extraordinary History and Mythology, Allure and Obsessions, Perils and Taboos of an Ordinary Meal.* New York: Macmillan, 1986.

Voeks, Robert. "African Medicine and Magic in the Americas." *Geographical Review* 83(1), Jan. 1993, p. 66(13).

Von Kahler Gumpert, Anita. "One Potato, Two Potato." *Americas* (English edition) 38(3), May–June 1986, pp. 35–39.

Walker, Benjamin. *The Hindu World.* 2 vols. New York: Frederick A. Praeger, 1968.

Walker, James R. *Lakota Belief and Ritual.* Lincoln: University of Nebraska Press, 1980.

Walker, Winifred. *All the Plants of the Bible.* New York: Doubleday, 1979.

Walter, F. Otto. *Dionysus: Myth and Cult.* Trans. Robert B. Palmer. Bloomington: Indiana University Press, 1965.

Wasson, R. Gordon. "The Last Meal of the Buddha." *Journal of the American Oriental Society* 102, 1982, pp. 591–603.

———. *Soma: Divine Mushroom of Immortality.* New York: Harcourt Brace Jovanovich, 1972.

BIBLIOGRAPHY

Wasson, R. Gordon, Carl A. Ruck, and Albert Hofmann. *The Road to Eleusis: Unveiling the Secret of the Mysteries.* New York: Harcourt Brace Jovanovich, 1978.

Waters, Frank. *Book of the Hopi.* New York: Viking, 1963.

Wellman, Frederick L. *Coffee, Botany, Cultivation and Utilization.* London: Leonard Hill, 1961.

Weltfish, Gene. *The Lost Universe: Pawnee Life and Culture.* Lincoln: University of Nebraska Press, 1965.

Werner, Alice. *African Mythology.* Vol. 7, Mythology of All Races. Boston: Marshall Jones, 1964.

Werner, Edward T. C. *Ancient Tales and Folklore of China.* Reprint. London: Senate, 1995.

Westfahl, Gary, George Slusser, and Eric S. Rabkin, eds. *Food of the Gods: Eating and the Eaten in Fantasy and Science Fiction.* Athens: University of Georgia Press, 1996.

White, Florence. *Flowers as Food: Receipts and Lore from Many Sources.* London: J. Cape, 1934.

Wilkins, John, David Harvey, and Mike Dobson eds. *Food in Antiquity.* Exeter, England: University of Exeter Press, 1995.

Williams, C. A. S. *Outlines of Chinese Symbolism and Art Motifs: An Alphabetical Compendium of Antique Legends and Beliefs, as Reflected in the Manners and Customs of the Chinese.* Rutland, VT: C. E. Tuttle, 1974.

Willis, Roy, ed. *World Mythology.* New York: Henry Holt, 1993.

Wilson, C. Anne. *Food and Drink in Britain from the Stone Age to the 19th Century.* Reprint. Chicago: Academy Chicago Publications, 1991.

Winzen, Damasus. *Symbols of Christ: The Old Testament, The New Testament.* New York: P. J. Kennedy, 1955.

Wittstock, Laura Waterman. *Ininatig's Gift of Sugar: Traditional Native Sugarmaking.* Minneapolis: Lerner, 1993.

Wood, Rebecca. *Quinoa the Supergrain: Ancient Food for Today.* New York: Japan Publications, 1989.

Yerkes, Royden Keith. *Sacrifice in Greek and Roman Religions and Early Judaism.* New York: Charles Scribner's Sons, 1952.

Young, Allen M. *The Chocolate Tree: A Natural History of Cacao.* Washington, DC: Smithsonian Institution Press, 1994.

Young, Gordon. "Chocolate, Food for the Gods." *National Geographic* 166(5), 1984, pp. 664–687.

Zuckerman, Larry. *The Potato: How the Humble Spud Rescued the Western World.* Boston: Faber and Faber, 1998.

BIBLIOGRAPHY

INDEX

Abraham, 250

Abundance, 47, 67, 76, 91, 94, 109, 133, 184, 188, 199

Acorns, **1–2**, 147

Adam, 10, 79, 146, 183

Adapa, 157

Adonis, 107, 131, 183, 245

Adonis, Gardens of, 245

Aegir, 33, 144

Aesir, 143

Africa, **253**. *See also* Bushmen; Congo; Ethiopia; Masai; Morocco; Nigeria; Rhodesia; Volta; Yoruba

Agatha, Saint, 237

Agave. *See* Pulque

Agni, 34, 46, 47, 100, 149

Agras (Agroi), 232

Agricultural observances, 20, 34, 52, 107, 109, 133, 199, 231, 245, 250

Agrippa, 154

Ahimsa, 4, 31, 44, 85, 93, 145

Ahura Mazda, 83, 99, 106

Ainu, 28, 29, 30, 46, 54, 82, 207

Alcoholic beverages, **2**, **3**(illus.), **4**, 49, 56, 61–62, 65

Aleuts, 84

Alexander the Great, 121

Algonquin, 141, 143, 233

All Hallows' Eve. *See* Halloween

All Souls' Day, 7, 54, 97, 174–175

Alligator and crocodile, **4–5**

Almonds, **5–6**, 55, 182

Amaranth, **6–7**, 42

Amaterasu, 200, 207

Ambrosia. *See* Nectar and ambrosia

Amrita, 46, 148, 158

Andean peoples, 66–68, 111–112, 121, 138, 186, 192, 227, 229. *See also* Incas; Peru

Anointing, 12, 163, 211

Anta, 200

Anu, 141

Aphrodisiacs, **259**. *See also* Love charms; Love potions

Aphrodite, 8, 11, 97, 131, 135, 173, 192, 210, 211, 245

Apollo, 79, 163, 165, 238

Apple of Discord, 8

Apple of Sodom, 85

Apples, **7–8**, **9**(illus.), **10**. *See also* Golden apples

Apples of Milos, 192

Apricots, **10–11**

Arabian Nights, The, 8, 205, 212

Arabs, 8, 18, 66, 70, 122, 135, 182, 200, 212, 216, 230

Archemorus, 169, 170

Arctic. *See* Inuit

Areca nuts. *See* Betel nuts

Ares, 182

Argentina, 57

Aristaeus, 58, 117

Arjuna, 35

Armenia, 10

Armenian apples, 8, 10, 230

Artemis, 79, 80(illus.), 163, 173, 184

Artichokes, **11**

Aryans (India), 42

Ascension Day, 7

Asclepius, 83, 155

Ashanti, 249

Asparagus, **11–12**

Assyria, 32, 95, 177

Atalanta, 167, 191(illus.), 192

Atargatis, 95, 107

Athena, 162(illus.), 163, 167, 173

Athenaeus, 59, 91, 131

Atlas, 167

Atonement, Day of (Yom Kippur), 103, 104

Attis, 6, 109, 179, 182, 183

Atum, 134

Aurora, 205

Australia, 86, 93, 250

Austria, 54, 172
Avalon, 10, 172
Avesta (Zoroastrian text), 213
Avocados, **12–13**
Awa. *See* Kava
Ayahuasca, **13–14**
Azazel, 103
Aztecs, 4, 6–7, 12, 34, 38, 39(illus.), 41, 42, 50, 54, 64–
    65, 71, 72, 73, 74, 95, 96, 98, 146, 147, 164,
    187–188, 228, 229, 235

Baba-Yaga, 42
Babylonia, 6, 10, 21, 93, 107, 117, 152, 177, 182, 183,
    245
Bacchus, 91, 187, 238, 246, 247(illus.)
Bachus, Saint, 110
Bagandas, 17
Baking, symbolism of, 41
Balche, **15–16**
Balkans, 117, 173, 250
Baltic lands, 186, 232, **253**. *See also* Estonia; Finland;
    Lithuania
Bamboo (shoots), **16**
Banana Maiden, 17
Bananas and plantains, **16–18**, 43
Banyan tree, 92, 93
Baobab, **18–20**
Baptism, 210
Barbatus, Saint, 237
Barley, **20–22**, 32, 33, 55, 193, 207, 244
Basil, **22, 23**(illus.), **24**
Bassari, 214
Bavaria, 63, 106, 161, 217
Beans, **24–25, 26**(illus.), **27**, 134, 146
Bear, **27–30**, 46
Bedouins, 140
Beef, **30–32**
Beer, **32–34**, 57, 98, 139, 144, 159, 193, 227, 239
Bees, 116, 117, 122
Bel tree. *See* Bilva fruit
Belgium, 27, 54
Belladonna. *See* Nightshades
Bellerophon, 38
Beltane festival, 53
Bengal, 231
Berries, in winter, 75, 217
Berry of the Valkyries, 159
Berserkers, 34, 159
Betel nuts, **34–35**, 71, 229
Bhairava, 83
Biblical accounts, 10, 11, 21, 54, 55–56, 58, 85, 104,
    110–111, 116, 122, 130, 139, 141, 146, 173–174,
    183, 210, 215, 241, 244, 250. *See also* Christians;
    Hebrews; Jews
Bilberries, 40

Bilva fruit, **35–36**
Birds' nests, **36–37**
Birth control, 155
Bison. *See* Buffalo
Bitter herbs, 63
Black color, 25, 44, 54, 70, 82, 83, 112, 136, 203, 212
Black Meteor Star, 217
Blackberries, **37–38**, 218
Blackfoot, 45
Bliny, 52
Blood, 6, 7, 29, 31, 37, 58, 64, 102, 144, 152, 166, 181,
    182, 200, 205
    and wine, 38, 246
    See also Blood and flesh; Blood sacrifice
Blood and flesh, 25, 27, **38–40**
Blood sacrifice, 39–40, 86, 110, 145, 146, 168, 215,
    246
Blueberries, **40**
Bodhidharma, 226
Bodhisattva, 202
Bohemia, 217
Bolivia, 186
Boreas, 179
Borneo, 240
Brahmans, 22, 31, 34, 44, 46, 86, 92, 133, 137, 149,
    155, 219, 240
Brain, 39
Bramble bushes, 37, 197
Brazil, 117, 138, 189
Bread, 38, **41–42**
Bread of Life, 157
Breadfruit, **42–43**
Breasts, 35, 36, 79, 187
Bretons, 8
Brewsters, 33
Brigit, Saint, 47
British Isles, 8, 11, 37, 49, 74, 87, 95, 118, 121, 170,
    232. *See also* Britons; Celtic lands; Druids;
    England; Ireland; Scotland; Wales
Britons, 165
Buddha, 92, 149, 202, 219
    death of, 154, 154(n)
Buddha's hand, 130
Buddhists, 4, 18, 31, 57–58, 60, 61, 63, 69, 76, 92, 99,
    130, 133, 137, 145, 158, 183, 195, 202, 206, 219,
    225, 226, 240, 263
Buffalo, **43–46**, 46
Bulgaria, 250
Buriat, 83–84
Burma, 36, 188
Burning bush, 37
Burundi, 148
Bushmen, 18
Bushongo, 138
Butter, 44, **46–47**

Cabbage, **49**

Cacao. *See* Chocolate

Cactus, **50**, **51**(illus.), **52**

Caduveo, 117

Cahuilla, 217, 241

Cake, **52–54**, 59

Calabash, 189

Calypso, 169, 170(illus.)

Canada, 87

Candy, **54–55**, 56

Cannibalism, 25, 27, 38, 42, 245, 264

Cardoons, 11

Caribou. *See* Reindeer and caribou

Caribs, 38, 175, 177, 179

Carob, **55–57**, 122

Carrots, **57–58**

Carya, 238

Cassava, 138

Cassava. *See* Manioc

Castration, 179

Catholic beliefs, 38, 210

Cattle. *See* Beef; Cows

Celebes, 39

Celery. *See* Parsley and celery

Celtic lands, 1, 10, 30, 33, 40, 47, 53, 54, 80, 105, 114, 174, 209, **256**

Centaur, 118

Central America, **256**

Cerberus, 83, 158

Cereals. *See* Grain

Ceres, 1, 245

Ceylon, 68, 122

Chaco, 57

Chamacoco, 234

Chang Tao-ling, 171

Chanoyu, 225, 226(illus.)

Cheese, **58–59**

Cheesecake, 59

Cheremiss, 132

Cherokee, 218

Cherries, **59–60**

Chestnuts, **60–61**

Cheyenne, 45

Chiang Yuan, 150

Chiapas, 15

Chicha, **61–62**, 112, 144, 193, 227, 229

Chicken, **62–63**

Chickory and endive, **63–64**

Chickpeas, 134

Childbirth, 61, 63, 93, 231

Children, 202, 203, 210, 217–218
  cooking, 42, 126

Chili peppers, 175

China, **253–254**. *See also* Buddhists; Taoists

Chinese gooseberries, 106

Chippewa, 76

Chkai, 116

Chocolate, 54, **64–65**, 82, 235

Christians, **257**. *See also* Holy Communion; Jesus Christ; Last Supper

Christmas, 106

Christopher, Saint, 79

Chrysanthemums, 96(illus.), 97

Chuales, 7

Chukchee, 154

Cinderella, 189

Cinnamon, **65–66**

Circe, 114, 117, 135, 230

Citrons. *See* Lemons and Citrons

Clairvoyance, 164

Clytie, 220, 221(illus.)

Coca, **66–68**, 112, 229

Coconuts, 43, **68–69**

Cocopa, 146

Coffee, **69–70**, 227

Cola nuts, **70–71**, 250

Columbus, Christopher, 64

Comox, 75

Confucius, 10

Congo, 138

Conjugal love, 132

Corinth, 153

Corn, 32, 61, 61–62, **71–74**, 98, 147, 193

Corn maidens, 71, 73

Corn mothers, 71, 73, 109

Corpus Christi, 112

Cortez, Hernando, 6, 64, 193.235

Cows, 30, 31, 32(illus.), 44, 46, 47, 149

Coyote (trickster), 2, 45

Cranberries, **74–76**

Cream cheese, 59

Creation myths, 31, 86, 89, 94, 116, 134, 146, 148, 189. *See also* Human origins; *individual food sources*

Cree, 76, 141

Crocodile. *See* Alligator and Crocodile

Crocus, 205

Crow, 228

Crown of thorns, 37

Crucifixion, 87

Cucumbers, **76–78**, 168, 188

Currants, 106

Currency, 64, 71, 174

Cybele, 177, 179

Cyclops, 58, 59

Cydippe, 191–192

Dahomey, 83, 214

Daijosai festival, 207

Daikoku, 195, 196(illus.)

Daikon, 195
Dandelion, 63
Danes, 89
Date plum, 176
Dates, **79–80**, 134, 141
Datura, 227
David, Saint, 165
Day of the Dead, 7, 97
Dead, foods for, **260–261**
Dead Sea, 85
Deadly nightshade, 159
Death, 24, 25, 27, 44, 58, 76, 83, 89, 95, 99, 131,
    134, 136, 147, 165, 169–170, 174–175,
    211–212
  and impotence, 131
    See also Dead; Death and rebirth; Death rites; Soul,
      spirit; Underworld
Death and rebirth, 20, 41, 42, 43, 66, 73, 74, 87, 107,
    109, 174, 179, 181, 218, 244, 245. *See also*
    Resurrection; Seasons
Death rites, 11, 97, 130, 169, 174, 195, 197, 199, 211,
    231, 240
Deer, **80–82**
Deipnosophists, The (Athenaeus), 59
Delphinus, 189
Demeter, 20, 21, 25, 42, 52, 54, 71, 74, 91, 107, 109,
    151, 152, 183, 185, 212, 244
Demons, 44, 45, 99, 100, 153, 159, 164, 165, 188, 203,
    211, 212, 213, 227, 231, 237
Denmark, 119
Depression, 251
Devil, 37, 153–154, 170, 210, 237
Devil's apple, 227
Devil's candle, 135
Devil's food, 153
Devil's plants, 241
Dewi Sri, 200, 201
Diana, 79, 191–192
Diodorus Siculus, 122
Dionysus, 2, 4, 49, 91, 97, 103, 111, 117, 154, 159,
    181, 188, 227, 238, 246, 248
Dioscorides, 114
Disease. *See* Ergotism
Divination, 8, 15, 31, 32, 49, 53, 63, 71, 83, 87, 106,
    112, 135, 159, 164
  rods for, 113–114
Doctrine of Signatures, 205, 262
Dog, **82–84**
Dogon, 94, 150
Dolls, 202
Dragons, 22, 180, 181, 234
Dravidians, 44, 205–206
Druids, 1, 32, 74, 86, 209
Drunkenness. *See* Intoxicants
Dryope, 95, 133

Ducks, 105
Dung, 46, 139

Earth goddess, 107, 109. *See also* Demeter
East Indies. *See* Indochina; Malaysia
Easter eggs, 87
Eden, Garden of, 10, 18, 99, 130, 166, 183, 192
Eggplants, **85–86**, 159, 230
Eggs, 63, **86–87**
  golden, 105
Egypt, **254**
Egyptian mulberry, 91
Elderberries, **87**, **88**(illus.), **89**
Elephant, 167, 223
Eleusinian Mysteries, 20, 74, 107, 152, 244
  games of, 109
Elixir of life, 33, 36, 46, 135, 144, 147, 158, 189, 206,
    225, 233, 238, **259–260**
Emu, 86
Endive. *See* Chickory and Endive
England, 8, 11, 27, 47, 87, 95, 100, 154, 155
Enlightenment, 91, 92, 125, 225, 246, 248
Ephedra, 213
Epic of Gilgamesh, 76
Epicureans, 59, 131
Ergotism, 21, 203
Eros, 197
Estonia, 21, 53, 92, 132
Ethiopia, 63, 69, 122, 214
Etrog, 129, 130
Eucharist. *See* Holy Communion
Euphoria, 248. *See also* Hallucinogens; Intoxicants
Europe, **256**. *See also* Baltic lands; Slavic lands;
    individual countries
Eurydice, 117
Eve, 10, 146, 183
Evil, 42, 44, 59, 87, 89, 94, 99, 114, 135, 146, 154,
    159–160, 161, 164, 165, 175, 183–184, 202, 223,
    227, 237, 241
  protection against, 24, 69, 77, 87, 89, 97, 99, 100,
    165, 166, 210, 211, 212, 219–220, 238
Exorcism, 171, 210
Eyelids, 226

Fagara, 175
Fairy food, 38, 196
Fairy rings, 153
Famine, 43, 45, 55, 139, 150, 151, 243, 249
Fava beans, 25, 27
Favism, 27
Feast of Age, 33, 105
Feast of Booths (Feast of Tabernacles), 130
Female symbols. *See* Sexual symbolism
Fenberries, 75
Fermentation, 56, 57, 61, 139, 144, 179

Fertility, **259**, **260**
   of earth, 27, 118, 179, 182, 185, 195, 218, 246
   and sacrifice, 73, 74, 103, 186
   of waters, 94, 210, 211
   See also Sexual symbolism
Festivals. *See* Harvest festivals
Fig tree, 87, 137
Figs, **91–93**, 147
Filbert nuts. *See* Hazelnuts
Finland, 29, 33, 34, 60, 116, 132, 196–197, 232
Finn (Celtic hero), 209, 239
Fire, 46, 47, 100, 153, 175, 216, 220
First-fruit festivals. *See* Harvest festivals
Fish, **93–95**
Flatulence, 27
Flemish, 166
Flesh. *See* Blood and flesh
Flood, 188, 189, 237
Flowers, **95**, **96**(illus.), **97**
Fo-shou, 130
Food injunctions, 25, 27, 30–31, 36, 38, 44, 62, 63,
   76–77, 82, 83, 85, 87, 93, 94, 116, 121, 145–146,
   147–148, 153, 165, 175, 183, 184, 187, 198, 239.
   See also Taboos
Foods
   cold/hot, 4, 121
   See also Mythic transformations; Shapes of food
      sources
Forbidden fruit, **261**
Fountain of Youth, 238
Fox, 228
France, 27, 61, 86, 230, 251
Frey, 8, 246
Friendship, 16, 34, 71, 177, 211
Frogs and toads, 66, **97–98**
Fruit of life, 166
Fungus, 21, 203
Future, foretelling of. *See* Clairvoyance; Divination;
   Prophecy

Gaduchi, 158
Gaelic, 147, 172
Ganesha, 17, 34, 35(illus.), 130, 212, 223
Ganges River, 123, 239
Garlic, **99–100**, 165
Gauri, 212, 231, 232
Genitalia. *See* Sexual symbolism
Gepetto, 241
Germany, Germanic peoples, 1, 2, 8, 27, 30, 33, 34, 42,
   54, 59–60, 63, 86, 105, 106, 113, 118, 121, 132,
   143, 150, 151, 153, 154, 159, 161, 165, 173, 175,
   196, 202, 210–211, 213, 217
Ghee, 44, 46, 47
Gilgamesh, 33
Gilyaks, 29

Ginger, **100–101**
Ginseng, **101–103**, 232–233
Globe artichokes, 11
Goat, lamb, and ram, **103–105**, 147, 161
Gold, 150, 218
Gold color, 100, 205, 206, 213, 230
Gold measurement, 55
Golden apples, 8, 129, 167, 176, 192, 230
Golden egg, 105
Good fortune, 11, 16, 18, 22, 24, 31, 59, 67, 133, 151,
   166, 195, 206, 219
Goose and turkey, **105–106**
Gooseberries, **106**
Gourds. *See* Pumpkins and gourds
Grain, **107**, **108**(illus.), **109**, 150, 168, 184–185
   last sheaf of, 202, 244
Gran Chaco, 117, 234
Grapes, **109–111**
Grass seeds, 146
Grasshoppers, 122
Great Spirit, 217, 218, 228, 250
Greece, **254**
Greed, 102, 232
Green snake weed, 164
Guatemala, 15
Guiana, 12
Guinea pigs, **111–112**

Hades, 107, 108(illus.), 151, 152, 183
Hainan, 69
Haiti, 167
Halloween, 49, 105, 114
Hallucinogens, 13–14, 15, 20–21, 50, 97, 153, 154,
   164, 199, 203, 227, **261–262**
Hansel and Gretel, 42
Haoma. *See* Soma
Haoma tree, 157, 213
Harvest festivals, 2, 40, 52, 73, 105, 107–108, 111,
   117–118, 119, 130, 131, 143, 161, 186, 195, 200,
   202, 212, 244, 250
Harvest Moon festival, 52, 173
Hathor, 31, 79, 91, 135, 147, 148(illus.)
Hathor-Sekmet, 33
Hatsuuma, 199
Hawaii, 40, 43, 82, 125, 185, 189
Hawaiki, 94, 224
Hazelnuts, 8, **113–114**, 209
Head-hunters, 39
Heart, 39, 50, 64, 74, 197
Hebrews, 6, 56–57, 58, 103, 104, 110, 122, 155, 184,
   211, 241
Hecate, 53, 82, 100
Helios, 118, 220, 221(illus.)
Henbane, 33, 159, 160, 213, 230
Heng O, 52, 65, 173, 176

Hera, 8, 103, 111, 129, 147, 167, 173, 182, 205
Herbs, **114**, **115**(illus.)
Hercules, 8, 9(illus.), 163, 167, 205
Hermes, 205
Herodotus, 66
Hesiod, 39, 168
Hesperides, Garden of the, 8, 9(illus.), 129, 167, 176, 192, 230
Hina, 68, 83, 93
Hindus, 2, 4, 17–18, 22, 24, 25, 30–31, 34–36, 44, 46–47, 54, 60, 63, 69, 73, 79–80, 83, 86, 91, 92, 93, 99, 100, 106, 123, 130, 133, 136–137, 144, 145, 147, 148, 149, 155, 158, 211, 212, 213, 219, 223, 230, 231–232, 233, 240, 263. *See also* Brahmans
Hippocrates, 25, 114, 239
Hippomenes, 167, 191(illus.), 192
Histoyre du Mechique (Olmos), 187
Hittites, 244
Holy Communion, 38, 95, 207, 246
Holy Land, 10, 177
Holy water, 210
Homer, 7, 58, 95, 117, 123, 133, 163, 169, 205, 211
Honey, 54, **116–118**, 158, 176–177
    from linden trees, 1, 132
Honeycakes, 158
Honeydew, 140, 140(n), 141
Hopi, 45, 93, 180, 217
Horse, **118–119**
Horus, 91, 94, 147, 165, 174, 183
Hospitality, 34, 71, 177, 211, 229
Hou Chi, 150
Hou-koua (constellation), 189
Hsi Wang Mu, 60, 170, 171
Hua Kuang Ta Ti, 152
Huai-nan Tzu, 238
Huckleberries, 218
Huitzilopochtli, 6–7, 42, 65
Human body. *See individual parts*
Human heads, 68–69, 85, 99, 186
    surgery on, 186
Human origins, 86, 94, 106, 109, 116, 134, 150, 153, 188–189, 192, 219
Human shapes, of food sources, 42, 102, 135, 136
Humans, transformations of, 5–6, 11, 13, 17, 37–38, 40, 50, 58, 60, 62, 63–64, 72, 82, 83–84, 93, 102, 106, 132, 133, 137–138, 146, 153, 155, 179, 182, 235, 238
Hungary, 117
Hunting, 28–30, 45–46, 80–82, 102, 197–199, 207–209, 242–244
Hyades (constellation), 13
Hyena, 18

Ibibo, 86
Ibo, 250

Ice and ice cream, **121**
Iceland, 8, 47
Ikshvaku, 76, 219
Iliad (Homer), 117, 205
Imana, 148
Immortality, **259–260**
    of earth, 107, 181
Impotence, 131, 151, 212
Inari, 199, 200
Incas, 38, 61–62, 64(n), 68, 71, 72, 111, 119, 172, 176, 186, 192–193, 220. *See also* Andean peoples; Peru
Incense, 65–66, 99, 164
India, **254–255**
    Vedic period of, 30, 31, 34, 46, 47, 83, 92, 117, 130, 132, 133, 149, 154, 213
    See also Aryans; Brahmans; Buddhists; Dravidians; Hindus
Indochina, 83, 84, 189, 200. *See also* Burma; Malaysia; Thailand; Vietnam
Indonesia, 36, 68, 200, 231
Indra, 2, 21, 31, 47, 69, 73, 144, 149, 158, 213, 219
Inebriation. *See* Intoxicants
Insects, **121–122**, 139–140
Intoxicants, 2, 4, 15, 32, 33, 34, 57, 64–65, 70, 95, 98, 114, 116, 125, 134, 143, 154, 159, 187, 213, 226–227, 229, 246, **261–262**. *See also* Hallucinogens
Inuit, 46, 198, 208, 242, 243
Iran, 62, 86, 106, 213, 246, 248
Ireland, 8, 10, 31–32, 37, 40, 47, 49, 83, 95, 105, 118, 119, 186, 187, 239
Iroquois, 141, 228
Irving, Washington, 57
Ishtar, 107, 238, 245
Isis, 79, 105, 107, 109, 147, 163, 173, 245
Islamic belief. *See* Muslims
Israel. *See* Biblical accounts; Hebrews
Italians, 99, 118, 189
Izanagi, 171, 201, 207, 215
Izanami, 171, 207, 215

Jaca tsariy, 112
Jack and the Beanstalk, 24, 26(illus.)
Jacob and Esau, 173, 174(illus.)
Jade, 238
Jains, 4, 31, 85, 99
Japan, **255**
Jasmine, 137
Jason and the Argonauts, 104
Javanese, 201
Jesus Christ, 87, 95, 104, 110, 183, 207, 210, 244
Jews, 63, 83, 87, 104, 110, 130, 183, 195, 211
Job, 11
John the Baptist, 55, 56(illus.), 122

Jonah, 241
Josephus, 85
Jove's apple, 176
Judas, 87, 88(illus.)
Jujubes, **123**
Juno, 237
Jupiter, 1, 25, 132, 237

Kachina, 45, 82
Kagami-mochi, 200
Kalevala, 33
Kami, 60, 77, 207, 246
Kanaloa, 43, 126
Kane, 43, 125, 126
Kappa, 77–78
Karok, 208
Karuebak, 138–139, 241
Kava (awa), **127**, 189
Khoi, 58, 122
Killing, act of, 145, 146
Kiribati, 68
Kitchen God, 55
Kiwai, 249
Kiwi fruit, 106(n)
Kojiki (Japanese text), 171, 206, 207
Koran, 123
Koreans, 102
Koryak, 154
Krishna, 22, 24, 30–31, 46, 47, 79, 91, 92, 116, 137,
    149, 223
Kronos, 107, 116
Kua Hsien, 76
Kuan Yin, 16, 200

Lacandon, 15
Ladon, 8, 167, 192
Lakshmi, 17, 22, 23(illus.), 34, 35–36, 68, 92, 93, 95,
    106, 133, 137, 201, 210, 212, 237
Lamb. *See* Goat, lamb, and ram
Land of milk and honey, 79
Lao Tzu (Lao-tse), 102, 180
Lapps, 58, 198–199
Last Supper, 41, 211
Leeks. *See* Onions and leeks
Legba (trickster), 83
Lemons and citrons, **129–130**
Lentils. *See* Peas and lentils
Leonardo da Vinci, 211
Lettuce, 63, **130–131**
Levi-Strauss, Claude, 229
Leviathan, 241
Li, 69
Li T'ien-kuai, 190
Lichens, 139
Life force, 27, 38, 40, 86, 141, 166, 182, 198

Life, interconnectedness of. *See* Soul, spirit
Lightning, 113, 153, 175
Limes and linden trees, **131–132**, 141
Linden trees. *See* Limes and Linden trees
Ling-chih, 154, 181
Lithuania, 60, 132, 237
Living creatures, noninjury of. *See* Ahimsa
Lo-phu, 58, 195
Locusts, 55–56, 122
Loki, 8, 161
Longevity, 16, 36, 37, 101, 170, 171, 172, 181, 206,
    234, **259**
Lotis, 95, 133
Lotus, 35, 95, **132–134**, 240
Love, 60, 114, 129, 137, 197, 237–238
Love apples, 135, 230
Love charms, 8, 11, 27, 95, 101, 191, 212, **259**
Love potions, 39, 63, 100, 117, 135, 159, 210, 230
LSD (lysergic acid), 164, 203
Lu Yu (Luwuh), 225
Lugh, 10, 40
Lughnasad, 40
Luiseños of California, 1
Lupercalia, 103
Lupines, **134**
Lycurgus, 49, 111, 169
Lysergic acid (LSD), 164, 203

Machinguenga, 139
Mad apples, 85, 230
Madagascar, 17, 200
Madhu, 116
Madness, 203
Magic, 5, 6, 18, 19, 20–21, 24, 25, 26(illus.), 27, 28, 33,
    36–37, 38, 43, 45–46, 47, 52, 54, 56, 57, 60, 61,
    67, 68, 70, 71, 80, 83, 86, 87, 89, 95, 97, 98, 100,
    101, 114, 116, 133, 139, 153, 155, 159, 188, 190,
    196–197, 206, 209, 212, 224, 230
Maguay. *See* Pulque
Magyars, 117
Mahadeva, 229
Maize God, 71, 73, 109
Maize. *See* Corn
Malagasy, 200
Malaysia, 36, 167
Man in the moon, 49
Manchurians, 232
Mandan, 45
Mandrakes, 33, **135–136**, 159, 230
Mangareva, 231
Mangoes, **136–138**
Manioc, **138–139**
Manna, **139–141**
Manu, 141
Maori, 94, 126, 249

Maple syrup, 54–55, **141**, **142**(illus.), **143**
Marco Polo, 58
Marduk, 177
Marigolds, 95, 97
Marquesas Islands, 43
Marriage rituals, 27, 34, 86, 113, 117, 129, 167, 182, 182–183, 191–192, 199, 206, 207, 210–211, 220, 231, 232, 237–238
Marriages, mythical, 40, 136–137, 150, 166–167, 195, 232
Mars, 100, 119
Marshworts, 75
Martin, Saint, 110
Mary, Virgin, 60, 183, 218
Masai, 47, 145
Maui, 94
Maui (trickster), 68
Maya, 12, 15–16, 64, 71, 72, 73, 82, 97, 98, 154–155, 164, 172, 175, 229, 233
Mayahuel, 147, 187–188
Mead, 2, 15, 33, 56, 116, 117, 132, **143–144**, 159, 213
Mead tree, 141
Meat, **145–146**. *See also* Ahimsa
Medea, 205
Medicinal powers, **262**. *See also* Doctrine of Signatures
Mediterranean, 40, 129, 161, 182
Melanesians, 34, 101, 224
Melissa, 116, 158
Melons. *See* Watermelons
Menoeceus, 182
Mercury, 40, 114, 132
Mescal, 227
Mesoamerica, 2, 50, 64–65, 71. *See also* Aztecs; Guatemala; Maya; Mexico
Mesopotamians, 30, 31, 33, 55, 79, 100, 109, 121, 157, 181, 182, 183, 238
Mesquite, **146–147**
Metamorphoses (Ovid), 151, 152
Mexico, 7, 15, 65, 82, 98, 122, 146, 153, 164, 227. *See also* Aztecs; Maya
Mhabharata (Hindu epic), 123
Michaelmas, 37, 105
Micronesia, 231
Middle East, 22, 85, 103, 104, 109, 121, 122, 130, 161, 182, **255**. *See also* Arabs; Armenia; Babylonia; Biblical accounts; Hebrews; Iran; Mesopotamia; Persia; Phrygia; Semites; Sumeria
Milk, 30(caption), 31, 36, 44, 46, 121, **147–149**, 158, 213
  breast, 131, 200
  coconut, 69, 147
  date, 79
  fig, 91, 93, 147
  pulque as, 187

Milk and honey, 250
Milkbird, 251
Milky Way (constellation), 107, 147, 149
Millet, 32, **149–151**, 207
Milton, John, 85
Mint, **151–152**
Mintha, 151, 152
Mithra, 62, 63, 91, 246
Mithras, 111, 220
Mohammed, 70, 71, 79, 122, 200
Mohave, 146
Momataro, 171, 172
Mongols, 58
Monkey bread, 19
Montezuma I, 65
Montezuma II, 64, 65, 235
Moon, 49, 52, 54, 65, 66, 93, 139, 158, 165, 173, 174, 176, 183, 213, 240, 250
Moon cakes, 52, 53(illus.)
Moors, 230
Moors' apple, 230
Morning glory seeds. *See* Ololiuqui
Morocco, 5, 182, 227
Moses, 58
Mossi, 150
Mother Earth, 61, 67
Mother goddess, 31, 69, 79, 91, 106, 118, 147, 148(illus.)
Motherhood, 31, 46–47
Mu-lein, 57, 58, 195
Mukat, 217, 241
Mulberries, **152–153**
Mundurucu, 138, 229, 241
Mushrooms, **153–155**, 180, 181
  fly agaric, 153, 154, 199, 213
Muslims, 4, 5, 70, 71, 83, 99, 123, 239. *See also* Mohammed
Mustard seeds, **155–156**
Myrtleberries, 40, 175
Mythic transformations, 5–6, 11, 13, 17, 37–38, 40, 50, 58, 60, 62, 63–64, 72, 82, 83–84, 93, 102, 106, 132, 133, 137–138, 146, 153, 155, 179, 182, 235, 238. *See also* Personifications of food sources; Shapes of food sources

Nana, 6, 182
Narragansett, 74
Natchez, 82
Native Americans, 1–2, 24–25, 29, 32, 54–55, 71
  and alcohol, 2
  of California, 1–2, 122
  northeastern, 82
  northwestern, 75, 82, 89, 93, 207–209
  Plains, 44–46, 221
  southeastern, 4

southwestern, 50, 52–53, 72, 146, 176, 180, 217, 221, 227
See also individual tribes
Natsiko, 82
Nature, sanctity of. *See* Respect
Navajo, 50, 74, 93, 180, 227
Near East, **255**
Nectar and ambrosia, 110, **157–158**
Nepal, 34, 136, 197
Neptune, 133
Nero, 154, 237
New Britain, 219
New Caledonia, 250
New Guinea, 68, 249
New Hebrides, 184, 239
New Year celebrations, 150, 220
Newars, 34
Nigeria, 70, 71, 82, 86, 214, 250
Nightshades, **159–160**, 175, 187
Nihongi (Japanese text), 206, 207
Nile crocodile, 4
Nile goose, 86
Nile perch, 94
Nile River, 20, 21(caption), 33, 73, 107, 147, 216, 239
Nineveh, 177
Niningi-no Mikoto, 200, 207
Niou (constellation), 168
Noah, 110
Nokomis, 143
Norsemen, 8, 73, 105, 141, 143, 144, 148, 161, 218, 239
North America, **255–256.** *See also* Native Americans
Nubians, 32
Nuer, 168
Nut (sky goddess), 31, 86, 91, 147, 149
Nuts of Jupiter, 237
Nuts of Knowledge, 209
Nuts. *See* Almonds; Betel nuts; Chestnuts; Hazelnuts; Pines and pine nuts; Walnuts

Oak trees, 1–2, 132
Oats, 32, **161**
Ocean. *See* Sea
Oceania, **256.** *See also* Maori; Pacific Islands; *individual countries*
Octli. *See* Pulque
Octoberfest, 33
Odin, 2, 8, 33, 34, 143, 144, 239, 246
Odor, 65, 99, 100, 129, 130, 152, 164–165, 215–216
Odysseus, 170(illus.)
Odyssey (Homer), 58–59, 95, 117, 123, 133, 158, 163, 169
Offerings, **262–263.** *See also* Dead, foods for
Oil, vegetable, 12, 155, 195, 211
Ojibwa, 55, 74, 141, 143

Old World. *See* Europe; Middle East
Olives and olive oil, **161, 162**(illus.), **163**
Olmec, 64
Olmos, Fray Andres de, 187
Ololiuqui, 15, **164**, 203
Olympian Games, 59, 163, 169
Olympus, Mount, 197
Onions and leeks, 99, **164–165**
Oomancy, 87
Orange blossoms, 166(illus.), 167
Orange color, 166
Oranges, 129, **166–167**
Orchids, 95, 97
Origin myths. *See* Creation myths; Human origins; *individual food sources*
Orion (constellation), 13
Orokolo, 250
Orpheus, 25, 86, 117
Osiris, 10, 20, 21(caption), 33, 42, 73, 94, 105, 107, 111, 147, 165, 179, 240, 245, 246
Otherworld. *See* Dead; Death
Ovid, 111, 117, 132, 151, 152
Ox, **168**, 215

Pachamama, 61, 67
Pacific Islands, 63, 68, 100, 122, 125, 184, 202, 219, 224, 231, 239, 249. *See also* Oceania; *individual countries*
Padma, 133
Pai-koua (constellation), 189
Pan, 179
Papa, 189, 224
Papago, 50, 146
Papua New Guinea, 184
Paradise Lost (Milton), 85
Parijata tree, 158
Paris, Judgment of, 8
Parsley and celery, 157, **169–170**
Parvati, 17, 106, 223, 229
Passover, 63, 87, 104, 195
Pastoral foods, 145
Patagonians, 118
Pawnee, 217
Peace, 13, 34, 91, 109, 125, 126
Peach wood, 171
Peaches, 60, 130, 166, **170–172**, 180
Peanuts, **172**
Pears, **172–173**
Peas and lentils, **173–175**
Pele, 40
Peonies, 97
Peppers, **175–176**
Permanence, 210
Persephone, 20, 21, 107, 108(illus.), 109, 151, 169, 182(illus.), 183, 237, 245

Persia, 59, 62, 70, 83, 91, 99, 111, 122, 133, 183.220
Persian apples, 8, 230
Persimmons, **176–177**
Personifications of food sources, 22, 24, 161, 187, 201, 202, 213, 232, 245
Peru, 62, 72, 82, 112, 121, 144, 176, 179, 186, 192, 220, 227, 229
Peyote, 50, 52
Peyote buttons, 50, 52
Philippines, 36, 197
Phoenix, 66, 79, 86, 100, 101(illus.), 209, 216, 234
Phooka, 37
Phrygia, 6, 177
Pigs, 105. *See also* Pork
Pilgrims, 75
Pima, 50, 146
Pine cones, 177
Pine resin, 179
Pineapples, **177**, **178**(illus.), **179**
Pines and pine nuts, 147, **179–180**
Pinocchio, 241
Piñon pine, 180
Pipal fig, 91, 92
Pitris, 211
Pizzaro, Francisco, 193
Plague, 203
Plantains. *See* Bananas and Plantains
Pleiades (constellation), 13
Pliny, 205
Pliny the Elder, 59
Plums, 60, **180–181**
Plutarch, 165, 184
Poisons, **263**
    antidotes for, 129, 155
Poland, 10
Polynesia, 68, 83, 93, 94, 126, 231
Polyphemus, 58
Pombe, 227
Pomegranates, 130, **181–183**, 213
Pommes d'amour, 230
Popul Vuh, 72, 73, 116
Pork, **183–186**
Poseidon, 79, 118, 162(illus.), 163
Potatoes, 159, **186–187**, 193
Prajapati, 46, 86, 137
Prometheus, 39, 146, 168, 215
Promised Land, 79, 104, 109, 116
Prophecy, 10, 50, 67, 68, 83, 86, 209, 238
Propitiation, 53, 69, 117, 184, 198, 206, 207, 209, 212, 220
Prussia, 161
Psychoactive preparations. *See* Hallucinogens
Pueblo, 29, 50, 72, 80, 81, 82, 176, 241
Pulque, 2, 147, 187, **187–188**
Pumpkins and gourds, **188–190**, 216(n)

Purifiers, **263**
Purity, 24, 34, 37, 60, 99, 100, 104, 123, 133, 210
Pyramus, 152
Pythagoras, Pythagoreans, 25, 27, 86, 103, 155, 215, 216
Quechua, 192
Quetzalcoatl, 54, 64, 74, 187, 188
Quiche Maya, 72, 116
Quinces, **191–192**
Quinoa, 61, **192–193**

Ra, 33, 86, 104, 105, 117, 135
Rabbit, 52, 66, 173, 188
Radishes, 57, 58, **195–196**
Rain, 57, 82, 98, 118, 122, 227, 240
    milk as, 149
Ram. *See* Goat, lamb, and ram
Rama, 123, 137, 158, 223
Ramayana (Hindu epic), 123, 137, 158, 223
Rapunzel, 196
Raspberries, **196–197**
Ravana, 25, 158
Raven, 89, 154, 242–243
Rebirth. *See* Death and rebirth; Resurrection; Seasons
Red color, 101, 152, 166, 181, 182, 183, 195, 197, 230, 231
Red Spider Woman, 217
Regeneration, 41, 46, 80, 93, 105, 163, 237
Reindeer and caribou, **197–199**
Renewal, **260**. *See also* Death and rebirth; Resurrection; Seasons
Reproduction. *See* Fertility
Respect, 28, 29, 50, 55, 80, 93, 143, 163, 189, 195, 198, 208, 209, 243. *See also* Ahimsa; Dead
Resurrection, 20, 24, 42, 46, 66, 73, 86, 87, 95, 104, 105, 107, 125, 134, 174, 179, 183, 185, 238, 240, 244, 245. *See also* Death and rebirth; Seasons
Rhea, 49, 116
Rhodesia, 20
Rice, 52, 66, **199–202**, 206–207, 212
Rikyu, 225
Rip Van Winkle, 57
Romania, 64, 105
Rome, **254**
Romulus and Remus, 92, 103, 147, 163
Root crops, 57, 58, 196, 232
Rose, 97
Rosemary, 33, 213
Roses, 97
Rue, 213
Rukmani, 137
Russians, 1, 42, 52, 113, 117, 118, 132, 133, 232
Rye, **202–203**
Rye wolf, 161

Sacraments, 38, 41, 52, 62, 185
Sacrifices, **262–263**
   wild/cultivated condition of, 151, 168, 262
   See also Death and rebirth
Saffron, **205–206**
Sagara, King, 76, 188
Sage, wild, 157
Saguaro cactus, 50, 51(illus.)
Saint Anthony's fire, 203
Saint John's bread, 55
Saint John's Day, 95
Saint John's Eve, 175
Saint Martin's Day, 106
Saint Michael's Day, 37
Sake, **206–207**, 246
Salem witches, 203
Saliva, 61, 144, 153
Salmon, 46, **207–209**
Salmon of Knowledge, 209, 239
Salt, **209–211**
Salt of the earth, 210
Samhain, 105
Samoa, 125, 224, 249
Samoyeds, 199
Sanctity of life. *See* Ahimsa
Sani, 25, 212
Santa Clara, 180, 241
Satan, 99. *See also* Devil
Satnami, 86
Saxons, 165, 217
Scandinavia, **256.** *See also* Norsemen; Vikings;
   individual countries
Scarab beetle, 134
Scotland, 87, 88–89, 147, 210–211
Sea, 36, 46, 93, 94, 95, 118, 134, 208, 210, 211, 219
   of milk, 31, 148, 149, 158, 213, 233
   See also Water
Seasons, 43, 52, 75, 105, 141, 143, 185, 195, 217, 244.
   See also Death and rebirth; Resurrection
Sedna, 198, 208, 242–243, 244
Seeds, 155, 181, 182, 187, 188, 211, 212, 220, 241
Semen, 25, 46, 93, 130, 154, 210, 228
Semites, 179
Seneca, 218
Senegal, 18
Sesame, 54, 55, **211–212**
Seth, 73, 94, 165, 183, 245
Sexual symbolism, 6, 8, 11, 12, 21, 22, 27, 34, 39, 54,
   67–68, 94, 95, 109, 130, 131, 133, 137, 153, 172,
   173, 210, 212
Shagana-Tsonga, 227
Shaivism. *See* Shiva
Shamans, 4, 13–14, 28, 50, 67, 74, 98, 100, 122, 153,
   154, 197, 199, 208, 227, 229, 231, 242, 243, 244
   rattle of, 243(illus.)

Shapes of food sources, 7, 41, 52, 54, 102, 135, 136
Sheep. *See* Goat, lamb, and ram
Shen Nung, 200, 215, 225
Shintoists, 206
Shiva, 18, 32, 35–36, 79, 83, 106, 123, 212, 223, 229
Siberia, 29, 82, 83, 154, 199
Siddhartha, 202
Sigurd, 132
Silesia, 153
Silk production, 152–153
Sirius, 216
Sita, 158, 223
Slavic lands, 1, 42, 53, 86, 105, 117, **253.** *See also*
   Russia
Snake, 214
Snow, 121
Sodom, 85
Soil, 231
Solomon Islands, 219
Solon, 191
Soma, 2, 21, 36, 46, 47, 110, 144, 148, 154, 157, 158,
   212–213, 238
Sons, 61, 137, 182, 188
Sorghum, **214**
Sorrel, 63
Soul cakes, 54
Soul, spirit, 95
   assimilation of, 29, 38, 39, 42, 82, 86, 103, 118,
     233, 248
   and communion with deities, 2, 3(caption), 13, 16,
     62–63, 67, 98, 134, 143, 144, 159–160, 164,
     199, 206, 207, 216, 227, 246, **261–262**
   as entity, 38, 260
   unity of, in life forms, 31, 58, 60, 77, 80, 106, 132,
     198, 242, 243–244, 264
   See also Ahimsa; Cannibalism; Enlightenment;
     Hallucinogens; Intoxicants; Life force; Mythic
     transformations; Sacraments; Sacrifices; Taboo;
     Totems; Transubstantiation; *individual food*
     sources
Soul water, 240
Sour gourd, 19
South Africa, 147, 227
South America, **256.** *See also* Andean peoples; Incas;
   individual countries
South Pacific. *See* Oceania; Pacific Islands
Southeast Asia, 36–37, 63, 84. *See also* Indochina;
   Indonesia
Soybeans, **214–215**
Spanish, 64, 229, 239, 241
Spica (constellation), 107
Spice birds, 66, 100, 101(illus.)
Spices, 114, **215–216**
Spirit. *See* Soul, spirit
Squamish, 75

Squash, **216–217**
Stars and constellations, 13, 107, 111, 147, 149, 150, 168, 189, 216
Sterility, 151, 152
Stimulants, 34, 64, 67, 69, 70, 71, 100, 229, 235
Strawberries, **217–218**
Strength, 4, 31, 37, 67, 100, 116, 154, 165
Sudan, 63, 148, 168
Sufis, 70
Sugar and sugarcane, 43, **218–220**
Sugaring, 143
Sujata, 149, 202
Sumatra, 202, 231
Sumeria, 76, 114, 141, 159, 215
Sun, 52, 53, 54, 61, 62, 65, 66, 68, 71, 86, 97, 100, 104, 105, 106, 118, 134, 166, 192, 210, 216, 218, 220, 232, 240
Sun cakes, 52
Sunflower seeds, **220–221**
Supernatural. *See* Soul, spirit
Surabhi, 31, 148, 149
Surgical techniques, 186
Surya, 116, 220
Susanowo, 200, 207
Sweden, 114, 132, 186
Sweet potatoes. *See* Yams
Sweets, 54–55
Switzerland, 7, 119, 172
Sycamore fig, 91, 147
Syria, 107
Szechuan pepper, 175

Taboos, **264**. *See also* Food injunctions
Tacuna Indians, 138
Tagaloa, 125
Tahiti, 68
Tairbfeis, 31
Talmud, 56–57
Tamarind, 137, **223**
Tamarisk tree, 139–140, 141
Tamils, 205–206
Tammuz, 182, 238, 245
Tangaroa, 94
Taoists, 79, 99, 102, 154, 170, 171, 180, 189, 190, 225, 238
Taos, 45
Taro, **224–225**
Tea, 95, 125, **225–226**, 227
Tea ceremony, 225, 226(illus.)
Tea Classic (Ch'a Ching) (Lu Yu), 225
Testicles, 25, 36, 39, 43, 97
Teutons, 1, 33, 95, 113, 217
Thailand, 36, 69, 149
Thanksgiving, 75, 106
Theogony (Hesiod), 39, 168

Theophrastus, 66
Theseus, 12
Thesmophoria, 52, 185, 212
Thessaly, 7, 230
Thisbe, 152
Thomas, Saint, 138
Thompson Indians, 220
Thor, 1, 31, 73, 105, 113(illus.), 175
Thornapples, 15, **226–227**
Thunder, 1, 31
Tibetans, 32, 47
Titans, 107
Tlaloques, 7, 74
Toads. *See* Frogs and toads
Toba, 241
Tobacco, **227–229**
Todas, 58, 189
Togo, 150, 214
Tomatoes, 159, **229–230**
Tonatiuh, 38, 39
Tonga, 126
Tortoise, 54
Totems, **264**
Totonacs, 235
Transubstantiation, 38, 41–42
Tree of Bodhi, 92(illus.)
Tree of Buddha, 157, 158
Tree of Knowledge, 91, 93, 146, 183, 189, **261**
Tree of Life, 55, 61, 65, 79, 80, 91, 93, 109, 123, 141, 147, 157, 158, 170, 171, 180, 181, **261**
Tree of Paradise, 123
Tree of Wisdom, 158
Tree of the Year, 79
Trees, 5–6, 17, 18, 19, 19(caption), 35, 68, 143, 147, 153, 157, 173
Trees of heaven, 158
Trepanning, 186
Tring Dayaks, 240
Trojan War, 59
Tsimschian, 89
Tsoalli, 6–7
Tuatha de Dana, 105
Tulasi, 2, 22, 23
Turkey. *See* Goose and turkey
Turks, 182
Turmeric, 206, **230–232**
Turnips, **232–233**
Turtle, **233–234**
Twelfth Night, 27, 175
Twilight of the Gods, 141
Tyrol, 132
Tzitzimitl, 187, 188

Uchu, 176
Udumbara fig, 91

Uganda, 17, 63
Uke-Mochi, 200
Ukko, 34
Ukraine, 118
Underworld, **261**
Unicorn, 234
Unity of life. *See* Soul, spirit
Unumbotte, 214
Urd beans, 25, 27
Urine, 46, 148, 154, 199
Usha, 223

Vaishnavism. *See* Vishnu
Valhalla, 33, 144, 218
Valkyries, 144, 159
Vanilla, **235–236**
Varuna, 21, 69
Veda. *See* India, Vedic period of
Vegetarianism, 31, 85
Veins, 99
Veneration, 18, 30–31, 50, 52, 61, 62, 83, 106, 145, 221
Venus, 95, 97, 173, 192, 197
Vietnam, 39
Vigilance, symbol of, 6
Vikings, 31, 105, 246
Vincent, Saint, 110
Vindemiatrix (in Virgo constellation), 111
Virgin of Guadalupe, 187
Virginity, 59, 116, 172
Virgo (constellation), 107, 111
Vishnu, 17, 22, 24, 30, 35–36, 46, 54, 85, 92, 93, 106, 123, 129, 233
Vishnu Purana, 158
Volsung, 8
Volta, 150
Vomit, 43, 241

Wakea, 189, 224
Wales, 165, 185
Walnuts, **237–238**
Wapaq, 154
Waste, 55, 243
Water, 93, 94, 118, 133, 209, 213, **238–240**, 262
  salt, 210
  well, 239(caption)
  See also Milk; Rain; Sea
Water buffalo, 43, 86
Water of Life, 149, 157, 171, 213, 238, 239
Watercress, 63
Watermelons, **240–241**

Wealth, 93, 113, 150–151, 184, 189, 219–220
Whale, **241–244**
Whanui, 249
Wheat, **244–245**
Whortleberries, 40
Wine, 2, 11, 21, 38, 50, 70, 110, 133, 149, 159, 190, 205, 227, **245–246**, **247**(illus.), **248**
  and blood, 246
Wisaka, 228
Wisdom, 37, 92, 114, 209, 238, 239
Wishing trees, 93
Witches, 37, 95, 114, 153, 155, 159, 170, 203, 227, 230, 237, 263
Wolf, 161
Wolf, she, 147
Works and Days (Hesiod), 168
World tree, 116(n), 143, 239
Woten, 154, 159

Xanath, 235
Xochequetzal, 95

Yahweh, 103, 104
Yaks, 47
Yam Spirit, 20
Yama, 25, 44, 83, 117, 129, 211, 223
Yams, 43, **249–250**
Yao, 84
Yellow color, 230–231, 232
Yemen, 70, 214
Yggdrasil, 141, 143, 239
Yi Yin, 153
Yin, yang, 62, 102, 105, 190, **215**
Yogurt, **250–251**
Yom Kippur, 103, 104
Yoruba, 82
Yoruba-Dahomey, 214
Yu Yin, 153
Yucca, 138
Yue Ping, 52
Yule (holiday), 105
Yuman, 146
Yungas Valley (Andes), 67
Yurok, 2

Zapotec, 164
Zeus, 1, 8, 39–40, 49, 54, 103, 111, 116, 129, 147, 153, 158, 167, 168, 205, 237, 245
Zoroaster (Zarathustra), 59, 62, 83, 99, 159, 213, 240
Zucchetina, 189
Zuni, 50, 81, 82, 93, 176, 227